SIGHT, SOUND, AND SOCIETY

BEACON SERIES IN CONTEMPORARY COMMUNICATIONS
David Manning White, *General Editor*

From Dogpatch to Slobbovia, edited by David Manning White
Agee on Film: Reviews and Comments, by James Agee
Agee on Film: Five Film Scripts, by James Agee
Culture for the Millions? edited by Norman Jacobs
Explorations in Communication, edited by Edmund Carpenter
and Marshall McLuhan
The Opinionmakers, by William L. Rivers
The Popular Arts, by Stuart Hall and Paddy Whannel
The Mechanical Bride, by Marshall McLuhan
Sight, Sound, and Society, edited
by David Manning White and Richard Averson

SIGHT, SOUND, AND SOCIETY

Motion Pictures and Television in America

Edited by
DAVID MANNING WHITE
and *RICHARD AVERSON*

BEACON PRESS   BOSTON

with much love for . . .
Ruth and Morton Wallerstein
Elizabeth and Anthony Barrett

PREFACE

Motion pictures and television have pervaded our lives with such rapidity and easy acceptance that it is difficult to consider modern civilization without them. So close are we to the daily experience of watching sight-sound-motion images that we have only begun to understand what that experience *does* to people individually, to the nature of their social collaboration, and to the culture they share.

The Editors of this book come from academic backgrounds rooted in the study of mass communication. In teaching courses dealing with the reciprocity between the various mass media and American society, we have recognized the need for a collection of essays such as this that gives primary attention to motion pictures and television. Accordingly, we have selected for inclusion those essays which we feel reveal the increasing interplay between the sight-and-sound media and American social institutions. Our hope is that this book will be read by both students in university communities and other interested observers of what appears on the small and large screens.

The contributors to this volume include creators of films and television programs, educators, government officials, political analysts, advertising executives, behavioral scientists, and critics. Some of the contributors regard motion pictures and television with considerable anxiety, while others feel these media have unmined potential. All of them, because they are involved in the "sight-and-sound situation," provide firsthand insights into the unique problems and opportunities that motion pictures and television raise for an open society.

As teachers of young people who anticipate careers in mass communications, the Editors are aware of the media's implications. As will become apparent, we have not refrained from voicing our viewpoints. Our intention is to present for examination all aspects, however complementary or contradictory, of the sight-and-sound situation.

Many colleagues and other friends have helped us by their generous interest, encouragement, and advice in locating material.

In expressing our gratitude to them we do not attach strings of responsibility for the completed volume. We want to thank, in particular, Manya Starr, Secretary of the International Writers Guild; Dr. Ronald S. Marquisee of Ohio University; and Professor Robert E. Summers of Boston University.

We owe an intellectual debt of many years' standing to Gilbert Seldes, to whom in a special sense this book is dedicated. Like many others concerned with the mass media, we have often turned to his critical analyses for scholarly guidance. It is his own affection for The Great Audience that kindled and sustains ours.

Our sincere thanks again to the contributing authors who have graciously permitted us to reprint their work.

We are greatly obliged to Marcia Cohen for her patience and skill in typing many manuscripts and for editorial assistance. She provided us with initial feedback and valuable recommendations.

To Catherine W. White and Max A. White we extend our deep appreciation for innumerable kindnesses, considerations, and cheerful attention to our needs during a summer of writing.

DAVID MANNING WHITE
Boston University

RICHARD AVERSON
Cornell University

September, 1967

CONTENTS

PREFACE   vii

SIGHT, SOUND, AND SOCIETY: AN INTRODUCTION *by David
Manning White and Richard Averson*   3

PART ONE   THE SCREEN AND ITS AUDIENCES   21

    I   *Media Managers, Critics, and Audiences* BY GILBERT
       SELDES   31
    II *Viewing: A Frame of Reference* BY ROBERT J. SILVEY   50
    III *What TV Is Doing to Our Children* BY WILBUR
       SCHRAMM   57
    IV *Television and the American Negro* BY S. I. HAYAKAWA   68

PART TWO   MEDIA AND MESSAGES   75

    V   *Communication and the Creative Process* BY WALTER
       LASSALLY   87
    VI   *Film and Aesthetics* BY ROBERT STEELE   92
    VII *Movies You Are Not Supposed To Dig* BY NORMAN
       N. HOLLAND   103
    VIII *Sorcerers or Apprentices: Some Aspects of the
       Propaganda Film* BY ROBERT VAS   115
    IX   *The Unreal World of Television News* BY HENRY
       FAIRLIE   127
    X   *The Louder Reality: Behind the Busy Mirror* BY
       DAVID T. BAZELON   137
    XI   *Television: Window on Culture or Reflection in the
       Glass?* BY AUBREY SINGER   150

PART THREE   SIGHT-AND-SOUND COMMUNICATORS   163

    XII *Passage to Hollywood* BY PAUL MAYERSBERG   173
    XIII *The Transient Olympian: The Psychology of the Male
       Movie Star* BY CLIFFORD ODETS   186
    XIV *Illusions and Independents* BY ANDREW SARRIS   201

XV   *Before Sinai, There Was Eden* by Loring Mandel   208
XVI *Broadcasting and the News* by Robert E. Kintner   213

Part Four   THE CONTROVERSIAL SCREEN   229

XVII   *An Outside Conscience for Television* by Harry S.
        Ashmore   239
XVIII *What's New, Copycat?* by Hubbell Robinson   258
XIX   *What's Bad for TV Is Worse for Advertising* by
        Fairfax M. Cone   263
XX   *National Jukebox or Educational Resource?* by Harry
        J. Skornia   271
XXI   *The FCC and Program Regulation* by Lee Loevinger   285
XXII   *How Drastically Has Television Changed Our Politics?*
        by Arthur Schlesinger, Jr.   302
XXIII *Beware of TV's Election Monster!* by Max Lerner   309
XXIV   *Violence in the Cinema* by Philip French   320
XXV   *The Film Writer and Freedom* by Michael
        Blankfort   335
XXVI   *Should American Films Be Subsidized?* by William
        Fadiman   344

Part Five   THE EXPANDING IMAGE   357

XXVII   *Wired for Sound: Teaching, Communications, and
         Technological Culture* by Walter J. Ong   365
XXVIII *The New Age of the Visible: A Call To Study* by
         Kenneth Winetrout   377
XXIX   *I Was a Teen-age Movie Teacher* by John M. Culkin   384
XXX   *A Program for Public-TV* by Lester Markel   396
XXXI   *Mass Media in the Year 2000* by Leo Bogart   409
XXXII   *Culture-Intercom* by Stan VanDerBeek   423

APPENDIX   The Literature of Motion Pictures and
Television: A Critique and Recommendations *by*
Richard Averson and David Manning White   435

INDEX   451

SIGHT, SOUND, AND SOCIETY

SIGHT, SOUND, AND SOCIETY: AN INTRODUCTION

MORE THAN 250 GENERATIONS AGO the Sumerians devised a system of written communication, the first step in man's attempt to preserve the external fabric of his culture by using abstract symbols. Within little more than the past half-century, hardly *one percent* of the time man has been using some form of writing for communication, he created the sight-and-sound media of motion pictures and television. Clearly these new media have altered man's attitude toward himself and his place in the universe, his relationships with others, and indeed the perspective of the entire human community.

Because of their inherent technological capacity to reach diverse audiences and their rapid acceptance by those audiences, the sight-and-sound media have aroused numerous conjectures, admonitions and prescriptions regarding their optimal role and function in an open society. Motion pictures and television have been described as "devices of societal consensus," "agents of social change," "tools for politics," and "instruments for education and enlightenment." All of these descriptions suggest the power of these media for persuasion, an assumption that is no doubt correct. Motion pictures and television may be utilized for all the purposes described above; and, indeed, a great deal of effort and money has gone into the study of their effects on opinion and attitude change, voting behavior, teaching effectiveness, and purchasing decisions.

Although any new major social phenomenon quickly generates discussion and controversy from opposing quarters, we can think of no products of man's inventiveness that have incited such a vigorous debate and concern as has the "moving image." Are motion pictures and television seeking—as some would say—nothing less than the death of the mind, the inversion of reality and dream, and the fulfillment of the "play ethic"? Or do they promise us enhanced perceptual skills by which we may probe our experiences, a deeper individual consciousness of being-in-the-world, more

3

binding human dialogues, and a new definition of social existence?

It is the premise of this book that we might better understand the interrelation between mass communication and American democracy if we consider motion pictures and television as a "total situation" involving the dynamic interplay among audiences and four primary institutions of our society: government, business, education, and the arts. The democratic "tension" and conflict of individual and institutional goals and imperatives shapes and largely determines those symbol-complexes appearing on small and large screens. Our opinion is that because motion pictures and television are forms of *mass* communication they provide a key to the ways by which American society *communicates with itself*.

Sight, Sound, and Society, therefore, is an investigation of the "total situation" of motion pictures and television in America. Our concern is with the historical and present points-of-contact between these four institutions and the sight-and-sound media; the ways audiences select what they see; the activities of communicators (such as producers, directors, and writers), and the capacities of these media for symbol transmission.

＊　　＊　　＊

We have stated that the total situation of motion pictures and television is one of conflict among various social forces. A major force is *the intentions of audiences*. Audiences are comprised of separate individuals who, although they share common viewing experiences, use the sight-and-sound media to satisfy their own particular purposes. There is no such entity as an "audience of fifty million"; this is a statistical mystique. In this so-called mass audience are fifty million distinct individuals, each of whom is motivated to fulfill his own needs, goals, and expectations of the future. From a wide range of offerings, he selects those films and television programs which will help him to achieve his objectives.

This interpretation of audiences regards man not as deterministically and mechanistically *pushed* by the past, but rather as a decision-making individual activated by his own free will and striving toward the personal realization of a future state of affairs. To the extent he evaluates all possibilities, and accurately per-

4

ceives with both head and heart the core of his problems, he makes the "right" decisions as to what he extracts and assimilates from the films and television programs he sees.

Obviously, what is "right" for a 13-year-old Negro boy in Newark, New Jersey depends upon his unique socio-psychological nexus. Whether television news coverage of racial violence in Buffalo a few weeks earlier served as a trigger-mechanism for his involvement in the Newark riots, or deterred him from participating by its focus on deviant behavior, depends on many complex facets of his personality. Indeed, such news coverage may even impel him to come to grips with the choice he must make.

A highly successful program, *Peyton Place*, for example, undoubtedly is watched by different kinds of people for different kinds of reasons. A teen-age girl might watch it to learn how to merge socially into the adult world; her mother might watch it because one of the characters has a parental problem similar to her own. Nor should we discount the likelihood that some people may watch *Peyton Place* to "kill time." But even killing time is intentional; it is a decision freely made, and descriptive of an individual's need.

Perhaps in mass communications research, we have devoted too much time (and money) analyzing only the surface content of motion pictures and television, assuming that a Western or a mystery *ipso facto* sets off a specific response in the viewer. But leading mass media researchers, such as Klapper, Bauer, and the Rileys, have emphasized the mediating factors between content and its effect on audiences. In short, the content of a film or television program is but one of many elements in the total mass communications situation.

* * *

We must recognize the importance of the sight-and-sound media *per se* as an additional force. Marshall McLuhan, whom some consider a Pied Piper leading all of us happy, enchanted children into an electronic wonderland, has stressed the different psychological effects generated by the various media of mass communication. He has reminded us that in our culture we have traditionally associated "linear" print symbols with psychological detachment. We read a book at our own pace, take the necessary time to reflect and ponder, and, so to speak, "control the speed of the message." Motion pictures and television, by virtue of their unique arrangement of sight-and-sound symbols, appear to be a replica of direct, sensuous experience; they seem closer to the flux of life itself. This semblance to life is especially characteristic of "live" television: within less than a second a televised signal can circle the globe, making viewers emotionally involved witnesses to events almost at the moment they are happening. Unlike our reading a book, the moving image prevents us from regulating the speed of the message. We cannot walk away from "live" television in the middle of a program and expect to pick it up the next day where we left off.

Although the total situation is far more complex than Mc-Luhan's simplistic paradigm that "the medium *is* the message," it is obvious that different media require different approaches. We have only to consider the adaptation of James Agee's sensitive novel A *Death in the Family* into the prize-winning play by Tad Mosel, and subsequently into a less successful motion-picture version, to understand the changes necessary when we use one medium of communication instead of another.

*   *   *

In addition to audiences and the media themselves as forces operating within the total situation, there are also the institutions of government, business, education, and the arts. All of these shape the messages of film and television, and it is the tension among all of these forces that is emphasized in the essays we have selected for this volume.

Like the print media of newspapers, magazines, and books which preceded them, the sight-and-sound media of motion pictures and television began as commercial enterprises. If we need to be reminded that they are still essentially commercial enterprises, a single issue of V*ariety* (July 19, 1967) removes any doubt. This authoritative trade journal reported that during the first half of 1967, advertising revenue for the three American television networks amounted to more than seven hundred million dollars, an increase of nearly fifty-five million dollars over the previous year. Such a figure, of course, does not include revenue of the more than 600 commercial television stations now operating in America. In regard to the motion-picture industry, which suffered a huge economic decline with the advent of television in the late 1940's, the total box-office receipts in the United States alone in 1966 was virtually a billion dollars—and 1967 was an even better year.

Although the business imperatives of the motion picture and television industries have always been subject to acrimonious criticism, we must recognize that without this profit-making incentive there would have been no theaters or television stations in the first place. It is the commercial thrust of American broadcasting that accounts for the more than fifty-four million American homes with at least one television receiver. We must also acknowledge that this same economic initiative provided the spur for research and technological improvement.

Yet the aims of business often run counter to the aims of other institutional forces in our society. For example, the Federal Communications Commission, representing government, imposes upon the commercial broadcaster an obligation to serve "the public interest." Television stations are permitted to operate only upon license from the FCC. Although the FCC has not laid down specific rules for programming and while it has not in any overt way censored program content, the fact that licenses must be renewed every three years compels the commercial broadcaster to accept his public responsibility. In this volume, Commissioner Lee Loevinger (pp. 285-301) discusses the issues involved in program regulation.

Another way that the FCC exerts governmental authority on the commercial (and noncommercial) broadcaster is the required adherence to technical standards of station operation. However, the effectiveness of the FCC as a regulating agency on television broadcasting is questionable.

Unlike radio and television stations, motion-picture theaters are not licensed by the Federal government. There has been, however, a steady governmental pressure exerted on the motion-picture industry. This has primarily been in the form of legal decisions pertaining to monopolistic practices and censorship. The

1950 Supreme Court Consent Decree and "divorcement" ruling prevented film producers and distributors from also owning theaters. The resultant increase of competition between "majors" and independent film-makers for theatrical "bookings" altered the subject matter of many Hollywood films. This is evident in the films of the early 1950's made by such producer-directors as Otto Preminger. As an "independent," Preminger produced films dealing with subjects which, because of the Production Code, major companies had avoided. After the "divorcement" decision, Preminger's *The Moon Is Blue* was widely exhibited in theaters which hitherto had been closed to the films of "independents." Even more noteworthy was the denial to this film of a "seal of approval" from the Motion Picture Association; in fact, the distributor of the film, United Artists, temporarily withdrew from the Association.

Another example is Preminger's *The Man with the Golden Arm*, which dealt with narcotic addiction, an area which the Production Code had prohibited. So successful was this independent film that the major motion-picture companies found it necessary to revise the Production Code in order to make other controversial films. Thus, the government's "divorcement" decision provided a catalyst for change (perhaps unwittingly) in an industry which was already suffering from competition from two sources: coast-to-coast television which was drawing audiences from theaters, and the influx of adult, foreign films.

Perhaps a less direct form of governmental influence on the American motion picture were the Congressional investigations of Communist "infiltration" in Hollywood. These investigations probably yielded few proofs, yet within the context of their time they served to deter producers and writers from dealing with subjects which might prove *politically* controversial. Because of their refusal to testify before the House Un-American Activities Committee, many creative people were "blacklisted" from Hollywood employment. Whether any lessening of quality in Hollywood films can be related to the loss of such people as Joseph Losey, Jules Dassin, and John Howard Lawson is, of course, speculative. But certainly this type of governmental scrutiny was not conducive to a favorable artistic climate.

Not all governmental influence on motion pictures has been

8

negative. Various Supreme Court judgments have extended the freedom of the screen. Two of the most famous legal decisions concerned the films *The Miracle* and *The Lovers*. Essentially, in these two litigations, the Supreme Court reversed its 1915 edict that motion pictures should be considered only as amusement; it recognized that motion pictures should be included within the mantle of the First and Fourteenth Amendments of the Constitution. In subject matter and their treatment, motion pictures now had the same latitude as the theater or books, and were not to be restrained by prior censorship. The result has been a rapid decline in all forms of film censorship on both state and local levels.

Another important force shaping the contour of the moving image is the educational institution. Stressing the incompatibility between commercial broadcasting and the educational needs of a democracy, many educators urged the establishment of a noncommercial "second service" television system. In response to these demands, during the "freeze" on television station allocation from 1948 until 1952, the FCC reserved a certain number of channels for noncommercial and educational television use. These stations have been operated mainly by community associations, by colleges and universities, and by state and local school systems.

To insure that educational stations remained outside the sphere of commercial interests, management of these stations was not allowed to sell advertising time. Unfortunately, the FCC did not, in return, provide a workable basis for these stations to support themselves. Those ETV stations which have managed to survive economically have had to rely on such fortuitous sources of funds as foundation grants, public donations, and "promotional" stunts. For example, WGBH, Boston's educational television station, relies on all of these means to stay on the air. One of its most successful gimmicks is an annual televised auction in which items contributed by stores or individuals are sold in order to raise $150,000. It seems unfortunate that the lifeblood of such an important station should rest upon these methods of fund-raising, however inventive and resourceful they may be.

One might ask whether now is not the time that the commercial broadcasting industry provide some continual and steady economic assistance to educational stations and raise them, in Fred Friendly's phrase, above the "malnutrition line." Such commercial television statesmen as Dr. Frank Stanton could well take the lead in a new rapprochement between business and education.

It was the financial dilemma of educational television which prompted the Carnegie Foundation to underwrite a germinal investigation of this problem. The 1967 report of the Carnegie Commission on "public television" proposed that Congress authorize a Federally chartered, nonprofit corporation that would receive and distribute funds to improve noncommercial television. To provide assurance of continuing funds, the Carnegie Commission recommended that a manufacturer's excise tax be placed on television sets. It is estimated that such a tax, beginning at 2 percent and culminating at 5 percent, would give the corporation an annual budget of one hundred million dollars within a few years.

The Carnegie Commission further suggested that the corporation be empowered to establish national centers for the production of programs for use by educational stations. These centers would be free to contract with independent producers, and their activities would supplement the excellent work of the already existing National Educational Television (NET), which operates on the minuscule budget of six million dollars a year provided by the Ford Foundation.

Acting upon the Carnegie Commission's recommendations, and after extensive hearings, Congress passed the Public Broadcasting Act of 1967. The bill sets up a 15-man Corporation for Public Broadcasting. Although the Corporation is authorized to receive $9,000,000 for initial operations, long-term financing is not yet assured.

New production centers will encourage experimentation in programming, which currently seldom happens in commercial television. Young writers, directors, and performers will find new opportunities for creative employment. We see such production centers as indirectly contributing to the improvement of commercial television as well as ETV. Audiences for programs such as Av Westin's *Public Broadcast Laboratory* might be extended, and, hopefully, such programming might provide a "quality" challenge to commercial television.

The proposals of the Carnegie report may alleviate charges that educational television has failed to live up to our expectations. Critics have pointed out that because the audiences for educational television are relatively small, the enormous amount of money required to maintain and program the now more than 125 ETV stations might be better used for other educational purposes. Further criticism has been directed at the programs which are offered by noncommercial stations. Because they are free of the pressures to please sponsors and advertisers, we have expected these stations to engage in more controversial topics and to be, as Robert Lewis Shayon has urged, "more daring." But thus far such programs as *The Mills of the Gods,* a disturbing Canadian documentary on the Vietnam war distributed by NET, are the exception rather than the rule. It is regrettable that the Michigan State University ETV station, for example, refused to telecast Malcolm Boyd's play, *Boy,* an indictment of racial inequality. One might understand the reluctance of a commercial station in East Lansing to schedule such a program, but certainly not a station appealing to specialized audiences. Apparently, self-censorship is not restricted to commercial telecasters.

Another criticism of ETV is that its programming is aimed toward elite audiences rather than mass audiences. Since these elite ETV audiences are usually more affluent and better educated than audiences for commercial television (as revealed in the findings of a recent Harris poll), it can be argued whether those who need education most are being served.

Because the mass communications media are of necessity concerned with reaching immediate audiences, it is difficult for some critics of popular culture to conceive of motion pictures and television as capable of creating any enduring art. Our usual conception of the artist is of an individual working alone to satisfy his own creative energies and oblivious to an audience. Also we are accustomed to thinking of art as something for hanging on walls of museums, or for stacking on library shelves.

Are the communication arts of film and television less art be-

11

cause they are designed to reach as large an audience as possible, because they reach masses of people? Indeed, does the quality of artistic endeavor decrease with popularity? Perhaps our view of art is too limited. It seems absurd to separate art from its social context. Whether we like to realize it or not, in every society the arts, too, are a social institution.

If we go back to the earliest civilizations, we find that they reveal themselves to us through their art forms. Recently, when a team of archeologists discovered the ruins of a 3,500-year-old Minoan city, they uncovered huge painted pottery jars as well as frescoes that appeared to be the work of a high civilization, perhaps the lost city of Atlantis. Through such art forms we can begin to share some of the feelings, aspirations, and outlooks of the 30,000 fellow humans who were buried beneath the volcanic ash at Thira. Marshall McLuhan has put it well in saying, "I think of art, at its most significant, as a DEW Line, a Distant Early Warning system that can always be relied on to tell the old culture what is beginning to happen to it. In that sense it is quite on a par with the scientific."

Like other institutions in society, the arts have their own identifiable characteristics: museums, galleries, training schools, advisory councils, and agencies. As the physical identifications of the institution of art become more prominent in our society, so will its demands for an equal voice in the workings of democracy become stronger.

Just as business, government, and education shape the configuration of the moving image, so does the art institution exert its own force. Some will deny that motion pictures and television, because of their roots in entertainment and amusement, are worthy vehicles of artistic expression. Yet, in agreement with McLuhan, we believe that motion pictures and television are a DEW Line helping us to understand what is being thought and experienced in this century.

If we had the opportunity to return to the time of Pericles by a Wellsian time-machine, to apprehend the temper of that age we might buttonhole someone on the street and ask him his opinions. Would they be valid opinions, and how much credence could we put in them? We would put a great deal of stock in them if he were a communicator whose work was seen by over seventy million people in a single night. For if seventy million people were willing to give an hour to viewing his work, this says something not only about his work but about the tastes of his fellow citizens, too.

Would Sophocles have been less an artist if television had been invented in fifth-century B.C. Greece, and if his plays reached mass audiences beyond the amphitheater at the Acropolis? We do not feel that the media of film and television in themselves deter the emergence of a new Aristophanes. In truth, we can't blame the mass media for the fact that our culture has not produced a genius of Shakespeare's magnitude since he died in 1616. For three hundred years, sans television and motion pictures, there still wasn't another Shakespeare. Perhaps his particular genius emerges only every four hundred years, and the next Bard of Avon may find himself working for David Lean or as a resident-dramatist for the National Broadcasting Company.

We have been dealing with the institutional nexus of government, business, education, and the arts within the total situation of motion pictures and television. We recognize that institutions are merely sociological abstractions describing groups of people with similar interests and engaged in similar activities. Institutions are, as Kenneth Burke suggests, "systematic attempts to carry out some plan or ideal." Each of the major institutions which are inextricably conjoined in motion pictures and television in America has its own ideals and ways of accomplishing them.

What becomes apparent to us as we examine the forces that shape the moving image is that each of these institutions—*intent on pursuing its own aims*—often contends with the other institutions. We do not regard the inevitable conflicts between government and business, or between education and business, etc. as necessarily detrimental to our society. The interrelationship of institutions in a democracy cannot be one of static synchronization or a well-oiled meshing of gears. It must be a *dynamic* interrelationship of tension and "strain" if social progress is to be made.

We acknowledge the need of the business institution to make a profit; its special use of the television medium is justifiable. On the other hand, we also perceive the equally urgent needs of government, education, and the arts. But while these institutions contend with one another to fulfill their aims, it is vital to our democracy that none of them so extends its sphere of influence that it gains exclusive domination of the sight-and-sound media.

An important section of this book, which we call "The Controversial Screen," will indicate the nature and extent of the problems engendered by this democratic institutional contention.

* * *

Also implicated in the total situation of motion pictures and television are those professional communicators skilled in the techniques of message-design: production, writing, performing, and reporting, for example. They are the rank-and-file troops who feel the brunt of the conflict among those institutions which vie for control of the moving image. Their activities and problems are discussed in the essays under "Sight-and-Sound Communicators."

Lillian Ross's astute book *Picture* and Merle Miller's *Only You, Dick Daring!* are case studies of communicators caught in the institutional cross fire. These books are typical of endemic pressures which force the communicator to compromise his optimal vision of what the message should be. Fred Friendly's quixotic career at the Columbia Broadcasting System is yet another example of a scrupulous communicator forced to make the choice between the business imperative of holding daytime television audiences of women, and the public-affairs value of a crucial national event. So intense was the cross fire between televising yet another rerun of *I Love Lucy* and his desire to carry the hearings of the Senate Foreign Relations Committee on Vietnam, that Friendly resigned as President of CBS News.

Sight-and-sound communicators face another kind of paradox. Unlike the writer of a novel, who alone arranges his words and chapters, or a painter who solely creates every inch of his canvas, the communicator in motion pictures and television is only one of many collaborators in the design of a technically complex message. He cannot be writer-director-actor-cameraman-sound technician at the same time: he cannot be a one-man team. The fact that there has to be a production executive to coordinate the many specialized contributions indicates the nature of this col-

14

laborative effort. This collective participation leads to a diffusion of responsibility toward the completed message.

So diffuse is this responsibility that disputes concerning the order and type size of "credit" listings often must be arbitrated between representatives of talent guilds and production companies. In many respects the sight-and-sound communicator sees himself as alienated from the finished work. He is always expendable; he can be replaced even during the production. In the demand to get the "product" completed his individual contribution is minimized. Whether Fred Zinnemann (or his replacement George Roy Hill) completed *Hawaii* was irrelevant: the motion picture "product" had to be ready for its set première.

Another problem area for the sight-and-sound communicator is that he often does not retain either artistic or entrepreneurial control over the motion picture or television program of which he has been an integral part. In the case of a film, the finished product may be far different from what a director, for example, anticipates. Darryl F. Zanuck of 20th Century-Fox edited the final version of the legendary *Cleopatra* without the advice of its director, Joseph L. Mankiewicz. Again, consider George Stevens' lawsuit against NBC for casually editing his notable film *A Place in the Sun* and haphazardly inserting commercials which he claimed mutilated its artistic unity. It should be added that Stevens' suit was denied.

These unpredictable circumstances in which the communicators must work are caused by a combination of the collaborative nature of film and television production *plus* the demands of anonymous stockholders for dividends. The chairman of the board of Gulf and Western Industries, which recently acquired controlling interest in Paramount Pictures, probably knows as little about making motion pictures as Adolph Zukor knows about public utilities. The average stockmarket speculator who buys some shares in Gulf and Western (or Transamerica, which a short time ago acquired United Artists) couldn't care less about either.

One final thought, which applies not only to sight-and-sound communicators but to other mass communicators such as a newspaper editor or a writer for a large-circulation magazine, is that they have only the vaguest knowledge of their audiences. The numbers they gain on a Nielsen rating, the box-office gross, these are the primary indices of successful mass communication. But we cannot emphasize too much that there is no such entity as a mass audience of forty or fifty million people who, to these communicators, must always remain nameless, faceless abstractions. In reality, there are forty or fifty million distinct individuals, each with his own personality, ambitions, and expectations. These individuals exist on the *other* side of the theater or television screen; only by an occasional letter of praise or damnation does the mass communicator become aware of these private identities.

          *   *   *

This book is not a collection of film and television criticism, at least not in the traditional sense. In it we do not suggest immutable standards for judging the "goodness" or "badness" of a film or a television program. Indeed, our emphasis on understanding the total situation of the sight-and-sound media is at variance with evaluations rooted solely in aesthetics.

Because television and motion pictures dominate the leisure time activities of most Americans, newspapers and magazines were forced to give these competitors space, and a new form of criticism came into being during the twentieth century. There are hundreds upon hundreds of so-called film and television "reviewers," and although we do not agree completely with Henry James's statement that "the practice of 'reviewing' in general has nothing in common with the art of criticism," he makes a salient point. We find too many commentaries posing under the guise of criticism which are merely extensions of publicity handouts. There is a great deal more depth required of the reviewer than the usual thumbnail plot synopsis and an arbitrary classification by Two Stars, Three Stars, etc.

Perhaps we shouldn't be supercilious about reviewers who last year were city hall reporters and who, because of a managing editor's whim, one day found themselves entertainment columnists. Unless such a critic is willing to rise to the challenge and responsibility of his new role, through studying the complexities of the sight-and-sound media and their relationship to his readers, his opinions can't be taken seriously. The best he can do is to disseminate his own uninformed notions, frequently corrupted by an all-expense-paid publicity jaunt to Hollywood or Salzburg, on an audience that needs honest, incisive, and knowledgeable interpretation of today's motion pictures and television programs.

The hundreds of run-of-the-mill reviewers only make us appreciate those television and film critics who take their work with the seriousness it demands, and who help us all to, in Henry James's phrase, "intellectually possess" the media. Lawrence Laurent, the distinguished television critic of the Washington *Post*, has provided aspiring critics of that medium with some guidelines concerning the vast store of information they must acquire. To the extent these factors affect television programming, the "complete television critic" must have an awareness of communications theory, history of broadcasting, governmental processes, advertising and marketing conditions, and public issues—in addition to being an expert in drama.

Mr. Laurent is not describing a paragon who does not exist, for these qualities are found not only in his own criticism, but in that of Jack Gould of the *New York Times*, and especially in the insightful work of Robert Lewis Shayon. The consistently high quality of Shayon's criticism in *Saturday Review* over a period of many years calls to mind Ezra Pound's comment, "It's only after long experience that most men are able to define a thing in terms of its own genus." Shayon continues in the tradition of Gilbert Seldes, having a deep concern for the social and humanistic consequences of television. In regard to motion-picture criticism the same qualities are evident in such writings as those of Andrew Sarris, Robert Steele, Penelope Houston, Paul Mayersberg, and Stanley Kauffmann, some of whom are represented in this book.

*   *   *

In his essay in this volume (pp. 384-395) John M. Culkin reminds us of Plato's analogy of the cave. Philosophically concerned with the problem of discernment between reality and appearance, Plato envisioned a cave whose inhabitants passed their lives watching shadows moving on a wall. So enraptured were they by this illusion that they repudiated the world outside the cave and embraced the shadows within. The "magic forces" responsible for this apparition were beyond their knowing.

The similarity between Plato's cave and our preoccupation with motion pictures and television is easily recognized. But even Plato could not have foretold the twentieth-century "dream machines" that conjure instant sight-and-sound images in our homes and theaters. Plato would have—as the "hippies" say—"blown his mind" at Expo 67's *Labyrinth* created by the National Film Board of Canada. Here, in a maze of winding passages leading to several viewing "chambers," audiences were, in Margaret Weiss's description, "defenseless against multiscreen sorcery and multisensory assault and battery." They became *involved* participants, not merely movie-watchers but movie*goers*, fused into a total film experience.

Fascination with the moving image is not unique to our time. Archimedes explored the optical effects created by sunlight refracted by a glass prism. Leonardo da Vinci, in a darkened room, examined how light rays entering through a small opening formed images. Although da Vinci's *camera obscura* began as a scientific tool for astronomers, it soon became identified with the arts of illusion and fakery. It is not surprising that one of the pioneers in motion pictures was a magician, Georges Méliès. In his A *Trip to the Moon*, Méliès employed a cinematic bag of tricks that are still used: multiple exposures, superimpositions, and animation by stop-action.

The *Labyrinth* of Expo 67 is an extreme example of what has been gradually occurring in the majority of our motion-picture theaters since the advent of various wide-screen processes. Cinerama and the less cumbersome Cinemascope initiated developments that may culminate in the eventual "disappearance" of the traditional proscenium that separated the spectator from the screen. In a physical sense, the wide screen complements what Daniel Bell has defined as "the eclipse of psychic, social and aesthetic distance"—which he regards as a distinguishing characteristic of our culture over the past century. The wide screen extends across the full range of our vision and is designed to, as the neon advertisements say, "engulf audiences." In the "ultrahigh fidelity" sensuous experience of a neighborhood circle-rama theater the viewer may indeed become both the spectator and the spectacle.

The television of the future may be no less "involving," as Leo Bogart's essay (pp. 409-422) suggests. We are promised free-standing, three-dimensional, full-color images delivered to our homes by lasers. Like the fireman's wife in Truffaut's *Fahrenheit 451*, by a talk-back device the television viewer may become a member of the cast of a Procter and Gamble soap opera.

What does this proliferation of "magic lanterns" portend? If Plato were living today he undoubtedly would be the leader of the elitist denunciators of the mass media. He would probably say that motion pictures and television are dooming us to lives spent before screens that are only mirrors of reality. Like the people in the cave, we would eventually lose all ability to differentiate between what is shadow and what is substance.

But let us also remember that the people in Plato's cave had their legs and necks chained from their childhood. They could "only see before them, being prevented by the chains from turning around their heads." Their curiosity to search for the truth behind those shadows on the wall was immobilized. They did not have the freedom to step outside the cave; they had lost the name of action.

Elitists like Plato, whether they be hypothetical philosopher-kings or some university intellectual who would rather be dead than caught watching *I Spy*, have no faith in the ability of lesser minds to discern between illusion and reality. In a democracy the individual is not enchained: There are no edicts from the State commanding him to attend Loew's Orpheum or to watch an NBC spectacular. Our society leaves ample room for a Henry David Thoreau, for whom the hills surrounding Walden Pond were always alive with the "sound of music." But our society also recognizes that the majority of Americans must be allowed to seek their own values, and that motion pictures and television may well help them to do so.

Moreover, because the individual is not shackled to the upholstered seat of his living room or neighborhood theater, he can become aware of—and disagree with, if he so chooses—the institutional forces outside the cave that shape the images within. If a television commercial hawking a patent medicine for hemorrhoids offends him, he is free not only to turn off his set, but to complain to the Federal Communications Commission; if he regards the sex and sadism of A *Fistful of Dollars* as a threat to the moral well-being of his children, he can leave the theater and complain to the manager. The institutions of a democracy are not beyond his reach; to the extent that he is willing to become involved in the workings of the mass media, his "feedback" is not a futile expression. Walt Whitman might well have been describing the mandate and the responsibility of audiences vis-à-vis motion pictures and television when he said, "The whole theory of the universe is directed unerringly to one single individual—namely to You."

We have emphasized that the total situation of motion pictures and television is one of conflict and opposing interests, which we consider socially valuable in a democracy. As libertarians, we believe, as did Milton, Jefferson, and John Stuart Mill, that only by engaging in honest debate will intelligent men recognize truth over lies and the morally viable over what is debasing and dead. This book, then, is a platform for discussion regarding the moving image in American society.

The participants in this "debate" who have written the essays we have selected for this volume represent those who are most directly implicated in the sight-and-sound media. They include producers, writers, professional critics, educators, government officials—all of whom share a common concern about the impact of motion pictures and television upon the lives of all of us.

PART ONE

THE SCREEN
AND ITS AUDIENCES

To have great poets, we must have great audiences, too.
—WALT WHITMAN

There was a child went forth every day,
And the first object he look'd upon, that object he became.
And that object became part of him for the day or a certain
  part of the day,
Or for many years or stretching cycles of years. . . .
—WALT WHITMAN

~~~~~~

THE AUDIENCES, THE VIEWERS, the people on the *other* side of
the screen. Why are they there? One thing about them we
can be certain of: they are not a homogenous, monolithic
mass dominated by some kind of statistical Groupthink. Each
individual sitting in front of a theater or television screen
watching A *Man for All Seasons* or *Mission: Impossible* has
his own reasons and motives for being there. Yet whatever
his intimate motives for viewing may be, a member of any
audience can watch only those motion pictures and television
programs that the "media managers" make available.

In his essay, "Media Managers, Critics, and Audiences,"
Gilbert Seldes probes what may be the crucial issue in mass
communications: What is the social responsibility of studio
heads, network presidents, and station and theater executives?
As dean of the critics of popular culture, Seldes challenges

21

the concept of "giving the public what it wants"—the dominant rationale given by the media managers.

The media manager of television, in particular, is perched on the tenuous fulcrum of a "cultural democracy" seesaw. How can he maintain the delicate balance between meeting the tastes of minority audiences and supplying programs which, as the ratings seem to indicate, appeal to majority audiences? Even though the preferences of large audiences may disappoint or repel him, the ever-present ratings give him a convenient rationalization. And if he occasionally feels a slight case of revulsion about catering to the statistical majority, the biweekly Nielsen reports assure him that he is doing his job. When he gives his carefully documented speech at colloquia filled with university students, his brow is the most furrowed as he bemoans the condition of television. A bright graduate student might well remind him of Shakespeare's words in *Richard II*, "Some of you, with Pilate, wash your hands, showing your outside pity."

But, in fairness, we realize that audiences themselves must share some of the blame, if any is due. Because the audiences of motion pictures and television are not known to the media managers, the prime source of feedback must be the sheer numbers of ratings and box-office receipts. If *The Fugitive* maintains over several seasons the highest "share of audience" in its time period, television's executives have some justification for assuming that this is a type of program which, indeed, interests the majority. When a carbon copy of this program, such as *Run for Your Life*, wins an equal "share" the managers feel doubly sure that they are supplying what audiences want. In motion pictures, as well as television, success breeds success—and cycles *ad nauseam*.

In a sense, "mass audiences" are their own cultural executioners; by choosing one program or film over another, they reduce the range of alternatives that might be offered to them. In mass communications, the tastes of majorities tend

22

to become self-reinforcing. One more caveat: as Seldes aptly states in the opening essay of this section, television ratings are not true measurements of program popularity; rather, they indicate preferences between competing programs that are *available* during any specific time period. Despite all the schedule juggling that networks contrive, a program does not necessarily carry its rating with it. For example, when *Ben Casey*, during the epidemic of doctors' programs a few seasons ago, was shifted by ABC from one night to another, its rating dropped substantially.

Unlike Gertrude Stein's immutable rose, ratings have different aromas for different people. We object to the critics who cry havoc at a 30-plus rating for a slick situation comedy, replete with canned laughter, and who shout hosannas when *Mark Twain Tonight* attracts a similar share of television households. They can't have it both ways; the latter is no more a judgment of The Public's taste than the former. All of the debate between media managers and critics concerning audiences is slightly reminiscent of Bernard Berelson's statement about mass communications research in general, i.e., some kinds of communication brought to the attention of some people, under some kinds of conditions, have some kinds of effects. To which we add, *sometimes*.

Despite this cynical-sounding summation of mass communications research, there are data which give us some indices on the television viewer and why he watches what he does. Contrary to the folk belief that commercial television is watched mainly by those of low socio-economic and educational background, a recently completed five-year study by TvQ surveys indicates that 98 percent of college-educated viewers watch television from at least one hour to more than 30 hours a week. The average number of viewing hours of the college-educated was 14.8. Also, the average number of hours watched weekly by families with incomes of $10,000 and over was 15.6. When classified into professional and managerial

SIGHT, SOUND, AND SOCIETY

categories, people in these high-status occupations watched an average of 15 hours per week.

There are many other studies of this type, of which the most comprehensive is Gary A. Steiner's *The People Look At Television*. This 1963 major study of audience attitudes presents some fascinating insights into the audience's reasons for watching television. Dr. Steiner ascertained that nearly 25 percent of the American public have guilt feelings about time spent with television, accusing themselves of being lazy and expressing related negative feelings, such as boredom and shame. At the same time, the same respondents to his survey indicated positive attitudes toward the medium, finding it a good way to relax, to be entertained and informed. Obviously, there is an ambivalence on the part of the television viewer.

Can we assume that motion picture audiences have similar responses toward watching films? The following incident, reported by the *New York Times,* illustrates the need for a comparable study. During the 1967 Israeli-Arab conflict, two bystanders were outside the Soviet UN mission waiting to see Premier Kosygin. One of them, a woman, advised the reporter, "Don't get too near the Russians. They'll stick a needle in you and that will be the end. That's what they are like." Queried where she got her opinion, she said it came from seeing the James Bond film, *From Russia with Love,* in which a woman commissar tried to jab 007 with a poisonous blade hidden in her shoe. A man standing nearby took issue with her, saying, "I like the film *The Russians Are Coming, The Russians Are Coming* better. That showed that the Russians are real people."

The ambivalence toward television which Steiner found in American viewers is also noted by Robert J. Silvey, head of research for the British Broadcasting Corporation, suggesting that this is a cross-cultural phenomenon. In his essay, Mr. Silvey raises the interesting (albeit disturbing to many) thesis that television viewing is, indeed, a form of *play*. Dr. William

24

Stephenson in his provocative volume *The Play Theory of Mass Communication* tells us that social scientists have been overly occupied attempting to prove that the mass media are more sinful than good. Contrary to the Calvinistic dictum that play is morally wasteful, both Stephenson and Silvey recognize that the freedom to "play" with television can be a means of self-enhancement. It is dubious, however, whether they would agree with Newton Minow's analogy between TV watching and "a steady diet of ice cream, school holidays and no Sunday school."

Silvey draws attention to another aspect of the viewer's frame of reference—the notion that television is "free." (Clearly, when one considers the initial investment and depreciation of the TV set, electricity bills, and the increased cost of advertised products, television is not "free.") His point is that if we had to drop a half-dollar in a coin-box attached to the set before we turned on the Jackie Gleason show, we might think twice about it. But as long as it's "free," and we're out only to play, all we have to lose is, perhaps, an hour's time.

Although it is extremely difficult to pinpoint the effects of the sight-and-sound media in any specific instance, adults are concerned with investigating their influence on our children. Perhaps we feel the need to believe that young people are more vulnerable to violence as portrayed in the mass media than we are. Actually, this is a debatable matter, and we might question whether a film like *The St. Valentine's Day Massacre* is not "corrupting" for adults as well as children. Unfortunately, the only characteristic that separates a great number of adults from children is chronological.

If children would only stick to *Captain Kangaroo, Bozo the Clown* and such television programs, we adults wouldn't have formed such "cleanup" squads as the National Association for Better Radio and Television and the Film Estimate Board of National Organizations. Nor would *Parents* Magazine feel the obligation to list monthly classifications of films suitable for children. But, as Wilbur Schramm states in "What TV Is Doing to Our Children," children quickly discover adult programs and soon prefer them. Above all, he adds, they prefer the more violent kinds of adult programs. Can this preference for violence be explained as the child's emulation of adult values, or can it be that Violence Readiness is not a matter simply of age but is there from the beginning? Freud might well agree with the latter. Whatever the explanation, most of us adults feel *certain* that the nebulous innocence of childhood would last a little longer if the sight-and-sound media had never happened. Before parents label the big and small screen as the *bête noire* corrupting their youngsters, they might do well to recall that Cain crushed his brother's head in with a rock without ever having seen James Bond, Clint Eastwood (the man with no name), or *The Untouchables*.

Besides their anxiety about the influence of mass media violence, parents also worry about the effects of films and television on the so-called *taste* on their children. It seems to us that adults who make the mass media the primary scapegoat if their children have "poor" taste are abrogating their own complex parental responsibilities. Television must be considered as only one of many taste-making influences within the social nexus of the home. The books on the shelf, whether *Valley of the Dolls* or Oscar Lewis' *La Vida*; whether the mailman brings *Life* or *National Geographic*, or perhaps both; the child's older sisters or brothers; and, most important, the parents themselves who too often are guilty of the old saw, "Do what I say, not what I do"—all are determinants of a child's taste. If we recognize all of them as comprising the social landscape of the home, then we can better understand Henry Adams' comment: "Everyone carries his own inch-rule of taste and amuses himself by applying it triumphantly wherever he travels."

26

Various studies of children's television viewing behavior indicate that the patterns of their taste are fairly well "set" by the time they are ten or eleven years old. If a child watches *Batman* on television, he probably also reads comic books with such heroes, and sees movies which coincide with his fantasies. The question of taste, then, involves program alternatives. Would a child, given the option of watching a program other than *Batman* during the same time period, abandon his supercharged hero? A partial answer was provided by Dr. Hilde Himmelweit and her associates in a long-ranging English study some years ago. When children had the choice of turning off the set or watching a program which did not promise to be very "interesting," they frequently chose to keep the set on. Significantly, they often found themselves *becoming interested*—which suggests that program taste can be broadened beyond the simplicities of a *Batman* if there is some "control." Himmelweit learned that when children were offered a choice of several programs on competing channels they invariably returned to the programs which they previously watched. Thus, although it sounds good to say if only there were more channels and types of programs available, children would have better opportunity to develop "taste," it isn't necessarily so.

Like adults, children relate themselves to television and are not reluctant to articulate their opinions. Charles Winick, co-editor of the Peabody Award-winning *For the Young Viewer*, studied children's television fan mail. By analyzing letters sent to NBC, Winick found that young viewers both praised and complained about television and also gave suggestions for new programs. One junior high school student wrote, "I would like to see the *Odyssey* in a series on television. Many people read myths and legends and it would make a good show." An eleven-year-old complained about authenticity as follows. "You and I both know that Billy the Kid was an outlaw. He killed his first man at the age of thirteen, and in the back! I hope that you will put in more of the truth because when my little sisters and brothers study about the heroes of the west, they won't know whether to believe TV or the book." Insofar as this youngster, with his sophisticated ability to separate fact from fiction, is representative of his peers, we can be optimistic about his taste.

No discussion of the people who watch the sight-and-sound media can neglect an examination of the significant minority audiences. One of the most perceptive statements of television's impact on such a minority, in this case the American Negro, is S. I. Hayakawa's essay which appears in this section of our book. Since television programs are aimed at the entire community, programs ostensibly directed to the white majority are also received by the Negro minority. To paraphrase a childhood poem, "I shot a TV signal into the air, it fell in homes I knew not where." If, as Hayakawa suggests, television is causing a cultural explosion, we should also recognize that such a force can have a fallout. In the case of the American Negro, the fallout may be the result of the much-maligned television commercial.

Wendell Johnson describes this kind of fallout in his well-known IFD paradigm—the triple-pronged semantic disease of Idealization ("Won't you drop in tomorrow to test-drive the new Chrysler?") which leads to Frustration (marginal employment) and which culminates in Demoralization or Despair (Newark, Detroit, Buffalo). We are not so naïve as to say that a continuous barrage of television commercials alone stimulated the terrible racial unrest of the past few years. But how long can a ghetto community be urged that "It's American to want something better!" without also being given access toward the realization of this ideal. Dr. Hayakawa sees clearly that advertising and mass production are pervasive democratizing agents. Day after day an unemployed Negro in Albany or Milwaukee sits in front of his television receiver and is told in dulcet tones, "You, too, can be beautiful, loved,

28

popular, and successful"—in short all the satisfactions of living in an affluent and Great Society. But when the Idealization is punctured by the cry of his sleeping child who has just been bitten by a rat, frustration sets in and his despair with democratic slogans becomes acute.

Although television programs and films are directed mainly to majorities, it is high time that we acknowledge that American society consists of people from different economic levels and educational backgrounds or what Herbert Gans describes as pluralist subcultures. Too often the media managers fail to recognize that these subcultures, each with its own life-style and values, exist. The highbrow and middlebrow subcultures have their programs, spokesmen, and indeed their own critics. But what about the Negro? Is his subculture being nourished by an occasional Bill Cosby or a Sidney Poitier, gifted as these actors may be, or an occasional film like A *Raisin in the Sun* or *Green Pastures*?

The problem of providing films and television for all groups of Americans, not just the so-called "average" man in Middletown, will constitute a continuing challenge for the sight-and-sound media. As Lancelot Hogben reminds us, when you have found that mythic creature who is exactly the "average" man, you must remember that there is 50 percent of the public below *and* 50 percent above him. Paul Ylvisaker summarizes this challenge to television in particular as follows: "If broadcasting could choose only one community need to serve in this decade of the Second Emancipation, it should be to fan the small fires of self-respect which have been lit in the breasts of the community's neglected and disadvantaged citizens. This year it was the Negro; next year, it may well be the Spanish-and-Mexican American."

I.

Media Managers, Critics, and Audiences*

GILBERT SELDES

Among the first to recognize the artistic and social significance of the mass media, Gilbert Seldes has shared his critical
insights through his major books, *The Seven Lively Arts*, *The
Great Audience* and *The Public Arts*, as well as in numerous
essays.

~~~~~~

THE MANAGERS OF THE MASS MEDIA have, for the most part,
shown what they think by what they do. But from time to time
the heads of studios and the presidents of networks have defined
their working principles. The following composite is offered as a
typical statement of the case for management.

> We are corporations engaged in business, with an obliga-
> tion to the public and an obligation to our stockholders. We
> do not think the two are in conflict.
> We have made our great successes when we have given the
> public what the public wants. We do not set up as dictators
> of taste; we cannot force the public to like what it does not
> like.
> We feel we have no right to devote our facilities to the
> production of entertainment for a small minority.
> We are aware of the fact that public taste is constantly
> changing. We try to keep abreast of—and often a little ahead
> of—these upward movements of public taste.
> We have ways of discovering what the public wants. They
> are not scientific to the finest degree, but we are constantly

* Reprinted from *The New Mass Media: Challenge to a Free Society* (1957),
pp. 54-67, by permission of the American Association of University Women
and the author.

checking our evidence. We test our offerings in private before they are made public; we submit them to the acid test of the box-office and the ratings; we are sensitive to every sign of public favor or disfavor.

By and large, we have found that most of the public wants, most of the time, sheer entertainment from the mass media. We think that if a significantly large number of people want to see a particular picture or a kind of program, we are genuinely working in the public interest when we supply these things.

We recognize a difference between ourselves and the suppliers of commodities such as food and motor cars and cosmetics. Our commodity touches the mind and heart of everyone, and we go to great pains to see that nothing hurtful is seen or heard. Here, too, we may make mistakes. But the public is quick to correct us.

In a democratic society such as ours we cannot win our great audience unless we respond to its desires.

We are businessmen and not ashamed of it. We are also good citizens and proud of what we have accomplished—and hope to do more.

The motion picture studios, the broadcasting companies, and the publishers of the well established mass-circulation books and magazines could not have remained in business if there were not a great deal of truth in the foregoing statements. It remains a question whether the rest of the truth—the case of the critics of the mass media—is not equally important.

In examining the managerial position, the following questions can be asked:

Is there a significant difference between "the public" and "the audience"?

How does a "want" on the part of audiences come into being?

How are wants discovered? Are they specific—for a particular kind or quality of picture or program—or general (for amusement, escape, and so on)?

Are other wants left unanswered in favor of those the mass media can most profitably answer?

Can the media properly be asked to call forth latent wants which cannot be satisfied without a financial sacrifice?

The basic position taken in the following pages is this:

A great many wants—different in kind and different in intensity—exist in all human beings.

These wants are general—for amusement, excitement, the esteem of one's fellow men, and so on. The desire to know more, to improve oneself, may coexist with a desire to have a lot of fun.

The average man does not know the specific way in which his wants may be satisfied. He shops around among the entertainments offered to him. The desire for "escape" may be satisfied by a Western movie or a slapstick farce or a polite comedy.

A latent want may become active.

An audience for particular kinds of pictures or programs cannot come into existence until it has had a chance to sample them.

By offering their wares, the mass media create audiences. When the wares are withdrawn, the audiences cease to exist; they become only potential audiences. When the wares which could satisfy a particular want are not offered and others are offered in profusion, the latent desire for the unoffered kind may dwindle or disappear.

Let us look at some illustrations.

The Creation of Audiences

An example of the process through which a diffused or latent want can become specific and active is the daytime serial. No one asked a cross section of the women of America whether they would like to have, as an accompaniment to washing dishes and making beds, a dramatic entertainment which they would have to listen to at the same time every day of the week, in which the plot was of astounding complexity, yet nothing very much happened on any single day and, if anything did happen, it would bring them to tears.

Actually, the daytime serial came into being after two people who were doing a chatter program in Chicago began to talk about what happened to them the previous day. Gradually these events were dramatized and separated from the actual people and attached to fictional characters.

33

No explicit desire for this specific kind of entertainment had existed. The desire that had existed was for diversion, for vicarious experience of romance, for someone to be companionable with while doing housework.* One of the commonest phrases used by devoted listeners to daytime serials is that they "visited with" Aunt Jenny or Big Sister.

A few years after the daytime serial became established, it virtually filled the morning and afternoon hours of the two largest networks, successive stories being piled on, one after the other. Those responsible, when criticized, said that women simply would not listen to anything else.

The facts were these. The total number of listeners to daytime serials was only a small portion of the number of women who were at home, had radios, and could listen. The majority of such women listened to nothing at all, and a small number listened to other programs (gossip, shopping advice, and so on). But the part of the audience that did follow the daytime serial was the largest group devoted to a *single* kind of program. They had come to like it, and indeed their devotion was great, but they had never in any sense asked for this kind of program. In short, the supply of daytime serials preceded and created the demand for them.

In 1934 William S. Paley, the head of CBS, told his associates that he would like them to arrange to broadcast the Sunday afternoon programs of the New York Philharmonic. When they objected that there was no audience for classical music, he replied, "If there isn't, we'll create it."

It is probable that in 1934 the number of people frequently listening to symphonic music was on the order of 100,000. Some ten years later, when the Philharmonic concerts became a sponsored program, the audience was estimated at perhaps 10,000,000.

The devotion of this audience was demonstrated when, a few years later, the network ceased broadcasting the Philharmonic directly from Carnegie Hall and used instead a recording at a later

* These are not the only satisfactions given by the daytime serial. The more significant ones are complex psychological factors, even more "diffused" than these mentioned. For instance, women were gratified to meet in the heroine someone of a higher level of wealth and education who seemed to have the same disturbances and frustrations.

34

time. The protests that followed were numerous and intense, and the original schedule had to be restored. This was one of the rare instances of successful public pressure, and it proved that a cohesive audience had been brought into being.

We now take up another case which, as if to make the contrast more dramatic, occurred on the same network. One of the most impressive of the sustaining programs of CBS Radio was *Invitation to Learning*, in which men and women of intellectual distinction discussed the literature and the ideas that have shaped the thinking of modern man. After it had been running about a year, the network publicized the fact that, although sixty-eight of the other programs preceded it in popularity, its listeners numbered about one and a half million men and women, some of them hearing it at noon in the East and some as early as 9 A.M. on the West Coast.

Here, again, is an instance of creating an audience. By all previous standards (Chautauqua, for instance), the existence of one and a half million individuals eager to learn about Aristotle, Newton, and John Stuart Mill was phenomenally gratifying. Not publicized, however, was the fact that only thirty-nine stations of the 136 associated with CBS carried the program. The others used the time either for programs of local interest or for commercial programs from which they derived revenue.

Allowing for all differences of situation, it is unreasonable to imagine that a program for which there was an audience in Des Moines could not have found one in Milwaukee or Bangor. The simple fact is that an act of noncreation in ninety-seven communities had occurred, parallel to the act of creation in thirty-nine others. Furthermore, the station in Los Angeles which is owned and operated by the parent network dropped *Invitation to Learning*; its audience, as an audience, ceased to exist. The power to create, therefore, would seem to include the power to withhold the act of creation and the power to destroy.

We should note, also, the managerial position that distinguishes between such a program as the Philharmonic and such programs as the daytime serial. In the first, the managers are eager to accept the credit for creating audiences by offering them some-

35

thing they had not known they wanted; whereas in the second, the managers say they had to present these programs because of a pre-existing want.

Before we analyze that position further, we can note the efforts made by the managers to ascertain the desires of the public.

Proof of "Popularity"

The makers of movies, and even more conspicuously the managers of the broadcasting business, have done considerable testing and research into what the audience wants. One method used by Hollywood is the direct question. "Would you like to see this combination of stars in a picture with this plot?" "Would you prefer this ending or that?"

Another method is the presentation of a virtually completed picture to an unprepared audience, to clock the laughter or observe the degree of attention. The audience is often asked to fill out a brief questionnaire. On the basis of these observations, pictures have at times been altered to be more responsive to the apparent wishes of the test audience.

It should be noted that the test group was a sample of the already existing audience. Moviegoers' responses could only predict what other moviegoers would say. They could not tell the researchers whether the very large group of infrequent moviegoers would be attracted by something different. As time went on, the people in the samples had themselves seen so many movies that their wants and likes had been channeled, if not actually "conditioned."

In radio, groups of people supposed to be typical of the audience would listen to a recording and press buttons indicating approval or disapproval at whatever point their emotions in either direction were stirred.

The producers in each case had to evaluate the responses of their test groups and to decide to what degree the expressed reactions were to be decisive. The correctness of their judgment was proved at the box-office in the case of the movies, and by the ratings in the case of radio and television programs.

In television, a polling of wants on a broader basis has been attempted. Viewers representing a cross section of the audience

36

were asked what they were not getting which they would like to have on the air. The investigators found after three or four years of television that apparently all wants were satisfied, with a small minority asking for new movies and Broadway hits as soon as they appeared. Again it was proven that the audience could not invent programs for itself.

Step by step with asking the public what it wants and pretesting programs before they are offered is the sampling of acceptance which ends up in the highly publicized "ratings." Various techniques are used to discover what programs people are watching, each of them based on the principle of sampling. The sample may be random: every fifth house in a block or every nth name appearing in the telephone book. It may be, on the other hand, a cross-section deliberately constructed to represent people of different ages, races, religions, educational levels, income groups, and so on, in proportion to their estimated number in the entire population. Respondents on the telephone are asked to what programs they are listening, if any. Interviewed at home, they are asked what programs they observed during the previous day (which adds the dimension of memory). Still another method is to attach to the set a device which automatically records every shift from station to station.

Criticism of ratings as inaccurate is often based on the variations in the positions given to various programs. The top one in System A may be third or seventh in B, and this leads to doubt of the method as a whole. In defense of the system it can be said that, given the margin of error usually allowed in handling such statistics, the ratings are probably right in the sense that they indicate the ten programs favored by most people, even if they do not agree as to the order.

Even if they are 100 percent accurate, do the ratings prove what they are supposed to prove? The answer of the researchers is that they merely present a set of statistics and the interpretation of the figures is not their concern.

But as the kind of entertainment we get from the mass media is largely determined by these measurements, and as they are often used to provide a kind of ethical basis for the way the broadcast media are operated, the meaning of the ratings is of central concern to us. For they begin as measurements of attention and, by semantic sleight of hand, "attention" is translated into "popularity" and "popularity" into the "satisfaction of wants"—which in a democratic society is taken as an ethical obligation the mass media must fulfill.

Actually the ratings do not measure popularity. They measure *preferences* only—between available and competing programs. They say that so many people, at this moment, found one program more acceptable than another. Since many people watch any program rather than none at all, the ratings also signify their preference for television over the absence of television.

The broadcasters are aware of this. They know that a program with a low rating is not necessarily "unpopular." It may be playing against an old established favorite, and the remedy is to place it in another time-period when it can achieve a higher rating. They know that some programs have high ratings because they follow other programs with large audiences—some 60 percent of which may continue on with whatever follows on the same station. The word "popularity," which calls up a picture of the great majority of people watching a particular program, is brought down to earth by the broadcasters when they are talking business.

All these things are known to the broadcasters, yet the ratings have a profound influence on the kind of programming we get. One reason is that no other useful measurement has been found. Another is that, with all reservations made, the ratings do correspond roughly to the known facts. There can be no doubt of the actual popularity of Milton Berle, for instance. He was talked about and imitated and mobbed at personal appearances. The ratings faithfully recorded the fact that twenty-one programs were placed opposite his time and failed to draw away his audience. (Some of them, showing promise, were shifted to easier periods and made good.) Sponsors out for maximum audiences are naturally displeased if their programs attract a smaller share—at the moment of broadcast—than a rival does.

One effect of the respect paid to ratings is that programs are often dropped before they can establish themselves. Another is that the style and format of high-rated programs are imitated and experiments discouraged because the sponsor-broadcaster wants

38

"a sure thing." A third consequence is the downgrading of programs—the addition of surefire material which may go against the grain of the original program in order to boost the rating. (This happened in the case of George Gobel. The originality of the program made him a popular figure but, in the race for ratings, new elements such as guests and slapstick were added and finally his program was merged with that of a popular singer.)

These are among the hard realities of the broadcasting business. We have still to consider a basic question. We are told that the American people spend more time listening to and watching broadcasts than at anything else excluding work and sleep. Does this indicate a very high degree of enthusiasm for radio and television?

We have seen that the ratings themselves indicate only a preference. It can be a preference for one program over another or a preference for television as against bowling or as against conversation with friends. The public apparently does want television. There is less evidence that it necessarily or profoundly wants the particular programs presented. It might take other kinds of programs—as the experience with classical music, for which there was "no audience," has shown. It has also been shown that there is a sizable audience for certain kinds of educational programs. When the University of Michigan broadcast over the usual commercial channels, it rolled up an audience of sponsorable proportions. And there is no way of telling what an audience, or the public, would want if its taste had not been formed by the programs between which alone it had to choose.

Wanted: A New Vocabulary

Since the whole ethical basis of broadcasting rests on the principle of service to the people—equated with giving the people what they want—and this, in turn, is "proved" by ratings considered as measures of popularity, it is clear that all these terms must be rigorously examined and detached from their overtones and associations. We have tried to do this in regard to the rating system in order to separate its operations from the highly charged concepts of "duty to the public" in a "democracy," with which statistics on preferences have little to do.

39

We can now turn to a final examination of the idea of what the public wants. A good place to start isolating the idea is half a century before our new mass media came into existence. When Edward Bok was editor of *The Ladies' Home Journal* he said, "The American public always wants something a little better than it asks for." We have here once more the concept of specific desires in the words "asks for"; it is again misleading because the proportion of the public, or even of Bok's subscribers, who were aware of their wants must have been entirely negligible. His rule can be reworded: "The American public will always gladly accept something a little better than most people think it wants." In practice, Bok not only gave women readers literary works of high caliber, along with a considerable amount of the second-rate; he actually put into his magazine things he knew they did not want. For a woman's magazine, in the backwash of the Victorian era, to discuss venereal disease was so offensive that 75,000 individual subscribers cancelled, there were newsstand losses, and advertisers threatened to drop out. No one had asked for this discussion; it was barely acceptable to the majority of the *Journal*'s readers. But as Bok continued to expose readers to it, first a willingness developed and then an interest, precisely as a desire for classical music and for daytime serials later developed in radio.

In the early days of electric lighting, all current was direct. It was an improvement over gaslight and most people, if asked, would have testified to their enthusiastic satisfaction. Few of them could have known of the possibility of alternating current. This improvement in power service was made by the industry without public demand. Perhaps the same obligation lies on the broadcaster. Perhaps the "satisfaction" or "popularity" of the present service is as irrelevant as the popularity of direct current was.

The public wanted direct current more than any previous form of power offered to it. The providers of power did not say that they were performing a sacred duty by giving the public what it wanted—and no more. It is not the concept of the public's right to get what it wants, but the use to which this concept is put that merits criticism. The divergent interpretations of "what the public wants" can be summed up like this:

EITHER	OR
Audiences exist	Audiences are created
Audiences = public	Public > audiences
(equals)	(includes and exceeds)
Demand precedes supply	Supply creates demand
The public gets what it wants	Audiences take what is offered
Wants are specific	Wants are general
Pre-tests prove audience wants	Pre-tests are limited to existing, not potential, audiences
"Ratings" prove popularity	"Ratings" indicate preference between simultaneous offerings
The audience wants little beyond what it gets	The audience is only moderately enthusiastic about what it gets
Only a small minority will accept "better" programs	No matter how good a program is, it will acquire an audience if presented often enough at the right time
The audience is always right	The managers' concept of the audience is often wrong

The Continuing Good

In fairness we must ask ourselves whether we, who so promptly recognize the tricks by which the managers of the mass media identify "what's good for the public" with "what's good for the people as a whole," may not simply be blaming them because they do not consider the needs and desires of the minority of which *we* are a part. The least we can do is to isolate "the public good" or "the public interest" from *all* partial or private goods and interests. We can make an abstraction to serve as a standard. Presently we will return to the concrete.

The life of a nation is a continuum in which the present is a link between the future it creates and the past it inherits. The public good *includes* the present good of the citizens but, in particular, it is that portion of the present good which is carried forward. The planted tree and the healthy child are part of the public good. The cut-over forest and the juvenile delinquent are not.

The intelligence of its citizens is an essential part of the

41

wealth of a democracy, part of the good out of which the future is created.

The power to distinguish between the transient and the enduring is used every day. It is displayed when a mother does not stop her child from crying by giving it the lighted candle it is crying for, and when a statesman jeopardizes his present popularity to protect the long-range interest of his country.

Under pressure, however, man may sacrifice the abiding good for immediate success. How can we protect ourselves against this danger?

It is to the interest of the managers of the mass media to incorporate individuals into a new entity, the audience, and to act as if the audience or the sum of all major audiences were identical with the public. Numerically this comes close to the actual fact, as 98 percent of all U.S. homes are equipped with radio receivers and 94 percent contain television sets. But the statistics do not tell the story in full. They isolate the public from its past and from its future, since the public *as audience* exists only in the present moment. But the *public*, if we think of it as the people who inhabit and will continue to inhabit the country, is the active force that carries the past into the future.

In addition to this distinction between temporary and enduring interests, we can also make a distinction between the *general* interest and all partial interests. We know that any one individual may have an interest identical with that of the nation, but that the national interest is *more* than the sum of all the immediate private interests put together. The national or public interest may be at any moment a compromise between conflicting group interests. In the long run, however, the public interest goes even beyond such compromises. *The public interest is to give life, which includes the power of adaptation and growth, to the essential values of the past so that they can form the character of the future.*

We need another name for the conglomeration of 200,000,000 immediate desires. To confuse them with the abiding interest of the nation is to invest our appetites with an almost religious dignity. These instant and common appetites are real and most of

42

them are legitimate. They are not, however, the only impulses of which people are capable.

In the present state of our society, and in connection with our special subject, we deal not only with the instinctive wants of the people but also with the manipulation of these wants. We deal with the power to encourage certain wants and to cause others to die away. We deal with a social and financial structure which is not in any large way obligated to consider any but the most instant satisfactions. Here is the central conflict.

The Two Positions

When Congress passed the law establishing a certain amount of control over broadcasting, it incorporated as basic three undefined abstractions: "The public interest, convenience and necessity." While convenience and necessity seem relatively practical, "the public interest" has defied the powers of philosophers to define. It has not, however, troubled the practical man, who has found no difficulty in identifying the public interest with whatever interests he thinks the public has at a given moment and, consequently, with whatever the broadcaster chooses to supply. The head of a network once gave this brief definition:

> The broadcasting of any radio program which a substantial portion of the available audience wants to listen to at the time it goes on the air is an example of broadcasting in the public interest.

The analysis we made of "popularity" and "what the public wants" permits us to translate this statement as follows: "We have the right to broadcast any program which even a small fraction of the available audience does not mind listening to, and it is in the public interest that we should do so."

In more philosophical terms, Frank Stanton, President of CBS, said:

> A mass media can only achieve its great audience by practicing . . . cultural democracy . . . by giving the majority of people what they want. . . . We find that most of the people, most of the time, want entertainment from their mass media.

43

The Stanton position is more complex because it brings in the concept of "cultural democracy," which is worth examining. But his other phrases point in the same direction as the first statement: "majority of people . . . what they want . . . most of the people . . . most of the time."

The opposing view is that the managers of the mass media are evading part, at least, of their responsibility if they let themselves be guided by "what most of the people want most of the time," which means only what one very large group of people of similar tastes are willing to accept most of the time. In this view, both a negative and a positive obligation lie upon those who control the media:

Never to present to the public, no matter how great the "demand," anything they themselves consider harmful; and

always to present to the public, no matter how small the demand, whatever they themselves consider good—and good for the public to have a chance to observe.

This is the extreme position of the critics. It is given here as the exact opposite of the extreme managerial position—that those who control the media have no obligation to the public which goes beyond their own inclination and profit. Most critics are ready to settle for less than the positive statement given above, and most managers are willing to concede the value, if not the absolute duty, of adding something above the lowest common denominator of taste.

But for the sake of clarity, it may be useful to contrast the two theoretical positions through hypothetical answers to some crucial questions:

Are the ultimate needs of the public met by satisfying the day-to-day wants of large audiences?

MANAGERS: Within reason, yes. The obligations of the mass media are to meet the daily wants of large majorities, and it would be improper to devote their powers to satisfying negligible minorities.

CRITICS: Not necessarily. The day-to-day wants do not necessarily represent deep-seated desires. Satisfaction of superficial

44

wants may be actually against the ultimate good of the public.

The individual members of the audience have many wants, differing in degree of intensity. Are the ones satisfied by the mass media the only ones worth satisfying?

MANAGERS: They are the only ones held in common by enough people to justify using the mass media. They are basic and legitimate. No known want is left unsatisfied, and it would be unfair to sacrifice the wants of the majority in order to follow the dictates of the superior few.

CRITICS: The satisfactions desired intensely by considerable minorities exist in the majority, also, in lesser degree. It is desirable to let people become aware of more satisfactions in life, and this can be done by giving them a chance to experience what the minorities already know.

Does satisfying the common wants tend to make all others less acute?

MANAGERS: Not necessarily. Other attractive ways of satisfying these other wants exist.

CRITICS: Inevitably. The latent appetite has no chance to be active if others are constantly fed. Desires difficult to fulfill can atrophy if unused.

Should the mass media make a deliberate effort to bring to the surface other wants and desires?

MANAGERS: Only those they can satisfy (which they often do, as in the case of classical music). Beyond that point, this is a function of our schools, churches, and other institutions.

CRITICS: Only those which are socially desirable—not such wants as lie below the threshold now accepted as a minimum (*e.g.*, desire for morbid thrills). Those lying above the present levels should be encouraged.

Within the framework of private enterprise, is there any obligation to offer entertainment which is not popular enough to guarantee a profit?

45

MANAGERS: No. There is, however, an obligation to provide vital information (in broadcasting).

CRITICS: Yes. Profit is made on the whole schedule (of pictures or programs) and it is not necessary to show a book-profit on each item separately.

On whom does the obligation rest to provide for the wants of considerable minorities?

MANAGERS: On those who find it to their advantage to do so. On the state (or other community-unit) if a public benefit is involved, as in higher education.

CRITICS: On those who have access to the majority and profit by it—*i.e.*, on the mass media.

Who is to prevent the presentation of entertainment of low intellectual or moral character if such entertainment turns out to be profitable?

MANAGERS: Public opinion as represented by the police power (not by prior censorship). By the workings of the competitive system, the offending material will turn out to be unprofitable.

CRITICS: Public opinion acting at random unless this proves ineffective—when it must be organized and spurred to action.

In the special case of children, who is to prevent exposure to excitements, diversions from schoolwork, and subject matter they are too young to evaluate properly?

MANAGERS: The parents. To compel the producer to do so would reduce the mass media to an infantile level.

CRITICS: Primarily the parents. But pictures should be publicly graded as suitable and unsuitable, and programs not for children should not be broadcast at inappropriate hours.

All of these divergences of opinion, to which many more could be added, indicate a fundamental difference in the value set upon the mass media. The management principle is that the media do not differ in essence from other forms of business enterprise, that their influence is counteracted by the prestige and effectiveness of other institutions, and that, unless they can be convicted of doing demonstrable harm, it is against the spirit of civil freedom to interfere with them. The extreme opposite position is that the mass media are a new and revolutionary phenomenon, that their power is incalculably greater than the combined power of all other institutions, and that the media have the power and, to an extent, the need to undermine all these others.

In sum, we discover that two divergent philosophies are in conflict here. The one embraced by the owners and managers of the media holds to a strict legal concept of rights. The other holds that the mass media are "affected with a public interest" and must be amenable to public pressure.

Assuming that the broadcaster is like the movie-maker in his corporate right to operate for a profit (so long as he obeys the law), we can ask whether it is good (legal or not) to use the vast powers of the communications machinery for less than their total potential social value. May not such a failure in itself be harmful to the public?

The Potential of Democracy

Let us say that the mass media are not being used deliberately to degrade the intelligence and debase the emotional capacities of the public. Let us say that in specific areas the amount of information reaching the public has been measurably increased and that, in some others, public taste has been markedly elevated by the mass media. Must we not also say that a vast market has come into being for entertainment of a quality so low that no one has ever said a word for it except that the public likes it (and it has not been proved actively harmful)?

As we get the answers to these questions, we seem to be listening to a debate on the meaning of the democratic process. And the debaters appear to be shifting sides. The critic, deploring the low quality of what the public accepts, is called anti-democratic. The producer who says the people are not capable of understanding anything better is called a friend of democracy. But the critic is the one who believes that the public has an infinite capacity to grow in maturity and intelligence, which is the foundation of faith in democracy. And any producer whose daily operations are predicated on a low estimate of his audience is, in reality, the enemy of the people.

47

Our democracy was formed in an age when men had come to believe in progress—in the possibility of improvement (if not of perfectibility). And we now meet a new concept of democracy in the arguments of those who proclaim themselves its friends—the concept of a people incapable of progress except in income and the gadgets they buy with their income. It is against this concept that the critic of the media, consciously or not, aligns himself.

The critic who is not the enemy of the mass media but is the enemy of the uses to which they are often put is bound to meet skillful and statistically formidable arguments. Among thém, one has specific bearing on the widely separated concepts of democracy we are discussing. It is that no acceptable standard has ever been set up, none can ever be set up, for the "goodness" of a program or picture. Obviously aesthetic and intellectual tests are inadequate. They shift with "the winds of doctrine" and criteria which would rule out the works of Charles Dickens are patently inappropriate for a popular medium. The critic must know how to evade the charge of being an intellectual snob—chiefly by not being one, and by having a clear concept of the very thing he is supposed not to have—standards.

The standard proposed is not applicable to a single picture or program as readily as it is to the whole content of the mass media. It is: *whatever engages more of the interests of the individual, whatever tends to enlarge his understanding of life, whatever makes him able to use more of his faculties and to "live more abundantly" is good*; and whatever limits, restricts, and diminishes is bad.

This returns us to the two concepts. One holds that it is enough to satisfy two or three basic wants among all those common to all men, and adds that it is impossible to evoke their interest in any others.

The second holds that all men have some capacity for growth, that this growth is stunted if only the desires they had as children are satisfied, and that the exploitation of these few wants is a crime against the dignity of human beings. It holds that in the heart of every man and woman lies the desire to be a complete person, not merely a bundle of second-rate sensations.

The first removes the distinguishing features of the individual and makes him a faceless unit in an audience. At its extreme point, in the purely commercial aspect of broadcasting, it is satisfied with creating a nation of customers.

The other insists upon the separate qualities of the individual which makes him valuable to whatever group or community he enters of his own volition. It looks forward to a nation of citizens precisely as Jefferson did—citizens capable of making themselves worthy of freedom.

II.

Viewing: A Frame of Reference*

ROBERT J. SILVEY

Robert J. Silvey is Head of Audience Research, British Broadcasting Corporation. Prior to his present position he was statistician to the London Press Exchange.

~~~~~~

THE TENDENCY FOR LUXURIES to become necessities is one of the familiar accompaniments of a rising standard of living. This is certainly what has been happening to television. The time is rapidly approaching when to the economist, if not to the moralist, television sets will have to be classed as necessities of life.

Prodigious though the "consumption" of television may be, the viewer does exercise choice, even if he can only receive one channel. And if he can receive several, choice is forced upon him, for he cannot watch all at once. How does he exercise this choice? Which program does he view and which ignore? And why does he exercise his choice in this way rather than that? What people view is more often discussed than why they view what they do; this essay is an attempt to introduce into consideration of this latter problem an aspect which is often overlooked.

The extent to which an individual views, and what he views, is clearly the result of an interplay of several factors. One of these is "supply": what people view is limited by what is available for them to view. Another is the individual himself and his circumstances: the kind of man he is, the kinds of needs and interests he has, the kinds of compromises he must make in the family circle, the times at which he is at leisure and so on. There is, however, a third fac-

* Reprinted fom *Contrast* (1962), pp. 212-6, by permission of the author and the publisher.

tor, highly important but too often forgotten, namely, viewing's "frame of reference."

It is often said that people don't buy television sets in order to be educated, but in order to be entertained. Advanced, as it usually is, as an argument against the broadcasting of whatever program the speaker happens to consider educational, this proposition is sterile because it is always possible to show that different people have different views, even to the point of finding educational programs interesting. It is, however, a useful reminder that, for the most part, viewing is a form of "play." This is a purely functional description. The essential characteristic which viewing shares with all forms of play is that it is normally an end in itself and rarely a means to an end. In this it differs not only from the work that one does in order to earn one's bread, but also from a great many other common activities, like household chores, the children's homework, or do-it-yourself, all of which are manifestly not ends in themselves but means to an end. That viewing is "play" is the first of three elements in the "frame of reference" to which I wish to call attention.

The second is that viewing is something which takes place "at home." It is a commonplace to say that the television performer must always remember that the normal audience round the set is small, most often only two people. What is less frequently recognized is that "home" has its own peculiar conventions of manners and behavior. Everyone knows that the "home" in which its members stand on ceremony and cannot relax is no home at all. For many it is the place where it goes without saying that you take your coat and tie off; where no one thinks you rude if you suddenly pick up a paper and read. It is the place where you do not have to lock the lavatory door.

The third element in the frame of reference is the fact that in practice it is "for free."

The influence which these elements exert upon any individual will naturally vary, depending upon what "play," "home," and "money" mean to him. Attitudes to play are not uniform. To the extreme Sabbatarian it is anathema on Sundays—and hence so will viewing be. Those who are still influenced by a Puritan upbringing sometimes have an uneasy feeling while they are viewing that they ought to be spending their time in a more improving activity. On the other hand, the child of indulgent parents who take the line that "he will only be a child once" will see no reason why, if he wants to, he should not watch television until he falls asleep from sheer exhaustion. Not everyone can relax in his own home, as many a badgered teen-ager would testify. There may indeed be "homes" in which one member of the family endeavors to keep up cultural pretensions in front of the rest. And the fact that viewing is free is unlikely to have much effect upon the man who does not have to think twice about paying $6.60 for a theater ticket. All the same, exceptions aside, there are prevailing attitudes towards "play," "home," and "money" and they have their effects on the general pattern of viewing.

The generally prevailing mores about "play" in our society are pretty indulgent. The "it's only a game" *attitude* is endemic about adult as well as children's play. "After all it doesn't really matter, it's only a lark . . . only passing the time." In short, "Why not? there's no harm in it." This is, of course, a pretty negative attitude, a far cry from regarding play as a potentially creative activity which, albeit an end in itself, is in fact quite as important to health as work. But in so far as people have this attitude, then they will not regard whether they view or not, or, if they view, which program they view, as really very "important."

For most people the fact that viewing takes place at home, and so is free from the restrictions imposed by the conventions which govern behavior outside the home, robs it of all sense of occasion and makes for a relaxed attitude towards it. The bored can switch off (or over) or wander into another room—how different from the theater or, for that matter, from the shop floor or the office. The viewer need not even look as if he is liking it; on the other hand he can laugh as loudly as he likes, or cry, without making a scene.

Viewing is cheapened by being "free," metaphorically as well as literally. This can work both ways, for whether or not we do not appreciate things we do not have to pay for, we tend to be cavalier about that which costs nothing. By the same token, we are not subject, when viewing, to the compulsive drive to get value for money; when we have watched a television program which turns out to be a waste of time, at least we do not have the added annoyance of feeling that we have also wasted money.

Bearing these points in mind, there should be nothing surprising in the mounting evidence about how people behave when television is on. It is a fallacy to visualize all viewers all gathered round sets in darkened rooms watching with absorbed attention, half hypnotized by the screen. It appears to be quite common for a television program to be given no more than peripheral attention; the so-called viewer may be reading or chatting with half an ear cocked "in case something interesting comes on." Indeed, one American research worker reached the pregnant conclusion that there was "no human activity which did not go on in front of the TV receiver."

Reinforced by the growth of a generation which cannot remember a time when the TV set did not stand in the corner, this attitude must be expected to grow. It is one which broadcasters have long had to accept. But if it must be accepted that there are powerful forces all making for a casual attitude towards viewing, with casual viewing as its consequence, it does not follow that viewing is not enjoyed. Far from it; the very factors which in one sense devalue viewing may, precisely because they encourage the viewer to be uninhibited in this field of behavior, enhance its attractions, give it a peculiar piquancy. It is, however, important to remember that the kinds of satisfaction which are derived from viewing are not confined to those which come from cognition of the content of programs. They may, for instance, come from the mere fact of sitting relaxed, with something not unpleasing to look at if you feel like it, but which you need not look at if you don't want to, from the feeling that it is "company," all the better for not requiring you to make any effort to be sociable, from the knowledge that your husband and family are all together in the same room and not out, goodness knows where.

Our frame of reference has an important bearing on the extent to which people view. None of the three elements of the frame of reference encourages restraint: quite the reverse, they all "sanction" as liberal a degree of indulgence in viewing as the viewer wishes. In this respect viewing is in sharp contrast with that of "work," whether this be work in a factory, an office, a kitchen

53

or a classroom. The essence of the working day, of chores, and of all the tedious obligations of life, is a compliance with a time-table laid down by somebody else or by circumstances. Freedom to view television as much as one likes and for as long as one likes provides an opportunity to restore a balance: to offset some doing-what-you-want against so much doing-what-you-must. This may well account, at least in part, for the fact that it is those whose daily work is dullest who tend to spend most time viewing television.

But apart from its influence upon the amount of viewing, what light does this concept of a frame of reference throw on the selection of one program rather than another? It is all too easy to see this in terms of a pattern of conscious choices. But it is only partially so. The viewer who always knows exactly what he wants, weighs with cool rationality the alternatives available to him and infallibly chooses that which he deems will satisfy him most, is no less a myth than the notorious "economic man."

Because viewing is play, at home, and for nothing, one of the pleasures it offers is that of not having to make decisions. Hence some viewers will always, and most viewers will sometimes, not so much choose as "drift," taking the line of least resistance. This may result in the set being "left on" to whichever channel it happens to be tuned or to the effective abdication of the right to choose in favor of a set of invariable habits.

Even if the viewer has the will to make a choice in terms of "enlightened self-interest" his choice may not be unfettered if, as is often the case, he is not alone. Here it is well to remember that all compromises between conflicting tastes tend to take the form of the lowest common factor.

But if the viewer, wanting to view, doesn't feel like drifting and can please himself, what then? The act of choice must be seen as an attempt to satisfy what I. A. Richards calls appetencies (desires which may often be unconscious) or, failing that, at least to avoid aversions. This act of choice will not always be easy, for both alternatives may to some be equally attractive—or equally repellent. The motives lying behind the choices ultimately made are a fascinating field of inquiry. Why, for example (to borrow Schramm's categories), are one man's appetencies most readily

54

gratified by "fantasy content" while another's are gratified by "reality content"?

The important point is that the frame of reference serves to release the viewer from any obligation to "better himself" or to consider his immortal soul. If you are only out to enjoy yourself why do it the hard way? This loads the dice against any program which stretches the mind or the imagination, which calls for thinking rather than feeling. Not only because such programs call for effort, but because notoriously all new ideas are potentially disturbing, for they may threaten the comfortable assumptions with which we cushion ourselves. By contrast, programs which make few demands upon viewers, and above all those which are built into a cosy framework of familiarity, minister positively to those needs for reassurance and emotional security which are in some measure universal. Raymond Williams quotes Coleridge's reference to "the two contradictory yet co-existing propensities of human nature, namely, indulgence of sloth and hatred of vacancy." Viewing, as a way of spending time, might almost have been designed to gratify both simultaneously.

If influences, mediated through the individual's circumstances, shape viewing behavior, that is not to say that they determine it. The eventual configuration of the pattern of any individual's viewing is what results from these "shaping" influences being brought to bear, within a context of a given output of programs, upon his unique personality structure, itself a product of his genetic endowments, accumulated experience, learned skills, knowledge, acquired tastes and habits, and social relationships. The extent to which each factor is responsible for this final configuration can at present only be guessed at. But what is certain is that the pattern of the public's viewing which is so familiar—the "lighter" the program, the larger the audience—is consistent with the hypothesis that the frame of reference plays a powerful part.

For those who care about television, who see it as a medium of communication through which cultural life can be enriched, this analysis may seem depressing. But to conclude that if this is how television is commonly viewed it isn't worth bothering about, would be a tragic error. The viewing public is now so enormous that even the least ambitious program is seen by an audience

55

which will be numbered in millions; and even if the majority of such an audience makes little effort to meet the producer halfway, those who do can be numerous enough to be the envy of any who hope to interest them that have ears to hear. As a means of communication television may be inherently "wasteful," but the prodigality of nature provides ample examples of "wastefulness" not being wasted.

One final point must be made. The nature of viewing's frame of reference is such as to render people's viewing behavior a poor predictor of the kind of people they really are. That viewing is play, that it takes place at home, and that it costs nothing, means that, at best, the way a viewer indulges in it reflects only one aspect of his nature. As well judge a man by nothing but the food he eats, the games he plays, or the Sunday paper he reads, as judge him solely by the programs he sees on television. People who only view trivia are not necessarily trivial people.

III.

What TV Is Doing to Our Children*

WILBUR SCHRAMM

Director of the Institute of Communication Research at Stanford University, Wilbur Schramm has been closely associated with Unesco as a consultant, writer, and adviser to governments. Among his many books are *Responsibility in Mass Communication* and *Mass Media and National Development*.

◅⌇◌⌇◌⌇◌⌇◌⌇◌⌇◌⌇◌⌇◌⌇◌⌇◌⌇◌⌇◌⌇◌⌇◌⌇◌⌇◌⌇◌⌇▻

ESTIMATES FROM DIFFERENT COUNTRIES indicate that the average child of elementary school and high school age (six to sixteen) devotes to television from twelve to twenty-four hours a week. Elementary school children spend, on the average, a little more time viewing than do high school students.

In the United States, where the most extensive measurements of viewing by children of different ages have been made, it is estimated that a child of three is already averaging about forty-five minutes a day on television. By the time the child is in the first grade (age five or six), he is spending about two hours a day in front of the television set. The time spent watching TV slowly increases with age and with later bedtimes, until a peak is reached at the age of twelve or thirteen when the average child is viewing about three hours a day. During the high school years (thirteen to sixteen), the viewing time decreases to about two hours a day.

This curve is consistent with other evidence on the subject, and the daily averages are not unlike those found in England or Japan. In England, it was found that children ten to eleven and

* Reprinted from *Unesco Courier*, February 1965, pp. 23-6, by permission of the author and the publisher.

57

thirteen to fourteen years old averaged about 1.9 hours a day, which is a little less than the American average for those ages. This may be because less television and fewer station choices are available in England. German youth, fifteen to twenty years old, averaged only seven to eight hours a week, or barely over an hour a day. It is not known whether this is a result of less television being available in Germany or of the age group selected or because there is a real difference in television's attractiveness to young people of different countries.

*   *   *

Wherever television becomes available for a number of hours a day it dominates the leisure time of children. Hilde Himmelweit, A. N. Oppenheim, and Pamela Vince in *Television and the Child*, based on studies made in England, have suggested several principles that help to explain the changes television brings about in leisure patterns. The activities most readily sacrificed are those which satisfy the same needs as television, but less effectively.

For example, younger children will go less often to the cinema when they have television in their homes; they will read fewer comic books, and read less magazine fiction; they will spend less time on radio. These activities meet about the same needs as television. But the reading of newspapers and non-fiction books will hardly be affected by television because these activities answer different needs than does television. Similarly, the adolescent's cinema-going will be less affected than will the younger child's, because for the adolescent the cinema represents a valued social experience, whereas for the younger child it represents television in a theater.

*   *   *

The impressive figure that emerges from the studies of television and leisure time is the enormous amount of time devoted to TV during childhood. An average child six to sixteen years old in any of the countries where more than a few hours of television is available and where children's viewing time has been measured in detail, can be counted on to spend between 500 and 1,000 hours a year in front of the picture tube. This is a total of 6,000 to 12,-

000 hours during the twelve school years. The larger of these figures is not far different from the amount of time an average child spends in school during those same years, taking into account vacations and holidays.

Effect on Taste. Because children spend so much time on television, chiefly on programs not noted for their cultural content, critics have wondered whether television "demeans" children's taste for entertainment. The research carried out has some interesting things to say on the subject.

When children begin at an early age to watch television, they usually start with children's programs—puppets, animals, storytelling, children's songs, and so forth. Very soon, however, they discover adult programs, and come to prefer them. Above all, they prefer the more violent type of adult program including the Western, the adventure program, and crime drama. The result is that, even in the early elementary school years, they view more adult programs than children's programs. This preference for adult programs has been reported from every country where a choice is available and where children's viewing has been studied. In the United States, it has been noted that as much as two-thirds of children's viewing was of programs in which adults make up the majority of the audience.

Children's taste patterns are fairly well structured by the age of ten or eleven. A child who likes a given kind of program on television will be likely to enjoy corresponding material in popular magazines or in films.

The question has been raised whether children "see what they like," or "like what they see." In other words, do they come to enjoy violent programs because no very attractive alternatives are available or do the more violent programs fill so much of the air time because children do not like programs which critics would say are at a higher "cultural level"? This question is by no means settled, but the research does contain at least one interesting finding relating to it.

Dr. Himmelweit and her colleagues found that when only one channel was available in England, and children had only the choice of ceasing to view or viewing a program which they did not expect to find very interesting, they often chose to see that program and became interested in it. Thus their tastes broaden and may be raised in average level. However, when choices are available, children tend to choose the type of program which they have previously found interesting and thus their tastes are hardened and narrowed.

Learning from Television. Abundant evidence has now accumulated that a good teacher can teach effectively by television, though no one contends that all the useful activities of education can be carried on by television.

There is real hope that instructional television may "enrich" many classes, that it may furnish expert teaching in fields where few experts are available (in the teaching of foreign languages in elementary school), that it may add new strength to home and extension teaching, and that it may be useful in some of the developing countries where teachers are in short supply.

Does home television cause a student to do better work in school? This is a hard question to answer. But there is little evidence that television helps children's school performance or that children's grades are poorer when they have television at home. Lower grades go with heavy viewing but the viewing is not necessarily the basic cause of the poor performance. The observation of most students of children's television behavior is that heavy viewing tends to be a symptom of stresses or frustration or unsatisfactory human relationships. The same stresses or unsatisfactory relationships might also reduce a child's efficiency in school, and the frustration of failing to do good work in school might result in heavier viewing.

* * *

Most of the debate, however, has centered not on the effect of television on school grades or on the effectiveness of instructional television, but rather on the incidental learning which children derive from the two hours or more a day they spend on entertainment television. Does television broaden their horizons? Does it teach them skills—desirable or undesirable? Does it give them a distorted view of the adult world?

The general conclusion, as summed up by Dr. Himmelweit recently in a statement concerning the British film inquiry, is disappointment that television does not teach children more than it does. "Surely a medium with such possibilities as television should be able to do more," she writes. "We should by now be able to point with pride to a younger generation more curious, better informed, more enterprising through having been able to offer them a window to the world. What is wrong? It seems to me a devastating indictment that while ten-year-olds still pick up some knowledge from television, by the time they reach thirteen only the dull ones do so, and that the television hold becomes less the more intelligent the child. . . . It must give even more cause for reflection to realize that these children view almost exclusively programs designed for family and adult entertainment. Is it perhaps that much of the evening's entertainment is at the level of a ten- to eleven-year-old?"

It was found in Canada that children in a television town came to the first grade of school with vocabularies about a year more advanced than children in a town without television. Half a dozen years later, however, the differences had disappeared, and the children with television knew actually less about public affairs (although more about entertainment matters) than the children without television. Here, as in other studies, it was found that in the early school years the bright children seem to learn more from television whereas after age twelve or thirteen the slower children seem to use television more and gain more from it while the brighter ones depend more and more on print. However, there is also some evidence that parents and teachers think the level of general knowledge is increased by television.

Studies of television content, of course, vary in their results from country to country but many of them point out that television brings a child face to face with adult problems long before he ordinarily would meet them, and in some countries this tends to give him a view of adult life that is distorted in terms of social class, desirable occupations, and violent ways of solving problems. To what extent this television world view becomes a child's real world view, affects his plans and expectations and preparations, and controls his behavior as an adult is not yet fully known.

When Does Television Affect a Child's Outlook and Values?
Television has its maximum psychological effect on children, ac-

cording to one of the ablest writers on the subject, when the values or viewpoints recur from program to program; the values are presented in dramatic form so that they evoke emotional reactions; they link with the child's immediate needs and interests; the viewer tends to be uncritical of and attached to the medium; and when a viewer, through his friends, parents, or immediate environment, is not already supplied with a set of values which would provide a standard against which to assess the view offered on television.

Thus, in order to predict the effect of television one must know something about the television and something about the child. A child with high aggression will probably make special use of the aggressive materials he finds in a television program. Many children may learn from a television crime program how a holdup is committed, but only a few children—for example, some who have psychopathic tendencies or have fallen under the influence of a criminal gang—are likely ever to make use of this information. For most children, television is a pleasing experience, a relaxation of tensions and relief from pressing problems; but to some it is a confusing experience because they are unable entirely to separate the fantasy world of television from the real world. Thus the same television program will not have the same effect on all children any more than will the same child derive the same effect from all programs.

But there is one element in the relation of child to program which seems rather more important than any of the others in determining what effect the program has. This is the extent to which the child can identify with one or more of the characters in a program.

Television and Delinquency. Most students of television effects on children are unwilling to say that identification or incidental learning from television plays any large part in causing delinquency or crime. The roots of this criminal behavior lie far deeper than television; they reach into the personality, the family experience, the relationships with others in the same age group as the delinquent or criminal individual. At most, television can be merely a contributory cause, and is likely to affect only the child who is already maladjusted and delinquency-prone.

Television may contribute by teaching a criminal skill which may be used when the individual decides to commit a crime. It may trigger off an act of delinquency by feeding a child's aggressive nature. Or it may encourage delinquent behavior by implanting an unreal idea of the importance of violent behavior in solving human problems. But in any of these cases television by itself cannot make a normal, well-adjusted child into a delinquent. This is the almost unanimous conclusion of research and clinical investigation.

The Effect of Violence. Because so much of the entertainment a child sees on television is violent, special attention has been paid by researchers to the possible effect of all this violence. The original hypothesis was that television violence might serve as a safety valve, by means of which a child might rid himself vicariously of pent-up aggressions. However, a series of experiments have now come out with exactly the opposite result.

The typical method used in such experiments is to frustrate a group of children so that they develop a high level of aggression. Then they are shown a film or a television recording of a drama in which aggressive behavior plays a prominent part. (In different experiments, the ending, the type of aggression, the nature of the character, and other elements of the story are varied.) A similar group of children, who have not been frustrated, are shown the same program. Then, the members of the two groups are given chances to express any aggression they may have—either by behavior or in tests of some type.

Invariably, there has been a great difference between the experimental and the control group. The children who were not frustrated (the control group) seem no more aggressive than they were before seeing the picture. But the children who were initially frustrated (the experimental group) have not reduced their aggression; if anything, they have built it up. They have in many cases found ways to express it.

* * *

We know that children with high levels of aggression are especially attracted to violent programs on television. If television now feeds rather than reduces children's aggressive tendencies and if it gives them hints as to how to take out aggression with fists,

63

knives, or guns, then an opportunity may come to use those weapons at a moment when they are angry. We assume this does not happen often because social norms teach them not to behave in such a way. But certainly there is little to make us believe that violent programs on television *reduce* the likelihood of violence in real life.

Suppose an aggressive child regularly identifies with a hero who himself uses violence to solve problems. For example, French investigators found that delinquent boys were very fond of a certain film hero who "fights . . . knows how to treat women . . . overcomes all obstacles . . . respects no moral code and frequently plays an ambiguous role; one can never tell whether he is on the side of the police or the side of the gangsters." Analyzing the reactions of the boys they were studying, they concluded that such a mass media experience as this is especially dangerous for juvenile delinquents or potential delinquents.

On the whole, the weight of the evidence is behind one researcher's conclusion that "the heavy dosage of violence in the mass media," although not a major determinant of crime or delinquency, "heightens the probability that someone in the audience will behave aggressively in a later situation."

Television and Maladjustment. One of the most important topics in the literature of television research is the relation of television experience to a child's social adjustment and his mental health. This has not yet been adequately examined because of the scarcity of clinical studies, and only tentative conclusions are possible.

There is ample evidence, however, that television sometimes frightens children, and of what kind of material is most frightening. But children often like to be frightened (witness the popularity of the roller-coaster!). And no scholar contends that television is likely to have a harmful effect on the social adjustment or the mental health of a child who enjoys warm and solid relationships at home and with his friends and who has no foundation of mental illness.

For this reason, parents have been advised that the greatest defense they can raise against possible ill effects of television is to make their children feel loved and secure at home, and to help

64

them to satisfactory relationships with friends of their own age. And so far as fright is concerned, parents can help their children to avoid programs that are too frightening.

Dr. Lawrence Z. Freedman, a psychiatrist, points out that most children in a reasonably stable environment do not confuse the make-believe world of television with the real experiences of personal and family relationships. "Most youngsters find the immediate personal relationships more compelling and rewarding than the animated, pictorial substitutes," he says. ". . . The intensity and psychic significance of the child's response to television is the reciprocal of the satisfaction he gains in the milieu of his family, school, and friends. One would predict that the less intelligent, the most disturbed youngsters and those having the poorest relationships with their families and peers would be most likely to immerse themselves in televiewing as escape and stimulus."

*   *   *

Does television make children passive and withdrawn? There is no proof that it does, although television clearly may contribute to passivity and withdrawal when there is already a tendency present. As Dr. Freedman points out, "when the automobile removed youngsters from the surveillance of their homes, we were concerned for their morals. Now television immobilizes them in the living room and we deplore their passivity." Nor is there any real evidence that television is good or bad for home life. It keeps children more often at home. But watching television in a group does not seem to make for a really strong group relationship; each member of the family reacts individually, more often than as part of a group, to the television he sees. The conclusion is that television is not likely either to ruin a healthy home relationship or rescue an unhealthy one. And a reasonable corollary is that the quality of a child's social relationships is more likely to control his use of television, than vice versa.

In general, the evidence on physical effects is negative. Television postpones average bedtimes a few minutes, but seems to decrease sleeping time very little because children who have stayed up later appear to go to sleep more quickly. It is true that there are reports of children who are frightened by evening television and unable to go to sleep, and of children who are sleepy in school because they have stayed up late at night to see a program, but none of the studies can find any evidence of widespread fatigue or other physical effect related to television. Indeed, there is some reason to think that standards of behavior set by the parents may have more to do than television with late bedtimes, and that if these same homes did not have television the children might still stay up late for other purposes.

Nor is there any evidence that television, viewed properly, has a bad effect on children's eyesight. Some specialists say that reading is as likely as viewing to cause eyestrain, and others that viewing is good "exercise" for the eyes. In general ophthalmologists advise children to view television in a room where the television receiver is not the only source of light, not to sit closer than six feet from the screen and to sit with the screen at approximately eye level. (The British ophthalmologists say, "eye level or slightly below"; the Polish say, "eye level, or a bit higher.") Even eye weariness resulting from protracted and improper viewing can be overcome in a short period of rest, a Japanese study found.

* * *

We are now rich in surveys, and except where a country which has not had a large survey wants a broad picture of the television behavior of its children in order to see how their behavior is different from that revealed by other surveys, there seems less need now for survey than for experiment. Perhaps the most obvious need is for additional close experimental and clinical studies of the effect which a given kind of television has on a given kind of child. It may be a long time before close, careful studies like these answer all the questions posed by the effect of television on children, but without such studies we shall never be able to say clearly and sharply what we are measuring and where our results apply. Whenever possible these studies should be extended over a period of years, so that we may begin to understand the cumulative effects of television.

Another aspect of television which deserves more attention is the problem of how to realize the potential of the medium. Some disappointment has been expressed at the fact that television has not completely fulfilled its potential as a window on the world, that it has not given us a better informed and more inquiring generation, and that it has merely provided the average child with two to three hours of daily entertainment.

Perhaps now we should study how to make the non-entertainment, non-fictional programs on television more interesting, so that they will attract their share of viewers and contribute their share of learning. And perhaps we need to study how taste is formed, so that instead of narrowing our children's taste around a certain level of entertainment we can broaden their television interest and encourage them to use television when possible as a window on the world rather than as a momentary escape from the stresses of growing up.

IV.

Television and the American Negro*

S. I. HAYAKAWA

The work of S. I. Hayakawa is well known. He is editor of
ETC.: A Review of General Semantics and author of *Language in Thought and Action*, and *Language, Meaning and Maturity*.

~~~~~~

INTERRACIAL communication is very much on our minds these
days when racial demonstrations are going on almost daily in cities
both in the South and the North. All problems of communication, whether between management and labor, white and Negro,
or nation and nation, have some elements in common, and it is
hardly possible to analyze one such set of problems without learning something about all of them. Furthermore, our success or
failure in interracial communication is going to affect profoundly
our success or failure in international communication.

The tremendous recent disturbances in Birmingham, Alabama,
in Cambridge, Maryland, in Chicago and Los Angeles and Detroit
and Newark have deeply shocked and upset many white people
who are saying, "Aren't the Negroes making steady progress? Why
all the sudden uproar?" Others are asking an entirely different
question, namely, why these demonstrations for civil rights hadn't
started long ago, with white people almost unanimous for so long
in ignoring the problem and pretending that it isn't there—seal-
ing themselves off behind restrictive covenants, moving to the
suburbs, and forgetting all about it. The shocked looks on the
faces of all too many white people in the past few months are very

* Reprinted by permission from *ETC.: A Review of General Semantics*, Vol.
XX, No. 4, pp. 395-410; copyright 1963, by the International Society for
General Semantics.

clear indications of the degree to which they have been shutting their eyes to what is going on—and also a clear indication of the necessity of shock tactics in order to wake them up.

The causes of any great social revolution are many and complex. But the student of general semantics will tend to look for the part that communication plays in any large social event. I think that most students of general semantics are familiar with the idea that the invention of printing—that is, a revolution in the techniques of communication—brought an end to the Middle Ages and ushered in the Renaissance. Before the invention of printing, when books were as rare as Rolls-Royces, the diffusion of knowledge, if it took place at all, was through a priesthood who told the people what was good for them to know. After printing, there was an immediate and widespread increase of that private vice known as reading, resulting in independent reflection and thought, so that in one area of life after another—in art, in government, in science, in commerce—new ideas began to blossom. The rise of one Protestant sect after another as people read and interpreted the Scriptures for themselves instead of relying upon the interpretations of a priestly elite was only one of the many manifestations of increased intellectual activity, and therefore increased social change and unrest, precipitated by the communications revolution brought on by printing.

*   *   *

Granting the validity of all that others have said and written about the causes of present Negro unrest, I should like to add another that has not been much explored. The great and revolutionary communications instrument of the present in the United States is television. What it has done to the nation has not yet been measured, and what it will eventually do cannot now be predicted. But there can be no doubt that it is already contributing much to social change, and that even greater changes now unforeseeable will result from television. A revolution in communications is always a far more important thing than is realized at the time. I wonder how many people have thought of the degree to which the revolution of rising expectations in Latin America, Asia, and Africa is due to the portable radio? In little villages all over

Africa, my African students tell me, people who formerly had almost no cultural contacts beyond the next village gather today around portable, battery-operated radios to hear the news from London, New York, Paris, Tokyo, and Moscow—and therefore they start wanting to become citizens of a larger world than they have ever known before.

Let us review some of the peculiar facts about television. In the first place, like radio, it bypasses literacy. It can be understood and enjoyed by those who cannot read and write. Before the advent of radio and television, to be illiterate was to be cut off from the world. But now the illiterate, whether in the Congo, in Mississippi, or in New York, can hear about and concern himself with matters which he formerly knew nothing about. Television especially has brought the whole big startling world into the lives and imaginations of millions who would never have been able to discover it through reading.

Secondly, television spread with greater rapidity among the poor than the rich in the United States, among the uneducated than among the educated. Long before upper-middle-class homes had made up their minds about the wisdom of buying a television set and exposing their children to it, forests of television antennae had risen above tenement homes in the depressed and slum districts throughout the country. In the socio-economic pattern of the spread of television over America, Negroes hold an important place. The poor and the uneducated being numerous in the Negro community, television spread with special rapidity among Negroes. I recall from about 1951 a telephone call I received from an almost illiterate Negro drummer—a friend with whom I had worked many times in giving lecture-demonstrations on jazz history. He called to tell me that he was broke, out of a job, and willing to work at anything to make a little money, and he gave this touching picture of his poverty: "Me and my wife just moved into this apartment, Doc. We ain't got a stick of furniture, not even a bed. All we got is our television set."

Television also holds for Negroes the additional advantage of providing entertainment at home, enabling especially the Southern Negro to avoid the indignities of the ill-kept, humiliating, separate balconies of the segregated movie houses of the Southern and border states.

Another important fact about television is that from the point of view of the producer it is a much more expensive medium than radio. Radio is cheap enough so that small groups can organize and pay for programs and stations of their own—foreign language groups, religious denominations, and the like. In almost every large city, therefore, there are all-Negro radio stations featuring Negro talent, Negro news, Negro church services. Television is too expensive to be supported by any such minority, hence all television programs are addressed pretty much to the whole community. This means that whatever the television set says to white people, it also says to Negroes.

*   *   *

All the foregoing facts tie in with another important fact, namely, that American television is commercially sponsored; it finds its economic support and justification in helping to push and promote consumer goods of all kinds. Hence television is always friendly, always beckoning cheerfully to the viewer, always inviting and alluring: "*Won't* you try our new cake mix?" "What did *you* think of the Governor's message to the legislature?" "Summer time is picnic time, and your picnic is not complete without our beer!" "You'll get a new taste thrill from our new filtered cigarette." "Do you know what Dean Rusk said in a speech in Paris yesterday?" "Won't you drop in to test-drive the new Buick?" "It's American to want something better!"

The spokesmen of the advertising profession continue to tell us that the moral and economic justification of their activities is that they create wants and stimulate demand and thereby increase the standard of living. I have little quarrel with this argument. Advertising and mass production are profoundly democratizing influences. They put standard, mass-produced goods into the hands of everybody. They tell everybody, "No matter how miserable your present condition, you *can* be as good as anybody else. You too can look attractive. You too can have a beautiful and spotless kitchen. You too can have an exciting and romantic vacation

71

through our thrift-plan holiday cruise. You too can enjoy all the satisfactions of living in our lush and abundant consumer economy!"

*   *   *

James Baldwin has said that the most difficult and bewildering thing about the white world is that it acts as if Negroes simply weren't there. There is a deeper problem than that of prejudice. The more serious problem is unawareness. Here, for example, is a television commercial telling what fun and excitement children can have if they can persuade their parents to bring them to such-and-such an amusement park. The commercial does not bother to explain that they need not come if they are Negroes. Here is another commercial inviting the family to hop into the car and drive just twenty-five minutes from downtown to Woodland Acres, the beautiful new residential development, where three-bedroom ranch-type homes are now open for inspection. It does not tell you that if you are Negro, these homes are not for you. Here is an advertisement telling you to order this new, sparkling soft drink with the thrilling new flavor. It doesn't tell you that if you are Negro, you will have to drink it standing on the sidewalk outside the cafe.

*   *   *

Now imagine that you are a Negro teen-ager, to whom the television set, with messages such as the foregoing, has been his constant baby-sitter and companion ever since he can remember. If you are this Negro teen-ager, you have spent more hours of your life in front of the television set than you have spent in school, according to the statistics given by audience research surveys. You do not know what your elders know, namely, which advertisements to heed and which to ignore as not being addressed to you. You only know that the friendly, friendly television set is always saying to you, "You are an American. You are entitled to eat and drink and wear what other Americans eat and drink and wear. You must think about the same political and world problems that other Americans think about. You are a member of the national community of Americans."

72

Then you discover, as you begin to go out into the world to shop for clothes, eat at a lunch counter, or apply for a job, that the culture is not willing to live up to its advertising. You discover that there is a caste system that the television set has told you nothing about—and that as a member of the wrong caste, most of the privileges of being an American, except for paying taxes and serving in the armed forces, are in whole or in part denied to you. So the Negroes are marching and picketing and demonstrating in protest. What would *you* do?

It is deeply significant that so many young people are at the heart of the current racial demonstrations. Teen-agers by the hundreds have been hustled off to jail by the Southern police—and they are singing and cheering as they go! Some Northern editorialists have asserted angrily that these young people are being exploited and used by unscrupulous Negro leaders to propagandize their demands. It still hasn't occurred to them that Negro leaders are not leading anyone any more. They are merely breathlessly trying to keep up with the revolutionary fervor of the young people.

I wonder if advertisers and television officials themselves know what they are doing to the public. Let them ask themselves as they preview a commercial how it looks and what it means to the 10 percent, or in some parts of the country, the 50 percent of their viewing audiences who are Negroes. I would like them to ask themselves about the ethics of offering for sale to the entire public goods and services which will be denied to Negro clients if they decide to buy.

*   *   *

Successful communication with our Negro fellow citizens must begin, as all communications must begin, with a recognition that words are not enough, that words must be the prelude to actions, and that actions must be earnestly considered and honestly proposed in the light of the full historical context and the present realities. What I am asking is that communications be based on a determination to carry through the moral purposes of the Abolitionists—to start a new Abolitionism—to abolish not only slavery, but the entire caste system that was devised to take its place. And here it might be well for all of us to remind ourselves that

73

historic Abolitionism has its Southern as well as its Northern sources: George Washington, Patrick Henry, Thomas Jefferson, and John Randolph were deeply opposed to slavery and looked forward to its ultimate extinction. Large numbers of Methodists, Baptists, Quakers, Presbyterians, and many other groups in the South fought against slavery as fervently as did the Northern Abolitionists.

In order to abolish the caste system, the present-day Abolitionist has certain advantages over his pre-Civil War ancestor. As I have said, we have in our times mass production, mass communications, and above all we have television. In order to maintain a caste system, members of different castes must not be permitted to communicate freely with each other, and they must also be separated from each other by receiving their communications from different channels. It would be difficult at this stage to devise entirely separate television channels for whites and Negroes, with special stations and special receivers for the two groups so that neither would get messages from the wrong channel. Besides, the necessities of mass marketing are structurally at variance against such a division of the national audience. Therefore, a powerful unifying force is at work to bring whites and Negroes together in their tastes and their aspirations, in spite of the best efforts of the White Citizens Councils and the Black Muslims. The impact of nationwide networks enables white and Negro, Jew and Gentile, Protestant and Catholic, to laugh simultaneously at the same jokes, thrill at the same adventures, admire and detest the same good guys and bad guys, yearn for the same automobiles, dream the same dreams, and therefore develop ultimately the same kind of value systems. From the television programs, Americans learn to see themselves as people not willing to be pushed around, and our Negro young people have learned that lesson, and they will be pushed around no longer.

The work that television has done cannot be undone—and we must go along with it gracefully and teach our recalcitrant neighbors to do the same.

PART TWO

MEDIA AND MESSAGES

Denk nicht zuviel von dem was keiner weiss!
Unhebbar ist der lebenbilder sinn;

—STEFAN GEORG

L'importance du cinéma, c'est qu'il est le
premier art mondial. La puissance de l'image
est victorieuse des différences de langue.

—ANDRÉ MALRAUX

~~~~~~

As RADIO, MOTION PICTURES, and television pervaded our society, it was inevitable that the nature of communication would become a central point of inquiry for scholars in many disciplines. The behavioral scientist was concerned primarily with the *effects* of the mass media, e.g., on voting decisions, purchasing habits, and attitudinal changes; the social scientist was concerned with how the manners and morals depicted in films, and later on television, were influencing the quality of our social fabric; the humanist and the aesthetician began to reevaluate art itself under the rubric of communication. What has emerged over the past quarter-century is an increasing emphasis on an interdisciplinary approach toward the study of communication, one that investigates the "total communications situation."

Because researchers quickly recognized the enormous complexity of mass communication, they began to formulate explanatory models and paradigms in an attempt to abstract the "process" of communication. One of the earliest and most

<div align="center">75</div>

widely used models was Harold Lasswell's *who—says what—through what channel—to whom—with what effect*. Valuable as the Lasswellian formula was, it implied that the communication process is unidirectional and that the message strikes the receiver as a kind of hypodermic needle. Subsequently, as we came to understand the role of mediating factors (e.g., "gate-keepers," group affiliation, and personality variables) we have reexamined the pioneering insights of the symbolic interactionists, W. I. Thomas and George Herbert Mead. They returned our thinking to the etymology of the word *communication*—which began with the Latin *communicatus*, or *shared*. Both parties in a communications situation—the sender of a message and the receiver—are involved; through shared symbols both participate and collaborate in the process by an exchange of meaning.

It is this collaborative activity between sight-and-sound communicators and audiences that Walter Lassally acknowledges as the basis for film communication. The central thesis of his essay is that audiences must share *emotionally* the intent of the film-maker. His position is similar to Ernst Kris's *Psychoanalytic Explorations in Art*. Kris sees communication as lying not so much in the prior intent of the artist-maker as in a subsequent recreation by audiences. In some cases, however, this emotional collaboration can be overly successful. For example, during Orson Welles's famous radio broadcast of October, 1938, *Invasion from Mars*, thousands of listeners shared too well the emotional quotient of the message (with traumatic results).

Granted that Welles succeeded beyond his expectations, his program was an anomaly; more often audiences share only a part of the communicator's intent. They are not always able to emotionally "read" the message and derive the exact intended meaning. This inability to achieve a one-to-one relationship between communicators and audiences is caused by such lacunae in the process which cybernetic-oriented communications specialists (such as Shannon, Weaver, and Wiener) call *noise*.

Noise may originate with the sight-and-sound communicator himself. As Robert Steele states in his contribution to this section, the film director must come to grips with the "machinery" of his medium. Unlike the painter, working solely with brush, paints, and canvas, the film director must recognize the technological hardware which stands between his conception and its realization. Cameras, lenses, lighting grids, moviolas, even the intricate operations of film laboratories are only part of the technology he must master. He must also be aware of the syntax of his medium (the language of "shots" and transitions) and all the conventions of structuring a sight-and-sound message. To the extent he has not learned the "grammar of the film" his intent will be distorted and unrealized.

But no matter how skilled a Fellini or a Howard Hawks may be in mastering the techniques of the film medium, we know that audiences bring a substantial amount of "psychological noise" with them. This exists in their predispositions, prejudices, and indeed their total personality makeup. We have all been in theaters where it appeared to us that people were laughing at the wrong places. They were emotionally "reading" something in the film that eluded us.

A major criticism of motion pictures and television programs is that they are often so easily understandable and so "tightly structured" that they reduce to the minimum the possibility of alternative interpretations. The viewer can anticipate the plot, the rhythm of the cutting seldom varies, the characters are stereotypes of stereotypes, and in some television comedies the canned laughter tells us when to chuckle. In such films and programs (which unfortunately constitute the bulk of sight-and-sound messages emanating from Hollywood and New York) there appears to be a tacit agreement between communicators and audiences that neither is going to impose too much on each other's collaborative energies. If this is the price we must pay in order to minimize *noise* and ensure that the message is emotionally perceived precisely as it was sent, perhaps the critics of mass culture have a valid argument.

Yet even within our much-maligned mass culture we are beginning to see a number of films that are "loosely structured" and which demand an active collaboration on the part of audiences. If the traditional Hollywood motion picture is, in McLuhan's terminology, "hot" (i.e., tightly structured), the 1967 American release, *Up the Down Staircase*, is decidedly "cool." While the film did not abandon the attempt to tell a story, the plot-line did not follow the usual sequence of exposition, rising action, climax and denouement. Instead, the film was composed of a mosaic of related incidents which had little temporal continuity. There were no conflicts resolved; and at the conclusion of the film the several concurrent themes were not neatly tied and packaged. *Up the Down Staircase* was "open-ended," and whether the young teacher was a success or failure was left to audiences to determine. The photography complemented the film's loose structure; the *cinéma vérité* technique of the unsteady hand-held camera drew viewers in "close" to the spontaneous flow of events.

Each of the contending institutions involved in the sight-and-sound media thinks it "knows" audiences best, and that it alone is able to determine what will be accepted and rejected. For example, the business institution may force inclusions in the message which the art institution eschews ("but will it sell?"); government and education may demand omissions (less violence and sexuality). What emerges is a film or television message that is often a compromise.

To risk a generalization, when the compromise is more favorable toward the business institution the film message is "hot"; that is, it is tightly structured and its meaning is easily grasped. However, when the compromise is more favor-

78

able toward the art institution the message is "cool." The films of the French "New Wave," of Fellini, Bergman, and Antonioni—the art films, which Norman Holland in his essay calls "puzzling movies"—contain little surface information and correspondingly more ambiguity and *noise*. To overcome this kind of *noise* and derive any meaning from a *Last Year at Marienbad* the viewer must involve, implicate, and emotionally extend himself. If he is unwilling to do so, he leaves the theater muttering to himself, "What does it mean?"

Yet even if the viewer is willing to enter into emotional collaboration with a film or television program he may be thwarted by another kind of *noise*, which may originate in the cultural differences between communicators and audiences. It is far easier for Western audiences to empathize with Orson Welles's *Macbeth* than with Kurosawa's version. The pace and cadence of a Japanese film, even from the hands of a master director, cannot be fully grasped unless the viewer has a deep understanding of Oriental symbolism and cultural traditions. Conversely, an American film shown in Japan may be equally misperceived. Indeed, when Edward R. Murrow was Director of the United States Information Agency he voiced his concern over the opinion of America which might be derived from our film exports. Although such techniques as dubbing and subtitling try to minimize the *noise* from cultural differences of languages, as yet we have no internationally understood syntax of sight-and-sound symbols.

In his discerning essay, Robert Vas describes how the film medium can be used as a powerful weapon of propaganda. Film is more than a photographic record of, in Lumière's phrase, "nature caught in the act." It is also a reality "sifted, pointed, and intensified." Sight-and-sound symbols can be so manipulated and juxtaposed that audiences can be emotionally tricked. While Vas considers all films to some extent persuasive, his prime concern is with the political propaganda film. While they clearly work toward different goals, the sorcery of Britain's *The War Game* is not unlike the magic of Italy's *Africa Addio,* Canada's *Mills of the Gods,* Russia's *The Cranes Are Flying* or the United States Information Agency's *The March.*

Just as when the "compromise" is more favorable toward business, so when the compromise leans more toward the political institution the result is a film-message that is "hot" and tightly structured. For example, in Eisenstein's *Alexander Nevsky* there is no room for *noise,* ambiguity, or alternative interpretations. The cutting, the casting, the photography, Prokofiev's score—the entire aural and visual montage—are deliberately designed and controlled to produce a "hot" message. The emotional energy flows mainly *from* the screen, requiring audiences to exert little collaborative effort. The viewer of a "hot" propaganda film is not unlike the passive shadow-watcher of Plato's cave. When Plato ostracized the artist from his ideal Republic, fearing the latter would emotionally manipulate the populace, perhaps he anticipated an Eisenstein, a Leni Riefenstahl, or even a John Grierson.

If films can "lie" and perpetrate "the big cheat," so can television, according to Henry Fairlie. However ardently the television journalist may strive for impartiality and "objectivity" in the reporting of news, the very fact that he *points* his camera and makes a selection of reality interferes with the veracity of his report. The result is that viewers may mistake the "excerpted reality" for the event itself. As a corrective measure, Fairlie urges that news commentators supply, for "audience steerage," *words* as well as pictures.

What Fairlie is touching upon is the "nature" of television as a communications medium. Although television is both sight *and* sound, it is not cinema; and although it has its technological and programming roots in radio, it is more than just pictures added to words. It is because television is neither fish nor fowl that its "proper form" is still being argued. Matching "content" to form is, to the television dramatist, an aesthetic problem; to the television journalist it is also a moral problem.

Many critics of the mass media decry the lack of commitment in television programs. They insist that television should refrain from being a "timid giant" and take strong positions on controversial issues. The charge is that even when television does deal with "serious" subjects, in documentaries and fictional social realism, such as *East Side/West Side*, the treatment is neutralized by an over-zealousness to present all sides. The result is that there is no dominant point of view from which a definitive conclusion may be drawn.

At first thought the labeling of television as a "timid giant" seems valid, but when we consider the pervasiveness of this electronic sorcerer and the alchemy of its images, do we really want the messages of television to be so "heated up" as to leave no room for alternate conclusions? Do we want television to become so bold a giant that it will overpower us emotionally and leave us no room for collaboration? Take, for example, a 1967 CBS Report, *The Homosexuals*. Some critics of television would have preferred that Mike Wallace, the moderator-reporter, had taken a strong stand (negative or positive) on this social problem, and made authoritative judgments. Instead, the program explored all aspects of the matter and left the decision to its audience.

If we deplore the fact that a Chet Huntley or Walter Cronkite do not vociferously editorialize on an electronic soapbox, and that many television personalities, such as Hugh Downs, appear to be bland and uncommitted, what is the recourse? Would we be willing for them to expropriate the power for propaganda which lies within their grasp? Fortunately, in our democratic system where no single institutional force, whether it be NBC or the FCC, can gain exclusive domination of the sight-and-sound media, the communicator cannot assume such power.

Similar charges have been made that Hollywood is uncommitted, that the American film should tackle racial problems more realistically than the romanticized A *Patch of Blue*, for instance. Even as television programs soft-pedal controversy, so do the majority of films. *Up the Down Staircase* is merely one example of an increasing "coolness" in motion pictures as well as television.

What is occurring is a creative cross-fertilization between motion pictures and television. Sight-and-sound communicators, such as John Frankenheimer, Tad Mosel, Richard Lester, Arthur Hiller, and Robert Mulligan, have worked in both media. There is also a mutual borrowing of both content and production techniques. The widely used *cinéma vérité* method of film-making that reduces editing in an attempt to capture "life as it exists" is an extension of tele-*vérité*. For example, as the batter in a "live" baseball game steps to the plate we hear, simultaneously voice-over, an interview that occurred the day before. In Frankenheimer's *Grand Prix* the same technique of dissynchronized time is used: we see the *present* race and at the same time, by a split-screen, the *past* preparation for the race.

This cross-fertilization, of course, works the other way. In Dan Melnick's television series *N.Y.P.D.* he deliberately imitated the jump-cuts, fragmented thoughts, and non-flashback narration of the films of Alain Resnais, Godard, and Antonioni. Although working in the hackneyed genre of the cops-and-robbers melodrama, Melnick believes that audiences "are more sophisticated than given credit, in terms of film techniques."

If Melnick's assertion holds water, the so-called average viewer, who might never consider seeing *La Guerre Est Finie* or *Blow-Up*, inadvertently will become familiar with the structure of the "cool" message. Hopefully, the more audiences accept the kinds of messages which require their collaboration, the less they will be inclined to tolerate the trite, tightly structured "copycat" film and television program.

Were media managers to be convinced of the wide acceptance of such experimentation in production techniques, we might see a fuller realization of the creative potential of the sight-and-sound media, sooner than any of us could ever hope.

In many ways the two essays by David T. Bazelon and Aubrey Singer, which conclude this section, focus on the philosophical base of this book. They raise the major epistemological question, *How do we know what we know?*, which has always been with us but which has become more crucial in the sight-and-sound age.

Kenneth Boulding has stressed that an important element in the dynamics of society is the optimism or pessimism of its visions of the future. These "images of the future" are largely determined by man's prevailing metaphor of reality. Within this metaphor man regards himself, imagines futures, and engages in actions to achieve his aims. If his interpretation of reality alters, so does his image of himself, his image of the future, and his patterns of behavior. The danger, as Boulding points out, is that when these images are self-justifying ones, man is reluctant to change them. Man risks becoming the prisoner of a dream wherein lies are truths and truths are lies and may be paralyzed in a metaphor of reality that is contrary to common sense, experience, and his own humanity. Just as men may be trapped in false metaphors so may their institutions and societies.

We do not know the precise relationship between the messages transmitted by the sight-and-sound media and man's interpretation of the reality of this century. We do not know by what complex procedure men construct images of themselves and images of the next hour, the next day, the next week. And despite the preoccupations of persuaders of every kind, we are not certain that by some men's manipulation of symbols other men's metaphors and images can be influenced. Yet because motion pictures and television are attracting large audiences in our society, offering viewers symbols not only as raw materials but as, so to speak, pre-packaged "codifications of reality," we cannot dismiss the possibility that these media are affecting our thoughts and actions.

What must concern us are the metaphors of reality inherent in sight-and-sound messages—the symbol-configurations which millions of viewers may be accepting as their own. If motion pictures and television are to contribute to the enhancement of man and the further development of our liberal-democratic society, their metaphors must be consistent with human potentialities. Their metaphors cannot be restrictive and false, and the images they project cannot be merely self-justifying ones.

We are often told that a prime function of the communications media is to uphold consensus within a society, to mirror our times and to provide us with, in Aubrey Singer's phrase, a "reflection in the glass." The problem is that in the interest of maintaining consensus and agreement we may become so cybernetically enamored with the feedback of our reflected selves as to preclude the possibilities of fresh ideas and innovations.

In his book, *The Broken Image*, Floyd W. Matson notes that as a consequence of the growth of scientific technology and the acceptance of a world-view emphasizing the regular, the repetitive, and the mechanical, the humanistic vision of man has been eclipsed. Lewis Mumford's "the whole man, man in person" has been displaced by a broken self-image. Matson regards this breaking of the human image as paralleling the loss of identity in the modern world and "the flight from autonomous conduct to automaton behavior."

The sight-and-sound media can be of greatest value to a democratic society if they are not merely "busy mirrors" but also "windows" on a universe of possibilities. They can help us to construct, as Matson urges, a new humanistic metaphor —a metaphor based on man's cumulative discoveries, a

84

metaphor more congruent to an American society whose traditional *élan vital* is resourcefulness and change, and a metaphor whose inherent individual, institutional, and societal images are open-ended with the free choice of decisions however difficult and experiments however perilous.

If the sight-and-sound media were to be successful in helping us to restore a humanistic metaphor of reality, with Bazelon we might ask: What assurance will there be that this metaphor is not "the big lie" and that the images projected within it will not turn out to be self-justifying and paralyzing? The simple answer is that we cannot know for certain—and this ambiguity is at the heart of the freedom which the humanistic metaphor thrusts on us. We can, in Erich Fromm's words, "escape from freedom" and surrender ourselves to conformity, automation, and an eternally closed system; or we can take our chances.

If we choose the latter, our responsibility to ourselves and our American society looms large. Because our democracy rests upon the "will of the people" and their participation in decision-making processes, the rightness of our choices depends upon the ability of each individual to define the problems that face us in this century.

It is by helping us define those problems that the sight-and-sound media can contribute most to the construction of a new humanistic metaphor. Motion pictures and television are indeed extensions of man's senses; they can provide audiences with those skills of perception requisite to minimizing our risks. To do so, they cannot be anything less than *mass* media. However one may deprecate or extol The Great Audience, we must recognize one undeniable fact: after centuries of being commanded and dominated by intellectual taskmasters, the *mobile vulgus* in America are free to make their own choices.

If The Great Audience in America is politically, culturally, and socially free, each individual has the right to choose his own metaphor of reality, his own images, and his own future-directed path.

In *The Italians* Luigi Barzini describes why Mussolini, almost to the very end, did not realize the defeat surrounding him. Prior to his public appearances, his corps of flatterers went forth—painting the fronts of buildings *Il Duce* would pass by, arranging the pomp and ceremony for his dedication of aqueducts that were incapable of being operated, and reinforcing the dictator's image of his self-grandeur and the image of a prosperous Italy. Because Mussolini did not have the intelligence to look beyond the reflecting mirror he was finally trapped in his own false metaphor.

The crucial question, then, of our sight-and-sound age is whether the messages of motion pictures and television will trap us in false metaphors or will help to further liberate us.

86

V.

Communication and the Creative Process*

WALTER LASSALLY

Walter Lassally is the photographer of many outstanding films. Among them are *Electra*, *A Taste of Honey*, *The Loneliness of the Long Distance Runner*, and *Tom Jones*.

~~~~~~

WHAT IS THE BASIS OF COMMUNICATION in the cinema? If there is a common factor which applies to, say, *South Pacific* getting across to its audience as much as it does to *Last Year at Marienbad* getting across to *its* audience, it is emotion. The basis of communication in the cinema is emotional, and once this has been recognized all sorts of enigmas can be solved. Emotion is the bridge between art cinema and mass cinema, which the intellectuals find so hard to cross; it is the reason why a film of any depth, such as *Viridiana* or *L'Avventura*, evokes such totally differing responses from different "intelligent" people; and the ability to respond emotionally to the stimuli of a film is as important an attribute for any film critic as a sharp analytical faculty.

The place of emotion in our modern existence seems to be badly misunderstood. Many people think that the intellect is in some way superior to it, that the latter should control, rather than balance, the former, and that to be open in one's feelings is not a thing to be encouraged as it leads to sentimentality or even mass hysteria. But any film worthy of discussion at all, and many a one that does not otherwise merit it, represents a strong emotional stimulus. In order to get something from it, the audience must be open and receptive to the stimulus; and in most cases the popular audience is, so films intended for this audience usually

* Reprinted from *Film*, Autumn 1963, pp. 18-24, by permission of the author and the publisher.

get across, provided the stimulus is within the range of experience of the majority and the material reasonably fresh. Not so with the art film, however, for many of the potential viewers of such a film, as well as the majority of critics, pride themselves on the appellation "intellectual" and partly shut themselves off from emotional experience by what they would call their analytical attitude.

Here follows a categorical statement: It is wrong to go to a film with an analytical attitude. Why? Because in a critical frame of mind one is not entirely open to the emotional stimulus of a film —some parts of oneself are open, but many are shut off by the self-imposed censor. A parallel with hypnosis exists here—one cannot be hypnotized if one isn't willing; and a film must draw the audience into its spell, must get it to participate in some sense in the action, not to sit back, arms folded, critical faculties sharpened to say: this is good, this is bad; this I accept, this I reject. By all means, do this afterwards, reviewing your experience of the film in retrospect—but you can never review an experience you have refused to allow yourself to have. It is like paying to go to a Turkish Bath and then looking at the steam through a plate-glass window to decide whether you like it or not.

Communication is like wireless telegraphy. It requires a transmitter and a receiver, and the latter must be tuned to the former. In practice, this means that the receiver must recognize the signal being transmitted, and this is only possible if it is within the receiver's emotional experience. The films of Bresson, Antonioni, and Resnais, for instance, do not fail to find a mass audience just because the latter is not intelligent enough, but because it is not sufficiently sensitive emotionally. Understanding, here, is not a question of being able to follow the story, but of being able to sympathize—to "feel with"—the characters and atmosphere or mood, having sufficient emotional range, in other words, to draw comparisons from one's own experience. This process goes on unconsciously as long as we are drawn into the spell of the film; it is only when some emotionally jarring element is presented that we are liable to be "thrown out," and to be led, perhaps, to an immediate rationalization such as "people don't behave like that" or "things like that shouldn't be shown on the screen."

88

In the appreciation of a film *during its projection*, intellect plays a much smaller part than the emotions, unless we deliberately keep the critical faculty active, in which case it is my firm belief that we are interfering with the proper natural process of communication and thus being unfair to the film into the bargain.

As this is a pretty categorical statement, let me expand it a little by looking at the creative process as a whole. Here again, to understand it, it is essential to have experienced it rather than to draw conclusions at second hand, for those who have never experienced it, and there would appear to be many such, will tend to believe that *all* creative processes take place *in the only way they can imagine*; that is by selecting, reshuffling and imitating that which has been created before, without the presence of that essential "original impulse" described below. But anyone who has experienced it in any field of artistic endeavor, be it music, literature, painting or film, will tell much the same story—they do not "think something up," they *feel* something strongly and seek to express that something in terms of their experience of life and of their chosen medium.

In the process of expression the intellect comes into play as well as the emotions and a large unconscious factor. Providing that the techniques of the process of expression do not seriously inhibit or distort the original impulse or idea, the "something" which the artist felt at the outset will be present in the finished work and will communicate itself to the viewer exactly in the proportion in which that same "something" is present in the latter. It is like a vibration being sent out: suitably tuned receivers will vibrate in sympathy, receivers tuned near the transmitter's wavelength will vibrate also, but less strongly (Rationalization: "with reservations") and receivers which have this particular wavelength coded "taboo" will emit a jarring noise ("I hate that sort of thing"). The intellect enters into this process only in so far as it has been a factor in the conditioning of the individual and has contributed its share to his present makeup. As a faculty, however, it moves much more slowly than the emotions and will always be late in any reaction to stimuli. So the *natural* process is to let the feelings feel first, not to hem them in with intellectual reservations and to analyze the result afterwards.

Of course the creative process is not often allowed to operate unhindered. Personality conflicts and the many pressures of an art awkwardly harnessed to an industry all too commonly prevent it. Instead of the original impulse being expanded and all its implications being worked out, factors like the probable audience reaction are often brought in at this stage to the inevitable detriment of the final work. The whole process may even be reversed so that something is concocted artificially from fragments of previous successes, clichés, and "sure-fire" situations which has all the hallmarks of an industrially manufactured product made to specifications statistically arrived at, and which will then be mechanical, fifth-hand and dead. Alas, a large number of films bear the evidence of this method of construction, which is the very opposite of the creative process—but the audience will be aware of this according to the degree of their emotional sensitivity. Again, only a small number of viewers (perhaps trained in what is called "film appreciation") will be articulate as to *why* such a film is bad, but many will reject it all the same, being instinctively able to differentiate between the phoney and the real.

Whilst the emotional basis of such films as *South Pacific* and *Guns of Navarone* is pretty clear, one might at first sight believe that the majority of the so-called art house films have a predominantly intellectual appeal. This is a dangerous half-truth, for on the emotional side, just as on the intellectual, there are many levels, and what would be represented on the one side as a high I.Q. would be equivalent on the other to greater emotional sensitivity and range. This, as a basic requirement for a proper appreciation and enjoyment of such a film, would take it out of the mass market just as much as intellectual incompatibility, but with an important difference. Were there such a thing as an Emotional Quotient, the distribution chart of high E.Q.'s in the population would look very different to that of high I.Q.'s and many a person with a low I.Q. would quite likely have a high E.Q. Here lies the clue to some intangibles such as why certain films go down well in the circuits as well as in the art houses (Chaplin, *The Quiet Man, The Wages of Fear*, etc.).

When attempts are made—as they all too often are—to analyze the art-house film from a purely intellectual standpoint, about the only thing that emerges clearly is the critic's emotional sterility. Emotional components of a film do not respond readily to analysis, for here sincerity or beauty must be the standard, not logic. Antonioni's oblique atmospheric statements and Buñuel's symbolism, for example, cannot be analyzed in terms of good or bad, right or wrong, for they contain, in addition to any obvious meanings, everything that the viewer may read into them. It is pointless to argue about what is, or is not, "really there" or to question the director about his conscious intentions. A symbol goes much deeper than any number of "explanations" of its meaning, and a sensitive artist will use this means of expression because it is at once less definite and immeasurably richer than any statement subject to the rules of logic. The ultimate, perhaps, in this form of expression is reached in a film like *Last Year at Marienbad*, which will have as many different interpretations and responses as there are viewers and *all* of them will be right. The emotional makeup of the viewer is the mechanism, the film's scenes the stimulus and the resultant reaction is as much, if not more, dependent on the nature of the mechanism as on that of the stimulus. A strong, unambiguous stimulus—custard pie in face or gun in nape of neck —will produce a pretty predictable mass reaction; a more subtle stimulus will require a more subtle viewer, and will, *of necessity*, produce a more individual reaction. Because creativity, sensitivity and individuality are somehow in line.

To create, it is first necessary to feel, and the same holds good for communication. The viewer's capacity to "feel with" the artist's intention is the key to his appreciation, so film critics ought to learn to sympathize (Greek: "to feel with") before they analyze. A little less vitriol and a lot more love. But lest they should feel this would lead to a lowering of standards and a sentimental approach let them ask themselves how it is possible to judge something you do not understand, and how you can understand anything for which you have no feeling.

Looking back over the few generally acknowledged masterpieces of the cinema, is it not strength and purity of feeling which they all have in common; and is it not the lack of this quality, sometimes called poetry, which excludes many a brilliantly clever film from greatness? There are no tricks in plain and simple faith.

VI.

*Film and Aesthetics**

ROBERT STEELE

Robert Steele is Associate Professor of Film at Boston University. He is a contributing editor to *Film Heritage.*

~~~~~~

GENERALIZATIONS AND PLATITUDES characterize much talk and writing about art, and an analysis of what makes film art cannot escape some of them. When we probe deeply enough, we discover that standards which we hold are vulnerable, and there is an invisible and inexplicable something in art which is a mystery. Analysis sharpens and uncovers, but its limitation is built in. Our tastes and judgments become more sophisticated by its pursuits, but it never leads us to an absolute finding.

The nature of art and film is such that we should be wary of critics and aestheticians who are overcertain of their analysis and judgment. Beating a drum for a favorite director or film is suspect. To the extent that a film professional loses his detachment to his own work as well as that of others, he has lost dependability. We need to use more care in describing writers as reviewers or critics. The distance between them is great, and their responsibility to themselves and the objects they evaluate differ. Readers need to be able to discriminate between film reviews and critics. Until they become attuned to their different natures, they will be baffled or incensed by the critic whom they think of as a reviewer.

Critics are rare compared to reviewers. Their evaluation of film art is not put before the public on newsstands. Writers for dailies and weeklies are reviewers. They say with one voice *Who's Afraid*

* Reprinted from *motive*, November 1966, pp. 6-10, by permission of the author and the publisher.

of Virginia Woolf? is a terrific film and its performances are smashing. The voice in the wilderness, on the other hand, that says the film is a fraud, and supports this conclusion with sound argument, may be the critic from whom one can learn. The film critic knows art *and* film. He is an aesthetician and has a scholarly stance. His subject matter—film—is so remote from science that it is difficult to think of him as a scientist; yet he is as responsible and conscientious as the scientist in using as much scientific method as he can muster for his investigation and analysis.

Popular writers about film usually have seen many films, identify with the form, and are thought to be critics. Frequently, less popular writers know less about film; i.e., they have not seen every film that was ever made or all the new films, but they know more about other things. Particularly, they know a great deal about the arts. Given their breadth of knowledge and interests, they may choose not to see a film that everyone is talking about, because they believe those critics who say it gushes with sentimentality and box-office formulae or because they prefer to attend a play, concert, or lecture.

We can never know what film art is or is not if we know film in a vacuum. The talented actor, writer, or director is a talented artist. Having become a human being whose mind and feelings respond and create as an artist makes him a special kind of person. He *is* a special kind of person and that is why his films are art objects. It is as difficult to say what a person or artist is as it is to say what film art is. All are recognizable; none is completely knowable.

An artist is the person who makes the film that is a work of art. Or, to put it another way, film art emerges from artists. Hordes of persons are active in film but the artist is rare. This makes film different from other arts and helps explain why film often bamboozles us. Artists among musicians, painters, and dancers are not as rare as they are among film-makers. There are scads of ways to work in film and make a living without having to be an artist or even a would-be artist. Many of our most successful film directors have learned a trade and have evolved some technique; but there is nothing in their makeup that would militate against their becoming successful executives in automobile or telephone industries. The same cannot be said about the present or past generations which have been devoted to other arts.

Most of our films are not made by artists, and, consequently, they are commodities which are as disposable as used paper cups. Because of their ignorance of art, their makers, in most instances, couldn't care less; usually, they are unaware of the triviality of their films. They are in a business and that business is not making art; however, the word "art" *is* tossed around, and professionals give each other awards which snow bumpkins who also know nothing of art. There is more in life than art, however, and art is not the most important ingredient in life. Therefore, all who go to movies need not demand that all films be art. It is the confusion willfully perpetrated by nonartists which strives to woo persons into thinking they are being given an experience of film art which is the occasion for castigation.

The nature of film-making itself has complicated the survival of artists who might choose to work with this form of expression. Had we never had an Industrial Revolution we wouldn't have to fret about film. Film is the only art form to be born since the prehistoric dawn of all arts. It is the art of the machine age, and its practice is dependent upon the mastery of machines made in factories by inventors, engineers, and technicians. Artists frequently are deficient in mechanical aptitudes. An achievement and a source of pride for the artist is his ability to change a tire on a car. A motor is more of a mystery than a wife to him. Some sculptors seem to be an exception to this plight of the artist, and sometimes their work shows it. Frequently, the sculptor, who is also a mechanic, produces work that looks like architecture—or as if it should be décor to be incorporated into a building.

Fellini, who I believe is a film artist, was so put off by the machinery that came between himself as a writer and the completed film, that he says for many years he never thought of becoming a director. He was pushed by Lattuada and Rossellini to change from being a writer to being a writer-director. He described the camera as a monster and admits he was intimidated by it. Like other film artists, he has made his way in film by getting a like-minded and formidable crew of technicians to pave the way for getting his thoughts and feelings on film. Many of the greats—

94

Griffith, Eisenstein, Dreyer, Vigo, Murnau, Clair, Renoir, Cocteau, Bresson, and Bergman—might never have been heard of as great directors had they not had the boon of talented cameramen and loyal technicians.

Because it takes so much more than a man with a typewriter or a camera to make a good film, and because of the clash between artists and technicians, film history is littered with uncompleted films—films that have been disowned by their "creators," because of broken contracts, lawsuits, and failures. Many who have had the intention, dedication, and personna of the artist have been defeated because they could not make their film alone, and they could not woo technicians to make their film the way they wanted it made. Thus, they fail. And justly they may blame the failure on technicians, the producer, the front office, the star, or the industry. Only recently in the United States have a few directors been given the authority and freedom, essential for the artist, to express themselves as artists by way of film.

The film artist selects raw material that is sensuous from which he creates his film. The raw material must be his material rather than someone else's. He may begin his work from someone else's novel or play, but he must have the freedom to handle it as his raw material. Either it emerges from his life or it is so deeply perceived by him that he can handle it with individuality and imagination. He can make a film only about what he knows and cares about. Best-sellers in fiction, award-winning plays, vehicles for stars, and fashionable modes (such as *cinéma vérité*) leave him cold. His raw material is similar to the raw material of all artists. This is not to imply that a film-maker does not get ideas from conversations with friends, newspapers, literature, or his dreams, so that his work will have a contemporary surface. But beneath the surface, there are strata that all artists everywhere may have used as points of departure for their creations.

Despite the film artist's inability to remember how to set and read an exposure meter, he must learn, if his films are to have sustained artistic merit, the mechanical and medial conventions of film. Always he wants to learn more, and takes great satisfaction in whatever technical competence he has mastered; he knows enough of his medial conventions to direct, rather than be directed

95

by, technicians. Film art has the chance of emerging when an artist conceives his raw material by way of the medial conventions of film. His knowledge of the medial conventions has rubbed off on his selection of raw material. He knows enough about film and other arts so that he does not select raw material that would work better on a stage or in a still-photography exhibition. He knows that cinema means *moving image,* and that moving images which tell a story, unfold a character, expose a problem, have the best chance of giving a viewer an aesthetic experience. He knows his medium sufficiently well to decide how he is to achieve image movement by way of moving objects in front of the camera, maneuvering the camera, and by editing. He has a sense of playing close-ups against medium shots, panning and tracking against staticism, black or white against color, music and speech against silence. He knows all of our greatest films and has done his best to discover what made them great. After he has mastered, as best he can, the medial conventions of film, then he is ready to break conventions by supplanting them with his own experiments. If they succeed they will become his and others' conventions.

The artist who knows his raw material, physical properties of picture and sound, his subject matter, and who is adept at handling and making filmic conventions, is ready to create. A film that is an art object has a chance of emerging into being. What the film-maker does creatively determines whether a so-called documentary film, a stock genre of thriller, Western, or horror fantasy, an arty addition to the short-lived *cinéma vérité* vogue, or a work of art is made. (The film-maker is not consciously determined to produce a work of art. That judgment will be made later by others. Rather, he is determined to do the best job he can by going as far and as deep as possible with his subject matter.) In the process of creating the film, the intuition, imagination, originality, empathy, and vision, of the film-maker will culminate into his artistic expression. Pictures hastily and expediently strung together —which for the majority would get by as a film—will not be acceptable to the film artist. He is in touch with a creative process telling him how his images should be linked together, so that they have movement and light rhythm which best reveal the dramatic substance of his subject matter.

MEDIA AND MESSAGES

It should be remembered that those American film-makers known as the underground or anarchist film movement are not motivated to give aesthetic experience to viewers by creating art objects. Either they don't know medial conventions, or they flout them. Their following is not looking for or wanting art; rather they seem drawn to non-art or anti-art. Or they may prefer the new and shocking. These film-makers have dedication and sincerity in their commitment to express themselves, and because this is a film age, they have landed on film rather than on older art forms. They use film for their ego fulfillment. Despite their mutual adoration and *avant-garde* posings, they have not made a contribution to film art. Their works are unimpressive as artistic expressions. They lack the intention, discipline, and maturity to create art. They have little or no money, and to make a good film, one has to have some money. Escaping from the commercial and industrial systems of film-making is laudatory and necessary, but the failure of many of our short films that are at war with Hollywood is that they are fighting our film past with crooked pins rather than paving roadways for future films. Obsessive repetition of devices such as a handheld, gyrating camera, flash frames, and tasteless nudity make their films self-indulgent and boring.

The film that is worthy of being called an art object has *content*. This is what the artist, by way of the formation of his subject matter, requires of himself in his film. Films, plays, paintings —all art forms—over and over, use the same subject matter. It may have to do with love, war, murder, self-sacrifice, nonbelonging, etc.; but because the artist is an individual with unique past experience and artistic intentions, his content is also unique. What he gives to the work of his personal taste, values, and modes of expression results in a residue of content. It is content that makes the difference between Dreyer's, Bresson's, and Preminger's films about Joan of Arc. It is the presence of content in a Bergman film, and its absence in the films of most American directors, that makes the former art and the latter commodities.

Content embodies the style of a director. Content is the reason Japanese films have a sameness that distinguishes them from those of other nations; and it marks the difference between Japanese films (cf. those of Kurosawa, Ozu, Ichikawa, Gosho, Shindo,

Teshigahara, and Mizoguchi). When a number of films from the same director appears to give a full expression of his personality, when they are so stamped by him that they tell us how he feels, what he thinks, and who he is, then we say he is an author of his films. While his film may be drawn from a novel or a play, it has ceased to be that novel or play and becomes the work of a Buñuel, Welles, or Bresson.

If a film is to have content, the director must have freedom to select and handle his material in the way he wishes; he must have the cast and collaborators of his choice. Because this is a privilege attained by only a few directors, we have only a few films, as contrasted to the thousands that have been made, which have the stature to enable them to endure as art objects. The content of a film takes the measure of a director, and by way of it he stands revealed nakedly as a shallow or serious artisan, a manipulator of tricks and gags or a creator of visions which have universal meanings.

The most destructive enemy of film art is imitation. An artist makes a film that is acclaimed as being original. Then he and others are prone to imitate it. Imitation suffocates originality. If a director succumbs to the pressure of a star, producer, or studio to "do it again," he exchanges hats with the hack. And when millions of dollars are at stake, we can't be too high and mighty by condemning the writers and directors who become victims of successful formulas. What began as their unique film content becomes sequels. Movement and change, along with the movement and change in life, get frozen. The word for "old woman" among the Eskimos means "frozen meat." She is a drag on those who survive because her ability to produce has gone. Her parasitic presence makes her death become desirable; in the past, she would be eliminated violently. Think of how many of our "successful" directors are "frozen meat": David Lean, Carol Reed, Fred Zinnemann, Vittorio De Sica, René Clément, Jules Dassin, Alfred Hitchcock, Vincente Minnelli, Elia Kazan, John Huston, Otto Preminger, William Wyler, George Stevens. Despite success or acclaim some have remained unfrozen: Chaplin, Dreyer, Cacoyannis, Renoir, Welles, Ray, Olmi, Reisz, Truffaut.

An artist, by his nature, cannot mark time. He is alive because

98

he is on the move, and the movement churning in him, which is the core of his creative process, prevents him from repeating himself. Jesse Lasky didn't know whom he was talking to when he asked Flaherty to bring back from Samoa another *Nanook*. Goebbels knew little of art and how artists work when he told assembled film-makers in Berlin that the Nazi "revolution" should be glorified by films like *Potemkin*. One would feel worse about the demise of Garbo's career had she proved herself to possess the stubbornness and passion of an artist rather than to let herself be used like a punching bag by a studio which sought vehicles for her. She is remembered for the artistry of her acting, her beauty, and her personality, but not as a great artist. She had the opportunity to prove she had the guts of an artist when *Queen Christina* was slated to be her next film. She had frozen meat for a director (Rouben Mamoulian), so when she said she was going to make herself up to look like Christina, her director fought her. Garbo wished to appear with a large nose and massive, masculine eyebrows. She said that Swedes would expect a real portrayal of Christina. She was informed that the studio was not making a film for history professors of a country with six million inhabitants, but that Metro wanted a movie that would command a world audience. Garbo capsized and repeated herself, but until her last film, because she was Garbo, she succeeded in repeating herself to an advantage.

In his postscript to *Lolita*, Vladimir Nabokov described how we should feel after we have had an encounter with art: "For me a work of fiction exists"—had he not been thinking of the novel, he could have said a work of art—"only in so far as it affords me what I shall bluntly call aesthetic bliss, that is, a sense of being somehow, somewhere, connected with other states of being where art (curiosity, tenderness, kindness, ecstasy) is the norm." Emily Dickinson could have been speaking about film art when she attempted to define poetry: "If I read a book and it makes my whole body so cold no fire can ever warm me, I know it's poetry. If I feel physically as if the top of my head were taken off, I know it is poetry. These are the only ways I know it."

When a viewer meets a film worthy of being called art, he participates in the creative experience of the artist who made the film. He is not a spectator observing from a balcony, but he is catapulted into the skin of the film-maker. He is in the film to such an extent that he is part of the film. The creative process at work in the film forces him into having a recreative experience, so that *he lives the film*. When this happens, E. M. Forster says, ". . . a man is taken out of himself. He lets down as it were a bucket into his subconscious and draws up something which normally is beyond his reach. He mixes this thing with his normal experience, and out of the mixture comes the experience of a work of art."

A work of art that mixes with our normal experience changes our normal experience so that we walk out of the cinema as different persons. Every time we are nudged by a great film, our normal experience, at least a bit of it, is transformed. We get something that sends us, in Forster's words, "beyond our reach." Rudolf Arnheim observed that, "we find ourselves in the presence of a work of art when the actors, actions, and objects of the foreground appear transparent and lead our glance to the basic themes of human existence."

Film art begins with an artist who, by way of his raw material and knowledge of and skill in using and making medial conventions, who, by way of his creative process (which involves his vision, intuition, artistic expression, and empathic grasp), forms and shapes raw material into subject matter that becomes a physically real object which contains content. But that is not all. The creative process and the work of the artist miss completion until they involve somebody. Films in particular are not made to be kept in a can, just as poetry is not written to be stored in a trunk (Emily Dickinson wanted to publish her poetry but was intimidated by those who thought it was not poetry). An exponent of the so-called Japanese underground film, who wrote the following in a promotional announcement of the film, is spouting nonsense: "Japan is the country of the *haiku*, that terse and inner statement, the meaning of which must be inferred. Communication is less important than consideration. The Japanese experimental film is traditionally intended for no audience at all."

The dichotomy made between communication and consideration in this statement is false. If the films are not intended for any audience at all, why do their makers wish to distribute them and hunger for income from them? Similar statements by other film-makers (Robert Breer is one) reveal this half-true way of defending films. Film-makers are inclined to say they made their films for themselves when their films are being attacked. The implication of their statement is: I made it for myself; who is to say I shouldn't; if I like it that is all that matters; you are not ready for it; who are you? This rationale sometimes is pulled out when an experiment has been tried that failed and should not have been shown to an audience—at least a paying audience of nonprofessionals. The truth in the statement is obvious. We do things for ourselves. We had better try to please ourselves and like what we do and get satisfaction from it. This is paramount. But films, by their physical, artistic, and economic nature (even more than music, painting, and poetry), are an art form that subsumes an audience—preferably a contemporary audience. This defensive film-maker is saying that mass audiences and commercial exhibitions of his work do not interest him. Good. He is to be admired. He is engaging in art for the sake of art and is willing to sacrifice its tangible fruits. But his vocation will be fulfilled, and his artistic expression realized, only as he displays his work before, at least, some friends or an elite audience. The communication-noncommunication battle now being waged among some artists results from an excess of talk and a paucity of thinking. Does anyone know of a film-maker who has made a film of which he is unashamed and refuses to show it; and doesn't he want and need at least a modicum of acceptance and appreciation for his work if he is to continue working?

A great film, one that is an art object, has significance that shakes us, at least a little, out of our normal experience and gives us a supra-experience. Because the artist has penetrated our beings with his being, it moves us beyond our past selves and opens us to new and changing selves. By way of a film, a film-maker communicates with himself, and if his self-communication does not become arrested, it emerges clearer, more direct, simpler, and certainly, more honest. To the extent he succeeds, he is on the move to greater achievements.

An artist cannot hate people and succeed as an artist. He has to harbor some hope that what he has to express may be communicated, at least partially, to someone else. Leonard Bernstein rightly observes: "Communication is a way of making love to people, or reaching them." He could substitute "conducting music" or "making a film" for the word "communication." He continues: "It's a most mysterious and deeply moving experience. Love and art are two ways of communicating. That's why art is so close to love." The great film artist is a great lover of himself and of other persons. The film that is an art object makes love to an audience by sharing aesthetic bliss with them. To be sure, this is a high ideal. But art is the métier of ideals. The high ideal, rather than being even somewhat irrelevant, is the alpha and omega of film art, because it shows us the way we wish to go.

VII.

Movies You Are Not Supposed To Dig*

NORMAN N. HOLLAND

Presently Chairman of the Department of English at the State University of New York at Buffalo, Norman N. Holland has written essays of film criticism for *Hudson Review*.

~~~~~~

LATE IN 1958, Janus Films released on a largely unsuspecting American public Bergman's *The Seventh Seal* and so started a flood in the art theaters of what seems to be a new genre in film, "the puzzling movie": *Hiroshima, Mon Amour; La Dolce Vita; The Lovers; Les Cousins; The Magician; L'Avventura*—to name but a few of these films, most of which almost dazzle with their richness, their sheer filmic excellence. As a genre, they represent perhaps the only sustained group of films after the advent of sound to be truly and overwhelmingly visual: these films look good like a cinema should.

Arthur Schlesinger, Jr., has suggested (in *Show* magazine) they are creating a new Movie Generation to replace those of us who grew up, cinematically, on the popcorn and cheesecake Hollywood classics of the thirties. Another reviewer calls these films the "undergraduate movies," and there is much truth in the adjective, if we extend it to include not only the four-year kind, but also the perpetual undergraduates on the other side of the lectern. These are indeed films that make their chief appeal to the academic and the intellectual.

But why do they appeal to anybody? If you stand outside an art theater as the audience comes out from a "puzzling movie," you will hear over and over again in a variety of phrasings and de-

* Reprinted from *The Journal of the Society of Cinematologists*, Vol. III, 1963, pp. 17-28, by permission of the author and the publisher.

grees of profanity, "What was *that* all about?" As a local joke has it, one Harvard undergraduate to another, "Have you seen *Last Year at Marienbad?*" The other, slowly, thoughtfully, "I . . . don't know." The feeling these films almost invariably leave us with is, "It means something, but just what I don't know," and the question I am asking is, Why should that feeling of puzzlement give us pleasure?

It doesn't, of course, to everyone. Popular as these films may be among intellectuals and academics, there are plenty of people who find them simply boring. At a somewhat more sophisticated level (I am thinking of the usual reviewer for the daily paper), we hear two kinds of complaint. First, these films make just one more statement of the moral and social confusion of the century. Second, we are likely to find a sexual indignation, for these films are rather strikingly casual about such matters. There were, for example, the two proper Bostonian ladies who went to see *The Virgin Spring*. During that appalling rape scene, one leaned over to the other and whispered, "You know, in Sweden, things are like that." And, in fact, sex in these films does tend to be either rape or mere amusement, a kind of bedroom Olympics in which neither the Russians nor the Americans stand a chance—only Common Market countries.

Sex and *mal de siècle*, certainly these films have them in abundance, but the quality that still stands out is the puzzlement they create. Contrast a film-maker like Eisenstein. He uses montage, symbolism, and the rest not very differently from the way the makers of the puzzling movies do, but Eisenstein aims to communicate his socialist and Marxist message; his symbols serve that end. The maker of the puzzling movie, on the other hand, as much as hangs out a sign that says, "Figure it out—if you can." His symbols serve not so much to communicate as to suggest or even to mystify. (Think, for example, of the devilfish at the end of *La Dolce Vita* and all the different interpretations of it.) Yet, despite the intentional mystification, we take pleasure in them just the same—these films are puzzling in more than one sense.

In particular, there are two ways they puzzle us. They puzzle us as to their meaning in a total sense. They puzzle us scene-by-scene simply as to what is going on in a narrative or dramatic way.

Let me consider first our puzzlement as to meaning— Why should these films, that seem almost to hide their own meaning, please us?

* * *

To answer that question, it helps to take a detour by way of the joke, an humble, but useful route through aesthetic problems, for the joke will serve as a model or prototype for more respectable literature. Jokes, for example, cartoons or limericks, all have a "frame," as serious literature does, and the frame leads us into an attitude of playful attention, a special combination of involvement and distancing, the aesthetic stance, just as the appearance of a poem on the page does or entering a theater to see a film. Jokes present us with the problem of form in a more acute way than even poetry does: no form, no joke, but clearly form alone is not what makes a joke funny. Jokes have content, that is, rational thought, social and moral purpose, but, clearly, editorial content is not what makes a joke funny, either. Rather, jokes get their response from some complex interaction of form and content, as, no doubt, the puzzling movies do.

In particular, jokes often have the same riddling quality as, say, a film by Antonioni. We have to solve some little problems before we "get" the joke—for example, the old saying "A wife is like an umbrella—sooner or later one has to take a taxi." The riddling form of the joke does two things. First, it draws and holds our attention to the joke. In the case of the puzzling movie, it draws and holds our attention to the film. Second, the riddling form binds our processes of intellection, creating a state of tension or damming up. The riddling form busies us with solving the riddle and so enables less relevant, less presentable thoughts prompted by the joke to sneak up on us, to take us unawares, as it were. So with the puzzling film: its enigmatic promise of "meaning" not only draws and holds our attention to the film; it also distracts us from the real source of our pleasure in the film, the thoughts and desires it evokes.

This, modern psychology tells us, is the real function of form in art. The neoclassic critics used to say form justifies content. A modern psychological critic would say, intellectual content justifies form and then form justifies emotional content. That is in the case of the joke, its promise that there will be an intellectual meaning, a "point," enables us to relax and enjoy a playing with words and ideas that we would ordinarily dismiss as childish or insane: intellectual content justifies form. At the same time, the play with words and ideas acts as an additional and preliminary source of pleasure. The pleasure in this play unbalances the usual equilibrium between our tabooed impulses and our defenses, and it provides the extra to topple those defenses—we laugh. In other words, the point (or intellectual content) of the joke justifies the form; then the pleasure we take in form allows another kind of content to break through, and we gratify some sexual or aggressive impulse we would ordinarily hold in check.

The same process seems to operate with the puzzling movie. The feeling we have is: "This means something, but I don't know what." "This means something," the first part of our reaction, acts like intellectual content in the joke—it justifies form; it bribes our reason to accept the incoherent stream of images or the incoherent narrative of the puzzling movie. Then, our pleasure in those images, the sheer visual beauty of the films in this genre, acts like form: it allows us to enjoy the forbidden content of the film.

But what is this forbidden content? In the joke-situation, we can usually identify the hidden impulse of hostility or obscenity that the joke works with. The content of the puzzling movie is not so easy to get at.

We can get a clue, though, from the adverse reactions to the films. Those reviewers and audiences for whom the puzzling quality doesn't work complain of two things: the casual attitude towards sex; the feeling that the films express in a peculiarly negative way the moral confusion of the age. For the disappointed critics of these films, the form didn't work, and the fantasies prompted by the film came through raw and repulsive: sexual promiscuity and a fear of moral confusion.

The sexual angle is the easier to see. These films are extraordinarily free about such matters—I am thinking of such scenes as Jeanne Moreau's taking a bath in *The Lovers* and *La Notte*; the striptease in *La Dolce Vita*; the scenes of lovemaking in *Hiro-*

shima; rape in *The Virgin Spring, Through a Glass Darkly,* or *Marienbad.* In effect, the puzzling quality of the films gives us an intellectual justification for gratifying the simplest of visual desires, looking at sexy things. This, I hasten to add, is a crude, first-order effect, but nevertheless a very important part of the appeal of even these very sophisticated and intellectual films. Or, for that matter, their lack of appeal.

In effect, the puzzling movies are an intellectual's version of the old DeMille Bible epic, where we gratify our sexual desires by watching the wicked Assyrians, Philistines, Romans or whomever carry on their grand pagan orgies, but we are justified by the ponderously moral content of the film. The Biblical frame allows us to gratify almost shamelessly the seventh and least of the sinful impulses. I say, "us," but no doubt I do you an injustice: no proper intellectual would be fooled by the crudity of the moral sop in the DeMille biblio-epic, and this is not the kind of form the puzzling movie gives us. The puzzling movie presents itself as an intellectual and aesthetic problem rather than a moral one, and then perhaps it does fool the intellectual in the same amiable way that jokes and works of art do.

* * *

We can see the process *in statu nascendi,* as it were, in Leslie Fiedler's remarkable review of a "nudie" movie, *The Immoral Mr. Teas* (in *Show* magazine). Mr. Fiedler, I presume, has reached the end of his own innocence and knows what he is doing. Even so, he looks at this film and finds in it "ambiguity," "irreality," "a world of noncontact and noncommunication." He treats this jolly and ribald movie as an index to the American national character, illustrates from it American attitudes toward the body, and (most strikingly) contrasts the nudity in *The Immoral Mr. Teas* with the more humane nudity in *Room at the Top* and *Hiroshima, Mon Amour.* In other words, Mr. Fiedler's astute analysis has erected such an intellectual "meaning" for this film (though it is scarcely above the level of a stag movie) that any self-respecting intellectual could go see it with a clear conscience and a blithe spirit of analysis. Mr. Fiedler does it with criticism; the puzzling film-maker does it with his camera; but, in either case, the intellectual promise of "meaning" justifies the simpler and more primitive pleasure.

Leslie Fiedler treats *The Immoral Mr. Teas* in intellectual and aesthetic terms, whereas the "meaning" that justified the content of the Biblical epic was its religious and moral "message." This shift from moral message to intellectual "meaning" is itself a source of pleasure in the puzzling movie, particularly for the intellectuals to whom the puzzling movie makes its chief appeal. After all, moral and religious issues have a strong and perhaps frightening emotional overtone. Aesthetic and intellectual "meaning" seems much more manageable. The notion that the moral confusions of this most trying of centuries can be shifted over to the very kind of aesthetic and intellectual puzzle that highbrows are adept at is itself a very comforting hope indeed. And again, confirmation of this source of pleasure comes from those in the audience who find no pleasure in this displacement: the films clearly deal with moral problems, but for those in the audience who cannot accept their translation of moral issues into intellectual ones, the puzzling movies seem merely to express moral problems without answering them, and these critics say the films just prove the sickness of the century.

So far, then, we have found three sources of pleasure in the way these films puzzle us as to meaning. First, we feel that somehow this film "means something," and that promise or content, a "point," enables us to take pleasure in the seemingly incoherent and puzzling visual form of the film. That preliminary visual pleasure in form combines with a less acceptable source of visual pleasure in content: peeping at some very erotic scenes. The combination of these pleasures from form and from content unbalance and override our usual inhibitions. At the same time, these films displace moral and social inhibition into aesthetic and intellectual demands for "meaning," something that intellectuals at least find much easier to resolve, and the puzzling quality so provides still a third source of pleasure.

This kind of economic analysis, however, seems highly abstract. Somehow, we are missing some of the essential quality of these films. Let's see if we can get closer by looking at the second source of puzzlement: not now as total "meaning," but scene by scene, the simple narrative riddle of, What's going on?

I have suggested that one of the brute, root sources of pleasure in these films is simply that of looking at sexual scenes. Yet sex in these films has a peculiar and special quality. Jeanne Moreau's bath scenes in *The Lovers* and *La Notte*—the first occurs in the context of a casual affair; in the second, her husband is simply bored by the sight. Similarly, the husband is bored by Romy Schneider's long and lovely bath scene in the Visconti episode of *Boccaccio, 70*, a visual feast but an emotional fast. The striptease in *La Dolce Vita* and virtually all the sex in that film is without any emotion but simple desire. Again, there is simply lust or hate in the rape scenes of *The Virgin Spring* or *Rocco and His Brothers*. The same quality shows in those seductions tantamount to rapes by the heroine of *Through a Glass Darkly* and by the nymphomaniac at the hospital in *La Notte*. The opening love scenes of *Hiroshima, Mon Amour* set out another casual love affair; the woman's voice drones on the sound track throughout the sequence much as the narrator's voice drones on in *Marienbad* debating with himself whether he took the woman by force or not. *The Seventh Seal*, perhaps the finest film in the genre, seems to vary this emotionless pattern, but not really: Bergman isolates sex *cum* love in the juggler and his wife, those who escape Death; while the knight and his wife, the squire and his girl rescued from rape, the blacksmith's wife seduced by the actor, they all show the same dogged lovelessness which seems to be the distinctive feature of human relationships in the puzzling movie.

This emotionlessness does not confine itself to sexuality, either. Think, for example, of the cryptic face of Max von Sydow in *The Seventh Seal* or Monica Vitti's classic mask in the Antonioni trilogy. These films are cryptic on the simple level of, What's he thinking? What's he feeling? The suicide of Steiner in *La Dolce Vita* reveals some underlying emotional reality his aesthetic and intellectual life had screened, but what? The disappearance of Anna in *L'Avventura*, her earlier cry of "Sharks!" in the swimming sequence—these tell us something about her inner life, but what? The long, circling walk of the lovers in the last third of *Hiroshima, Mon Amour,* the fashion-plate style of *Marienbad,* the disguises in *The Magician,* all show us cryptic outward actions as a substitute for inner emotions not revealed.

*   *   *

All through the puzzling movies, in other words, we are seeing events without understanding their meaning, particularly their emotional meaning. We are simply not permitted to become fully aware of what is going on emotionally. This sensation, though, is not by any means a new one, special to the puzzling movies. In fact, these films duplicate an experience we have all had, one which was at one time irritating, even frightening, a constant reminder of our own helplessness in the face of forces much bigger than we. I am thinking of the child's situation, surrounded by a whole range of adult emotions and experiences he cannot understand. "What's that man doing, Mummy?" is a not inappropriate comment on the whole genre of "puzzling movies."

Typically, the child does not even have the words with which to grasp these adult emotions and experiences, a circumstance these films duplicate by happenstance. That is, they are all foreign-language films which put us again in a position where the big people, the ones we see on the screen, have all kinds of complex experiences which they speak about in a language we cannot understand (at least those of us who bestowed our time in fencing, dancing, and bear-baiting instead of the tongues). Even for those who spent some time with the tongues, these films make us regress, grow backward, into children a second way by their intentionally visual and filmic quality. They take us back to the picture-language of the comic strip, of children, and of dreams.

There is still a third way these films take us back to the child's frame of mind: in sexuality. The child's dim awareness of adult sexuality very much resembles the sexuality of the puzzling movies. He can see or, more usually, imagine the physical act, but he cannot feel the whole range of complex emotions and experiences the adult knows as love. Rather, the child understands the act of sex as something associated with violence and danger, as we see it, for example, in *The Virgin Spring; Rocco and His Brothers; La Dolce Vita; Hiroshima, Mon Amour; Last Year at Marienbad; Les*

Cousins; and the rest. The child is aroused at his sexual fantasies and a bit afraid at his own arousal, as indeed we ourselves tend to be at a puzzling movie. Further, the child's general uncertainty about the adult world finds a focus for itself in his uncertainty, arousal, and fear at this particular area of adult life—sexuality. It serves as a nucleus for his total puzzlement at adult emotions and actions, just as the sexuality in the puzzling movies serves as the nucleus of the total atmosphere of mysterious, baffling emotions and motivations.

In various ways, then, the puzzling quality at the story level of these films takes us back to a childhood situation of puzzlement, but presents it now as an intellectual and aesthetic puzzle rather than an emotional one in real life. "This event obviously says something about the emotional life of these people, but I don't know what, and it's only a film anyway." The film puzzles, disturbs, presents us with an emotional riddle, but puts it in an intellectual and aesthetic context. Further, it transforms the emotional puzzle into precisely the kind of puzzle that an "undergraduate" audience might feel it could solve, an intellectual and aesthetic puzzle, instead of an emotional one. In other words, not only do these films take us back to childhood disturbances; they seem to say we can master those disturbances by the strategies of our adult selves, our ability to solve aesthetic and intellectual puzzles.

The puzzling movies hold out to their intellectual audiences the possibility of mastering childish puzzlement by the defenses of the adult intellectual. For example, most intellectuals have a good deal of curiosity. The reason psychologists offer is that their early attempts to solve the puzzles of childhood became a way of life. In technical jargon, infantile curiosity became sublimated into the intellectual and aesthetic curiosity of the adult. Now the puzzling movie comes along and enables us to do or think we can do just what our life-style has been wanting to do all along: solve the riddle of emotions and sexuality by purely intellectual means. Would that we could!

The puzzling movies play into the intellectual's life-style in another way. Academics and intellectuals often present the appearance to other people of "cold fish," the reason being that it is very typical of the highly intellectualized person that he puts up a barrier between sensuous emotional experience and the intellectual problems with which he concerns himself. The puzzling movie enables him to do this again—to put aside the emotional mysteries of the film and see it coldly, in intellectual terms. In short, the puzzling movies, precisely because they are puzzling, take us, as any great work of art does, along the whole spectrum of our development from infancy to adulthood; or, at least, they do for most of their "undergraduate" audience.

There is, though, one special reaction that deserves notice: some critics feel no uncertainty at all—at least on the narrative level. The usual review of an Antonioni film, for example, in a film magazine or a literary quarterly will tell you scene by scene and scowl by scowl what each of the characters is thinking at every given moment. For this kind of person, there is no mystery in the puzzling movie, or, more properly, his careful observation of the film enables him to say that he has seen everything there is to be seen. There is no mystery—he understands the emotional riddle. This response offers a variant but no less pleasurable way of overcoming that residue of childish bafflement in us—instead of shifting it to an adult intellectual problem, the critic simply says it doesn't exist at all: there is no puzzle. I have seen it all and understood it all; there is nothing to be puzzled—or frightened—by.

* * *

To bring them all together, the puzzling movie turns its puzzling quality into pleasure in two large areas. First, it presents itself as an aesthetic mystery: What does it "mean"? As in a joke, the oblique promise of a "point" enables us to relax our demand for coherence and take pleasure in the incoherent visual form of the film. Then, that visual form lets us take pleasure in the sexual content and, at the same time, shifts any moral qualms we might have to intellectual and aesthetic qualms. Second, the puzzling movie presents us with a mystery on a simple narrative or dramatic level: What's going on? This second kind of mystery duplicates a child's feeling of bafflement at the adult world around him, but translates that preverbal emotional bafflement into an aesthetic mystery that a sophisticated, intellectual audience, no longer children, can feel confident about solving.

There is a lesson here about movies in general, for all movies take us back to childhood. They give us a child's pleasure in looking at things, which we, as film critics, respond to in our demand that the film be true to its medium, that it be visual. Similarly, the film takes us back to a preverbal stage of development; and, again, as critics, we demand that the picture makes its point, not through words on the soundtrack, but through pictures. Most important, however, there is that certain feeling people have, that looking at a film is somehow "passive." In fact, of course, the film involves no more passivity than reading a novel or watching a play, and yet there is something akin to passivity in the cinematic transaction.

Wolfenstein and Leites, in their classic study of the psychology of the movie audience, find part of that sensation of passivity in the audience's "peering with impunity" at the big people on the screen: "What novels could tell, movies can show. Walls drop away before the advancing camera. No character need disappear by going offstage. The face of the heroine and the kiss of lovers are magnified for close inspection. The primal situation of excited and terrified looking, that of the child trying to see what happens at night, is recreated in the theater; the related wish to see everything is more nearly granted by the movies than by the stage. The movie audience is moreover insured against reaction or reproof from those whom they watch because the actors are incapable of seeing them. The onlooker becomes invisible." (*Movies: A Psychological Study*; Free Press, 1950).

The actors, in short, can't fight back, and that is one way the film seems a "passive" medium.

The other side of the coin is that we can't provoke the actor. Unlike the stage situation where the length of our laughter, the solemnity of our listening will affect the actor's performance; unlike the television situation where we can turn the box off, get up for a beer or what not, we have no such effect on the film which grinds away its twenty-four pictures a second as relentlessly as Niagara Falls. We are powerless, as we were when we were children, to change the doings of the "big people." Now, though, we are immune; the giants on the screen cannot affect us, either. Our regression is safe, secure, and highly pleasurable.

This regression to the safe but powerless child, it seems to me, is the reason people feel watching a film is somehow "passive": the big people cannot act on us; we cannot act on them. This regression, of course, is a key source of pleasure not only in the puzzling movies, but in *all* films, and especially those which, like the puzzling movies, make their appeal visually, that is, those in which the preverbal element of the film is especially strong.

In fact, we could define filmic achievement in terms of what it does with this visual, preverbal element in the situation of safe helplessness induced by the motion-picture situation. In the case of silent comedy, the action on the screen says to us, in effect, "This mysterious preverbal world of violence and disaster is really harmless—it's all right." Eisenstein's films and others of the montage school say, "This mysterious preverbal world you see is meaningful. You understand it and you respond to it emotionally and morally." The puzzling movie says to us, "This mysterious preverbal world you see, though you don't understand it, still, it can be solved." The puzzling film pleases us because it is, in the last analysis, as all art is, a comfort.

VIII.

Sorcerers or Apprentices:
Some Aspects of the Propaganda Film*

ROBERT VAS

Robert Vas frequently contributes essays of film criticism to
Sight and Sound, the journal of The British Film Institute.

∿∿∿∿∿∿∿∿∿∿∿∿∿∿∿∿∿∿∿∿∿∿∿∿∿∿∿∿

PROPAGANDA, WE TEND TO THINK, is something we live with, inevitable and inescapable. The Central European proverb "I
caught a Turk—he won't let me go" fits the situation perfectly.
The word "propaganda" has acquired all sorts of overtones during
the last quarter of a century; and along with this extension of
meaning has grown up that basic mistrust which is our only
weapon of defense against it. What on earth could be more suspect than film propaganda? Cinema itself may be called a cheat
against reality, but the way the propaganda film operates is a double cheat—it is, in effect, nothing but the sad story of how they've
pulled the wool over our eyes.

To raise the moral issues and contradictions involved in this
kind of film is yet another task. Did it fertilize the art of the cinema, or work against it? Did it liberate or shackle cinema's powers
of expression? We are bound to ask more questions than we can
hope to answer. But this article is intended as a sort of subjective
reconnaissance of only a few aspects of the subject, mainly those
concerned with the creative side rather than with the equally important questions of audience response. Enough if it helps to prepare the ground for a more disciplined and organized attack on
this contradictory and menacing subject.

* Reprinted from *Sight and Sound* (1963), pp. 199-204, by permission of
the author and the publisher.

Grierson's classic definition, "Propaganda is the art of public persuasion," does justice to the concept and views it with patience and hope. But this was written in the early thirties, when propaganda films in Britain meant socially conscious educational material about aero-engines, slums, or the six-thirty postal collection. To propagate was the same as to sow the seed of general knowledge. With the film "a single say-so can be repeated a thousand times a night to a million eyes. It opens a new perspective, a new hope to public persuasion." One cannot but feel a certain nostalgia for this period when all our handy definitions were born; when such concepts were still pure and uncorrupted, offering themselves up to clear-cut classification.

As early as 1931, Paul Rotha had enough apt examples to lay down a categorization which is still perfectly valid. "Film propaganda," he wrote in *Celluloid, The Film Today*, "may be said to fall roughly under two heads. Firstly, there is the film which wields influence by reason if its incidental *background* propaganda. Secondly, there is the *specifically designed* propaganda film, sponsored as an advertisement for some industry or policy." And it was in the same essay that he put into words the idea that inevitably comes to mind when thinking about this subject: "In one form or another, directly or indirectly, *all films are propagandist*. The general public is influenced by every film it sees. The dual physio-psychological appeal of pictorial movement and sound is so strong that if it is made with imagination and skill, the film can stir the emotions of any audience." John Grierson put it all more dramatically: "No form of description," he wrote, "can add nobility to a simple observation so readily as a camera set low or a sequence cut to a time-beat."

This is why film and propaganda *had* to meet. Cinema is reality sifted, pointed and intensified; propaganda is a sifted, pointed, intensified idea used for a specific purpose. And their cooperation was a genuinely mutual one. First involuntarily, then more and more consciously, they have always leaned on each other. When cinema first became aware of its own language and power, it was, in fact, through propaganda. From then on its great moments were also those of the "art of persuasion."

Perhaps it all began with the committed way *Birth of a Nation* was put together: the construction of, say, the scene of Lincoln's murder, provoking hatred for the assassin and sympathy for the unsuspecting President. The scene of the liberating Klansmen intercut with the lynch gang makes an even more outspoken (and in fact contradictory) propagandist statement. And closely allied is Kuleshov's famous experiment using a single shot of Mosjoukine's face apparently reacting differently when juxtaposed first with a shot of a plate of soup, then a coffin with a dead woman, and finally a little girl playing with a funny toy bear. Isn't this innocent little trick a key to all the more sinister ones that were to follow? It was the young Soviet cinema which used it first, along with all those other methods which the textbooks call the basic principles of the art of the film. In Eisenstein's *Strike* (1924) we find the first intuitive, crude formulation of almost everything that has followed up to the present day, from the sheer elementary power of moving images to the most complex metaphors and abstractions.

It was an intellectual urge which made Eisenstein seek out this language; but he was also a propagandist, in those days, even a pamphleteer. It was the effort to achieve propagandist simplicity that encouraged him to think in symbols like The Capitalist and The Proletarian—and so to explore for the first time the cinema's ability (and in a way necessity) to work in terms of types. It was the loose, undisciplined, Mayakovskyish propaganda which enabled him to conceive his film with only an intellectual continuity, and allowed him to ramble freely between the naturalism of the rubber hose sequence and the grotesque and puzzling abstraction of the gnomes, or to link the shot of the slaughtered bull to a clumsily infernal tableau of massacred workers. *Strike* was the first resounding exclamation mark in the history of the cinema, as well as the first haphazard specimen of its intellectual capacities.

Editing, as Eisenstein used it, is a way of showing one's true colors. A cut is a kind of helpful conflict, a harmonic contrast between two shots. A cut in *Potemkin* between the boots of the Czarist troops and the desperately fleeing crowd is a plea in itself: a division between good and evil done with the intensity which only a propaganda film can afford and only a sharp cut can put over. And it was out of this propagandist immediacy that one of the cinema's most versatile and dynamic means of expression emerged.

This was the first common ground between film and propaganda, and led to the first turning-point in their history. Before *Potemkin*, film propaganda was used only rather intuitively. Through the artistic success of Eisenstein's film the Soviet cinema became aware of its own possibilities as a worldwide propagandist, and from then on developed them consciously. Even the Master himself could afford to ramble freely within the enormous and more propaganda-conscious concept of his masterpiece, *October*, only after *Potemkin* had shown what could be achieved. It was this newfound awareness which introduced the milk separator as a dramatic hero, or encouraged Dziga Vertov to let his propagandist camera go for a carefree stroll. Film as Art was born.

The West, too, found similar common grounds. *All Quiet on the Western Front* in a way summed up the American cinema and foreshadowed the increasing social awareness of the thirties. In Britain, the propagandist impulse gave the Griersonians their "generous access to the public." Buñuel made propaganda when he explored the horrors of *Las Hurdes*. And in the Germany of the Weimar Republic propaganda was the essence and spice of artistic expression, through the idealistic plea for poor *Mutter Krausen*, through a Brechtian stylization of Rich and Poor, through the sober realism of *Westfront 1918* and the conscious message of *Kameradschaft*. In Mother Russia the Dovzhenko of *Earth* and *Ivan* used propaganda to achieve ends more personal than those desired by the regime, but there is otherwise much to criticize or disregard in Soviet cinema, until *Chapayev* found a way to combine the useful with the truthful. In these years it really does seem true that "all films are propagandist," whether knowingly or unknowingly. The hit song in *42nd Street*, "I'm Young and Healthy, Full of Vitamin A," was like a sad dedication for a world running full speed towards a new war; and the puckish ingenuity of Disney's *Three Little Pigs* helped America to confront the Big Bad Wolf of the Depression. The artistic conscience still dared to hope that it could help.

*   *   *

MEDIA AND MESSAGES

Then comes the paradox, so sad and so revealing. Though propaganda in the early thirties was conscientiously aimed at social progress, the period's crowning achievement is at once a powerful rebuff and a Machiavellian masterpiece. With *Triumph of the Will* (1934-36) education turned to deliberate misteaching, and the whole idea of propaganda moved towards the era of Goebbels and notoriety.

Leni Riefenstahl's film was a diabolic combination of reality and stylization, Wagnerian mysticism and present-day immediacy, beauty and threat, commanding *tableaux vivants* and an overpowering urgency of movement. Above all, it was a masterpiece of timing. What makes a propagandist film truly great is perhaps this recognition of the right moment, the precise point at which it can assert itself most forcefully. Miss Riefenstahl aimed the superman idea towards that man-in-the-street who, in a confused and disillusioned Europe, was almost waiting for an order to obey. Propaganda had meant goodwill, generalized humanism with all its limitations. Against this, Leni Riefenstahl's film set a firm statement, replacing doubt by military certainty, problems and hesitations by an unambiguous exclamation mark. People who saw the film must have felt that when those in charge were so *sure* about where to put the camera, they could not but be right. . . .

But *Triumph of the Will* also came as a reminder that the real propaganda film can't stand half-measures. It cannot really afford to let us think, and is consequently a totalitarian form of expression. After the final fadeout we are supposed to go straight into action, to seize the nearest spade and begin to dig (as I am always prepared to do after the tremendous last scene of Turin's *Turksib*). Propaganda may have helped Eisenstein to contribute in a general sense to the language of the cinema, but in *Triumph of the Will* Miss Riefenstahl went right back to the core: she liberated the elemental power of direct propaganda and crystallized its full meaning. Her film makes everything that had gone before look merely committed or argumentative. While making full use of Eisenstein's techniques for pictorial rhythm, his flair for symbols or the handling of crowds, she cheerfully rejects his intellectual conscience. To hell with it! Let's have the *real* stuff! And instead

119

of the Master's sophisticated exclamation marks (put down, one feels, with a gold-nibbed fountain-pen on fine paper), here boots thunder out the message on the Nuremberg pavement. (This image of marching boots, indeed, could be taken as the trade mark of the propaganda film: it keeps popping up regularly every ten years.) Here was sheer pagan pomp, shorn of the ballast of humanitarian mental reservations. Reality and symbol walk in step with each other to a thunderous marching rhythm, and for the first time history is used in a direct way to shape history.

Editing, too, takes on a different role. Soldiers marching down a street may be just a bunch of men, but a film shot of their trampling boots expresses *power*. So the editor doesn't give a damn about hidden visual connections, about contrasts or intellectual metaphors. His job is to perform a "simple" cheat: to make two boots out of one, and a victorious regiment with an ideology out of a few lines of marching soldiers. And indeed if those boots, so irresistibly aligned by the editor's scissors, had marched down from the screen, Europe would have been trampled under within a week. . . .

This, then, was the ultimate: something that holds together what has been achieved before, and finds its consummation in a dazzling display which can lead nowhere (except to imitation). *The Triumph of the Will* was really the Defeat of our Infallibility: a symbol of how propaganda has contributed to the natural language of the cinema and led it, simultaneously, to the brink of an abyss of difficult moral questions.

*   *   *

The film made us aware, as nothing else could have done, that here we have a dangerous weapon which can easily misfire. The genie had at last escaped from the tiny bottle and loomed over our heads, monstrous and powerful, ready to carry out any service—if we knew how to handle it. Intellectual and artistic conscience was bound to ask itself whether we are masters of our own strength, or merely the sorcerer's troubled apprentices.

One question mark begets another. Isn't it opposed to the essence of art, which searches for a *universal* truth, to lift out one single, allegedly useful truth and use it perhaps to subvert others?

Is such a violent and arbitrary shaping of reality simply immoral, a misuse of democratic ideals? Or can it, because of its crisp immediacy, help to fertilize a vigorous, committed form of artistic expression? Is it a good or an unhealthy sign, for instance, that the same single image of the Nuremberg Rally can be used by Miss Riefenstahl for agitation, then in the British *Swinging the Lambeth Walk* as a piece of scathing irony; that many years later it can be applied (by the Thorndikes, in East Germany) as Communist propaganda, and that finally (after 27 years!) it can be used by Erwin Leiser in an attempt at sober evaluation?

If I feel that everyone must find his own answers to such questions, this is not an evasion. The answers depend largely on personal judgments about aesthetics and politics, on whether one sees art as firmly rooted in its own age or floating in the vacuum of the absolute. The artist, we said, searches for "a universal truth"—but is there any such thing? Everything that rises to the level of artistic truth is bound also to be a private truth, something which the artist has first recognized for himself and to which he gives a new and personal meaning. And who can tell, in any case, where art ends and propaganda begins? After the war neorealism turned a clean page, trying to rehabilitate this whole besmirched concept, to look for the universal truths and to assert its genuine commitments. But again comes the question: where is the borderline between a propagandist and a committed cinema, and does it even exist? Whenever a cinema becomes socially conscious, sooner or later it is bound to be transformed into propaganda. Are *O Dreamland* or *Los Olvidados, Pather Panchali* or *La Terra Trema*, "only" committed films, or do they qualify as more direct persuasion? Commitment seems to be the word which legitimizes propaganda. But art is an outcome of an immense will to communication. And involvement—why whitewash it?—*is* propaganda.

There may be a difference, though. One may well expect honesty from a committed artist, but not necessarily from the maker of a direct propaganda film. The product is of too dubious a moral value. Yet the question remains worth asking: is it necessary for the propagandist-artist to believe in what he or she is doing? Miss Riefenstahl has repeatedly declared that she knew nothing about the objects of the Nuremberg Rally film—and yet she was able to blend the work of 120 people over a two-year creative period into a breathtaking artistic unity. Can we believe her? Can the thing be done by sheer talent alone? And do we have here a case of intensified commitment or just another monumental and painfully absurd cheat? The moral wilderness of film propaganda is certainly the worst place in which to look for artistic absolutes. Its language has been polished through upholding the bloodiest ideas of mankind, and it seems a fitting product of a world in which it takes an almost physical effort to remain neutral.

Let us grant, however, that it may be possible. And even if all art is more or less propaganda, we can still ask in reverse whether propaganda is art. Many people would give a negative answer. If we *do* live in such circumstances, they would argue, amidst such unstable social, moral, and aesthetic values, then that is all the more reason for the artist to remain impartial. But for the artist to seal himself hermetically into a baroque castle and float in a dream world of the absolute seems to me a blind, cowardly and comfortable form of self-deception. And it strikes me as a kind of propaganda in itself—perhaps the worst kind. It talks about an attitude which it lacks the guts to uphold. The involved artist is concerned to strip life bare and to take his chances; but the other will prefer to dress up a skeleton in decorative clothing. He may find many "absolute" qualities in the *mise en scène* of *Triumph of the Will*: for him art creates its own laws and these justify its aims. But this, it seems to me, is the attitude of the intellectual *Übermensch*. And there isn't a baroque castle on earth, or any laws of art, which could hold out against those marching boots.

There is a fascinating dialectic to be observed in the question of how far propaganda is a product of its times and how far it can influence them. Political and social circumstances may produce an artist who exerts an influence (as Miss Riefenstahl's film doubtless did); the circumstances then change, and the new situation throws up its counter-artists. The very intensity of the propaganda genre means that it carries its own antidotes with it, so that each period seems to fight out its own particular battle between two different kinds of propaganda. Early Nazi films find their opposition (only seemingly indirect) in *L'Espoir* or *La*

Grande Illusion. In the moral wilderness there is still a continuous line pursued by the progressive conscience: in post-war documentaries about hunger and want; in neo-realist films standing for basic human rights; in the conscience of American journalistic films during the McCarthyist era; in the intellectualism of the French documentarists; in the attack against old standards by the Free Cinema group. Such continuous conflict is one of the things that helps to keep the genre alive.

It is typical of the anarchistic rootlessness of film propaganda (and a compliment, too, to its versatility) that its greatest works have a way of emerging from what seem to be the least promising circumstances. Eisenstein's intellectualism came out of (and almost in spite of) a bloody revolution. Riefenstahl's work emerged from (and against) the desperately humanist atmosphere of the thirties. And out of the Second World War came the incarnation of the humanist artist, a poet as noble, mature, and controlled as Humphrey Jennings.

Jennings' subjective style was perfected at precisely the moment when the general language of the propaganda film was at its most direct. War seems to be the test, to some extent even the harvest, of propaganda. Both involve uncompromising and totalitarian concepts. And to loosen up such a state of emergency in the arts, at a time when everything is gauged to the tight bark of a military command, is in itself an act of real courage. But this kind of liberation, with its rejection of all imperative symbols, was precisely the essence of Jennings' art. He recognized that true patriotism (and also good propaganda) can have its roots in the conscious temper of the people rather than the showy trappings. Riefenstahl tramples her awed audience underfoot; Jennings lifts them up again into humanity. Riefenstahl's propaganda quickly exhausts the few superficial symbols of its ideology; Jennings looks for the inner heartbeat of his country in troop trains, factory canteens, wheatfields, fire stations, National Gallery concerts. At long last propaganda was flowing again from the most intimate beliefs and visions of an artist. Even the most stubborn purists might be reassured that public persuasion *can* be an art.

For the umpteenth time in its own history alone, *montage* once more takes on a different role. For the old trickery of two-boots-for-the-price-of-one, Jennings substitutes something much more flexible. Like a Debussy or a Renoir, he finds fresh associations of pictures and sounds, discovers an airy music of images to mirror a sea of moods, connections, contrasts, episodes in the life of his country at war. The historic moment creates its own symbols: a barrage balloon; Myra Hess playing Beethoven ("German music"); the bare, empty walls of the National Gallery. For the poet, these are simply observations made in a particular context: nothing and therefore everything. And perhaps this is why, once the war was over and the intensity of the circumstances had vanished, Jennings could never really recapture this rare poetic amalgam of the ordinary and the extraordinary.

* * *

Similar contradictions are apparent in the screen propaganda of the present day. As the world political climate became more and more gloomy during the fifties, so film propaganda grew scared of its own power and responsibility. Soft, mild, middle-of-the-road film-making became the style. The political situation, fertilizer of propagandist art, was itself too desperate, and faced with the elemental problem of sheer survival everything became ridiculously oversimplified. Symbols seem to be produced on the assembly line, and concepts like The Bomb, The Wall, The Button themselves neutralize any kind of artificial symbolism which propaganda could provide. The marching boots of the old stereotype simply can't keep up any longer. Nor, I think, would Jennings' gentle poetry be able to catch up with and confront the situation. And while on the surface things may appear to be oversimplified, beneath this surface the atmosphere is more confused and complex than ever.

The easy way is to make the most of the simplified situation by accepting it at face value. It has become too easy for anyone with a few sympathetically progressive ideas to become a passionate benefactor of mankind. The Humanist tag may be tied to a Kramer or a Chukhrai—provided it is spelled with a capital H. Make a neutral film about the last people surviving on earth, première it in a 15-nation saturation booking, and you become the greatest prophet that money can buy. Make a film about Innocent Blond Ivan caught up in the Inhumanities of War, and you will win all the top prizes at San Francisco. . . .

But perhaps we help to foster this image by ourselves becoming gradually more and more immune to human misery. In Japan they have made a wide-screen, color, stereophonic epic about the annihilation of mankind by nuclear war, addressed (as a new type of publicity stunt) directly to Messrs. Khrushchev and Kennedy. Even in the thirties this could have seemed a disturbing, thought-provoking Wellsian vision: now we just smile at it and make a quick comment on the clumsiness of the special effects . . . And why not? We can watch the genuine real-life horror, all the painful superlatives which our contemporary existence can produce, at home in our slippers, after tea. And after close-ups of the killing at Leopoldville; the earthquake in Iran; the public execution of a head of state in a television studio, all laid at our feet by the unsurpassable magic of the telephoto lens and the cathode ray tube, what price a *Las Hurdes* in the cinema?

Yet here seems to be the root, and also the solution of the problem. Great things may have become everyday things; the capital letters may have been hacked to death. Isn't this, then, the precise moment when an artist should step in, should reassess the bloated and overworked concepts by subjecting them to his own personal viewpoint, treating them with that indefinable plus quality that only an artist can contribute? It is impossible to intensify the exclamation mark slammed down by a single shot of a heap of human hair at Auschwitz—but at the same time it *can* be intensified into a *Night and Fog*. By just looking around "you have seen nothing at Hiroshima"—and that is why Resnais strove for and achieved so much more than that. This is the way Franju's *Hôtel des Invalides* attacked, and Buñuel, Ichikawa, *Two Men and a Wardrobe*, *Vivre*, *Actua Tilt* and many others.

True, it is a question whether this long overdue invasion of conscience, and the return to an Eisensteinian intellectual humanism, may bring death or regeneration to this fundamentally totalitarian form of expression. A few years ago many devotees of the genre praised to the skies the effective Communist propaganda films made in East Germany by the Thorndikes. Perhaps they seemed like the last of the Mohicans: the defenders of the "real stuff." But, I feel, the quieter, sometimes hesitant, voice of awakening conscience means much more now than a few smart pranks with the editor's scissors or some bombastically effective pictorial harangue.

Perhaps the whole concept of film propaganda, in itself and in relation to its audience, will soon have to be reassessed. Films by Chris Marker and Jean Rouch illustrate the close links with television, but also the film's own superiority to it. In these works, at long last, propaganda is being written in lower case rather than in the old capital letters. And at a time when history so visibly outruns us, is formed, reformed and indeed deformed before our eyes, the real aim of propaganda ought to be to determine (and no longer to confuse) the place and role of human beings in our topsy-turvy universe. It's in this way that the genre could be rehabilitated.

But in the meantime there is something we can benefit from right now. If propaganda, with all its dangers, reminds us of the need to face up to the world we live in, urges us not to remain neutral but to try to adopt a standpoint, then let it come. It will help us to build up our own resistance. After all, it was *we* who allowed ourselves to be cheated.

IX.

The Unreal World of Television News*

HENRY FAIRLIE

One of England's best-known political commentators, Henry Fairlie is responsible for the term "Establishment." He has reported from Washington for the London *Sunday Express*.

〜〜〜〜〜〜〜〜〜〜〜〜〜〜〜〜〜〜〜〜〜〜〜〜〜〜〜

NONE OF US has ever seen Alexander the Great emerging from his tent. If there had been television in his day and we could look at the tape, would we know him any better, as we think we now know a John F. Kennedy or a Lyndon B. Johnson when we see them, on television news, emerging from a convention?

None of us has ever heard Julius Caesar speak. But if there had been radio in his day and we could listen to the recording, would we know him any better, as we think we know something important about Franklin D. Roosevelt from his fireside chats?

The answer is far from clear. Of all historical evidence, the public presence of voice or of physical appearance is the most revealing but can also be the most misleading. Yet the problem of historical evidence is raised every night on television news, when we are asked to accept what we see and hear as genuine. It is raised especially by the two most important television news programs in the United States: Huntley-Brinkley on NBC, and Walter Cronkite on CBS. Millions of people have to decide not so much whether they can believe what they are told but whether they can believe what they see flickering in front of them.

"The evidence of their own eyes": but that is precisely what is not available to them. What *is* available is the evidence, first, of the camera, making its own selection, dictating its own terms;

* Originally published as "Can You Believe Your Eyes," in *Horizon*, Spring 1967, pp. 24-7. Reprinted by permission of the author and the publisher. (Copyright, 1967, by American Heritage Publishing Company, Inc.)

and it is the evidence, then, of the small screen—still the best description of television—which in turn dictates to the camera. Can television, by its nature, ever tell the truth?

Amid all the pretentiousness of his theorizing, Marshall McLuhan is right to this extent: the medium is the message. Television does not merely create news. That is an old business, practiced for generations by newspapers. Television creates its own events, something even the most imaginative newspaper reporter cannot do. The newspaperman can only create words, and however powerful they may be, words do not *happen* over the breakfast table as television *happens* in a living room. Thomas W. Moore, ABC's president, came very near to the point when he said: "It is difficult to retain one's perspective when, without leaving the security of our living rooms, we become witness to such startling events as the assassination of an assassin, or a war in progress."

It is because television *happens* in this way that people begin to think that the small excerpts from life which they see on the screen in their living rooms are more "real" than the life which they experience around them. There is a vital margin of difference between saying, "Did you see the report in *The New York Times* of the massacres in the Congo?" and saying, "Did you see the massacres in the Congo on television last night?" The first remark implies only that one has seen a report (which may conflict with a report from another source). The second implies that one has seen the event itself. However carefully television is used, it cannot avoid this deception.

It is doubtful whether it is ever easy—sometimes whether it is ever possible—for a newspaper or television reporter to report an event. He can report incidents, and it is the nature of incidents that they can, and do, happen in isolation. But the true meaning of an event depends on all of its known and unknown causes, on all of the known and unknown incidents that contribute to it, and in the process, cease to be isolated, and on all of its known and unknown repercussions. The whole of an incident can easily be described; the whole of an event may escape even the historian.

If this is a difficulty that confronts the newspaper reporter

128

from day to day, it is one that the television reporter can rarely overcome. For the newspaper reporter possesses a flexibility that the television reporter does not have. He has flexibility because he can move without the paraphernalia and encumbrance of a camera or a camera crew. He has flexibility because he can reach where the camera cannot reach: the camera can never go "off the record."

The newspaperman has flexibility, above all, because words are flexible and the length of a story is flexible: the one able to qualify, even in the shortest parenthetical expression; the other capable of imposing its own perspective. But however carefully chosen the words of a television reporter, they can never properly qualify a spectacular picture; and however discriminating the apportionment of stories in a television program, they are in length too nearly the same.

Incidents are usually in the open; the whole of an event, often obscure and private. Not only is the core of television the public and the spectacular, but there is an important sense in which television has a vested interest in disaster. From the point of view of a good story, both newspapers and television prefer covering a major strike to negotiations which prevent a strike. But it is possible for the newspaper reporter to make negotiations almost as exciting a story as a strike itself: by word of mouth, he can collect a picture of the comings and goings which are the essence of negotiation and, by his words in print, vividly describe them. But what can television do with negotiations? It can only show pictures of people arriving at a building and people leaving it. However colorful they may be—and the modern business executive is not normally colorful—this does not make exciting viewing.

Violence is the stuff of television, and the question of how to deal with it is the most important one confronting the medium.

To be sure, the same question confronts newspapers; but the impact of violence—whether a boxing match, a riot, or a massacre—is much greater in a moving picture than in a still picture or in descriptive prose. Violence is movement—the raising of an arm, the smashing of it on someone's head—and movement is what television cannot help emphasizing.

129

In covering violent situations, three distinct characteristics of television conspire to intensify both its special problems and the special temptations to which it is exposed. There is, first, the limitation of time. A lead news story in a paper such as *The New York Times* may take twenty minutes to read; in a popular newspaper or a tabloid, as many as ten. There simply is not this time available in television news. In the reporting of all news, this means concentration to the point of distortion. In the reporting of violence, it means concentration on the violent incident to the exclusion of the whole event.

An outstanding example of such distortion was the police attack on civil rights marchers at the Selma, Alabama, bridge in March, 1965. I was not present myself. But I do not know one reporter who was present, and whose opinion I trust, who does not point out that there was first a prolonged period during which police and demonstrators faced each other, without violence, in an atmosphere of unbearable tension, and who does not agree that the tension had to break in the form of police action.

Television news—except in special features and documentaries—did not, and could not, show this preliminary encounter. Three minutes of film is an extended sequence in a news program, and the time is best filled with action, not inaction. On the other hand, a single phrase in a newspaper story, placed correctly, where it carries weight, can put even an extended description of violence in perspective.

The point of such perspective is not to excuse any eventual police brutality, but to explain it. Without this explanation, whether implicit or explicit, one begins to think that brutality is automatic, that the police will always behave in such a manner; demonstrators begin to think that they can, and should, goad the police; and the police begin to think that, since restraint is so frail anyhow, they may as well give way to exasperation from the start.

There is, secondly, television's tendency to produce self-generating news. The problem arose most notably during the disturbances in Watts; but it has arisen, again and again, whenever there have been similar disturbances in other cities. However spontaneous the original outbreak of violence, an external provocation is added once it has occurred. That provocation is the presence of television cameras in the middle of the trouble spots.

This is especially true on the night after the original outbreak. Then, as dusk gathers, television cameramen and reporters move into the streets looking—literally looking—for trouble, and the crowds begin to play up to them. Their presence is very different from the presence of newspaper reporters, who either roam around, hardly distinguishable, or lounge in bars until they hear that action has broken out somewhere down the block. Television, merely by its presence, helps to create incidents and then itself remains part of the happening. There is no doubt that this participation occurred after the first night in Watts, and that it occurred again last summer in Chicago.

But in order to create on the screen the impression of continuing disturbance, of continuing riots, television needs only one incident. One spectacular incident of violence can occupy a two-minute sequence in a news program just as impressively as a series of incidents. Much of the Watts film is a classic example of this: showing that it needs only one defiant boy and only one hotheaded policeman to suggest that a neighborhood is aflame.

In this connection it seems worth pointing out that a newspaper reporter's dishonesty—or imagination—can be a great deal less dangerous and provocative than a television reporter's. The newspaper reporter, after all, need only create—or exaggerate—a story in his own mind. But the television reporter must create—or exaggerate—it in actuality: he must make it a happening.

Finally, in this matter of violence, there is the size of the screen: the limitations which it imposes, the temptations it offers. At the end of the summer of 1966, television news showed some alarming pictures of white men and women in the Chicago suburb of Cicero screaming abuse at some Negro marchers. Their hating faces—a dozen of them, perhaps—filled the screen. They looked as if they were a representative example of a much larger crowd. But anyone who was there knows that these particular whites were only a small part of the crowds in the streets; and that the crowds themselves were only a small part of the total white population of Cicero. To this vital extent, television that night distorted badly.

What all this amounts to is not only that people sitting in their homes begin to think that all police are brutal, that all demonstrators are violent, that all disturbances are riots, that all crowds are aggressive; the fact that they usually go through each day without either meeting or themselves displaying violence becomes less real to them than the violence on the small screen.

Anyone who has appeared regularly on television knows that complete strangers think they have actually met him. They smile or nod at him in the street or across bars; they approach him and shake his hand; they even ask him to drop in when next he is around their way, as if they really believe that he has been in their homes. It is this imaginary "real" presence of television in people's living rooms which is the background to the whole problem. Surely much of the feeling of living in a condition of perpetual crisis, and the agitation arising from it, comes from a sense of being a witness to a world which is more actual than the routine world in which one lives.

Television can create not only events out of incidents, but movements and people. The television news coverage of the Meredith march across Mississippi, during the couple of days when I accompanied it myself, constantly appalled me. It was near the beginning of the march, when it had barely gotten organized, and when the numbers were few and the individuals composing the numbers were anything but impressive.

All the familiar hazards of television reporting were displayed. A straggling column—it was at the time little more—could be made on the small screen to look like an army. When the cameras were rolling, the marchers pulled themselves together and played the role expected of them. The several civil rights leaders strode in line abreast, at the head of their enthusiastic followers.

The real story of the Meredith march was not this unified demonstration at all, but the fact that it produced the deeply significant clash between different factions of the civil rights movement over "black power." Newspapers felt their way to this story and were, by the end, reporting it fully. It was a story which, for the

MEDIA AND MESSAGES

most part, was taking place in private meetings where the cameras could not reach. But then when television at last caught on to the fact of "black power," it inevitably exaggerated and distorted it. Film is expensive. Getting film ready for a news program is a hurried job. The result is that in reporting any speech the television reporter and cameraman make an automatic, almost involuntary, selection. They wait for the mention of a phrase like "black power," and on go the lights and the film rolls.

But, given the length of the usual sequence in a news program, that is all. The impact is far greater than that of any selection made by newspapers. By constant reiteration on the small screen day after day, the slogan of "black power" was elevated into a movement. It was suddenly there. It had suddenly happened. "Black power" switched the cameras on, and in turn the cameras switched the movement on. It was a classic case of self-generating news.

Stokely Carmichael, of the Student Nonviolent Co-ordinating Committee, could not have emerged so rapidly as a national figure without television. (SNCC is a master at using television.) But he is not the only example of television's ability to create—or destroy—people. No one, I think, questions that Governor Ronald Reagan is the creature of the television cameras, just as previously Actor Ronald Reagan was the creature of the movie cameras. John Morgan, one of the British Broadcasting Corporation's most experienced television reporters, returned from the California gubernatorial campaign in 1966, amazed at Reagan's professionalism in the television studio, and the use that he made of it to dictate camera angles and even the moments for close-ups.

Much of the poor impression that President Johnson has often made is the direct result of his comparatively poor television "image." The close-up, especially, can distort in the crudest way and make what is simply unprepossessing actually repellent. In fact, in considering the impact of the close-up, one can notice the vital difference between television and the movies; between what is legitimate in the cinema and illegitimate in a living room.

Movies are intended to be, and are taken to be, larger than life. Sitting in the theater, one does not imagine that what one is seeing is real. The close-up in the movies, therefore, is a legitimate *and understood* distortion. But a distortion it is. We never do see anyone in real life as close in as the camera can go, except in one position and in one activity: when making love. There is no reason why President Johnson, or any other public figure, should have to pass this private test in public. Moreover, not only does the close-up bring one ridiculously close to a face, it shows it in isolation. It removes the general bearing; it removes the whole man.

Perhaps the most striking demonstration of the power of television to create personalities is one that most people will think also demonstrates its power for good. For a comparatively short time three men seemed to bestride the world: John F. Kennedy, Pope John XXIII, and Nikita Khrushchev. Their impact, all over the world, was quite out of proportion to the length of time any of them held office. In a few years they had made as great an impression as Queen Victoria had in sixty years. This was the work of television.

Television news is new, and we have not yet got the measure of it. Its hazards are numerous: some of them are inherent in the nature of the medium, and are likely to be permanent. Others are more technical and, with technical advances, may be removed.

Camera crews are costly, and costly to move about; this automatically imposes a preselection of news far more rigorous than it is in a newspaper. Film costs impose a second automatic selection. Time on the screen is expensive, and this imposes a final selection. Again and again, when I have been making news films with a camera crew, I have wanted to utter over the pictures, "It was not like this at all."

However paradoxical it may seem, the only immediate answer to most of the problems of television news lies not in pictures but in words. Given the powerful impact of the pictures, the words covering them must provide the corrective. Most television reporting just describes the pictures, and by doing so, reinforces them. But the object of words in television news should be to distract from the pictures, to say: "It was not quite so. This was not the whole story." Pictures simplify; the object of words should be to supply qualification and complication. Pictures involve; the object of words should be to detach the viewer, to re-

134

mind him that he is not seeing an event, only an impression of one.

The manner of delivery—especially of the "anchor" men in the studio—is as important as the substance of the words themselves. There is something very professional and very engaging about the television manners of Chet Huntley and David Brinkley and Walter Cronkite. All of them, in dissimilar ways, cultivate a deadpan approach. In Huntley, it is made to suggest a judicial impartiality; in Brinkley, an ironical detachment; in Cronkite, an unfailing common sense. Each of them by his manner reinforces the impact of the pictures over which he is speaking, suggesting that they can be taken at their face value.

Only now and then, when Brinkley's irony is allowed to break loose into that overnourished flicker of a smile, is the value of the pictures ever questioned. The vital role of the television reporter or commentator is to make watching as difficult as reading, to invite the viewer to make comparisons and judgments from his own experience so that he never reacts by assuming that he is seeing actual life.

That television news can do some things remarkably well, especially in full-length features and documentaries, that those involved in making television programs are conscientious and skillful, does not touch the main problem. Television news holds a mirror up to the world in a way that newspapers never can; and the world is beginning to believe that it can recognize itself in it. Life is not made up of dramatic incidents—not even the life of a nation. It is made up of slowly evolving events and processes, which newspapers, by a score of different forms of emphasis, can reasonably attempt to explore from day to day.

But television news jerks from incident to incident. For the real world of patient and familiar arrangements, it substitutes an unreal world of constant activity, and the effect is already apparent in the way in which the world behaves. It is almost impossible, these days, to consider any problem or any event except as a crisis; and, by this very way of looking at it, it in fact becomes a crisis.

Television, by its emphasis on movement and activity, by its appetite for incident, has become by far the most potent instrument in creating this overexcited atmosphere, this barely recog-

135

nizable world. The medium, to this very important extent, has become the message; and the message is perpetual stimulation, perpetual agitation, perpetual change. The world it creates is a world which is never still.

Many of our unnecessary anxieties about the way in which we live, about the fearful things that may happen to us, might be allayed if television news began, now and then, to say: "It has been a dull day. But we have collected some rather interesting pictures for you, of no particular significance." Television news has a deep responsibility to try to be dull, from time to time, and let the world go to sleep.

X.

The Louder Reality: Behind the Busy Mirror*

DAVID T. BAZELON

David T. Bazelon is by training a lawyer and an economist. Among his publications is *Power in America: The Politics of the New Class.*

~~~~~~

MOVIES WERE a false community. But they were a community of a kind. This was the edge they held on the reality of the time.

How they did it, was to postulate a concentrated ninety-minute super-reality. Later, they reached for a three-and-a-half-hour one. But only after the coming of television was the double-feature consolidated into the blockbuster. The effort did not avail: the blockbuster is nothing but gorgeous and edited television: and television—being, unlike the original movie form, an invasion of the home—is presuming to become a fairly complete substitute for undefined reality. Being "complete," its dynamic is to be busy rather than precise or concentrated. Indeed, television has been so busy becoming what it is that, compared to what the movies were, it is decidedly retrograde. It consists mostly of serials, which are mass-produced B-movies in which standard parts are utilized. This creates both lowered costs of production and also the hypnotic endlessness which, thus far, defines the medium. I think this is no more than a primitive beginning, however —movies, too, began with serials—and that the louder reality of the recreated world now based on television remains substantially undefined.

To be weighty and historical for a moment, the encroaching

* Reprinted from *Review of Existential Psychology and Psychiatry* (1966), pp. 143-53, by permission of the author and the publisher.

problem of the quality of our lives can be characterized as that of industrial Byzantinism. Briefly, the opportunities for affluence will make idiots of us all, if we do not let the barbarians in. So much power and resource as America now possesses cannot simply be placed in some kind of power-and-resource bank, there to be held against a rainy day. Such deposits destroy the banker—and all of us within the affluent sector are bankers of a kind, whether we know it or like it or not. The kind of surplus-for-living we in America have now had thrust upon us, is a dynamism, a continuously threatening transcendence, a monster and a master beyond all previous ones. Happiness, I must tell you, is not a warm puppy: it is the white teeth at the front end of the tiger whose tail we hang onto for our very lives.

While we have been thinking over the character of our new lives, the tiger has led us into fabulous rituals. Ritual, we should remember, is the only non-money life-bank known to man. And it is a bank, history often tells us, from which withdrawals are neither encouraged nor facilitated. Then what happens? Well, first there's a run on the bank; then the priests or bankers are detested; in temporary puzzlement, people live a little in down-to-size, hand-made realities; some actual history occurs; and finally somebody starts a new bank.

Our popular culture, now centered around television, will always be deeply compelling because it is our only community with our inferiors, especially including our inferior sense of ourselves. The factor to reckon with here is that genuine community can never be elitist: community reaches to the limits of identification. That is the present definition of community as it was formerly the obvious definition of God. If I choose *Partisan Review* instead of television (I don't, incidentally), I am simply expressing my putatively superior taste in a choice between two false communities—because I have to have at least one to get through the rest of the day—just as intellectuals of previous periods ordinarily ended up choosing one false god or another.

In the law, we say that the rationalistic hypocrisy accompanying pragmatic change is the "genius of the common law"—and, considering all of the other possibilities, it is. Beyond law, with conscious human beings generally, we may say that the tendency

138

to heresy is the special genius of human history. Our popular culture is a hodgepodge of heresy—an incompetent outpouring of the human demand for a god for each period of the day. At one moment, it will be the miracle of a new detergent or toothpaste or mouthwash or shampoo; at another, the need is for a long sojourn at the wailing wall of domestic misuse; later, an avenging angel waves a tommy-gun or a Colt .45 in the direction of solvency; then a half-hour of teen-age barbarism convinces us again that age is not the ummitigated disaster it seems to be; just before bedtime, serious men reassure us as to the complexities of history which indicate, very likely, another such day as this one was (some of the shrewdest political nuances occur in the weather report, if you listen carefully); and then, with the louder reality silenced, we are free to roam beyond the busy mirror of the present—all the way into the warmer unreality of the movies of our youth.

With such programming, Richelieu might have succeeded in creating a France beyond the recurrence not only of the wrong Louis, but even of Charles de Gaulle.

Art of any kind, even the best kind, is a re-representation, a misrepresentation—in sum, a false community. But at its best it is a *true* false community. You find this a contradiction? I wonder why? Truth is a function of mentality: the truest truth of all is not the slightest bit of a substitute for the littlest banal piece of reality. And real community is an event, not an idea. But false community is an idea—that is why it is false. Some of these ideas, however, are better than others. And one or another is necessary, because we do not survive well without at least one. Therefore, we are in the business of making judgments of value as among false communities. Therefore, some are even truer than others.

Perhaps all art and even all consciousness, no matter how we play with the truth, is a re-representation of reality. In my present daring mood, I am tempted to agree with Charles Péguy, who said: "Everything begins in mysticism and everything ends in politics." However that may be, as mechanical devices lead us closer to a fuller verisimilitude, a process of once-slow change finally overwhelms us: *the reality being re-represented is lost.* Modern politics, then, would be an attempt to recapture reality through action—mysticism the attempt to do so by standing still (achieving inaction) creatively.

The initial loss of reality is much facilitated by living in cities, where the traditional reality of nature is obscured in its own physical re-representation—as brick and mortar, and chrome and plastic, and other fantastical materializations. Interestingly, natural community is one of the early losses of the city: cities are made up of migrants. The abandonment of natural community is part of the price of admission to the never-ending recreation of human nature and its environment, which is the drama of the city.

But verisimilitude—whether by mechanical device or by the more laborious and dangerous method of building a city—is tyrannous and objectionable. Indeed, it can be totalitarian. To be brief, it presumes an identity between idea and fact which we are not used to, which is presented without our permission or participation, and which is strangely less believable as it becomes truer. I think this explanation helps to explain, for example, the response of abstract art to the advent of photography: the more serious people became more and more hysterical in their effort not to be "taken in" by encroaching verisimilitude. I think that ordinary and less serious people have, with the ordinary and less serious means available to them, responded similarly to the encroachment of the city.

What is the difference between a city, and the photograph of a city? I suggest that the difference lies in the quality of belief bestowed on each: the initial unreality of the city is certified as "real" by the photograph. And these issues of belief are different from others in that both are presented as unalterable facts rather than as subjective notions produced by other human beings. To someone who has never lived in a city, the photograph of one would be taken as an imaginative offering or imposition—as somebody's idea of something. But if you live in that city, the photograph will very likely be taken as fact-truth—and is felt to be the same kind of imposition as the city itself is. Conceive the city as the alterable fault of City Hall, however, and you may walk away from the photograph muttering about lousy artists or presumptuous cameramen. And—here Péguy is clearly correct—you cannot finally and seriously do the one without also doing the other. Man-made realities and their misrepresentations cannot be kept separate.

As with the arts of the city, so with the managers of verisimilitude— Who runs City Hall, and with what ends in view? More precisely, with what image of *me* in mind, if any. And what can I do about it if I don't like it. (That is, what can I do about it besides learning to like it.)

Note that under the effects of modern technology, the previously clear line between environment and culture is obscured. And that line, further note, is a basic one, since it separates dream from actuality. Now wait a minute, you reflect in a cool objecting mood, if that particular line were lost, everybody would be nuts —by definition. We don't have the time or the courage to face that issue directly, but I would suggest that the line has indeed been obscured, whatever that may do to our definitions; and that the issue replacing this previously compelling and obvious one is a choice of acceptabilities—nearly a matter of fashion. It is we on the outside who decide who is to be put away on the inside—or *vice versa*—and we change our minds on this subject frequently, and according to the vagaries of fashion. Certainly fashion, and other indeterminate compulsions, have already created acceptances and disallowances as to the content of cities, of environment/culture, of who is in and who is out of almost anything. And these choices are not based on any simple Rouault-line between figure and background, dream and actuality.

Religious cultures provided handicraft public dreams—and also the handmade conventional line between these and reality. With active photography and the movies, our public dreams became subject to the startling dynamics of industrialism. When mechanical verisimilitude replaces mysticism, the dream is unleashed upon reality. The difference between a lyric poem and six hours of television is a difference past comprehension. Without much comprehension, we can confidently say that it is different men who take each as their different cultures. I would now like to characterize these industrial dreams, and indicate some of the avenues of solution for the unitary persons who—because of the nature and need of community—understand that they must live as *both* these different men.

Technology does with our dreams what it does with other aspects of our lives—it rationalizes the production of consumption items and administers their application. But our dreams present the most intractable material with which the rational administrative order must deal. Also, the American gluttony for dreaming far surpasses our world-famous predeliction for creature-comforts and shiny objects. All this has the consequence that in the production of dreams our rational administrators rise to levels of incompetence they seldom achieve elsewhere. I tried but could not bring myself to agree with Newton Minow's characterization of television as a "vast wasteland": he saw it as an unsuccessful effort at adult education. Viewing it more pertinently as Dreamsville, USA, the candid observer is struck not with the absence of discussion shows and other cultural events, but with the helpless messiness of the programming. It is one big bowl of chop suey, resulting from the frantic pursuit of a buck by means of the primitive manipulation of happenstance. It is like an unending visual magazine put together by a team of overworked, drunken editors who refuse to speak to each other about any subjects except gross receipts, dividend disbursements, and year-end bonuses.

For instance, given the terms of the game, I don't object to the commercials. They are often enough technically superior and visually more interesting than other segments of the endless show. They certainly consume no more time than one spends finding the text in *The New Yorker*, or distinguishing between the ads and the pictures in a picture-story in *Look*. Apart from big events like the Kefauver or McCarthy hearings, and the great assassination weekend, most of the artistic innovativeness of television has been in connection with the commercials. As for the rest, it is mostly derivative—lifted bodily from the movies (probably half the TV time in the country is devoted to movies, anyway) and the ancient art-form of parlor visits by strangers. Even the big events are not that much better than the commercials, when the organization has time to get the equipment in position and plan the representation, as with the Churchill funeral and the Johnson Inauguration.

It is true of our national popular culture generally that the manipulation of the dream and the representation of objects of consumption are hardly separate aspects of the same thing. Mostly, they *are* the same thing. Remove either, and the other will be changed substantially. Which is why I always preferred movies to *The Ladies' Home Journal*. In pre-television movies, the presentation of consumption items was skillfully woven into the text, so to speak. In this, it was more like the photograph of a city, and less like an ordinary real estate ad with pictures.

It should be clear by now that I am one of the old-fashioned fellows: I used to "go to the movies," and doing so was important to me. I think the movies were the "pure case" of popular dream culture—that is, the two decades or so of American talkies, ending with the triumph of television in the fifties. I saw the end coming in 1951 when I was in law school, and my classmates were a few years younger than myself. After dinner, one of them suggested we all "take in a flick." I didn't know what he was talking about, but I was game for anything in those days, so I agreed. I was horrified to find out he meant let's all "go to the movies." How I learned to detest that phrase! It meant the end of my movie-going days. I was damned if I was going to lower myself to "taking in a flick"—which, it turned out, meant first preference for a French or Italian film or an American thing compounded of the worst elements of each—something as awful, say, as *The Barefoot Contessa*. I withdrew in dignity, nurturing my hard-earned honor as a former slave to movie-going. "Take in a flick," yet! *Me* —who had seen a hundred and seventy-five Tom Mix serials, every Bogart since *The Petrified Forest*, and every Cagney since *Public Enemy*.

The central institution in American society is something called "Success"; and its sustaining myth has been Individualism. The movies that were important to me, I now see with hindsight, were a development of the post-Depression fate of the myth of American Individualism. I bought my ticket and entered the communal darkness of the theater in a state of desperate loneliness; I dreamed along with millions of other communityless Americans; and I believe that most of us emerged, after two decades, older and wiser and more shrewdly adjusted, as individuals, to the louder reality of the city. We dreamed our way past the dangerous edges of the myth. I don't think Hollywood ever intended to give us that much for our money. In the delirium of dollar-fever, they goofed. It was as if the machine answered the machine-tender with something like sympathetic consideration. Because of the difficulties of administration and the accompanying distractions of making a buck, this is potential in all dream-machines, I suggest—even television. Machines, like children, mirror the underlying *Us* when and if we fail to interfere effectively.

The real difference between high art, and the lower commercial or industrial stuff, is the quality and effectiveness of the interference. We will return to this point in a moment; but first I want to tell you about what happened in the movies, especially from *Little Caesar* to *The House on 92nd Street*. It is relevant to the subject we are speculating about—the relation between reality, the actor, and mechanical devices of rerepresentation.

The simple form of the myth of Individualism in the movies appears as the Cowboy. For background, I will only suggest that the Cowboy was romanticized because Mr. Horatio Alger Himself became unbelievable. Before that, the actual cowboy was a dirty bum—a hobo, a seaman, a social Houdini. Anyway, after Cotton Mather and Horatio Alger, the Cowboy became the Purest Thought of which Americans were capable. He was a fellow with a horse, a frying pan, and a gun. His basic connection with anything real or recognizable was the gun: the horse was a farmer's memory, and the frying pan dispensed with women altogether. He had one change of clothing. But he had the gun: this was the single symbolic connection with the city, with complicated civilization. In many of the best Westerns, the chief character is the gun —especially to be mentioned is that sophisticated but loving rendition of the crypto-Western, *Destry Rides Again*.

The Western is not hard to understand—it is almost as pure and obvious, in the American context, as Hemingway's hunting and fishing scenes. The aesthetic problem was to engage this emotional stream of myth closer to home, as the farmers' stay in the city lengthened into decades. The occasion for the solution was the apocalyptic Depression, and the symbol was the Gangster. In essence, the Gangster was a denuded Cowboy: his horse had been shot out from under him, somebody had taken away his frying pan, and all he had left was his gun. And no scenery: the picture begins with him arriving in the City. He gets off the bus with one change of clothing and the gun, and there are no Open Spaces: this being the City, all "spaces" must be opened by him.

Probably the greatest single piece of movie criticism written in this country was the five pages in *Partisan Review* by Robert Warshow, called "The Gangster as Tragic Hero." Nearly twenty years later, I find it as startling and brilliant as on the first reading. Bob Warshow was a friend of mine: as were the two other leading American critics (after the *Hound and Horn* group and Otis Ferguson), James Agee also dead, and Manny Farber still kicking. Farber is unequalled in being able to perceive a significant piece of business in a film; Agee's rhetorical enthusiasm for film as an art form is equalled only by the aesthetic criticism of the twenties. But Warshow saw film just as I did, only better: he saw it as a bonanza of an opportunity to penetrate the emotional history of one's own time. Which he did, as for instance in his brief essay on the gangster film.

Warshow begins with the proposition that there is a duty to be happy in America, and that our organs of mass culture naturally undertake to meet this responsibility. Then he notes the just-as-natural countervailing force in our culture, the need "to express by whatever means are available to it that sense of desperation and inevitable failure which optimism itself helps to create." This the gangster film has done in unparalleled fashion: "From its beginnings, it has been a consistent and astonishingly complete presentation of the modern sense of tragedy." The genre consists of a repeated pattern which "creates its own field of reference." The gangster film does not concern "real" gangsters: "What matters is that the experience of the gangster *as an experience of art* is universal to Americans." And that is because "The gangster is the man of the city . . . carrying his life in his hands like a placard, a club . . . he is what we want to be and what we are afraid we may become." The essence of the gangster is that he uses violence to achieve success, but he "is doomed because he is under the obligation to succeed, not because the means he employs are unlawful." To succeed is to be alone—"the successful man is an outlaw"—and if you are alone you will be killed. Thus, with the gangster catharsis enacted, we value our failure.

The gangster film itself had a definite death: it was so in tune with its audience, unconsciously, that it could not be repeated successfully today. When Edward G. Robinson as *Little Caesar* dies in 1930, his last words are pure brutal wonderment—"Mother of God, is this the end of Rico?" Some years later, in *The Roaring Twenties*—a film about the end of the gangster era—Cagney lies dead on the street in front of a cathedral, and a cop with a notebook in hand asks the dead man's girl, "What was his business?" "He used to be a big shot," she says. The final and absolute end of the gangster film I date, however, with Cagney's *White Heat*, circa 1949, in which the basic idea of the gangster was self-consciously psychologized. In this absolutely wild film, the mother was the head of the gang, and Cagney is loudly psychotic from the first reel. And he dies not in the traditional burst of submachine gun fire—he is blown up in an oil factory, grinning hideously as the flames, etc., etc.

Meanwhile, the general development of the myth of Individualism and the problem of Success was creatively refurbished in 1941 with the great private-eye film, *The Maltese Falcon*. Here, American City Man is no longer a gangster, but not yet a soldier or a cop. He is positioned in between. Indeed, everything is ambiguous about him except one thing: he wants to do a competent job. This is his substitute for big money, big success, big sex, big anything. He can die, it is clear, only through lack of male cunning and other incompetence. With the private-eye film—hundreds of which were made during the forties and early fifties—the City Man has become a semi-professional with a code of competence centered around the job-at-hand, which affords control over his environment *and* his own impulse to get too much out of life. I date the end of this genre with Mickey Spillane, whom I would rather not discuss at length.

Meanwhile, the cop-film arrived, during the War, with *The*

House on 92nd Street. Here, Individualism is the permissive gift of organization. Law and order triumph as teamwork and machinework: it is a highly bureaucratized form of law and order. The fascination of these cop/organization films consists in the variety of machines and the efficiency of organization: you identify with these, not with people. A recent and very successful example of this type has been *The Untouchables* series on television, high-grade B-movies which presumed to go back and rewrite the gangster film from the viewpoint of a law-gang. Now, with something like *The Man from U.N.C.L.E.,* this genre encroaches upon science fiction, becomes bizarre as well as sophisticated, and includes a charming layer of silliness. Efficient organization, I predict, is becoming funny in popular culture—not yet the high macabre humor of *Dr. Strangelove,* but still increasingly funny in a bizarre way.

Well, where are we? I think my overall point has been that dreams, and the ideals and ideal-images they contain and enunciate, are a large part of the louder reality, and properly so, whether or not we think we are participating in a religious culture. In a man-made world which includes integrally the machine-made re-representations of it, dream is so much a part of reality that we need a new approach for those occasions when it is still important to distinguish the two. Let me put it another way: Technology is transcending traditional religious dualism by destroying nature, both inside man and in the outside world. The result has been to unleash dreams and dreaming upon the destroyed worlds. The one virtue of dualism was that it presumed to keep dreams off the streets. Nothing can presume to do that now. So the "new approach," I feel, must follow Freud's prescription for dreams, which I take to have been affording them greater acceptance and applying a higher order of criticism to them. And this must be done socially and politically—on the streets—and not just in the dream-doctor's quiet study.

My suggestion has been that mechanical reproducing devices merely facilitate the unleashing of dreams by: 1) fostering the deception of verisimilitude; 2) compounding the cultural felony by, so to speak, photographing a photograph; and 3) reproducing the disorder of the management of the city in the "pictured" re-representation of it—on television, for instance, by the absence of the artist—so that it is no longer true enough that in dreams begin responsibilities. In sum, tape and film are magical only if you are not yet aware of what technology has *already* done to the world. With that awareness—but only with that awareness—they become stimulatingly ordinary, and may even be a means of salvation, since they are especially suited to the imaginative manipulation of technologized reality.

And what about the quieter realities of cultural elites? Fine, no problem—except one. That is, how to establish communication between all dreaming realities, and the possibility of community among all dreaming men. That is an old religious problem, now reconstituted on a new technological basis. Indeed, the pattern repeats itself startlingly, on the new basis. Where once the church introduced great distortion in mediating between God and man, we now have the corporations and other bureaus for the administration of dreams and ideals. Instead of the Borgia popes, we had L. B. Mayer and some others; and now, I am sure, have numerous curia of network executives, and so on. Elites-out-of-communication, for one reason or another, tend to become corrupt—one way and another. Especially in America, which is a democracy *or else*: can you imagine this country without its belief in democracy—without that potential, or preoccupation, or whatever it is? The mere thought is enough to make one's head spin. In a democracy, one must always search for the proper relation between popular and other values—between the worlds made by lesser men, and the superior worlds imagined by our elites. But never either/or: that would be crazy.

And especially in America, the better elites perform a great function—sometimes nobly at great cost to themselves, and sometimes less nobly in spite of themselves. Snobbery is their problem: but their value is that they are concerned with *form*—old form, fresh form, frenzied form, form without content, but nevertheless form. And that is very important for us, with our general lack of inherent form in American life. So, view them, if you must, as laboratory technicians of form, and try to forgive them their bad democratic manners, and the fact that, spinster-like, they tend to dry up sooner than their coarser fellow-countrymen.

148

The future of American culture, as with everything else in this country, lies with the great organizations—which, incidentally and lest we forget, are still made up of individuals, I think. In popular culture, I expect to see giant diversified entertainment organizations—"private" commissariats of culture. Notice how block-booking quickly reappeared, after more than a decade of movie antitrust litigation, in network television—which, with its great captive audience, is little more than block-booking. With all our dreams held in these fat organizational arms, we may one day look back on the historical mess of Hollywood movie-making as a great Golden Age—because the director, or the producer, or even the great star who carried the script in his face, was a single aesthetic organizing factor unavailable to the NBC-MGM-Time, Incorporated, of the future.

It may soothe us to imagine what may lie behind *all* the busy mirrors: it is the terror of creation. And I rather think this is primarily the terror of creating more and better mirrors, before the reflection of life, in our unanimal settings, ends. I wonder what else it might be?

Anyway, we are too busy or too vain to abandon the mirrors. I know I am. I remember pausing on my way out of the Loew's Sheridan in New York City some years ago, after having submitted to a real stinker. I shook my fist at the screen: "You win this time, damn you! But I'll be back." And I will.

XI.

Television: Window on Culture or Reflection in the Glass?*

AUBREY SINGER

Aubrey Singer is head of the television outside broadcasts, feature and science programs of the BBC, which he joined in 1949.

~~~~~~

TELEVISION IS something by our times, out of our times, for our times. It reflects the virtues and faults of our times.

Its electronic principles were conceived by the prophets of technology about the same time that practical radio was being demonstrated, that Einstein was laying the basis for the exploitation of matter, that concepts of anthropology were shifting to concepts of sociology.

Television was conceived at the end of the century when man's curiosity was optimistic, charitable, and untarnished, when man still believed in God, in man, in laissez-faire economy, and in the rigidity and essential firmness of the world around him. Although this world was changing with increasing pace, Marlowe's lovely lines written in the last half of the sixteenth century fit the vision of man and the ambitious aspirations of the times.

> Nature that fram'd us of four elements,
> Warring within our breasts for regiment,
> Doth teach us all to have aspiring minds:
> Our souls, whose faculties can comprehend
> The wondrous architecture of the world:
> And measure every wand'ring planet's course,

* Reprinted from *The American Scholar* (1966), pp. 303-9, by permission of the author and the publisher. (Copyright, 1966, by the International Center for the Communication Arts and Sciences.)

> Still climbing after knowledge infinite,
> And always moving as the restless spheres,
> Will us to wear ourselves and never rest,
> Until we reach the ripest fruit of all,
> That perfect bliss and sole felicity,
> The sweet fruition of an earthly crown.

There it is, the reconciliation with environment to reach felicity through knowledge.

But in the fifty years from the turn of the century, in the fifty years that television has grown from an idea to fulfilled reality, man has changed and his ideas have changed his environment. Earth, air, fire, and water lost their place as observed and simple absolutes two hundred years ago. It has taken this time for a new idea, the equivalence of space, time, energy, and mass, to become their substitute.

Those old four fundamental elements, those archetypes of our environment, today are held in low respect. Earth is consumed for minerals, moved by the mountain, shaped, bored into, synthesized. Air is flown over and above, liquefied, solidified, split into constituent gases; its climate is altered, its heat and cold ignored. Fire is made small before the power of the nucleus: man can imitate the sun. Aqualung, bathyscaphes and permeable membranes are letting us return to our beginnings, to the sea that was the womb of life.

In fifty years man has not merely come to control environment at will. His familiarity and dominance now hold it in contempt. After all, when an astronaut can fly through space, when a picture can be transmitted around a planet or from another planet, when a jet can fly from London to New York in a few hours (and all this was developed within the last two decades), it is not surprising that man should have suffered an implosion of his horizons. Our personal and terrestrial worlds are no longer large enough—the immediate world has given way to the desperately desired imminence of the future world. "Give us this day our glimpse of tomorrow."

But when we look at tomorrow we have lost our vision of Utopia. Consciously people are led to believe the promised future is here. Unconsciously they suspect the vision of new bright lands has vanished forever. Along with our vision of Utopia we are losing our capacity for anger and indignation with what we see going on around us.

In his book *The Dehumanization of Art*, Ortega y Gasset says in a memorable passage: "A fundamental revision of man's attitude towards life is apt to find its first expression in artistic creation and scientific theory. The fine texture of both these matters renders them susceptible to the slightest breeze of the spiritual trade winds."

Architects, designers, composers, scientists, and writers are being buffeted by the spiritual hurricane which is shaking our times. Compare the words of Marlowe's sturdy vision which I quoted earlier with E. E. Cummings' poem written with a profound sense of anxiety sometime in the 1940's.

> What if a much of a which of a wind
> gives the truth to summer's lie;
> bloodies with dizzying leaves the sun
> and yanks immortal stars awry?
> Blow king to beggar and queen to seem
> (blow friend to fiend: blow space to time)
> —when skies are hanged and oceans drowned,
> the single secret will still be man

The belief in the human spirit remains but is surrounded with a deep unease, perhaps inspired by those zephyrs of the first half of the century—relativity and quantum mechanics, psychiatry and sulphonamide, and the new knowledge of the impermanence of the universe. None of this gives a static vision—it speaks of the new relationships and resonances with which the human psyche has to reconcile itself.

And the last verse, in a spasm of buffeted prophecy, foresees our twenty postwar years and the new revolutions that were to come:

> what if a dawn of a doom of a dream
> bites this universe in two,
> peels forever out of his grave
> and sprinkles nowhere with me and you?
> Blow soon to never and never to twice

(blow life to isn't: blow death to was)
—all nothing's only our hugest home;
the most who die, the more we live

There's the spiritual jet stream for you. There's U-235 and plutonium, A-bombs and H-bombs, and amino acids, computers and all the paraphernalia of our moments caught in a poet's glimpse at the start of our epoch.

The poem hints too at the new changes in quality produced by the changes in quantity and the organization of quantity. It hints at mass culture in all its impact, at cinemas, national newspapers, radio and paperbacks and television and tape recordings, at punched cards and computer codes. It hopes against hope that man himself will come through all this and retain his identity.

But it's too late, for surely the point about our present-day condition lies in the Marxist tag, "A change in quantity brings a change in quality." Philosophically debatable perhaps, but tenable when one looks at the changes our new techniques have wrought in modern urban society. The change in the number of man has produced a change in the quality of man. Somehow, compressed and crowded urban man is losing his individuality and becoming a cell in a larger organism.

In fact, for man to survive (and he needs nothing less than a lost Utopia really to achieve survival) he is being forced to accept (albeit and surprisingly rather willingly) a degree of organization that can lead to nothing less than insectivization. The dull routines and social customs of mankind are amenable to statistical measurement and indeed organization is now planned to facilitate this measurement. Within this framework the individual turns in on himself and frenetically tries to assert his individuality and, up to a point, the more he tries to do this the more he is a subject for statistical study. From the world of things man is moving to the world of probabilities.

Television is of all this, the twentieth-century born and bred product of our society. By our times, out of our times, for our times. Its electronic principles may be fifty years old but the persuasive networked home entertainment we know today began twenty years ago in 1945. Then there were perhaps a hundred thousand sets in the world. Now there are about one hundred and fifty million. Then it covered a few urban areas in experimental form. Now it is possible to ring the northern hemisphere.

Theoretically a picture could originate in Tokyo, be sent across to Vladivostok, thence to Moscow, through Europe to Britain, across the Atlantic by satellite, across America by landline, across the Pacific by satellite and back to Tokyo. Puck said he'd put a girdle round the earth in forty minutes—that old Shakespearean square! Television can girdle the earth in about a fifth of a second, and it's no longer a miracle. Along with our contempt for spatial environment has come a loss of wonder. *Sic transit gloria imago mundi*—thus passes the glory of the image of the world, and man looks around and wonders who devalued his psyche.

Those who sense this loss react strongly; for instance, television has become the chopping block for the liberals. While in the 1930's they indulged in political or social activity, now their attentions and frustrations are turned on the mass media, with special emphasis on television. If juvenile delinquency increases—blame television; if there is any decline in moral standards—blame television; if man feels cheated in any way by this society he has created, then the blame is turned on television.

In one aspect, and alas its most common aspect, television as practiced today is just one of the many windows through which we observe, transmit and reflect our valuation of society to each other. If indeed there has been a change in the quality of life, if indeed our times have belittled our stature, the television medium in this aspect only responds to and reflects the social climate. It has little to do with the initial creation of a spiritual trade wind. It is only a sort of air conditioner that processes and gets this wind into homes more quickly.

There is, however, another aspect of television. There are times when television acts in its own right, when it evaluates the new Renaissance in its own terms, when it uses its power of communication not merely to convey other people's images but rather to create out of its potentialities its own genuine statements. This is the television at which we in television have got to aim. When we do we can claim equal responsibility with those who create the values of society. With architects, authors, scientists, designers, film-makers, with all those who create and communicate original work.

If we avoid enlisting in the creative spearhead, then television abandons itself to the role of reflector. If we in television do not have the courage to speak our own mind—utter our own statements—then there are plenty who will buy our time from us, for communication, like nature, abhors a vacuum.

If television chooses to take the side of the creative talent, it joins with those trying to reach a new relationship with the shifting face of society and the fading importance of environment. It will react to the different visions of how this might be achieved. For the poet: "The single secret is still man." For the composer: It can be as escapist as romanticism or as brittle and "switched on" as the new sound. For the artist: Let a Francis Bacon painting speak for itself. For the architect: Let me quote from a recent publication: "We are concerned not with architecture or town planning but with the creation of environment for every scale of human association." (Saadrach Woods, 1963.)

Perhaps the architect speaks his mind most openly. At least he admits he wants to tailor the cosmos. He might be accused of the sin of pride but he latches on to the important truth that man must continually strive to live in a homeostatic relationship with society as well as environment. For it is this aspect of feedback, and control by feedback, that has become more important to our creative thinkers than the old indefinable frozen moment when things were still against a sharp background.

This is the new relationship in which television must share, the new relationship of man to his world, of man to art, the new-found relationship of man to mind. Recently in a BBC program we asked a psychiatrist to define mind:

> *Interviewer:* If the mind can influence the body to make a father experience the discomforts of pregnancy, how do you define mind, Professor Trethowan?

> *Professor Trethowan:* Well, that's very difficult. Mind: mind is a function of the brain, it's a function of the sensory organs which feed it, it's a function of the motor organs which give it expressions. Mind, I think, is communication. Communica-

tion between man and his environment, communication between man and himself, communication between man and
man. Mind is feeling and knowing. Knowing comes from the
barrier of consciousness and mingles with the other contents
of the deeper parts of the mind, is reflected back again like
sound from the ocean floor where it breaks consciousness and
modifies knowing once again. What we see here is mind as a
continuous oscillating, fluctuating process, it's a cybernetic
process, there's a feedback between man and his environment,
a feedback between the inner man and the outer man.

These new thoughts, these new relationships and resonances
are what concern us today. Perhaps we've not lost our vision of
Utopia. Perhaps it's changing. As man changes. Perhaps what we're
all a party to is a struggle between man and mankind: the point of
evolutionary decision between Homo sapiens and (dare I coin the
word) Homo cyberneticus.

If television is to play its part in helping man define his role
then on its part society must know what to expect from this electronic window—whether merely to expect a reflection from the
glass or whether to expect a good view of the cultural country-
side.

What is the role of television? It's difficult to define. At its
most ordinary it acts as an extension of vision. It relays routine
information, routine entertainment, routine education, into the
drawing rooms of the audience. At its best it bestows insight. It
heightens perception, reveals new relationships and brings with it
a new view of our daily lives.

Television is rapidly becoming one of the main contributors
to the stream of information that makes up the feedback from
the world to man. In taking over, ruthlessly and with compulsion,
television processes other media and tends to drown them out.
Before the electronic age there was a time when the channels of information—painting, music, literature—were held in balance and
did not draw on each other very much. Mass communications, especially television in its routine moments, now draws relentlessly
from all other media, from films, from literature, from graphic
design, from theater, from events. In doing so—both because of
its limitations and because of the frequency and thoroughness

with which it does so—television is tending to act as a great leveler, a sort of tomato ketchup on a feast of culture.

If this is so then all the more do we have to be wary of the ubiquitous images of television. Those images are aggressively sociable and the medium that carries them technically complex; because of their easy acceptability and the facility with which they reach us in our homes these images become more credible, more important, than the reality they represent. Television supersedes reality and this new reality, this electronic picture, is a pale and transient thing compared with some of the images lying around our cultural supermarket. For instance, have you ever seen a TV picture that was really beautiful in the same way that some photographs are outstandingly so? In TV there is little or nothing that is pictorially beautiful. I suppose it has something to do with the size of screen, lack of definition and transient nature of the medium.

No, television is at its best when it's not trying to ape other media and achieve goals outside its limitations. Television is at its best in raw direct communication between people with things to say. Television favors the articulate and scorns the dumb. In television, unlike the movies, a word is worth ten thousand pictures. Television's real discovery has been the extrovert personality, the bridging of distance, and, above all, the immediacy of the happening.

While there are advantages and disadvantages inherent in television itself, the mere business of operating the medium carries its own share of mixed blessings.

At the moment there are several limitations in the number of frequencies available to television operators. This of course means that under present legislation in the United States and in Britain there is a limit to competition.

Making these channels available to the largest audience entails large financial outlay on capital equipment and high operating costs. Nevertheless it has been discovered on both sides of the Atlantic that television is amenable to the same management principles as any other mass distribution process. These principles require that the largest potential audience for a given type of

157

program be reached at the lowest cost. Television by any present criterion of efficiency is too expensive to exist in a vacuum.

The managers of TV running their enterprises on a basis of profit or cost effectiveness are well aware of these problems. However, as they shuffle their programs on the chessboards of their schedules, they are aware that in the eyes of their critics the competitive search for audience, the rate at which television swallows material, and the sheer amount of air time to be filled tends to make them play down to lesser cultural levels, supporting complacency rather than satisfying aspiration.

Obviously there is a large measure of truth in the criticism. But these problems are worldwide—television's costly and complex technical facilities tend to lead to a homogeneity of product on the one hand and on the other have far outstripped our knowledge of the audience.

We know some things about our audience. In most cases we consider it to be very large. This is the mass audience the advertisers and professional managers of television are interested in.

On the other hand the audience is very intimate and very small—the family circle grouped around the television set. This is the audience that the television producer should be interested in. For television is an intimate dialogue, a two-way interacting variable between producer and receptor: "a continuous, oscillating, fluctuating process, it's a cybernetic process, there's a feedback between man and his environment, a feedback between the inner man and the outer man." Forgive me for again quoting that definition of mind but that's what television should be about, and I suspect that in the case of a successful program "the oscillating processes" at both ends of the system produce an intellectual resonance in audience and also in producer.

To take an analogy from another area, this small intimate audience is the fundamental particle of which the mass audience is composed. Like the fundamental particles of physics it is subject to indeterminancy. That is, if you try to experiment with it the mere act of experimentation alters the nature of the experimental subject and therefore renders the experiment valueless.

The prime arts work at this quantum level. Composers, authors, painters don't try to gratify an audience. They try to com-

158

municate. If they communicate to a large number of those quanta of society so be it, but it is not their prime purpose in life. And it is working in this area of uncertainty and unpredictability, of having to rely on intuition rather than knowledge, that distinguishes the artist from the craftsman.

But for the manager with a large competitive stake in television this is a most unsatisfactory state of affairs. He can't afford failure and therefore he invokes mathematical statistics, for while the individual is unpredictable, the mass is only too subject to measurement.

Consider a scene that for me is even more important than those old visual clichés, the A-bomb explosion at Alamagordo or the rockets shooting up from Cape Kennedy: the grounds of Naworth Castle in England. It was under a rock overhang on those grounds in the year 1889 that Francis Galton first formulated the idea of mathematical correlation: an idea that made it possible to represent by a system of numbers the degree of relationship or of partial causality between the different variables of our ever-changing universe.

That picture should be the icon hung in the office of every television manager, for by using the techniques based on Galton's flash of intuition he can with some degree of safety ensure a mass audience for his product. And not merely this. The fabricators of his product have made it so bland that it suits all palates, for the ultimate discovery is that the television he has made to please a national mass audience will, with adjustment of language, gratify an international audience and travel with ease from country to country.

In view of the fact, this odd thought occurs to me. C. G. Jung proposed the idea of a collective unconscious. I wonder if the spread of television is not more than playing its share in the formation of a collective conscious. As people for the first time really see each other on the screen, on one hand they might get an idea of each other's humanity, but on the other the process whereby man becomes a cell in an organism inevitably will be speeded up.

I have stressed that television is something created by our times for our times. We live in an age where the information about our world is increasing exponentially. We live in an age where man is graduating from machines that amplify his energy and assist his muscles, to machines that amplify his mental capacity and assist his intellect in the control of his surroundings.

Television is something new and persuasive, one of the two media that can keep pace with the times. Perhaps the formation of this collective conscious is just the first step in the new directions that man is taking.

Recently in one of our BBC programs we did a story on trends in science fiction, interviewing many authors. Since this genre had already predicted flights to the moon and telecommunication satellites as far back as 1910, we asked these writers what areas concerned them at this moment. Their answer was robots! And they saw man building parts of his robots into himself.

Clearly they see the emergence of "Homo cyberneticus." The new trend, this spiritual trade wind, is already discernible. Western man is desperately trying to come to grips with the machine. He sees his individuality being submerged in a tabulated mass, his ideas being catalogued in a memory store, his actions being predicted in the banks of calculating transistors. This trend explains the popularity of television shows that depict man in a dominant friendly or understandable relationship with a machine: *The Man from U.N.C.L.E.*, the James Bond stories. It also explains pop art, op art, recent sculpture and science fiction.

Unlike other intellectual revolutions, in which the thinking only slowly percolated through the strata of society, this revolution is likely to go quickly. Television has already started the work of feedback and information with unrivaled rapidity. But in operating at the predictable mass level, in so consciously attempting to please, the medium is throwing away opportunities, all too often wasting its potential in internal rivalry, failing to attract the best talent and thus not providing the motivations expected of any leader.

This situation grew out of the beginnings of radio, for this first precursor of television started in an atmosphere of hotly debated political compromise. In the United States it was decided that it should remain in the hands of private enterprise, in Britain it was thought too big to be dominated by advertisers, and so we started the BBC, whose independence was assured by the unwritten checks and balances in our own constitutional process. Since that time American antitrust laws have broken up one network. We in Britain decided that monopoly was stifling and brought in a second television system, this one based on advertising.

Systems that have grown out of compromise are not necessarily the answer. They are too big, too heavily involved in getting audiences in order to prove their efficiency and justify their capitalization. Yet can any other system provide the amount of high standard continuous entertainment, information and education in such a widespread manner?

Why has nobody attempted to undertake a design study of a television system in present-day terms? I don't know what such a study would produce but the specification outlining the parameters of the design might be as follows:

"Mankind needs a system of television communication so designed and controlled that communication can occur between all levels of our audience and all levels of the culture represented by that audience. The audience should be able to select from any of these levels when and as it wishes. In order to achieve this, ways should be explored to ensure that the costs of television apparatus and production come down, thus reducing the operator's need for large audiences and enabling him to design programs for the unit rather than the mass."

The rub of the design problem would be to prevent such a system from becoming an Orwellian nightmare, for such a window on culture would be a two-way affair in which the image might well increase its transcendence over reality. Television receivers would become communicators; not only would they receive local network and international programs, but by means of wave guides (to provide the channels) and small cameras and cheap video recorders they would become a link between the viewer and his personal world, between the home, the library, the bank, the office, the shops and, of course, the Government.

To design such a machine is problem enough, but to design a system (no! let's call it a medium) not merely for social communication but also capable of responding to the whole range of values and spiritual needs is problem indeed. It is the very heart of

161

the design challenge and of our present dilemma. For the paradox is surely this:

On the one hand mankind needs a large "machine" element in order to integrate with the new cybernetic culture so eagerly awaited. These machines—mechanical, mathematical, and social —are utterly essential if mankind is to come to grips with and accept his new environmental surrogates, the equivalence of space, time, energy, and mass.

On the other hand, man—the individual man—recognizes that in using these machines and adapting himself to their techniques, he must assume their attributes. This is the moment of terrible truth, for in gaining "the sweet fruition of an earthly crown," the individual risks submerging his humanity and becoming a digit in a socio-cybernetic system.

As a television man I know where I stand. I believe that it is not the job of mass communication to pander to mankind. Rather we should use our ubiquity to seek out and service the individual.

I believe that television, given the opportunities, can be more than of our times, out of our times, and for our times. I believe it can be ahead of our times, providing crucial leadership, fostering man's awareness of his position, providing the feedback that enables us to utilize the full spectrum of our total vision. It will be and should be an open window on our culture, helping to ensure that "the single secret will still be man."

PART THREE

SIGHT-AND-SOUND COMMUNICATORS

Now the heroes were plenty and well-known to fame
In the troops that were led by the Czar
And the bravest of them was a man by the name
Of Ivan Petruski Skavar

—ANONYMOUS

~~~~~~

PAUL MAYERSBERG, in the opening essay of this section, urges us to remember that whether or not we accept it, the sight-and-sound media are primarily businesses, and to work in them communicators must respect their conditions. To respect such conditions often involves a struggle for survival in the institutional cross fire between commerce and art.

In the short history of Hollywood there have been plenty of heroes: producers, directors, writers, and "stars"—and their fame was spread over the land by the artillery of publicity and flack. But they were all "transient Olympians," and when the pseudo-battles were over, they took away their scars and Oscars. Some died in the fight—Griffith, Garfield, Monroe, and Tracy; others retired to fairer shores to live on the income from television reruns. Some hung on to parody themselves in horror films, and it was sad to see what *really* happened to Baby Jane.

The czars who led the Beverly Hills brigade also began to vanish. Mayer and Selznick died, and no one could fill their power gap; others were relieved of their command as

Gulf and Western absorbed Paramount and Seven Arts took over Warner Brothers. When the remaining Hollywood czars admitted that they couldn't lick television, they hotly embraced the electronic bride. Her dowry included contracts for *Bonanza, Batman,* and *Beverly Hillbillies;* new income from the syndication of films that had long been forgotten and relegated to the vaults, and a chance for old stars to pick up pocket money by endorsing coffee or vitamin pills in commercials. Even if it were only a marriage of convenience, the old Hollywood bridegroom waited, with the Giaconda smile: within a few years "live" television virtually was dead, East had gone West, and every night was Saturday Night at the Movies.

The marriage of Hollywood and television gave birth to new moguls, who, although not so flamboyant as their sires, inherited the old problems as well as some new ones. The economic pressures from the box office are just as great. But the "box office" isn't just a little glass booth in a theater lobby anymore; it's every television set in fifty-four million homes. Turning off *Hogan's Heroes* has the same economic effect on Hollywood as passing up *The Dirty Dozen.* Moreover, this extended concept of the box office is no longer restricted to the United States; the international market for syndicated television series is a lucrative one. Australian television alone is a fifteen-million-dollar-a-year prize for American telefilms. The American motion picture is no longer a stay-at-home industry.

The central theme of Mayersberg's essay is that "the manipulation of money in film production can be as crucial to the end product on the screen as the manipulation of the script or the camera." However one may regard cinema as Art with a capital A, it is also Business with a capital B. As one of the leading European film critics, Mayersberg visited Hollywood; but unlike most, he kept his eyes objectively open. He describes Hollywood's dominant mystique as an ambivalence between "the dream of success" and "the romance of failure." In Hollywood, where Sammy Glick is still running hard, Mayersberg found that Success is the American Comedy, and Failure is the American Tragedy.

Even as the old Hollywood czars relinquished command to the new moguls, the traditional "star system" faded, too. Who can forget the photograph of Louis B. Mayer surrounded by his stable of stars—Gable, Garson, Rooney, Garland, and the Taylors (Robert and Elizabeth)?

As Clifford Odets reveals in his brilliant composite of the Hollywood star, they were all carefully launched. They studied elocution and fencing at the studio drama school, and algebra if they were minors; they danced at Ciro's; they attended the premières and waved to the fans. Louella Parsons chronicled their rise to fame from walk-on bits in "B" pictures, to supporting parts, and finally to their first big starring roles. And when they had made it, Paul Hesse posed them for the covers of *Photoplay*, and their feet were immortalized in the cement of Grauman's Chinese theater. They were all carefully teamed, farmed out, and traded. If they began to believe their own press clippings too much and if success began to spoil them, they were suspended until their naughtiness cooled.

Where else but in Hollywood could Ivan Petruski Skavar, the son of a drunken Pennsylvania coal-miner, become the nation's Number One box-office draw? So long as he had broad shoulders, flashing eyes, and looked good in tights, the corps of press agents could always add an acceptable Anglo-Saxon name like Robert Farrar. So what if Bob had a blemish on his right cheek? The camera could always photograph his left profile, or shoot him in soft focus.

But the halcyon days were over. Competition from television and the economic effects of the 1950 "divorcement" decision forced the major companies to curtail their production schedules. The peak years of 1943 and 1944, during

165

which nearly 400 pictures were made each year, were never to be equalled. Not until the middle 1960's were the box-office grosses of the World War II years even approached. The emphasis on wide-screen "road show" films with increased admission prices contributed largely to Hollywood's economic comeback. Two films of the mid-sixties, *The Sound of Music* and *Dr. Zhivago*, overtook the financial success of the long-standing *Gone with the Wind*.

With the decline in production, the major studios such as MGM and Twentieth Century-Fox could no longer afford to maintain their expensive stables of contract players. Relieved of their contractual obligations, the stars of "The Golden Dozen," as Odets termed them, began to free-lance. James Stewart, Elizabeth Taylor, John Wayne—and, of course, Robert Farrar—went "independent" and demanded a share of the profits of the pictures in which they appeared. Some like Kirk Douglas and Burt Lancaster established their own production companies which enabled them to take advantage of capital gains clauses in the filing of their income taxes.

Another postwar change in Hollywood was the rise of the "package" deal. Giant talent agencies, such as the Music Corporation of America and William Morris, were able to offer a major studio a combination of writers, stars, and directors, all of whom were represented by the agency. The agent thus became a significant force in production. So extensive became the packaging activities of MCA that antitrust action by the Justice Department forced MCA to choose between talent representation and its production interests. MCA chose the latter, under the corporate name Revue. Today, what started out as a talent agency, combines the old Universal Pictures, Decca Records, and kindred merchandising enterprises into a gigantic entertainment empire which straddles both the motion picture and television industries.

Like the stars, many directors at the major studios were freed from exclusive contracts. They, too, went independent and became a part of package deals. Under the old Hollywood system the creative contribution of the director was usually minimized: the film was a "producer's picture" and was billed primarily as a Samuel Goldwyn, a Jack L. Warner, or a David O. Selznick production.

In the European cinema the film is a director's picture, and we associate *La Strada* with Fellini and *The Seventh Seal* with Bergman. Because of the *auteur* theory of film criticism which emphasizes the corpus of a director's work, a John Ford, an Alfred Hitchcock, and an Elia Kazan are receiving wider recognition. The best representative in the United States of this particular critical approach (which originated in the French *Cahiers du Cinéma*) is Andrew Sarris.

This important American critic has addressed himself to what has been called the Independent Film Movement and its relationship to the mainstream of Hollywood motion pictures. In his essay in this volume and elsewhere, Sarris asks some important questions: What makes a film independent? Independent of what—Hollywood commercialism, a plot and story-line, the need to be "entertainment"? And at what point, Sarris asks, does independence descend into license?

These questions are particularly pertinent when applied to an evaluation of the anti-Hollywood "underground" films of Andy Warhol, Kenneth Anger, and Bruce Conner, to name a few of the New York-based film-makers.

Although ardent Hollywood haters, the "underground" film-makers have generated their own pantheon of demi-czars, demi-gods and demi-goddesses such as Jonas Mekas, Mario Montez, and Nico. Their temple is not Grauman's Chinese theater but the Film-Makers' Cinémathèque.

Although for many observers "underground" films are

167

associated with the circus atmosphere of Happenings and psychedelic mixed-media presentations, this is an unfair simplification. In spite of the epicene phonies who attach themselves like sucker-fish to the latest anti-Establishment fad, there are sincere and gifted film-makers like Stan VanDerBeek, Stan Brakhage, Shirley Clarke, and Lionel Rogosin who are trying to build a viable "Hollywood on the Hudson."

One thing needs to be clarified: this group cannot be labeled by the work of a single film-maker, and the term "underground" is itself ambiguous. Does the "underground" film deal merely with what Sarris terms "intimations of shock and salacity"? (The two most successful films in this genre were Warhol's *The Chelsea Girls* and Anger's *Scorpio Rising*.) Or should we define "underground" films as those denied exhibition in commercial theaters in places like Terre Haute, Indiana?

However we define it, and even if its devotees think avant-garde applies only to their work, the "underground" is only one aspect of continuing experimentation in the American film. Although the Film-Makers Cooperative has been striving for wider distribution of "underground" films, they are still being exhibited only in the largest metropolitan areas and on college campuses. It should be noted, however, that attention to the "underground" film among campus film societies is only a small part of a wide-ranging interest in film-making by young people. These same societies also screen the works of Chaplin, Dreyer, Welles, and Richardson.

The future sight-and-sound communicators may well come from UCLA, Boston University, New York University, or the Annenberg School of the University of Pennsylvania rather than from the East Village studio-lofts where the High Priests of the Underground are testing how far Art can go before it collides with the permissiveness of the First Amendment. By providing the financial wherewithal for advanced film study and by establishing a "second circuit" for dis-

168

tributing the work of talented young film-makers, the newly formed American Film Institute may quickly enrich the non-commercial as well as the commercial cinema in America.

It is a truism that even the best director and the most popular star needs a good writer, and this is as apparent in television as in motion pictures. But is there a shortage of good writers in these media? No, according to contributor Loring Mandel. Comparing the writers' garden of Eden in the early days of television to the present Sinai of the vast television wasteland, Mandel feels there is no place for original drama in a medium which thrives on reheated "formula" scripts which are "prepackaged, presold and predigested."

There was a time in the late 1940's and early 1950's when television gave us a real sense of creative excitement; but ten years later it was so far behind us that we refer to it nostalgically as television's "Golden Age." *Playhouse 90, Studio One, Philco Playhouse,* and *Kraft Theatre* afforded opportunities for writers like Paddy Chayefsky, Tad Mosel, and Loring Mandel himself. It is probably true that not all of the "live" plays of the Golden Age anthology series had the artistic quality of *The Mother, Thunder on Sycamore Street,* and *My Lost Saints,* to name a few. But there was a mood of the exploratory and the experimental in all of them, as producers, directors, and writers jointly sought to utilize television's potential for creating a new form of American drama that was neither theater nor cinema. As Hubbell Robinson has said, "It was not the individual programs of the Golden Age that made it shine, so much as its spirit; for it was, it seems to me, a time of creative ferment in the medium. . . . There was a spirit of adventure in the air. And most important of all, there was room for failure."

A resurgence of drama on commercial television may yet happen. Robinson's *Stage '67,* although not all programs of the series were dramas, tried to revive some of the old creative ferment. George Schaefer's *Hallmark Hall of Fame,* although relying too heavily on the tried and proven, maintains a high standard. *CBS Playhouse* has commissioned new plays by Reginald Rose and Loring Mandel. Hopefully, a new generation of Horton Footes and Robert Alan Aurthurs might emerge from the American Broadcasting Company's scholarship program at the Yale Drama School.

The Yale-ABC project is a prime example of how the institutions of business, education, and the arts can mutually benefit each other. Another instance of collaboration between business (in this instance, CBS) and the arts was the telecast of Arthur Miller's *Death of a Salesman.* The production itself cost $450,000, while air time amounted to another $250,000. The sponsor, Xerox, in this unusual case for a drama, paid the air-time cost only; CBS-TV undertook the cost of the program as well as an additional $500,000 for promotion. The success of *Death of a Salesman,* in terms of audience-response and critical ovation, more than justified the expense.

Thus far we have been discussing sight-and-sound communicators who work primarily in the areas of the story film and drama. Unlike most motion pictures, not all television programs are intended as entertainment. An equally important function of the television medium is to report and interpret the news. David Brinkley has noted that while television has its roots in such entertainment ancestors as Cecil B. DeMille and *Amos 'n' Andy,* its heritage also includes Fox Movietone Newsreels and radio commentators such as Raymond Swing, Elmer Davis, and Father Coughlin.

The extent to which television is being relied upon for news and information is indicated by the various public surveys conducted by Roper Research Associates. Asked where they got most of their news about world events, respondents in a 1967 survey answered "television," and when asked to name the information medium in which they placed the most credence, the answer was the same.

As a veteran newspaper reporter and columnist, who later became an outstanding electronic journalist, Robert E. Kintner describes in his essay the problems and challenges of operating a network news division. During his tenure as President of NBC, he helped to establish its strong position in news and public-affairs programming. He pays tribute to Elmer Davis and Edward R. Murrow who epitomized the ability to cover the news in a "calm, intelligent way." If Davis and Murrow injected opinions into their broadcasts, which, of course, they did, such opinions were invariably backed solidly by facts. It is the ability to "write, report, speak, edit and put it all on the air" which Julian Goodman says typifies the quintuple-threat man in television news.

The racial riots during the long, hot summer of 1967 particularly challenged television's obligation to report the news responsibly. Network news executives urged their reporters to prevent incidents which the presence of cameras and microphones might precipitate. News crews were instructed to approach trouble areas in unmarked cars and to be unobtrusive. Cameramen were ordered to cover their lenses if rioters appeared to be performing for television audiences. William Sheehan, in charge of television news at ABC, admonished his staff to maintain perspective in their stories. He said, "We don't want to give the impression a whole city is aflame just because someone started a bonfire. It may be stating the obvious that ABC wants nothing to do with staged stories. If you miss an element, don't ask for a repeat."

Television journalists recognize the social impact of documentaries examining racial problems as well as regular "hard news" coverage. In August of 1967, when racial tension was high, Richard Salant of CBS News decided against rebroadcasting the documentary, *The Tenement*. This was done at the urging of several affiliated stations in major American cities. Originally aired during the previous February, the program told the story of nine Negro families caught in the frustration of poverty and hopelessness. Because the racial situation was explosive, CBS postponed rebroadcasting *The Tenement* because it might well have ignited further riots.

Sight-and-sound communicators are the specialists called upon to design the messages of motion pictures and television. As Dr. George Gerbner has suggested, the message is the "coin of the communication exchange." If, in McLuhan's truism, the medium is the message—the producer, the director, the writer, and the performer are indispensable messengers.

XII.

Passage to Hollywood *

PAUL MAYERSBERG

Paul Mayersberg is a frequent contributor to *Movie* and *The Listener*. He is the author of *Hollywood: The Haunted House*, a collection of his film criticism.

∿∿∿∿∿∿∿∿∿∿∿∿∿∿∿∿∿∿∿∿∿∿∿∿

To EUROPEANS, Hollywood is a country of the mind, like Africa in the last century. If the green hills of Africa once represented a dream of contentment, so the brown hills of Hollywood today represent a dream of success. Sammy is still running, as hard and as fast as he ever did. But just as there is a real Africa far from contented, so there is a real Hollywood far from successful. In fact, I have never been to a place as respectful of success and as despising of failure as Hollywood in sunny southern California.

Everyone I spoke to on my visit was concerned with success in one way or another, the need for it or the search for it. Success was sometimes referred to as the American Tragedy or the American Comedy, depending on whether the person offering the opinion was a failure or a success. The director Donald Siegel, whose talent in my opinion is considerable, is by Hollywood standards a failure. Among the good movies he has directed are *Riot in Cell Block 11*, a documentary-style feature on life in a penitentiary; a science-fiction picture called *Invasion of the Body Snatchers* which does not let the allegoric elements get out of hand; and a war movie, *Hell Is for Heroes*, a portrait of the war hero as psychopath.

I asked Don Siegel how he got into the movies and he replied:

* Reprinted from *The Listener* (1966), pp. 887-90; 922-4, by permission of the author and the publisher.

173

"I don't like that question! First, because it'll reveal my age, and, secondly, there's only one way to get into the movies and that's to have relatives. Unfortunately, I did not have relatives, so I had to start at the bottom. That's a bad idea too! If you start at the top and work your way down to the bottom, at least you've been at the top. Having started at the bottom, I don't think I'll ever reach the top."

By contrast, here is the voice of success. Stanley Kramer: "After I got out of the army I intended to write the Great American Novel, or a play or something. Then, I met a man with fifty million dollars. . . ." The irony in this comparison between Don Siegel and Stanley Kramer is manifold. Kramer started to produce about the same time that Siegel began to direct, just after the war. Both started small in terms of budgets, but whereas Siegel's films have remained small, Kramer's have got bigger and bigger. Kramer may in fact have lost the companies he has worked for fifty times as much as Siegel, but because he thinks and acts big, Kramer will always be forgiven by the studios if he makes a flop. Because Siegel finds it difficult to act as an entrepreneur he also finds it difficult to get film assignments, and he now seems resigned to television, where he functioned as producer of the series *The Legend of Jesse James*. This puts him into the $100,000-a-year income bracket, but does not satisfy his soul. With films like *Judgment at Nuremberg* and *Ship of Fools* Kramer finds himself in the $500,000-a-year class, with no soul to satisfy anyway, only pretensions.

When discussing Hollywood, the question is always raised: is it really possible to write or direct a picture which will be a success at the box office (or B.O. as *Variety* unflinchingly calls it) and also a success artistically? Can one be an entrepreneur, which is virtually *de riguer* in Hollywood, and also retain one's integrity? The answer to both questions is that it is very hard. Truly gifted people, like Alfred Hitchcock or John Ford, can do it sometimes, but for most directors with some talent the combination of wide success and significant critical recognition happens about once, or at the most twice, in a whole career. It happened to Richard Brooks with *The Blackboard Jungle*. But he did not succeed without a struggle of the classic Hollywood type. Here is part of his account of it:

174

I was still under a seven-year contract when the story of *Blackboard Jungle* came along, but I refused to compromise in the MGM manner of photography, cutting, casting, or anything else in that picture. That was the first one where I had the chance to say, No, I don't want to do it, except this way. But there was trouble. They were not going to release it because the New York office said, "It's a terrible picture, it's not good for anyone to see it." They sent me an added scene, in which Glenn Ford, the teacher, goes to the police or the principal and says: "You think we've got trouble here. You ought to see the juvenile delinquency in Russia!" I said: "What has Russia got to do with this story? This story I know. I've been to these schools as a kid and I know this story. What're you talking about Russia for?" And they said: "We don't want anyone to think we're criticizing America." "What's wrong with criticizing America? We're Americans. I'm not going to shoot that scene, you'll have to get another man in. If the public doesn't like it, that's something I can't help."

After Brooks's *Blackboard Jungle* there followed a score of movies about teen-age delinquency. Success breeds success. Nicholas Ray, the director of *Rebel without a Cause*, once said: "There is no formula for success, but there is a formula for failure—try to please everyone!" From the money Richard Brooks received as a result of the success of *The Blackboard Jungle*, he was able personally to buy the rights to both *Elmer Gantry* and *Lord Jim*, the latter taking him ten years to set up. Brooks probably has something of the personality of Stanley Kramer, and is I suspect a pretty good entrepreneur, but unlike Kramer he does not try to please his audience by making them feel good or superior. There is much more of a personal point of view on a subject in Brooks's films, rather than a standard liberal view that you get in Kramer. Brooks feels some personal responsibility towards his subject and the audience, but he does not see himself as a universal conscience like Kramer in *Judgment at Nuremberg* or *Ship of Fools*.

The responsibility of Hollywood to the American people, to democracy, and to the world at large has been stated in a classic manner by that apostle of responsibility, Cecil B. DeMille:

When leaders of nations tell us—as the highest officials of Egypt and Burma have told us—that as boys they derived their conceptions of the world, their ideas of right and wrong, from American motion pictures, they bring home to us our awe-inspiring responsibility. It is a sobering thought that the decisions we make at our desks in Hollywood may intimately affect the lives of human beings, men, women, and children, throughout the world.

Thinking about an audience that way, the Hollywood way, has probably done more to destroy the old Hollywood world of the moguls, like Jesse Lasky, Louis B. Mayer, and Harry Cohn, than any other single thing. And it is odd because this is what they were fighting for, apart from personal power, a position of responsibility like senators in Congress.

In some ways the decline of the tycoon era has been a good thing. Studio policies as to the films they will make are no longer subject to the whim of one man. The personal vendettas of these men which sometimes, allegedly, ended in murder—these are of the past. Clifford Odets' play *The Big Knife* isn't a true picture of Hollywood any more, and principally because the contract system for players no longer has the force it used to. Blackmail is not a threat when contracts are so much looser, and free-lance activity among writers, directors, and stars has become the norm. One reason why Marilyn Monroe died so poor was that for years she worked for very little money. Because of her long binding contract at 20th Century-Fox, no matter how important a star she became at that studio she was unable to earn much more than a starlet.

*   *   *

However, the director, Delmer Daves, who has films such as *Dark Passage, Cowboy,* and *3:10 to Yuma* to his credit, has been under contract to Warner Brothers for most of the thirty years he has spent in the motion-picture business. Delmer Daves had this to say about his contract years:

It's become a way of life. I worked with Jack Warner on over twenty-six films as writer or director or producer-director. While he saw the rushes every day—he's very conscientious about that—I never got any interference. And I had the privilege of preparing my own cut, over which I was never hurried, and which was shown at the preview. After that Jack Warner usually combined his own opinion with that of the preview reaction and we would go over the picture together. Of course, he had the final say. He owned the company which was putting up the money. He could have asked me to re-shoot if he wanted to. He never did though. The trend in Hollywood now towards producer-directors is the result of efforts by directors who have suffered under the yoke of contracts. You can't blame them if it's been oppressive, but in my case it hasn't been. I haven't had any impulse to escape, although I must say I have played doctor for him in taking assignments that were not exactly to my liking. But he gave me more opportunities than any other person. He gave me my first chance as a director in 1943 with *Destination Tokyo*. So, when he got into trouble with pictures like *A Summer Place*, *Parrish*, and *Susan Slade*, these were done as gestures of gratitude to the man.

In what Delmer Daves says one can see why some people might mourn the end of the tycoon era in Hollywood. Heads of studios are still powerful, but they are elected. There is no air of the divine right of kings about these new organization men. Their names do not strike terror to the heart. With a team of grey flannel suits under him, the organization man is always fighting for his job. He is unlikely to have anything of the benevolent despot in him. And that is a pity, because the cinema is not totally an industry, and casual ruthlessness does not finally pay off. Patronage is needed today as much as it ever was. The old-style studio boss would be more likely to stand by his opinion, and not bend when the wind blew. He could be a mortal enemy. But he could also be your best friend. The organization man will never make enemies if he can help it. He is too frightened. Today's enemy might so easily be tomorrow's ally. But, on the other hand, he will resist real friendship, because the situation might arise in which he may have to sack his best friend.

*   *   *

The production of *Cleopatra* symbolized the death-knell of old Hollywood. The extravagance of the budget and the glamour of the subject itself, the wild publicity and the future of a whole studio in jeopardy, a million dollars for the star and her on-screen off-screen affair with Richard Burton—all this makes up a wonderful picture of Hollywood in decline. As a matter of fact I rather think that this was at the back of the mind of the director, Joseph L. Mankiewicz, who has previously had things to say about show biz in movies like *All About Eve* and *The Barefoot Contessa*, and who is well known as a critic of the Hollywood system. The story of Cleopatra is, after all, the story of a great civilization in decline—Egypt. Egypt was as essential to the Roman Empire as Hollywood is to the world film industry. Yet in many ways both seem outmoded, decadent, wasteful. One might go further and say that at the time *Cleopatra* was made Europe was a threat to Hollywood as Rome was a threat to Egypt. As it turned out, *Cleopatra* marked the end of the short-lived period in which Rome, the capital of European film-making, did seem to be taking over from Hollywood as movie capital of the world.

One important result of the *Cleopatra* business was that it drew the attention of the public to the possible costs of motion pictures. In the sixties the cost of production in Hollywood has risen sharply to such an extent that many big studios are beginning to make films in Europe where costs are about a third cheaper, even after the expenses of travel and transport have been met. This may not, on the face of it, sound very radical, but the motion-picture industry was until recently one of the most stay-at-home in the United States. The reason was the studios' fear that they might lose control of their pictures. Not only is it difficult to watch over the expenditure of money if a film is being shot thousands of miles away, but it is also difficult to supervise the individual producer or director and ensure that he or they are providing the kind of picture the studio wants.

The cost of a motion picture is divided basically into two parts, what is called the "above the line" cost and the "below the line" cost. "Above the line" refers to the salaries or fees of the actors, the cost of the property, the original novel or play, and the development of that property, that is to say the screenplay, and also the fees of the director and producer of the picture. In other words, "above the line" includes all the lump sum payments

178

for work on the picture. "Below the line" means the cost of actually making the film: the raw materials, the laboratory processing, the wages of the technicians, in fact everybody doing day-to-day jobs on a picture, from the art director to the hairdresser.

Once upon a time it was thought that the cost of films was primarily dictated by the stars' fees: big star, big budget. This is no longer true. The star's fee is after all a fixed sum, however high. But the technicians are paid by the hour. So hold-ups and slowness of production result in overtime for the technicians and with the rising labor costs this can alter the face of the budget. As a matter of fact, a very small percentage of Hollywood films is brought in on budget. It is not unusual for a fairly average technician to earn $700 a week. The lighting cameraman can earn $2,800 a week on a major picture. Time is what costs money in the cinema. How else could a film like *The Collector*, which takes place on virtually a single set, cost almost three million dollars? The film had no big stars. It had an expensive director, William Wyler, but that was the chief cost above the line.

*　*　*

Labor is comparatively cheap in western Europe, and extremely cheap in eastern Europe. For example, Roger Corman shot an outdoor adventure film in Yugoslavia called *The Secret Invasion* with a fair cast, including Stewart Granger, Raf Vallone, and Mickey Rooney, for about $500,000 which was about the same budget as *Nothing But the Best*, an urban black comedy made in England by David Deutsch and Clive Donner with Alan Bates and Millicent Martin. On the other hand, Martin Ritt managed in Ireland to spend over $4,200,000 on *The Spy Who Came In from the Cold*, starring Richard Burton. Hollywood has always been extravagant and that is part of its appeal. But you can be too extravagant: that is to say, you can make a picture which stands little hope of getting its money back at all. *Lord Jim* is an example of this. It cost over $8,000,000. The film was a total disaster at the box office. But even if it had been a great success, it is doubtful if it would have made a good profit. What Columbia, the studio who produced the film, was obviously hoping for was another *Lawrence of Arabia*, which, despite its cost, estimated at $12,600-

000, still made a fantastic profit. Similarly, it is immaterial what the cost of a James Bond movie is. The gross in 1965-6 of *Goldfinger* was $42,000,000. When the film is re-released it will almost certainly become the biggest grosser in the history of the cinema, overtaking *Gone with the Wind.* In the sixties the cinema as an entertainment has made a big comeback, and this has encouraged ever-increasing investment.

The money for Hollywood films comes not from Hollywood but from New York, referred to in Hollywood as "back east." Motion pictures are financed by banks, principally, I suppose, the Bank of America. The bank puts up some money and requires a high rate of interest in return. It is therefore extremely important to get a film out around the cinemas as soon as it is completed. If a film is held up too long it costs the production company a great deal of money. Apart from the good name of the company seeking a loan from the bank, it is the duty of the company to explain to the bank why they should invest in a particular picture. It is possible that Columbia told the bank in New York, when seeking the money to finance *Lord Jim,* that it was a film like *Lawrence of Arabia,* a high-class prestige adventure picture with Peter O'Toole. What they probably did not explain was that the hero was in reality a coward and a failure. I believe that this was the real undoing of *Lord Jim* at the box office, though I personally thought highly of the picture.

The point is you can make a picture about a man who fails (to some extent Lawrence in the film version was a failure), but either it must not be obvious that he fails, or the film must be made for a smaller budget because it simply cannot appeal to huge audiences. If you make a film on the grand scale it must sport values and attitudes that are popular and appealing. There is nothing wrong with unpopular viewpoints, but you are in grave danger if you spend too much money trying to promote them. Whether one likes it or not, the cinema is a business and in order to work in it effectively (that is to say, to go on working in it) one must respect its conditions. I would say that the conditions of film-making as constituted at this time should be interpreted as the nature of cinema. One cannot talk of cinema as art. It is at least 50 percent business, and as a result of my visit to Hollywood I am convinced that to omit this aspect from movie criticism is to tell but half the tale.

I am not trying to say that it is impossible to criticize a film without knowing how much it cost. That would be nonsense. The cost of a film is merely a fact. What is important is the effect of the cost. The development in film production methods, moving away from Hollywood to tell stories on the actual locations on which they are supposed to happen, has an effect on the style of Hollywood films. For example, *The Spy Who Came In from the Cold* is a European as well as a Hollywood film. The fact that two of the chief characters are avowed Communists, and yet are not the heavies plotting to overthrow the free world, is an important step towards a wider, more complex, view of life as expressed on the screen in a major American film. One could speculate that had the picture been made in Hollywood it might have had a very different emphasis.

So money, the desire to save it, or to make it, exercises an influence for good as well as for bad in the cinema. The manipulation of money in film production can be as crucial to the end product on the screen as the manipulation of the script or the camera.

If you had to pick one man in the Hollywood hierarchy, one figure from the mythology of Hollywood who most completely represented its dilemma, it would be the Hollywood writer.

Of course, the writer is nowhere near the top of the Hollywood hierarchy because he seldom has any power and nobody knows his name, but he has come to be regarded as the conscience of Hollywood, as the man who can see both sides of the coin. The writer is the bridge, if a very rickety bridge, between Hollywood and real life. The writer appears in his habitual role of the conscience of the crowd in Elia Kazan's film A *Face in the Crowd*. Mel Miller (played by Walter Matthau) is a pipe-smoking, bespectacled, world-weary, sentimental, cynical writer-reporter who has seen it all. The writer is traditionally a man who is strong in the head and weak in the arm. He knows, he understands, but he cannot act.

Dalton Trumbo came close to describing the typical Hollywood writer when he said: "The system under which writers work would sap the vitality of a Shakespeare. They are intelligent enough to know that they are writing trash, but not intelligent enough to do anything about it." But the writer's position is not the result of a fault of intelligence. It is a lack of strategic power on the one hand, and a lack of personal willpower on the other. The writer has to some extent grown accustomed to his weak strategic position, and he has come to romanticize it. So he does not fight too hard against it.

Often when reading even critical writing about Hollywood you come away with the impression that the romance of Hollywood is success and the attributes of success. That is only part of the story. The romance of failure can be almost as attractive. Certainly it has psychological compensations. You might, as an unsuccessful writer (by which I mean a man not working on the projects that he wants to), feel freer than a successful writer, the man who earns a lot of money, because you are less frightened of the fall. Fear of failure can be more demoralizing than failure itself. There is, too, a certain glamour in failure—heroism even. A failure in Hollywood can still be surrounded by more glamour than a success elsewhere. In the end it seems impossible ever to de-glamorize the glamorous.

The ambiguous relationship between success and failure is undoubtedly the major theme in Hollywood life. In the old Hollywood, success and style used to go together. When a major studio came up with a picture that proved to be a success, they followed it up with others like it. This still happens, but without the style. Now it is virtually impossible to identify a studio by the kinds of films it makes and the way it makes them. In the early nineteen-thirties, for example, Warner Brothers produced movies like *Public Enemy, Little Caesar,* and *I Am a Fugitive from a Chain Gang.*

Apart from representing the personal work of the individual writers and directors, these pictures also carried the hallmark of the studio that made them. They shared common subject matter; the world of gangsters and criminals and enemies of society. They had a certain social content that was (and still is) widely regarded as box-office poison. The life-style of the gangster hero was attractive to a large public as the glorification not just of the bad-man but of the outlaw figure and of the thrills and spills of private enterprise.

These movies shared a common recognizable style: they were dark, low-key, violent movies, displaying the sordid environments of Chicago tenements, back streets at night, state penitentiaries, and smoke-filled, ill-lit speakeasies. Visually, the films had a harsh look to them (in direct opposition to the popular comedies of the time). The whites had the glare of naked bulbs and the blacks conveyed the menace of perpetual night. Contained in this vivid contrast of white and black, with few gradations of grey, was the timeless drama of good versus evil, simple and appealing. With these movies Warner Brothers established a formula for success.

But once you have exploited the formula and the public has become bored with it, what then? You could switch to a different formula as Twentieth Century-Fox did with their first (*the* first) movie in Cinemascope, *The Robe*. Without a precedent they decided on a biblical adventure in order to exploit their innovation. They could have made a big war movie, or a big musical, or a big spectacle of any kind. They opted for a semi-inspirational picture, and it turned out to be a good choice, a trend-setter for the next ten years. Fox wanted something new (for them) in terms of subject because they had something new technically. *The Robe* was a clean break. But supposing you wanted something new, but did not want to drop the continuity of your previous success. What then? This was the position that Warners were in after the cycle of gangster movies had run its course.

Warners adapted certain elements of their gangster formula of the thirties to create a different but related pattern for their pictures in the forties. The gangster film became the melodrama, the black thriller. Al Capone gave way to Sam Spade. What *Little Caesar* was to the thirties *The Maltese Falcon* became to the forties. The starkness of the black and white gangsters gave way to the softer, more subtle, greys of private eyes and independent operators.

But the world of crime was still the hunting ground of Warner Brothers. Perhaps the key to their new formula lay in the personality of the actor who incarnated its protagonists, Humphrey

183

Bogart. In the thirties after *The Petrified Forest* (1936), Bogart did not turn out to be an altogether convincing heavy. He used to end up playing second fiddle to James Cagney, as for example in Raoul Walsh's *The Roaring Twenties* (1939). Bogart's death scene in *The Roaring Twenties* looks ludicrous: he simply did not know how to die with a whimper, which was what the part called for. Bogart's appeal was his stoicism, his acceptance of the world and the way it was. The thirties gangster was not a stoic but a man of uncontrolled energy who could not accept the world the way it was.

In 1940 Raoul Walsh made the film which was to be the successful transition from the character of the gangster to the character of the independent operator, and he used Humphrey Bogart to do it. The film was *High Sierra*. The chief personality trait of the independent operator was a certain lazy acceptance bordering on resignation. He had the demeanor of a man in semi-retirement. *High Sierra* described the autumn and winter of a gangster's life, his last "job." This time Bogart was playing a gangster who had become resigned to the world and who had ceased to believe that he could change its appearance with a Thompson. In *High Sierra* Bogart had his first solo lead part and the movie established him as *the* Warner Brothers actor of the forties: he subsequently appeared in *The Maltese Falcon, The Big Sleep, To Have and Have Not* and *The Treasure of the Sierra Madre* (in which he was again miscast as a hothead).

Interestingly, *High Sierra* was co-scripted by John Huston whose first film was *The Maltese Falcon*, which was made a year or so later and firmly established the principles of the new Warner Brothers' formula for success. In the footsteps of Raoul Walsh and Howard Hawks, Huston brought respectability, and perhaps a dangerous self-consciousness, to a type of adventure-thriller that represents one of the greatest achievements of Hollywood cinema.

Other companies have from time to time managed similarly clever transitions from one formula to another without sacrificing their image or style. Metro-Goldwyn-Mayer moved from comedies in the forties to musicals in the fifties. L. B. Mayer had always felt that humor and charm and prettiness were essential elements in the formula for successful family entertainment. The apotheosis of the Metro-Goldwyn-Mayer style is to be found in *High Society* of 1956, which was a remake as a musical comedy of Metro's 1940 success *The Philadelphia Story*. Scores of lines from the original script remained unchanged. Those that were changed were solely to accommodate Cole Porter's songs.

Recently Warner Brothers returned to the scene of some of their past success with *Harper;* it was a big success. As yet it has not been followed up and there are no hints that it will be in the near future. It may be that Paul Newman, whose stylish relaxed performance contributed so much to the picture, is unwilling to commit himself to a series of films that might type him dangerously.

At the moment the American cinema, Hollywood cinema, seems to be going through a period of isolated successes. The great contemporary genre, the spy movie, is conspicuously free of the style of any particular studio. Every studio, major and minor, American and European, has produced spy movies and milked the universal formula for success. In other words, studio strategy is coming to replace studio style. This is the fundamental difference between old and new Hollywood. New Hollywood is opportunistic and mercurial. Old Hollywood was stick-in-the-mud, stupid but stylish. Now Hollywood is like Raymond Chandler's description of Los Angeles as a city with the personality of a paper cup.

XIII.

The Transient Olympian:
The Psychology of the Male Movie Star*

CLIFFORD ODETS

A distinguished playwright and long-time Hollywood resident, Clifford Odets wrote for both the Broadway theater and the screen. Among his numerous plays are *Golden Boy* and *The Country Girl*; his scenarios include *None But the Lonely Heart* and *The Sweet Smell of Success*. He died in 1963.

~~~~~~

ROBERT "BOB" FARRAR is one of the dozen most wanted men in the world today. He is a movie star of the first magnitude, however, not a criminal—a "top grosser," sharing his Olympian position with roughly a dozen other male stars, loosely referred to these days as either "the Big Ten" or "the Golden Dozen," such stars as Burt Lancaster, Glenn Ford, William Holden, Frank Sinatra, Marlon Brando, Kirk Douglas, Cary Grant, Rock Hudson, Tony Curtis, Robert Mitchum, Jimmy Stewart, Jack Lemmon, John Wayne, and Gregory Peck.

While all these men are not exactly wine from the same barrel, they nevertheless grow on vines rooted in the same soil; so that it is both possible and probable that, like choice Médoc types, they must share qualities and flavors. Their differences from each other, however, are myriad and not insignificant. Bob Farrar, for instance, neither owns nor flies his own plane, as several of the others do. Some of them, after glum marriages, are now raising the small riots of bachelorhood; but Bob, along with most of the Golden Dozen, is a squarely married man living in a square

* Reprinted from SHOW Magazine, April 1963, pp. 106-7; 130-3, © 1963 Hartford Publications, Inc. Reprinted by permission of the publishers and the Odets Estate.

house, likely enough with the children of two marriages or even more. Any further qualities and habits shared by these men are probably morphological and coincidental.

Farrar was raised in a small Pennsylvania town, under the cloud of a boozing father and a managerial, moralistic mother. She used to say that Bob would follow in his father's footsteps. This felt probable to even Bob himself (his mother had built into him a sense of worthlessness equal to none), as he quit high school, loafed around, ran errands, tinkered with cars and, surprising in one so uncommunicative, went haying with some of the best girls in town. His combination of "silent strength" and the air of a "lonely boy" (to leave unmentioned his blue eyes with their veiled voltage) was apparently as irresistible then as it is now, when his annual income often approaches the million-dollar mark. In his late teens, Bob, tramping through several states, was already that strange alienated American type, the transient "passing through," cloaked in an atmosphere of rebellion and the laconic—a short-order cook, or the itinerant village carpenter (or auto mechanic), all of his tools and possessions wrapped in a work apron. Bob added to the type a shy charm and a slow, warm, intermittent smile.

It was four years of navy in World War II which gave Bob some adult integration. Endowed with plenty of native shrewdness, never stupid so much as hopeless and low in self-esteem, he began to look out objectively at people and study a little. After he began to frequent a modest bar-restaurant in lower Manhattan (after demobilization), an attractive if slightly older waitress (Miss Butch in person!) took him over. Mothering and dominating, Kay seemed at first a mere whistle stop to Bob, but it ended, to his surprise and dismay, in the terminal of marriage. Loafing, egged on by his nagging wife, he went along one day with a pair of the bar's habitués and, aided by the GI Bill of Rights, found himself being educated in an acting school.

Boxed in by dialogue and an acting partner, Bob was hopelessly awkward and inexpressive. Without tools in them, his large capable hands were clumsy and rigid, although by now they have learned a convention of grace or the casual palliation of pockets. And yet, as his wife insisted, there were his size, his good looks and the fetching smile. A Hollywood talent scout agreed just enough with Kay to suggest that Bob look him up if he ever came out West. That one year was enough for Bob, and he quit the school and, making a clean sweep a few months later, he quit the marriage, too. He felt for Kay anger, guilt and some sentimental gratitude; the relationship had been hectic and crowding—four bare legs in one bed didn't make a marriage! And Bob has never changed: restriction and nullification set his teeth on edge.

Early that summer, Bob hit Chicago. The cheap lodging houses held their usual attraction for him. He felt at home with these homeless men, relaxed and articulate; these types never crowded him or made demands. He liked to walk the streets and watch the active life; a few times he drew books from the library or visited a great art museum for a baffled look. But most of Bob's spare time was spent watching old movies. Precursive stars like Cagney, Fonda, and Gary Cooper excited him most; the sophisticates, Boyer and William Powell, left him unimpressed.

That fall, buying himself a secondhand suit—Uncle Sam still paying the bills—he found himself painting scenery and playing a few bits with a Chicago little theater. Although Bob was not taken seriously as an actor, his unconscious air of apology and modesty (when sober!) easily won him friends. He found himself living with a not ungifted ingénue of pathos. Himself somewhat inured and self-unaware, he was stolidly surprised at how many problems one girl could have. Even today, Farrar feels burdened by anyone with "problems"—they make him uneasy. Life should be simple and clear, not complex or difficult.

Later that year, a local newspaperwoman "befriended" Bob. Naturally, the ingénue did not care for that and there were sharp and hysterical clashes. The winter winds were blowing bitterly off the Lake that year, and Bob, who had built in himself by now a *dolce far niente* philosophy—Bob, poor as always in the art of human constructs—packed his itinerant's suitcase and disappeared. Both women received the same telegram: LEAVING TOWN, THANKS FOR EVERYTHING, BOB FARRAR. Years later he discovered that the ingénue had suicided a year after they parted.

In New Mexico, after several months of loafing, he settled down to pumping gas and built himself a car from spare parts.

Bob was eating well and finding his usual sort of friends. But a secret compulsion bothered him: he liked to go down to the Albuquerque Santa Fe station a few afternoons a week and watch the westbound Super Chief make its daily stop. It was not until he stolidly watched his tenth or twelfth movie celebrity strolling the platform that he understood the cause of this strange compulsion: he was aching with a yearning he could not deny—it led him to Hollywood ten days later.

Joe Angst, the talent scout he met in New York, had turned agent. He was then, as now, a shrewd little man, who seemed to have no eyebrows or eyelashes, the eyes looking at you in a neutral, not unfriendly, detached way. Vague and disinterested as he was then, Angst claims today that he recognized Bob's potential the moment he entered his office. Actually, he saw the boy's awkwardness, the owlish embarrassment covered with an attempt to "play it cool"; Bob was obviously without money or friends, and yet the likable thing filtered through. Angst was looking for clients, and a few vague promises or advice might bind the boy to him just "in case." He flatteringly talked Bob down with: "Look, son, you're an actor with New York experience. Forget all this hooey about extra work. In this town you don't get anywhere by the back door! Drop in and see me once a week—something might happen."

In over 20 years that is the only contract that Farrar has ever had with Joe Angst. For it was only six weeks later that the agent asked Bob if he could ride a horse. Bob, never having so much as touched one, hesitated. Angst smirked: "Anyway, you look as if you can. Get over to the riding school and keep your mouth shut." In 12 hours Bob not only learned how to ride but later looked more like a cowboy than anyone else in the film. His part, while it had very few lines, ran through the entire film; furrowing his brow like a puzzled boxer dog, he kept Gary Cooper in mind, and that overlay, plus a hesitance of speech, integrated his own qualities into a noticeable performance.

That beginning was followed by several similar parts, each limited but effective, until Al Friskin, a shrewd independent producer of cheap Bs, put Bob under personal contract. Now Farrar was playing leads written to fit his type. That type, as the pro-

189

ducer might have seen it, was a physically bulkier if less sensitive Fonda; certainly less finished, but with the same male detachment and reserve, homeless, a stubborn, fighting hero of lost or unpopular causes, with a dash of something boyishly forlorn—the combination gearing rewardingly into American folkways, the total type representing that strain of individualistic idealism that runs like a half-submerged thread through our American life.

Fourteen cheap pictures later, ten of them Westerns, but all of them like the shiny synthetic satin used in coffins—not to be seen again after that brief mournful hour—Joe Angst realized that Farrar could become a big star if he might be associated with important "properties." The important properties came when, for tax benefits, Friskin sold Bob up the river to a major studio during, as it happened, a period of general industry retrenchment. Magically, Bob found himself nearly the top male player on an important lot. Despite Angst's now fully aroused obstetrical skills, a major setback occurred with Farrar's first high-budget picture. The film was a financial bust; even worse, the young star showed in it as a gawky amateur. The puzzled disappointment was general; and, as of old, Bob wanted to hide his head or hit the road again. It was Angst who finally pointed out that his client was not yet ready to play a sophisticated gentleman in a dinner jacket; he was not a William Powell and never would be!

The studio crowd ruefully agreed with Dr. Angst's diagnosis, but months passed before Bob was given a new assignment, this time sensibly in a prison locale film. Here Bob, as if throwing his previous humiliation and inchoate anger into the part, played in garments that fitted him. He was so outstanding as the bitter leader of the inevitable jailbreak that the studio quickly renewed his option with a raise, stock-piling more than a dozen properties for him. Three of them used prison locales, but with the added twist that their hero was a wronged, innocent man, as the priest and warden had suspected all along. Bob would not travel the grim last mile, like Jimmy Cagney, a cock of the walk till the end —it was not his type.

Today Farrar smiles when he recalls those early, protesting days of "What? Back to the jute mill again?!" But he knows that those old stereotype films began his real career—they were the scaffolding under his present high position among the Golden Dozen. And in a business where gratitude is conspicuous by its absence, Bob is deeply grateful to his agent's good sense and advice, Angst standing today *in loco parentis* to the actor. This Christmas past, Bob gifted him with a Rolls-Royce, but what is that in Beverly Hills, where every day producers' and stars' wives go grocery shopping in them?

Adele was an airplane hostess when Bob met her. Not until they married did he realize that under her assured, competent manner and pertly attractive face, there lurked an almost hopeless neurotic. Even today, after three children and 14 years of marriage, Bob is baffled by this woman. Recently, returning slightly tight from a late party, he found himself snarling at her: "Why don't you stop complaining? That's your destiny, to be a mother! What the hell should I do, thank you for it?" To which she shouted back, "And what's *your* destiny? To be a sonofabitch!" What bothers Bob is that between what *he* wants and what *Adele* wants there is always a mysterious difference; and about this "difference" he, like the most ordinary American husband, always feels guilty.

Uncomprehendingly, Bob knows that the stars who have married European wives fare better—at least their marriages are not ones of mutual attrition. The European wives of actors like Greg Peck and Kirk Douglas are female and self-respecting women, who live more with the "human facts" than their American opposites. While not necessarily compliant, neither is the European woman forever scrutinizing her husband's private life for sins. She knows that she holds her husband with the home, the children, and the circle of friends she brings together. More importantly, knowing that a woman can seldom get into a man's central reserve, she cleverly draws a larger circle around him that takes *him* in. She understands that a man's work is his honor, not to be fingered or tampered with; and, *most* importantly, she mothers both him and his talent, instead of competing with them.

While there are exceptions, the American movie wife, of course, runs headlong and often despairingly into all of this. Usually a hypomanic, she excessively takes care of the children, may become notable for her "good works," lives in resenting, resisting and half-hysterical rhythms, and is usually no more able to construct the marriage than, in this case, Bob is. No matter how Adele verbalizes it, she virtually is asking Bob to neglect large worrisome aspects of his career and give that extra time to her; she accuses him of not loving her, of secret rendezvous with other women, of being a poor father, of not encouraging her to bolder self-expression, of smothering and driving her to drink. In turn, Bob is patient, guying, guilty or outraged—when he comes home after an exhausting day's work and she looks at him like cold rain, he often wishes, at the age of a youngish 45, he'd not been born! That *desideratum* unfeasible, he develops craftiness and responds with a vague politeness, cold punitive silence and, most often, a tone of comic self-deprecation.

Adele, however, is not without a case. Married to a major movie star, she is joined to a man who has himself on his mind most of the time. Then, she is never sure that she is living up to the position of being Mrs. Farrar; a simple, informal person, institutionalized behavior is expected of her. Her relationship with the three servants, for instance, depresses her. She shares with Bob the national ideal of democratic affability and leveling but feels that for all her "niceness" the servants walk all over her. Unable to control or order them about competently, she ends by angrily firing them, blaming her timidity on them. Black or white, sometimes Filipino, they are bored, cynical and shiftless professionals, who have worked in many movie homes.

Bob likes best about his wife that she has given him three children: and when he looks at the feminine frailty of their only girl child, seeing in her a more delicate version of Adele, he knows (the shocking division of community property aside) he can never divorce his wife. It touches him that she walks flatly and rapidly, a little crouched, as if hurrying to catch a high ball; and it moves him that after all their roustabout times together she is still somewhat prim without realizing it. He knows that like himself, as lonely and exasperated as she can be, that Adele wants to be a good human being, to do the "right thing." Finally, exactly like himself and his peers, he knows that Adele feels herself to be an *impostor;* probably this pretenders' style of life will last, but how did they ever get here!

Notwithstanding, from all the domestic storms Bob stays semi-detached and reserved. He has his elaborate "work room" where he studies his lines; there are the health club, the horses and cars, the tennis court and golf links. Once or twice a year, he can blessedly slip off alone for a few weeks on a "promotion tour," making publicity appearances in a dozen key cities for a picture he partly owns. Without knowing it, Farrar has begun to live by the morality of self-advantage and personal convenience at any cost. He has acquired that deadening and uncreative habit of judging others only in terms of his own needs: "Is this guy good for me? If not, the hell with him!" In this way dozens of human beings are wiped out, becoming distorting mirrors of his temporary needs and satisfactions. Bob now shares with some of the others a silent, efficient and foxy face, somewhat metallic and self-purposive; a handsome male face, like a kit of burglar tools, carefully aligned and calibrated, calculated precisely to the impress it will make.

It is an open secret that Bob Farrar and many of his glittery friends are not happy men. In his pensive hours, Bob wonders how this happened, for like most Americans he equates success with happiness. He is unable to share the more classic French view, expressed by Jean Renoir in conversation: "Maybe, my friend, when you were given so many other gifts, you must grow used to the fact that happiness is not among them." Bob does realize that his elevation contains its elements of crucifixion. He is unable to understand why he should be accountable to anyone who holds a press card; privacy (and a personal vagarious life) is something that he remembers in caged hours with a heavy ache. Again and again, as if magnetized, he is pulled back to a stern sense of being dominated and boxed in at a time of his life when he should be completely free. He struggles and blusters, trying different approaches and postures, but he still knows that, inclusive as gravity, he is the prisoner of his audience, those unseen millions whose tastes have made him what he is.

Probably what Robert Farrar does not realize, along with his fellow Olympians, is contained in the remark of Matthew Arnold, "Life is not a having and a getting, but a being and a becoming." Perhaps Bob, and some of the others, are really big, splendid, stupid men, few of whom had adequate backgrounds for the "aristocratic" positions they hold. Once Bob's career began in earnest, like love and battle, it drew power to itself; but he came unprepared for victory, an "upstart" without breeding or values. This is one reason why Bob's substance seldom lives up to the niceties of his present manners. While he is not unimpressed by the folklore of himself, he is uneasily disgusted that people make too much of him. Bob's feelings about this echo Debussy's dismay: "Our era has a peculiar trait. We run after people who have scarcely learned to walk." He may not admire Marlon Brando, referring to him once as a "pregnant monk," but he envies the elaborate valve system by which Marlon keeps out any urgencies other than his own sensations and opinions. Justly, Bob sees himself as steadily besieged and intimidated by a swarm of favor-seekers; his curt, overriding response clouds much of his native sweetness and generosity.

Since Farrar so much prizes his independence, it is surprising how little he recognizes in himself the contradictory fear of losing others' affection, regard and goodwill. One could say that, along with his fellows, he makes an enormous career of not being disliked. He may not see it so, but *basically operative* in his life is the sad and sometimes tragic fact that our country is a place where its high and gifted citizens, even men of genius, are expected to have the easy accessibility, the glib politeness, the transparent and uncomplicated behavior of gas station attendants. Bob's whole life is adjusted to meet that expectation; but since he is also his own person and, as a film star, must make a mature and authoritative impression, exhausting strain is implied. What results is something "deadpan," self-conscious and self-ironic, ritualistic, a painful corseting-in which justifies the phrase "the uniform of the star." To get away from it all, a Robert Mitchum, who began in the same decade as Farrar, has moved out of the state; Glenn Ford lives alone on a hill, like Cary Grant, who spends half his time in Europe; Brando skulks alone in odd, cheap restaurants; and a Burt Lancaster restricts his growing family to the periphery of Hollywood things.

In *other* harmful ways, the world, its hurly-burly and practicalities, are too much with Farrar: he has become more businessman than actor. Heading his own company now, he buys books, reads scripts and budgets, hires writers and directors—the itch for big profits spreads dangerously across his life. Seldom inviting his soul to loaf, unless in competitive games, his actor's appetites and imagination weaken in exact proportion to his mercantile increase. Each year he lacks more the significant mood and temperament, the mystique, that make an interesting actor. Of course, "There is powerful temptation in money," as Mr. A. Lincoln writes in a letter. Consider that Sinatra receives $1,050,000 for his performance in a single film, before it even recoups its costs. Cary Grant's deal is similar, with the entire film reverting to him after seven years. Tony Curtis, merely gadding about, is reputed to have become a millionaire over the last few years. Lancaster had his first million long ago, while William Holden owns properties all over the world, Africa included.

As an actor, Bob inclines to stay with the accepted image of himself. He gives you few surprises, but he is considered good goods, a standardized, expensive package. His pictures may encompass a dangerous war mission or an adaptation from Sir Walter Scott; a recent one was a "Hitchcock subject," while the last was a slick, successful submarine yarn, what Bob calls a "bread and butter picture," implying that the others are possibly works of art. Twice in the past Bob did make an arty film for a small fraction of his usual fee. He was trying to prove to himself and others that he was an actor of depth and range. The films failed because of their inorganic and split approach to "unpopular" but serious subjects; and Bob's public didn't want him to lose the girl, walk with a limp or try to characterize some puzzling native Parsifal.

With Angst's help, Bob was quickly convinced that "good pictures" don't sell, and it is doubtful that he will ever repeat those two "spiritual retreats." After all, why should Farrar become before his time *magni nominis umbra*, the shadow of a great name?

195

Or as Dr. Angst put it, what is the sense in antagonizing your public and your financing associates? Bob only reluctantly agreed with this; for he naively continues to think of "art" as a hat or cloak which may be worn and removed at will, never realizing that art is an atmosphere in which the artist lives every day of his life, the very respiration of his being. Whatever their other problems may be today, you will never feel about Farrar, as you do with Lancaster, that he is always ready to take a chance with a disagreeable character role; or that, like Glenn Ford and perhaps Gregory Peck, he plays out of some never quite forgotten idealistic view of things. Bob will never have Brando's intellectual hunger and curiosity, and it is doubtful if they will say of him, as they do of Mitchum, that he quietly is becoming a better actor every year. It is perhaps to some of the others rather than Bob that we shall have to look for small budget pictures, aimed at a mere adult fraction of the audience. Only a few of these Olympians might be enough to *make American cultural history* if they placed such adult pictures *centrally* in their plans instead of seeing them as mere slumming trips. It is not enough for a matured man of Cary Grant's obvious talents to say of a long string of highly successful comedies, based on mere anecdotes, "Well, you know, they do make a lot of people happy." Especially today, a deeper purpose should animate some few among this Golden Dozen.

As a performing actor, Bob, like most of the others, is a clever journalist. He will skillfully report you the outline of a character's life, but fall down on the emotional or spiritual atmosphere of the person and the scene. As an actor, Bob shares with the other Olympians a sort of instinctive good taste—do less rather than more. This comes not only from a repugnance to "hamming," or from the typical professional ease and authority, but from the movie performer's almost feline sense of fitting gracefully into the film frame, particularly in the tighter shots. It goes without saying that Farrar is a "straight" or personality actor, Bob being Bob if he plays a submarine captain or a Roman Caesar—only the makeup and the costume change. Unlike their English counterparts, our stars are virtually without a sense for character or period style. It is doubtful if more than four of them could walk across a stage with enough aplomb to be called actors in the theater sense.

Farrar's working habits on a film are solid and diligent. Like most movie stars, the habit of concentrated work is now ingrained in him, as in cooks and peasants. A shooting schedule of from eight to perhaps 14 weeks leaves him little time for anything but work. Unlike some of the others (who will make a ballroom of a set), Bob frowns on socializing during working hours; a good captain, he likes to run a tight ship. The shooting weeks usually see a quiet family life at home. Retiring early, Bob may horse around with the kids, glance at their homework or take them out for a quick restaurant dinner; or, trying to learn his lines, he may be annoyed by their noisy intrusions. If he is depressed by how the work is going, he may during these austere weeks turn to Adele for solace; and these are the times the marriage is kindest to them. "She is a good egg," he says to himself, as she dozes off in his arms, the sleeping children and the silent home so substantial around him. If everything else vanishes (and who can tell?), *this* is left.

Friday and Saturday nights, with no work the next day, are the socializing nights. Interlocking and reciprocating dinner parties are usually arranged by the wives of the busy movie men with whom the Bob Farrars associate. These social evenings are unintentionally clannish and excluding, the cliques formed by income and position, or by mutuality of interests, these ranging from picturemaking and finance, tennis, respect for each other's identity and opinions, art collecting, a shared friendship for the New York guest of honor; or simply because the wives are chummy, sharing the same prejudices and enthusiasms.

In the main, a certain few homes excepted, these relaxing and friendly dinners, often followed by a private projection of the latest film and amiable chitchat (if not a card game), are so barren of human and cultural significance as not to be believed. Seen in smaller groups, many of these men and women are delightfully attractive and stimulating company. Together, however, one supposes that they mute and dull each other by an unconsciously held pact that since they are all special and privileged, of equal rank, gift and fortune, no one is to exceed or "top" the other on pain of probable excommunication. Only an intrepid few (Danny Kaye and the witty Billy Wilder are fair examples) dare brighten these deferentially shadowed evenings with undimmed wattage. The lesser dinners, peopled by the agents, petitioners and various of the "palace guard," are dreary simply because none intends to outshine or contradict the *obiter dicta* of the star-host, sometimes a man of infinite platitude.

As of old, Robert Farrar thinks of himself as a simple, uncomplicated man, actually almost daring you to see him plainly for the complex, anxious, difficult and exasperated man he really is. He shares his world's ideal that the human personality should work, "get across"—in any season he is for total competence at any cost! As barricaded, secretive, and cautious as a man can get, he nevertheless thinks of himself as open and candid. Seeing himself as broad and ample, worldly tolerant in a word, he is too often chary, provincial, and narrow. Notably resourceful and enterprising in his work, or the perfection of his golf or tennis, with his wife he faces or examines nothing but what he is forced to face; he inclines rather to spend thousands of hours in the covert avoidance of painful scenes. Self-respect in another usually bothers these men (unless he is himself a truly self-respecting man as, for example, Jimmy Stewart is); it smells to them of heresy and hubris and must be chipped away with little digs and quips.

Sometimes when you meet Bob later—his secretary had called you at the last minute to break an appointment—Bob apologizes to you with a stiff face, feeling the possible pressure of a "black mark," but he apologizes exactly as if you had done *him* harm. His apology, it seems, demands apology. No matter how Bob wrongs, uses, or scuffs you, he "defies you not to love and admire him" (as someone said of Balzac). He is impossible to pin down, his mind so busy with a hundred expedients, projections, and cautions that he becomes expert in evasive non-committal commitments; or he coquets instead, really a form of conciliation, asking that you understand his dilemma and judge him not too harshly. Although he is usually deadened by glut to the articles and people of his environment (while pretending enthusiasm for all!), it is a different thing with Farrar and his children. He feels for them

198

the glimmering sympathy that unhappy, guilt-laden adults often have for children. Bob, perhaps unwisely, buys his boys anything they want, including a season's box at the ball game; and about the elfin Debbie he tells cute stories, exclaiming softly with shiny eyes, "How do you like that for a feminine little bitch!" With those he likes, including his agent, he establishes an attitude of affectionate, kidding deprecation.

For better or worse, these stars radiate real *charisma*, and they know it; but uppermost in their abashed minds, and Bob's, is the fear of being considered pretentious or too outstanding. Perhaps they hear the harsh voice of Demos crying, "God hates a chesty man!" They will contort themselves into pretzels to seem reasonable and average, and, if they act contrarily, it is in defiance of this very fear. They dress expensively but colorlessly in public, assuming a blank anonymity and, the very crabs of fashion, walk sideways into restaurants and airports. Outside their moats they hide, most of them, their natural pleasure in being rich and famous, as if this state of grace implied imbecility or incest. Parenthetically, when they do a good deed or public service, their press agents are instantly alert to illustrate Mark Twain's thought that "When some men discharge an obligation you can hear it for miles around." Only the personalities from another time, the Robert Frosts and Carl Sandburgs, have been not afraid to be personalities or express distinct differences from their fellow man.

Many bridges to be crossed, the toll charges of stardom are incredibly expensive, in at least two cases even tragic. After the Napoleonic helter-skelter, the biggest grabbing time before our own, De Vigny wrote: "Beware of men who rise quickly." Bob might justifiably paraphrase that to read, "You men who rise quickly, beware!" For this Olympian senses that high up, *isolated*, the first million lusting to join itself to a second (cohabitation is the first law of money!), a man can forget easily that the free exercise of *all* his human faculties are the main purpose and reward of life. Farrar's sensitivity often may be inarticulate and undirected but, like a wistful boy staring through a dusty window, it is always there, asking for friends to trust, models to admire, yearning with an ache it never quite understands. Bob's semipetrifaction disturbs him more than he can say. Only an arid, philosophical pest

199

could blame him and his fellows for wanting to keep their brilliant careers aloft. It is when the Career and its ways become Theology that it should be spoken—not unsympathetically—for what it is.

XIV.

Illusions and Independents*

ANDREW SARRIS

Andrew Sarris is film critic of the Village Voice and editor of the English-language edition of Cahiers du Cinéma. He is the author of Interviews with Film Directors.

〰〰〰〰〰〰〰〰〰〰〰〰〰〰〰〰〰〰〰

THE MYSTIQUE of the Independent Film movement in America has always nurtured itself on a hatred of Hollywood movies. Indeed, if Hollywood had never existed, we would have had to devise another code name for vulgarity, mediocrity, and the sweet corruptions of capitalism. Intellectuals mention Hollywood, like Broadway and the bustling Parisian boulevards of theater-going Philistines, only for its pejorative implications. But Hollywood is more than a state of mind; it is also a geographical absurdity to the cultural elite of the East Coast. Consequently, though many relatively experimental films are shot on the West Coast and many relatively commercial films are shot in New York, the illusion persists in some quarters that everything shot east of the Rockies is Art and everything west is Kitsch.

This regional prejudice is only one of the distorting elements that afflict supposedly serious discussions of an American alternative to Hollywood movie-making. Much anti-Hollywood rhetoric is basically anti-movie as well. Attacks on the star system serve also as attacks on all acting and story telling beyond the newsreel-level narrative of Potemkin. Perhaps the most outrageous distortion of all is the use of "Hollywood" to apply only to movies one doesn't like. Thus Quo Vadis is a Hollywood spectacle, but Citizen Kane is an American film. The effect of this dishonest dis-

* Reprinted from Saturday Review, December 24, 1966, pp. 23-5, by permission of the author and the publisher.

tinction is to magnify the vacuum that exists for enlightened moviegoers.

Already those of us who regard ourselves as enlightened movie-goers find it difficult to keep up with all the film footage offered for our inspection. Where, then, is the pressure coming from for more and more movies, however independent? Certainly not from audiences, at least from the evidence to date. While experimental films are hanging on at best in marginal engagements, *The Sound of Music* and *Goldfinger* demonstrate hallowed Hollywood principles as vulgarly as anything has in the past, and their grosses are much greater. *David and Lisa* is cited as counter-evidence for the independent movement. A closer inspection of *David and Lisa* reveals an extremely sentimental treatment of clinical material, affecting performances by Kier Dullea and Janet Margolin, and the awkward manner of an ostentatiously inexpensive production. Even so, *David and Lisa* was fortunate enough to open during the New York newspaper strike, and consequently escaped the peril of a Bosley Crowther pan. The question remains: Is *David and Lisa* what we have been waiting for all these years as an alternative to "Hollywood"?

If not *David and Lisa*, then what? *The Balcony? Finnegans Wake? The Savage Eye? Private Property? Ladybug, Ladybug? Night Tide? Crazy Quilt? Hallelujah the Hills? Scorpio Rising? The Chelsea Girls? Nothing But a Man? One Potato, Two Potato? Salt of the Earth? On the Bowery? The Connection? The Cool World? Goldstein? The Brig?*

*   *   *

Each of these seems to have been conceived at least partly as a rebuke to Hollywood. Of this group, only *One Potato, Two Potato* has approached the commercial success of *David and Lisa*, and *One Potato, Two Potato* is easily the most sentimental of the lot. It did much better, for example, than *Nothing But a Man*, which lacked the sensational advertising gimmicks of *One Potato, Two Potato*. As much as we say we need more films about the Negro's role in America, the public apparently prefers to be titillated rather than edified on the subject. *The Chelsea Girls* and *Scorpio Rising*, the most successful films of the so-called underground movement, both have profited by intimations of shock and salacity.

This is not to say that commercial success is necessarily indicative of artistic abdication. The problem is that the mainstays of the Hollywood ethos—sentimentality, sensuality, sensationalism—seem to reappear in the Independent Cinema. In fact, people looking for Something Different often have worse taste than people looking for the Same Old Thing. If the subject matter is sensational enough, esthetic distinctions become irrelevant to the audience as the reviewer is reduced to a reporter. Where social themes are involved, the critic is tempted to cater to the prejudices of his readers. It would take a brave soul indeed to report that *Nothing But a Man* has moments lacking in inspiration. Hollywood's disgraceful treatment of the Negro seems justification enough to encourage a less condescending approach to the subject. Thus, good intentions are the great alibi of independent films both after they are released and before they are financed.

There is some truth to the truism that it is easier to find backers for a million-dollar movie than for a hundred-thousand-dollar one. Faced with this financial paradox, the independent filmmaker may be tempted to fall back on moralistic cant if not downright propaganda in his sales talk. Nowadays, with universities and foundations entering the field of motion pictures, an arty sales talk has become indispensable to the independent or beginning film-maker. Even the major studios are showing more interest in this approach as the glibness of Sammy Glick seems to have found a new home in television.

The time may be approaching, however, when the big problem of the independent film-maker will be less production than distribution and exhibition. Counting the films in repertory, there is now more footage available than any one person can see in any one lifetime. Cameras and film stock are becoming less expensive, and young people are becoming increasingly camera conscious. How will this surge of cinematic energy be channeled in the future?

A great deal depends upon the role the critic assumes in promoting new works. Up to now most film critics have preferred to accept the decisions of the film industry with undue passivity.

If a film, however worthy, can't find a theater, it is treated as a non-film and goes unreviewed, unreported, and unremembered. When films by Jean-Luc Godard, Robert Bresson, Ingmar Bergman, and Michelangelo Antonioni have been completely passed over for American release without any critical outcry, what hope can there be for unknown American film-makers to have their wares shown and judged? It is not enough for the Crowthers and the Crists to editorialize about what is wrong with Hollywood. If they sincerely wish to change things, they must encourage distributors and exhibitors to take greater risks. Unfortunately, such encouragement could constitute collusion, and most critics prefer not to become involved with the financial workings of the film industry. This attitude is quite proper, but hardly helpful to the aspiring outsider.

*　　*　　*

The Independent Cinema should not be judged too harshly by those who expect an alternative to Hollywood to materialize out of thin air, lofty ideals, and drafty lofts. One must keep the marginal role of the Independents in perspective. It isn't fair to expect the American Underground to produce a *Breathless*, a *L'Avventura*, or an 8½. For one thing, we don't need an American *Breathless*, an American *L'Avventura*, or an American 8½ any more than we need a European *Citizen Kane*. For another, Godard, Antonioni, and Fellini are closer to the Establishment than to the Underground. American artists must find their own forms and statements, not imitate the currently fashionable styles and themes from abroad. It is possible that certain artists will never be able to function effectively in the cinema. New York, in particular, seems to be more a town of painting, sculpture, writing, and photography than a movie town. The distinctive New York sensibility of Burroughs, Mailer, Kerouac, Ginsberg, Rauschenberg, and even Warhol has not yet established a cinematic equivalence. Perhaps it never will—Warhol's candor and compassion as the Flaherty of the fey and the foul notwithstanding.

Nonetheless, the Independent Cinema will continue to have an indirect influence on the Establishment Cinema. Films such as Jack Smith's *Flaming Creatures*, crudely put together for a pittance, probably have done more to liberate Hollywood from its idiotic self-censorship than have all the pious editorials on the subject. By making the unthinkable thinkable, Jack Smith's outrages against decorum extend the boundaries of artistic freedom. Similarly, sympathetic and even favorably biased treatment of the Negro helps break the barrier of timidity in the mass media.

If the Independent Cinema continues to disappoint with its advance claims and heroic rhetoric, part of its problem is its failure to preserve some of the genuinely creative gains of Hollywood film-making. The classical economy to be found in the works of Ford and Hitchcock, the expressionistic flourishes of Welles, the unobtrusive cutting of Lubitsch, and the crisp cutting of Lang are swept away by the vulgarities of the front offices. Thus many independent film-makers preach the virtues of simplicity, but lack the technical skill to express even their simple-mindedness simply. And too many academicians still confuse crudity with sincerity.

Jean-Luc Godard, quoting Degas, recently said that art must be discouraged. We don't need more bad movies, particularly bad movies posing—painfully—as art, nor do we need any more bad artists. We will get them just the same, but we don't have to encourage them. What we need are higher critical standards among those whose task it will be to sift through the enormous output of the next decade for a small handful of masterpieces.

To achieve these higher standards, we will have to modify some of the more persistent illusions of the Hollywood-haters:

1) *Realism is the only valid style in the cinema.* As Harold Rosenberg has observed, realism is only one of the fifty-seven varieties of decoration.

2) *Dramatic and narrative elements are alien to the medium.* Documentaries from *Nanook of the North* to *The Chelsea Girls* will find a privileged place in the cinema, but films that tell stories will always form the bulk of most movie-going biographies. Actors and actresses will never be replaced by abstractions.

3) *Artistic freedom is inversely proportional to the size of the budget.* This argument is less fashionable today than it was in the forties when the avant-garde was more strident in its avowed anti-commercialism. An artist such as the late Maya Deren con-

sidered herself in revolt against the mass media. An artist such as Andy Warhol considers himself more an accomplice of the Establishment than its antagonist. If anything, Hollywood is now more fashionable than European artiness.

4) *Frankness of expression is an index of the artist's honesty and sincerity.* Perhaps, but frankness can also be the last refuge of the imbecile. The problem of what can or cannot be said or shown on the screen is more complex than we once imagined. Tact, discretion, and even repression have probably helped artists shape their work into more meaningful forms. There is more awareness of sex in D. W. Griffith than in Roger Vadim, as there is more in Henry James than Henry Miller.

5) *The mere locale of movie-making determines its ultimate truth and beauty.* In some seminars, Sidney Lumet is introduced as an independent film-maker, although he functions as a Hollywood producer-director working away from Hollywood. Hollywood films were being turned out in New York well into the thirties, and one recalls the Paramount Astoria studios and the Hecht-MacArthur-Coward-Woollcott consortium in *The Scoundrel* with special fondness.

6) *Documentaries and short subjects will someday constitute a meaningful challenge to Hollywood's alleged hold on the masses.* Television is now the logical medium for the socially oriented documentary, and short subjects will always require some form of subsidy.

7) *Colleges and foundations will be more reliable judges of talent than the traditional movie studios.* Judging by the published tastes of most film academicians, Pauline Kael's wildest fears about the fun-killing potentialities of academicians seem fully justified. If anything, the relatively respectable auspices of Academe may discourage more daring enterprises for the sake of conventional exercises in the service of an esthetic that atrophied somewhere between *Caligari* and *Potemkin*.

Ultimately, we must not expect too much from post-Hollywood cinema. The King is dead! Long live the King! New vulgarities will arise to replace the old. New sentimentalities will bedevil our sensibilities. The temptations to compromise will take subtler and more devious forms. And one day we may quite possibly look back on the Hollywood cinema between 1915 and 1966 as the Golden Age of film-makers with a flair for telling a story with feeling and expressiveness. The Independent Cinema! It will have suffered the final disease of self-expression—subjective dispersal.

*   *   *

We will have thousands of honest film-makers, but no conventions and no generally comprehensible cinema. Program notes will be handed out at every showing. Even the old movies will be encrusted with commentaries and secondary scholarship, and there will be a bright essay in *Partisan Review* about how modern film-makers can't tell stories anymore. It will be called "Movie-Movie/Fable, Fable," and we will have come full circle from the late Siegfried Kracauer's theories on film. For the present, however, we critics must content ourselves with finding some order in the coming chaos.

XV.

Before Sinai, There Was Eden*

LORING MANDEL

Loring Mandel has written for the stage, motion pictures and television. His *Do Not Go Gentle into That Good Night* was recently presented on *CBS Playhouse*.

〜〜〜〜〜〜〜〜〜〜〜〜〜〜〜〜〜〜〜〜〜〜〜〜〜〜〜〜

REST EASY. I want to allay all your apprehensions. I want to announce that the writer shortage has been cured. More than that, it probably never happened. It was most likely a psychic block —a kind of operational spasm that caused producers and columnists to say "Writer" when they fully intended to say "Market" all along. There *is* something called "Writer Shortage," but that's a purely anthropometric matter which many of us helplessly acknowledge. The need for talent is always greater than the supply, true, but the lack of respectably intelligent drama is not from a lack of willing and able playwrights.

In my experience, none of the media—television, films, the stage—is starving for writers. No one starving for nourishment could sustain himself on predigested food, and if drama is in demand to any great degree it is drama that has already been developed, tested, prepackaged, and presold. One symptom of this illusory dearth of writers is the inevitable question, "Why have you abandoned ————?" (fill in the blank with the medium for which you last wrote an original drama).

"Why Have You Abandoned?" is a favorite among interviewers; it feeds the writer's vanity while providing a forum in which the interviewer can develop his own prejudices within his subject's quotation marks. "Why Have You Abandoned?", in fact,

* Reprinted from *The New York Times,* July 16, 1967, Section D, pp. 13, 17. © 1967 by the New York Times Company. Reprinted by permission of the author and the publisher.

208

SIGHT-AND-SOUND COMMUNICATORS

was the suggested topic of this piece. I demurred in favor of this, my own prejudicial account. It's my experience that it is most often the writer who is the abandoned party, and like many another orphan of life and literature he spends an unconscionable amount of time searching out a medium he can call Mother.

My first produced work was in television. It was a very deliberate selection that I made. Sitting in a Chicago advertising agency office watching the Kefauver hearings, aware of the way the entire city stopped work for three days to watch them with me, I was convinced utterly that the potential power of communication by television was many orders beyond that of motion pictures and the distant Broadway stage. For a writer who wishes to communicate, I reasoned, this must be the place.

I still believe this today, but it must be said that the TV medium has hardly moved a step toward realizing that potential. In fact, "medium" has become a word more suited to television than to anything else. When it was possible for me to move to New York, I did so. I submitted scripts and outlines and sought out story editors. I spoke with producers, directors, agents and even critics. Almost without exception, those I met were eager to help me. There was then a feeling that the outer limits of the allowable were the outer limits of the possible. New shows were drawn from new concepts. There were no formulas. Perhaps because the motion picture industry was initially hostile to the idea of television, radio people were in charge and they were generally an imaginative bunch. In radio, imagination was a necessity; radio drama demanded that one of our senses do the work of all five.

But all that early eagerness and vitality of television seemed to have an automatic cutoff, like an electric coffeemaker. Maybe what was happening then was really a race between television's potential for communication and television's potential for making money. Making money won, and once it was ascendant it never lost hold. Creativity was the loser, and was put into place as one of the components of a large organization primarily devoted to commercial goals. There have been momentary swells of activity among the captive creative, but always within the commercial perspective and never high enough or sustained enough to cause serious alarm. And as television settled into its pattern of eliminating risk to its corporate growth, the formulas took over.

All of those writers and directors and producers who were rushing forward to explore the borders and expand the meaningfulness of television looked over their shoulders for a moment to see if the main troops were behind them, and found that the main troops had stopped and consolidated long long beforehand. Eden had become, like the Sinai of today, a Vast Wasteland—and the writers of the vanguard, now wandering the desert looking for their units, were asked by numberless columnists, "Why Have You Abandoned Television?"

For the writer who stayed in television, conditions had changed. I remember one isolated incident when I was new and excited, explaining to a story editor my idea for a documentary on the life of Leadbelly, the remarkable Negro composer and folk singer. The story editor enthused at great length about the possibilities, agreed that he would approve the show and get it on, and then added, "but of course we'll have to make him a white man." A shock, but funny, then. I got some mileage out of the story, too, until it became commonplace. Negroes, of course, are now seen regularly on television in natural color, but in roles most often bleached. And controversy is doled out in careful doses.

A script I wrote for *CBS Playhouse* is a singular exception (in my experience) to the prevailing pattern—concern with quality became once again legitimate. But while *CBS Playhouse* is a significant step, I can't say it is an advance over what we once had—up to seven and one-half hours every week of live drama.

So a writer seeks another medium. If he has an idea that will not fall within the narrow limits of the allowable on television, why not the Broadway stage? No corporate giants there. In fact, I find it generally agreed that only nuts enter the legitimate theater in the hope of enjoying a profitable business while employing legitimate business methods. The theater is still like a Mom-and-Pop store—a small delicatessen, perhaps—in a supermarket society. The analogy seems real enough to me. Off-Broadway theater is Op, while the Great White Way is an early canvas by Edward Hopper. In order to keep the business afloat, as in pre-supermarket days, one must still starve the help (who steal you blind, anyway), pay protection and insurance money to various enforcers, go out of business on a regular basis, mark down the losers and turn over the inventory fast, water the drinks and sauces, and then stand in front of the store to pull in the passers-by. Maybe it isn't Edward Hopper at all, it's George Price.

I think, however, it totally true that the theater is being revolutionized (largely without knowing it), caught in a graphic example of what Buckminster Fuller—in a more profound context—called "the Einsteinian dynamic norm." Everything, that is, is in motion . . . change is normal . . . normality is kinetic, not a stable condition at all. This is not merely to say that theatrical forms are changing, but that audiences are changing and even that the nature of the theatrical experience is changing. You don't have to read McLuhan to guess that an audience raised on staged drama will be different from an audience raised on televised drama. The amounts of participation and concentration, to give only two factors, are enormously different in such audiences.

The decline in romantic fiction and the rise of documented non-fiction in books and periodicals is, to me, another symptom of the same revolution. It takes no heavy analysis to see what has happened to non-comedic fiction on the American stage; you don't have to look any farther than the last season. Only one drama is now playing a Broadway stage, "The Homecoming." Even with a chestful of medals, it is far from a sellout. It is a play that demands a kind of participation and exposure from its audience, and any accountant—certainly the accountant at the Music Box—can show you that *that* audience just isn't around any more. Maybe they're in Uganda. Could it have been prophetic that the Music Box was originally built without a box office? No, the theater isn't starving for good dramatic writers, but rather for audiences.

*   *   *

Are they starving for writers in Hollywood? Film (called Product by its enemies and The Flicks by its friends) is exciting, no question, and it would be hard to deny the evidence that the most creative and experimental work is being done by film-makers. But film-makers are no longer the corporate entities which used to conceive, create, and distribute their magic movies to the grand palaces of Balaban and Katz, twinkling in the old Midwest. Even then, writers were considered semi-skilled technicians, hardly creators. Working for a studio in the thirties and forties was like six months in a locked room; today it is frequently like six days in a revolving door. The opportunities for a writer who wishes to sell an *original* idea, treatment or screenplay to a studio or a studio-contract producer are so few as to be statistically meaningless. Writers are almost always hired to do adaptations of stories, novels, articles, essays, old films and old screenplays, stock footage, someone's aberrant conceit—or to come in and chew over a piece of meat one or more writers before him have choked upon.

Original screenplays today are done either on speculation or in collaboration with financially acceptable directors and/or stars, packages usually put together for the values accorded their names or faces rather than for the strength of the creative idea. Sometimes, writers are parts of these teams, and the work is good. I know producers who spend many hours each week reading original writing in the hope of finding a certain winner . . . but certainty being a far rarer commodity in Hollywood than talent, seldom is an original screenplay thus done. Instead, the writer is hired to rewrite. In motion pictures, I think it reasonable to say, the rewriter is in great demand. The writer is merely a candidate. It is strictly a buyer's market.

I'm perfectly willing to be wrong. Perhaps we writers are really a shoddy and talentless crew. Perhaps we are living in one vast Abner Dean cartoon, writers and producers walking naked and unidentified in all directions looking for one another and endlessly defeated. Perhaps we have not reached that Jamesaubrian Equilibrium where Entertainment and Art and Profit have joined hearts and hands. Perhaps producers are scrambling for my phone number right now and I really have abandoned something.

XVI.

Broadcasting and the News*

ROBERT E. KINTNER

Robert E. Kintner was Secretary to the Cabinet and Special Assistant to President Johnson. In this essay he describes his experiences as president of the National Broadcasting Company.

~~~~~~

ON ELECTION NIGHT, 1960, the news desk at NBC received an unexpected telephone call. The voice at the other end of the line identified itself as the Associated Press, and it wanted to ask a favor: "When you run down the board, could you keep the figures on the screen a little longer? You're going so fast we can't copy them."

Less than a quarter of a century before, the Associated Press had established a secondary service to supply radio stations with brief reports, mainly synopses of the detailed items that moved to the newspapers on the AP's trunk wires. Newspapermen in those days—and I was among them—regarded broadcasters as upstarts, whose idea of legwork was to run out and buy all the newspapers so they could read the headlines over the air.

In all fairness, as I have learned, the radio networks were trying. At the urging of William S. Paley, then president and now chairman of CBS, a Columbia News Service had been established as early as 1933, General Mills picking up half the bills, CBS the rest. Columbia News died in less than two years, but by then CBS executive Ed Klauber and news manager Paul White were planning the great staff that would dominate broadcast jour-

* Reprinted from *Harper's* Magazine, April 1965, pp. 49-55, by permission of the author and the publisher. Copyright © 1965, by Harper's Magazine, Inc.

nalism in the 1940's—Ed Murrow, Elmer Davis, Bill Shirer, Howard K. Smith.

But nobody in the trade really took broadcast news seriously in the 1930's. I was working in the New York *Herald Tribune*'s Washington bureau and later writing a column with Joe Alsop, and he didn't even own a radio. I had one, but the only things I listened to were President Roosevelt's fireside chats, *The March of Time* on Sunday nights, and a fellow on Mutual who gave advice on family problems, a program so grotesque it was amusing.

Up until 1939 Washington newspapermen wouldn't let radio correspondents into the House of Representatives or Senate press galleries. The way we saw it, if the broadcasters wanted somebody to tell the news from Washington, they could pay a working newspaperman to give a talk every once in a while. They did, too.

But by 1960, the press associations were admittedly getting their election figures from broadcasting. It was a milestone, though not quite the end of the road. After the 1962 election, the AP appointed a committee of managing editors to explore ways to make the wire-service reporting of election returns more competitive with broadcast coverage. Then, last June, on the night of the California primary, the AP found itself moving a midnight bulletin that Rockefeller had gone into the lead. Our NBC team had just left the air (it was three o'clock in the morning, New York time), having reported on the basis of far more complete returns that Goldwater was the winner. Forget the projections— this was the real vote. The next day, the early editions of afternoon papers in the East carried an AP election story that was, simply, wrong. Ironically, our early-morning radio news programs followed AP rather than our own people in California, so they went wrong, too.

The wire services thereupon decided that if they couldn't lick us they would join us. A few days later Wes Gallagher, general manager of the AP, and Earl J. Johnson, vice president and editor of UPI, waited outside the office of CBS News president Fred Friendly, while representatives of the three television networks met to hammer out their own agreement on a pool to gather election returns in November. When the networks had settled among themselves, Gallagher and Johnson were invited to join the meeting and to arrange for the press associations to have access to the pool as nonvoting partners and to contribute a share of the cost. In the future, the press associations will have a vote in any such syndicate, and they should have had one last year. This job must now be done collaboratively; no one company can afford the accuracy and speed the public demands and should get.

In 1936, the year of the Roosevelt landslide, the total NBC revenues for *two* networks (the Blue, now ABC, and the Red) came to $38 million. In the year of the Johnson landslide, the NBC News Division—one of the company's five operating divisions—alone *spent* $53 million. Among them, the three networks last year spent more than $125 million to present news-as-it-happened, reports on news, and special programs probing at the facts behind the stories. On election night, the Network Election Service, combining the resources of the three networks and two press associations, employed 150,000 people to gather data.

*   *   *

The results show. In a survey taken by Elmo Roper's organization, more people answered "television" than anything else to a question on "where you get most of your news about what's going on in the world." Even more significant, to me, were the answers to the question, "If you got conflicting or different reports of the same news story from radio, television, the magazines, and the newspapers, which of the four versions would you be most inclined to believe?" Of those who had an opinion, 44 per cent chose television and 15 per cent radio; fewer than 30 per cent chose newspapers.

Competition between newspapers and broadcasters no longer exists in a true sense. The day of the EXTRA is gone—a broadcaster can put the same news on the air, in starker detail, hours faster than a newspaper can set a banner headline and a one-paragraph bulletin, print the paper, and get out onto the newsstands. For such fast-breaking big stories as deaths, key votes in Congress, verdicts in notorious trials, people are going to turn a dial rather than hang around waiting for a delivery truck.

Still, the papers can cover much *more* news than television, and do a more complete job on almost any story. The last few years have seen a rash of newspaper strikes—in New York, in Cleveland, in Detroit—and we have all learned that no amount of broadcasting makes up for the absence of the daily paper. NBC's toughest competitor, Walter Cronkite, once put it this way: "Daily newscasts can only supplement newspapers." There are time limits on the programs and on how much the average viewer wants to hear about a given story. "In the daily newscast," Cronkite said, "I rarely use a story of more than 175 words as a straight on-camera report. Even a film report seldom runs over 350 words. At the other end of the scale, a front-page story in the *New York Times* runs to one thousand words or more." NBC's experience on *The Huntley-Brinkley Report* is similar.

Today, the principal competition between newspapers and broadcasters is for personnel. The networks have used both the papers and the wire services as recruiting grounds for their own talent—in fact, Bill McAndrew, executive vice president in charge of NBC News, doesn't like to hire people without press experience. "City editors," McAndrew says, "teach them the importance of middle initials, getting the address straight and how to write a simple declarative sentence. Without that, they're no use to us." Four to five years is usually enough, and the people the broadcasters take are the people the papers should be trying to keep.

*   *   *

Obviously, a man needs a lot more than a sound newspaper background to be a television correspondent. He has to be acceptable on screen. It's heartbreaking to see an excellent reporter fail as a broadcaster because he isn't articulate on his feet or his appearance is unsettling. (Or he doesn't have sense enough to keep his jacket on and wear long socks.) A top man needs other talents, too. Julian Goodman, vice president of our news division, talks about "the quintuple-threat man—he can write, report, speak, edit, and put it all on the air." Particularly in the more remote bureaus, in Africa and Asia, the reporter has to be a "producer-correspondent," taking on himself all the responsibility for the words and pictures that tell the story. Perhaps the most accomplished practitioner of this new profession was George Clay, who died in Stanleyville, murdered by the Congo rebels, on November 24, 1964.

The new breed of correspondent, as much as the extra money we are willing to spend, accounts for the great jump in the quality of broadcast journalism since the war. Many of the newscasters of the 1930's, though they might be reporters when doing other jobs, were strictly script readers on the air. Lowell Thomas is the greatest sight reader who ever lived; sometimes he would come to the studio only a minute or two before broadcast time, pick up the document, and go right to the microphone. He had been a newspaperman, of course, and he could write—but not for radio. One year he was given an award for radio writing; generously, and publicly, he turned it over to the late Prosper Buranelli, the man who actually prepared his scripts. Gabriel Heatter wrote more of his own material, but he didn't do much digging. He got his "Good News Tonight" from the Transradio News Service, whose ticker was installed in his home.

But there was something about the disembodied voice coming over the radio that made people sure they were getting inside stuff. Bill McAndrew remembers an evening when he called Congressman May, then chairman of the House Armed Services Committee, and May said, "Bill, I can't talk with you now. Gabriel Heatter is reading some manpower figures on the radio, and that's something I want to know about."

This air of omniscience, given freely by the microphone, was a terrible temptation to broadcasting columnists who really had their own chains of contacts below the surface of the news. When I took over the news division of the newly formed ABC network in 1945, its prime properties were Drew Pearson and Walter Winchell, who supplemented their newspaper earnings with once-a-week fifteen-minute broadcasts.

Winchell and Pearson, who then drew the largest pay in broadcasting news, are extremely well informed, their sources ranging from Presidents to thugs. When I went to ABC they also had the largest audiences of any commentators. They had been on NBC's Blue Network, and when the chain was sold to Edward J. Noble, the Life-Saver king, their contracts were part of the deal —some said because their broadcasts were so hard to handle.

217

Both were politically liberal, and they expressed their opinions on the air in the strongest terms. Still, despite hundreds of threats, the record of successful libel suits against them is virtually blank.

With commentators like Pearson and Winchell, ABC needed conservatives to balance its schedule. For this purpose we had George Sokolsky and Paul Harvey from Chicago and Henry J. Taylor, who was engaged directly by General Motors. The revenues from these sponsored shows gave us a little margin to build an ABC staff that would take no sides, politically. When Elmer Davis was about to leave the Office of War Information, we hired him. We also brought in, from CBS, another top newspaperman, John Daly, to head the news department and to offer competition to NBC's John Cameron Swayze and CBS's Doug Edwards.

Bob Sarnoff and I—and, I think, Bill Paley and CBS president Frank Stanton—feel strongly that news broadcasters should not use the camera and microphone to expound their personal views. Men who prepare and present news programs should be full-time members of the news staffs, and broadcasting managements, in turn, should assume complete responsibility for the handling of the news. I have always felt that Elmer Davis and Ed Murrow were the men who first gave broadcast journalism real stature and importance, in the early years of the war. They used a new medium to cover the news in a calm, intelligent way. Both did, at times, inject opinion in their broadcasts, but their basic commodity was hard news, carefully interpreted, and such opinion as they did express was based solidly in fact. Both found support for their positions in unusual public acceptance of their personalities.

When I came to NBC in 1957, I found the company ready to develop a big, aggressive news division. Everyone, especially Bob Sarnoff, who was then president, was annoyed and embarrassed by the general belief that CBS was doing a better job than NBC in news and public affairs. He wanted to fight and was prepared to spend money. I sometimes find myself agreeing with the critics who say that network competition in the entertainment area has bad effects on the quality of the bread-and-butter television drama or comedy series. But in the area of news and public affairs, competition is wholly beneficial. I have three television sets in my office, one for each network, built into a wall cabinet. While watching the screens, I can control the sound with a dial by my desk, and if another network has a story we don't have, or seems to be doing a story better, I like to know why. McAndrew tells me my record is thirty-five memos to him in a two-day period.

We compete for prestige, for public attention, and for public acceptance, and the rivalry among the networks has an intensity that has not been seen in American journalism since the days of Hearst and Pulitzer. Competition drives us to abandon commercial programming to cover a fast-breaking story, with or without sponsorship. It sends us after the unusual story, like the films of the Yemen royalists in battle, which ran five minutes on *Huntley-Brinkley* and cost $20,000. Goodman says, "We're still sending people to find Livingstone in Africa." I'd like to think we would do it even if CBS weren't breathing down our necks, but it's true that in television news, competition is the mother of initiative.

By the time I came to NBC, the bell had tolled for the original television once-a-night news show, an announcer reading bulletins and showing still pictures or films purchased from newsreel companies. Advertisers were beginning to learn that it was the better part of wisdom *not* to seek control over the content of news programs: the best answer to the complaining customer was, and is, "We have nothing to do with the show; we don't even see it before it goes on the air."

Planning NBC coverage of the 1956 political conventions, some bright lad (many claim the credit) had hit on the idea of teaming Chet Huntley and David Brinkley. That fall, they went on with their own fifteen-minutes-a-night news report, opening, incidentally, on the day when the Suez crisis broke and topped the continuing story of the Hungarian revolt. During his tenure as president of NBC, Sylvester "Pat" Weaver had launched the *Today* show, which has been deliberately and gradually news-oriented to become the most influential continuing public-affairs program on the air, partly because of its early-morning time slot, when important people can see it while breakfasting or dressing. Seven out of ten Congressmen watch *Today* as do many officers in the Executive branch.

In a relatively brief time, we have built a news gathering, processing, and presenting organization with eight hundred employees scattered throughout the world, all of whom, except for a few stringers in remote spots, are fully employed by NBC and owe no allegiances anywhere else.

*   *   *

Because you have to maintain speed, you particularly need responsible people on television. When I worked for the *Herald Tribune*, I'd see what everybody had said in the afternoon papers, what AP and UP and the Washington *Post* were going to say the next morning, and then I'd get started writing at six o'clock; I had all the time in the world. And editors would read it before it got into print. In television, there is little or no time to edit a fast-breaking story. You rely on the ability and judgment of the man on the scene, whose "copy" goes direct to the viewers at home.

A first warning of how sensitive broadcasting could be was sounded on a Walter Winchell show in 1934. A bulletin came in and, as any broadcaster then would have done, Winchell read it— there had been a fire in a Dartmouth fraternity house, and nine students were dead. Instantly, telephones rang at stations all over the country, frightened people calling to find out whether relatives or friends were among the victims.

Today, NBC will not announce a plane crash without first getting the details of exactly which flight was involved, on which airline, heading from where to where. Our news staff is alerted by an inside intercom system, but nothing goes on the air. This one can be handled by policy, but many others can't. We were the last network to announce that President Kennedy was dead, though I believe we had the first definite statement of the fact. One of our sound men, at the hospital, got on the line with the words, "They say he's dead." We sent him back to get positive identification of his "they" before we would broadcast the news.

Correspondents and producers need solid judgment, too, on the question of what is and what isn't news. Every afternoon at 2:30, producer Reuven Frank opens the direct line between David

Brinkley's offices in Washington and our news division on the fifth floor of the RCA Building in New York. For two hours, a half-dozen senior people in the Huntley-Brinkley team (there are forty-one all told, employed on this show alone, plus the services of all other NBC reporters) debate the question of which stories are important enough to demand inclusion that night, which features should be taken from the shelf, what should come out first if a story breaks between 4:30 and 6:30. Frank maintains what he calls a "magazine department," stories which are or look likely to be timely, but need not run on any given evening. "Like the Spanish pressure on Gibraltar," he says, "it's not something that stops people from eating their lunch, but it's interesting, and they ought to know about it."

*　　*　　*

Like the newspaper, the news program is the predestined victim of events staged for publicity. Producers have to live with this problem, decide for themselves whether a refugee rally or an American Nazi party is worth time on the air on a given day. An organization without any real membership could picket a political convention and stand a chance of putting itself, at least briefly, before a huge public. A network news division must rely on the editorial judgment of experienced people on the scene, whose decisions are final because the story goes right out on the air. Frank occupies the "slot" at national conventions, and decides whether the real news value lies in the interesting characters demonstrating outside the doors or in the speech somebody is making inside.

The area of greatest and most complicated responsibility is that of news analysis and interpretation. The NBC network does not editorialize, and we do not employ "commentators." Our aim is to present the news with enough background to make it comprehensible. But every reporter knows that when you write the first word, you make an editorial judgment. Different reporters covering the same event and gathering the same information will write different stories.

Still, there is a line somewhere between interpreting and editorializing. Nobody can draw it precisely—Paul White once tried to, in a rule book for CBS, and correspondents found themselves crossing it all the time, though they were not in fact editorializing. The best you can do is hire responsible people and editors and supervisors, drill into them that you don't want their personal opinions, and then let them go.

Questions about the fairness of interpretation are most likely to arise in connection with what we call "actualities," and most people call "documentaries." Some of these programs are not controversial at all, like Lou Hazam's portraits of Vincent van Gogh and Shakespeare, Lucy Jarvis' tour through the Louvre, George Vicas' story of the French Revolution.

But often programs expose a scandal (like David Brinkley's *Great Highway Robbery* or CBS's *Biography of a Bookie Joint*), or go behind the slogans in a big fight (like Robert Northshield's and Chet Hagan's three-hour program on civil rights, Irving Gitlin's dissection of the welfare battle in Newburgh, New York, or the CBS documentary on birth control). Many programs take an important story from the recent past (the U-2 episode or the Cuba missile crisis) and try to see it for the first time under the eye of eternity.

Such programs raise hackles, and they should. Their producers' responsibility is not to be bland and unobjectionable but to present all the major angles of approach to a controversy. The correspondent should confine his comments to highlighting the issues, but, of course, the issues are what *he* sees as the issues. Like the judge addressing the jury, he does not attempt to tell the audience which witnesses to believe; he assumes that people can spot untrustworthy testimony. Editing the film, the director and producer should neither protect people from their own folly nor cut back and forth for the purpose of making someone look foolish. Men who live with a story for weeks or even months almost inevitably become identified with one side or another, and it takes great professional acumen and self-restraint to make a fair program.

We have had to defend a number of programs against attack by government officials, industry associations, political groups.

222

In every case, I think we have done so successfully—that is, we have demonstrated not that the programs were right in every interpretation, but that they were factually correct, reasonable, and fair.

In a few cases, I think it can be said that the medium's need to simplify for a big audience—coupled with a general-news reporter's inevitable lack of expertise in a specialized subject—leaves us open to legitimate accusations of superficiality. We admit we need more experts, and we are trying to get them, even though most good reporters hate to tie themselves down to any one subject. And, of course, the big financial rewards in broadcast journalism lie in a reporter's establishing himself as a personality, which he can't do if all he reports on is, say, medicine.

*   *   *

Somewhere between the regular news show and the studied "actuality" is the program which presents events as they are happening or takes a longer look at today's news. These programs have been television's finest hours; they are what the medium is made for. They range from the glory of space shots to the tragedy of a President's assassination and a nation's mourning, from the malevolence of a Mafia renegade testifying before a Senate Committee to the good cheer of an Inaugural parade. These are done live, supplemented by tape and film, and people work on them until five minutes before they go on the air. Obviously, the authority and prestige (indeed, the legal liabilities) of the company must be given trustingly into the hands of a few producers, editors, correspondents.

Such programs can be called into being at any time—McAndrew has authority to drop the regular programming and take over the network for news whenever he feels it necessary, though normally he checks first with me. The specials are more expensive than most people realize. Beyond the costs of time and production, there is the additional, sometimes brutal, expense of preempting a scheduled, sponsored show—paying the producer for the program that didn't run. This "preemption cost" is always absorbed by the network. Without the help of Gulf Oil, which has given us a commitment to pay part of the costs for instant specials and leaves racks of commercials with us to run in such programs, the burden might be too heavy for the network to bear.

All these programs must be ours, from top to bottom. We must know all the people involved in the production; we must have someone to hold accountable for every piece of work that goes into the show. If humanly possible, we will shoot our own film, though sometimes we have to buy film from others (for example, the six hours of pictures of Communist China made by two French cameramen, which we edited down to one hour and fitted to a script by staffers). And we have an absolute rule against broadcasting any news or public-affairs shows made by outside producing companies.

Occasionally, packagers come to us with documentaries and with sponsors for them, and we refuse to accept. We cannot undertake the responsibility of presenting actualities to a nationwide audience unless we have detailed supervision. The risks are too great. We cannot know enough about where the information came from, or about how the cooperation of the participants was secured.

Making public-affairs programs is an immensely complicated business. You are always asking people for cooperation; they grant you access and spend considerable time with your crew without being paid for it. The network must know, more certainly than it ever can with an outsider, that the process has not compromised its integrity. We had a revealing demonstration of this difficulty one afternoon, when a capable outside producer showed us a program he had made about American missiles. It was a good job. The producer assured us that it was ready to run, that he had already made the changes demanded by the Department of Defense.

"Oh," said Bill McAndrew. "Security?"

"No," said the producer. "Editorial." We turned down the program.

By far, the most complicated clearance arrangements NBC News ever made were with the Soviet government, in connection with *The Kremlin*, George Vicas' brilliant exploration of the history of Russia through art treasures of the Russian sanctum. After much negotiation, the Soviet government gave us access to areas of the Kremlin that had never been photographed, and Soviet historians and art historians helped with the script. They insisted on our employing Russian camera crews and technicians, but we supervised the entire activity. They wanted to develop the film themselves, but they permitted us to fly it out to Paris for that purpose because it was Eastman Color and they did not have proper facilities for handling it. The cooperation from the Red Army was superb. Russian soldiers set bonfires outside the windows of the museums to help us simulate an episode from Napoleon's occupation of the city. The Red Army chorus learned a Czarist hymn and sang it as a musical background for a painting of the funeral of a Czar. In return, we gave contractual guarantee that the film and the script would be shown to the Soviet government before we ran the program and that we would make any changes necessary for historical accuracy. They would have a week in which to propose changes.

The week passed, and we did not hear from them. On May 8, 1963, four days beyond the week's limit, we received a laconic telegram from Soviet Radio and Television announcing that "we categorically object against the showing of the film in its present form." Meanwhile, Vicas in Paris received a telephone call specifically protesting the Czarist hymn and denouncing the statement in the script that the Palace of Congress was "built with the assistance of architects from the Western World." Since the statement was correct, and the hymn did not fall into the category of "historical accuracy," we rejected the protest and informed the Russians that we would broadcast the program as it was.

Six weeks later, a detailed memorandum of complaint arrived from two eminent Soviet scholars. Mostly, they were picking nits ("About the guns should be said not 'abandoned,' but 'taken as trophies'"). Among the more general objections was that the program was not really nonpolitical, as we had promised, because it concentrated on the Czars themselves "without any mention of the social classes and forces whose policy they represented and carried out." Julian Goodman wrote a reply stressing that "at no time in its negotiations with Soviet authorities did NBC profess to represent Marxist positions. . . . References to NBC in cur-

225

rent Soviet writings provide ample evidence of our network's non-Marxist character."

We went ahead. I doubt strongly that any independent packager would have done so—or would, indeed, have got its films out prior to complete clearance by Soviet authorities. There is an interesting comparison to be made between *The Kremlin*, representing the independent judgment of NBC News, and the various recent documentaries from China. These were put together by impeccably non-Communist Western packagers—but their bargaining position was much weaker than ours.

While we were having our troubles with the Soviet Union over *The Kremlin*, two of our White Papers—*The Death of Stalin* and *The Rise of Khrushchev*—turned out to be unexpectedly expensive for NBC News. We were thrown out of Russia, our correspondent was expelled, and our bureau closed. For a year and a half we were handicapped a great deal in our news coverage. CBS and ABC got things out of Moscow we couldn't get. CBS, by the way, found their victories almost as distasteful as we found our defeats. Richard Salant, then president of CBS News, called McAndrew and generously offered the use of their bureau and their people in Moscow. McAndrew turned him down because we were afraid that if the Russians got wind of it they would throw CBS out, too. Khrushchev was personally angry at NBC. One of our Russian diplomatic contacts once told us he was afraid even to reopen the discussion of whether the question should be reopened.

We were allowed to start up again in Moscow, at the beginning of this year, only through the direct intervention of Secretary of State Dean Rusk. From the beginning, Rusk took this expulsion as seriously as he would take the closing of a U.S. consulate. He negotiated the matter personally with Foreign Minister Gromyko.

* * *

Rusk's conversations with Gromyko show one strand of the tangled interrelationships that have grown up between government and broadcasting during the great expansion of television. It is important to the State Department that millions of Ameri-

226

cans who rely on NBC for news coverage shall not be deprived of information from Moscow. It is important to the President that the White House be plugged directly into the nation's television transmitters. President Johnson has turned over space in the White House to be equipped as a studio by the networks. The networks are spending a million dollars on this job, and hereafter will spend half a million a year on engineers to keep the room "live" and ready for use at any moment. Washington newsmen call it "The Little Theater off Lafayette Square."

Every public figure wants to use television as much as he can, and where public figures are in conflict television is in the middle. Nobody has written precise ground rules: definition is lacking in many important aspects of television's relations with the legislative, executive, and judicial branches of government at all levels. And unlike newspapers, broadcasting stations and networks live within the great penumbra of government authority.

PART FOUR

THE CONTROVERSIAL SCREEN

Where there is much desire to learn,
there of necessity will be much arguing,
much writing, many opinions.

—JOHN MILTON

I have heard of some kind of men that
put quarrels purposely on others to taste
their valour.

—W. SHAKESPEARE

~~~~~~

TELEVISION AND MOTION PICTURES, in our time, have generated their own catalog of dispute and their own dictionary of issues. The debaters are the supporters of the major social institutions involved with the sight-and-sound media. The National Association of Educational Broadcasters, NAF-BRAT, the FCC, the National Catholic Office for Motion Pictures, the Television Information Office, the National Citizens Committee for Public Television—from all such quarters come spokesmen with diverse opinions, platforms, and "solutions."

One group with a deep interest in the special issues raised by the mass media is the Center for the Study of Democratic Institutions. In the opening essay in this section, the Center's Harry S. Ashmore underscores the perennial controversy surrounding the quality of television programming. He sees the "loss of excellence" in commercial television as inversely related to a rise in profit. Ashmore's solution to the problem

229

is the establishment of a "board of jurors" to serve as an "outside conscience" for television.

Ashmore's complaints are familiar, and they are echoed by many sight-and-sound communicators who have given television some of its memorable hours and who, despite discouragements, have not forsaken the thinning electronic vineyard. In his own analysis of television programming, producer Hubbell Robinson recommends in his contribution that any attempt for television to "break through the fog of *kitsch*" must be spearheaded by the medium's top-level managers.

Many critics who hold television programs in low esteem feel the fault lies with the advertiser. Their conviction seems to be that the "big spenders" in television such as Procter and Gamble, American Home Products, and General Foods participate in an organized conspiracy to pervert the national taste. Speaking from the point of view of advertising, Fairfax M. Cone suggests that sponsor influence on programs would be lessened by adoption of a "magazine concept" of rotated commercial announcements.

Spokesmen for the educational institution are not without their own mettle and platforms. Going beyond the issue of raising the level of television programming, Harry J. Skornia questions the very foundations of the American system of broadcasting which has more often favored the aims of business than the goals of education. He raises the argument whether the Federal Communications Commission as it is presently constituted can provide the regulation and direction necessary for an integrated system of American broadcasting that gives education its fair share of the electromagnetic spectrum.

Lying at the root of the debate surrounding the living-room screen is the recognition that broadcasters do not *own* the channels that they use. Because station management must apply to the FCC to receive a license to operate, broadcasters are more *trustees* than owners. The awarding of a license to competitive applicants is usually based on promises to meet programming responsibilities toward the public. Curiously, what the FCC gives it never takes away. When station licenses come up for renewal, the Commission does not measure performance against promises. The establishment of a specific FCC method of comparing performance and promise —or the refusal of license renewal for poor performance— might, as Jack Gould suggests, indeed make waves.

So incoherent is FCC policy on programming standards that a question heard with increasing frequency is whether the Commission is obsolete. The Communications Act of 1934 is apparently not broad enough to cope with the technological expansion within the relatively brief time of its operation. The awarding of licenses to broadcasters is merely one aspect of the Commission's responsibilities. The new ultrahigh frequency facilities, the proliferation of community-antenna television systems, communications satellites, and even telephone rates and regulations—all of these tax the limited resources and personnel of the agency.

Yet, if the solution to an outmoded FCC is the broadening of its regulatory powers, where will we draw the line between intervention in programming and overt censorship? How can we maneuver our democratic way between the Scylla and Charybdis of program censorship from Washington and the patent irresponsibility of 30 Rockefeller Plaza? Lee Loevinger, in his contribution to this book, urges us to believe that the success of our seamanship will depend ultimately upon our willingness to keep faith with the media managers. Even though Loevinger himself is a member of the seven-man Commission, he believes that the maintenance of a viable, democratic social philosophy cannot rest upon the discretion of any governmental agency, no matter how benevolent. This is to say that we must have confidence in the checks and balances which are inherent in the contending influences of the institutions concerned with sight-and-sound media. This requires patience—with the pluralism of our social fabric, with the maturation of a public philosophy on the part of the media managers, and especially with the evolving sensibility of The Great Audience.

The controversy surrounding the home screen is not confined to the entertainment function of television. Clearly, as a reporting medium television is a major instrument for public information, particularly in the area of politics. While the traditional stumping around the country is still a necessary part of the political campaign, there is increasing reliance on the use of television to persuade potential voters. "The fall madness," in Herman Land's phrase, of an election year brings the preemption of "regularly scheduled programs" by political speeches as well as the flurry of one-minute "paid political announcements." In his essay, historian Arthur Schlesinger, Jr. questions whether such use of television is producing a better-informed electorate or reducing our politics to "a mixture of high-pressure salesmanship and beauty contests."

The importance of television in the strategy of political campaigning is acknowledged by Theodore H. White in his *The Making of a President: 1964.* "Here is where the audience is," he writes; "here is where the greatest part of the money is spent. . . ." According to Herbert E. Alexander of the Citizens' Research Foundation, the "money spent" by Republicans and Democrats for political broadcasting (television and radio) in the general election period of 1964 was 24.6 million dollars, four times the costs of the 1952 period. Political talk (unlike political promises), Alexander reminds us, is not cheap.

Campaign expenditures for political uses of television is money well spent if the persuasive impact of the medium is considered. Pollster Elmo Roper has reported that 57 percent of the voters in the 1960 Presidential election acknowledged the "influence" of the Great Debates between Kennedy and Nixon. Of an additional 6 percent (four million voters) who stated that their decision was directly based on these debates, 72 percent voted for Kennedy. Considering that Kennedy's margin of victory was only 112,000, it is obvious that big money and electronic persuasion go hand in hand.

Did the confrontation between Kennedy and Nixon provide audiences with what Howard K. Smith called a "spiritual X ray" of the candidates, or was Max Ascoli's phrase, "an electronic nightmare," a more accurate description? It is too early in the continuing history of political television to venture categorical opinions. Wisely, in 1964 there were no Johnson-Goldwater debates, since a nationwide dialogue between these two wits might have disenchanted the electorate from even going to the polls on November 4. Discounting cosmetics, remodeling of an "image" by Charisma, Inc., and five o'clock beards, the more germane question of the value of Great Debates will be answered only in subsequent elections, providing the two opponents are willing to risk the game for the candle.

With the recurrence of the "fall madness," especially during Presidential campaigns, the media managers of television conduct their own campaigns for relaxation of governmental restrictions on the political use of television. Their *bête noire* is Section 315 of the Communications Act, which requires broadcasters to give (or sell) equal air-time to all candidates for public office. The broadcasters argue that if Section 315 had not been suspended during the 1960 Presidential campaign, the Great Debates could not have taken place. Moreover, broadcasters feel that the First Amendment should grant them the same freedom of operation as it affords the print media. In truth, were a governmental agency to force the nation's press to grant equal newspaper or magazine space to all political contenders, there would be an irrepressible brouhaha on the part of publishers and editors.

Robert W. Sarnoff, chairman of the board of NBC, considers that an additional shackle on the "giant of television journalism" is the excluding of television cameras from such places of public affairs as the Congress, the Supreme Court, and other judicial and legislative chambers. This, of course, brings us directly into the thorny issue of Canon 35 of the American Bar Association, which not only excludes television apparatus but newspaper photographers as well. The larger problem of the individual's right to a fair trial has to be weighed against the public's right to know, and, in truth, there are extremely valid arguments on both sides.

In its zeal for the public's right to know, television journalism is forcing American politics to adjust to the ability of the medium to rapidly report election returns. The high-speed computers used by network "voter profile" experts to project election results have raised an unprecedented dilemma. What is at issue is the susceptibility of men's minds. The coast-to-coast telecasting of such projections, based on a minute raw-vote count from key areas, may not only influence the decision of voters *before* they go to the polls, but may actually deter them from voting for or against what seems a *fait accompli*. As Max Lerner states in his essay, we have not so much to fear from the fallibility of the "monster" computers, but rather from their success. A possible solution lies in the proposal, strongly endorsed by such media managers as Dr. Frank Stanton of CBS, to stagger the closing of polls in each state, so that time differentials could be evened out.

Perhaps one of the most serious problems generated by the pervasive sight-and-sound images is how to deal with the portrayal of violence. But television and motion pictures do not have an exclusive hold on the exhibition of aggression, brutality, and vicious behavior. Despite the infamous *Bus Stop* episode on television, "A Lion Walks among Us," in which a nineteen-year-old Fabian hacked an old man to death with an axe, or the shocking stabbing in the shower in *Psycho*, nothing in the sight-and-sound media can match Shakespeare's *Titus Andronicus* as a horrifying bloodbath. Because

234

there is no Federal Communications Commission which licenses motion picture theaters, up to now the theater screen has had an edge over the home screen in depicting violence. If 1967 saw a *St. Valentine's Day Massacre* or *Bonnie and Clyde*, such films were only following a Hollywood tradition that went back to *Scarface* or *Little Caesar* thirty years before, The margin may be narrowing, moreover, as films like *Psycho* continue to be released through syndication to television stations.

Nor can we be so casuistic as to exonerate the sight-and-sound media from their social responsibility with the rationalization that gunning a man down is as old as Cain and Abel. According to Dr. Konrad Lorenz, famed naturalist and director of the Max Planck Institute, man alone among animals kills his own kind. This Lorenz attributes to the evolution of coded electro-chemical signals which were developed in the human brain nearly two million years ago when the earliest humans roamed the African plains.

If we recognize that these murderous propensities exist within the human psyche, to what end is it humanely legitimate to utilize this pathology for purposes of "kicks" and thrills? We are not suggesting that the only salubrious themes for films and television programs should be of the *Lassie Come Home* variety, for obviously master films such as John Ford's *The Informer* or Fred Zinnemann's *High Noon* demand the depiction of physical aggression. Indeed, as Philip French describes in his essay, the nature of the film medium is peculiarly suited to the portrayal of violence. Camera movements, the altering size of images, and the techniques of editing to create juxtaposition and montage, all are specially adaptable to telling an aggressive story whether it be a Western, a gangster melodrama, or a war epic.

Still, we may legitimately ask, how specific must motion pictures and television be in their quest for realism. How much of the gory action must occur within the frame? If

Euripides or Sophocles could create great *and* popular art while telling a grim story and yet sparing audiences the gruesome details, is it lese majesty to suggest to Otto Preminger or Roy Huggins that today's audiences do not require every minute recital of ferocity?

A brilliant contemporary critic of American morals, Tom Wolfe, has charged that the mass media are promulgating a "new genre" of mass perversion which he calls *porno-violence.* The theme of this new pornography is not sex but the portrayal of sadism, masochism, and mayhem. Commenting on Wolfe's term, Paul Weber, writing in *America,* believes that television news coverage of racial riots, or the war in Vietnam, has contributed, perhaps unwittingly, to this pornography of violence. The sight-and-sound porno-violence, he suggests, "fantasizes the desire, present deep in every man, for easy, violent, but forbidden, solutions to complex problems." Obviously, this kind of porno-violence, which is almost inextricably bound up with news and the public's right to know, is going to be very difficult to control. Whole new areas of self-censorship in the interests of moral concern and responsibility are being thrust upon the media managers of motion pictures and television.

Almost from the beginning of the motion picture as a mass entertainment medium, various agencies, councils, and "censor boards" have expressed concern with the content of films and have attempted to exert some types of restraint. This extended beyond overt sex-violence to such matters as the depiction of the clergy, narcotics addiction, or miscegenation. The relative effectiveness of such groups was contingent upon their various and arbitrary definitions of what constituted sacrilege, immorality, and profanity.

Because these agencies operated in a grey area, their "decisions to ban" were always open to subsequent reversal by courts of law. As a result of various legal decisions, principally by the Supreme Court, the traditional censorship board has

236

been reduced essentially to acting in only an advisory capacity for municipal and state legal authorities.

The major intention of censorship efforts has always been to safeguard the sensibilities of the young. Proposals for enforced "classification" of films as to their suitability for children, similar to the British system, has met with consistent opposition from the Motion Picture Association of America. Unwilling to refuse ticket money from minors, the best the Association has come up with that even remotely resembles classification is the advertising tag, "Suggested For Mature Audiences." Since the local exhibitor feels no responsibility for defining what "maturity" is, such labels often serve as an enticement to young moviegoers rather than a deterrent.

On the other hand, classification by any agency raises the danger of a renewal of prior censorship insofar as films must be submitted for someone to evaluate them. One result may be that close decisions would be decided in favor of the "Adults Only" category. It is also conceivable that motion picture producers would be timid about making controversial films that might receive an "adult" label and thus deprive themselves of revenue from exhibition to wider audiences.

In their opposition to censorship over the sight-and-sound media, the usually contending institutions of business and art are in the same camp. For business, greater freedom increases profits; for art, it augments the possibilities of enlarged creative activities. To pursue his vision of man, Michael Blankfort says in his essay, the writer-communicator has the obligation to oppose all limitations to freedom. And even though the film and television writer works under "industry codes" as a condition of employment, Blankfort argues, this does not mean that he accepts them.

Throughout this book we have tried to show how certain major institutions in our society exert influence over the moving images of the sight-and-sound media. In this section the special problems surrounding and generated by these

237

media are discussed, particularly the responsibility of motion pictures and television to society at large. The final essay of "The Controversial Screen," perhaps more than any other statement in this volume, encompasses the central issues we have examined.

Recognizing that the art of the motion picture is as important a contribution to American culture as music, ballet, and the theater, William Fadiman proposes a unique solution to the doldrums in which the American film finds itself. His bold suggestion is that creative activity in the American film be *subsidized* by grants from citizens' groups, foundations, government, and even business itself. He finds it ironic that so promising a development as the American Film Institute has a budget of approximately five million dollars for its initial three-year tenure, while American symphony orchestras received from the Ford Foundation alone in 1967 the sum of eighty-five million dollars. The originality of Mr. Fadiman's proposal is enhanced, in our eyes, by the fact that he is a vice-president of a successful film and television corporation rather than some detached idealist calling from his ivory tower.

We have talked at some length about the contending institutions of business, government, education, and art, and feel that a certain vigor comes from a dynamic competition among them. Yet we should not overlook the advantages to the sight-and-sound media (and to American audiences as a direct beneficiary) of a closer dialogue among these institutions. It is precisely for the possibilities of such a dialogue that William Fadiman outlines the framework.

XVII.

An Outside Conscience for Television*

HARRY S. ASHMORE

Harry S. Ashmore has received a Pulitzer Prize as editor of the *Arkansas Gazette* and the Sidney Hillman Award. He is currently chairman of the executive committee of the Fund for the Republic and the Center for the Study of Democratic Institutions.

∼∼∼∼∼∼∼∼∼∼∼∼∼∼∼∼∼∼∼∼∼∼∼∼∼∼∼∼∼∼∼∼∼

THE CRITIC of the mass media suffers a peculiar occupational hazard that usually leaves him sounding as though he were speaking in an echo chamber. His audience knows in advance what he is going to say, and he knows how his audience is going to respond: most of those on the business side of communications will dismiss him as uninformed, or a malcontent, or both; the creative workers will generally agree that he is probably right but offers no practical solutions; and the bemused public will pay no attention at all.

It is not easy to take a detached view of the communications system, and to consider its several parts. We have become enveloped in something like a seamless web of sight, sound, and print, and the media have trouble locating their own places in the endless expanse of words and images.

The physical manifestations of the technological revolution have been accompanied by even more significant psychological traumas. So long as newspapers remained the dominant mass medium, their proprietors held automatic place in the top tier of the power structure, and their exclusive ability to create and withhold celebrity conferred an eminence that touched even rela-

* Reprinted from *Mass Communications* (1966), pp. 28-39, by permission of the Center for the Study of Democratic Institutions and the author.

tively lowly editorial workers. In less than a generation, these proud men have found themselves shoved into second place by an electronic upstart born of an unholy union of Hollywood and Madison Avenue.[1]

Already the new dispensation has made it possible and perhaps even necessary for newspapers to do a good many things their proprietors thought they couldn't do. Simple-minded sensationalism, long accepted as a necessary evil by the most ascetic editors, has just about gone by the boards. Such remaining repositories of the zam! bam! whowie! headline and smart-aleck editorial line as the New York *Daily News*, the Chicago *Tribune*, and the San Francisco *Chronicle* are conspicuous anachronisms in the expanse of restrained typography and generally responsible, if incomplete, reportage that stretches from coast to coast. "I could get you a raft of American papers and clip off the mastheads and defy you to tell where they are printed," says Executive Editor Norman Isaacs of the Louisville *Courier-Journal*. Mr. Isaacs de-

[1] Commercial television broadcasting began in 1946, with six stations serving 8,000 families. As of January 1, 1966, the Television Information Office of the National Association of Broadcasters offered these "dimensions of the medium": Some 54,000,000 homes, or 94 percent of all family units, are equipped to receive television; multiple set ownership brings the total in use to 67,000,000. There are 700 stations on the air, with another 124 under construction and 179 additional applications on file; the current expansion was fostered by FCC regulations which by 1970 will equip 80 percent of receivers for Ultra High Frequency reception, as well as the present standard Very High Frequency. NAB expects the spectrum to close out again with 1,000 stations, 823 commercial and 179 educational. The year-round per family average of daily television viewing is now estimated at five and a half hours, rising to six and a half hours in midwinter; the estimate for grade-school children is twenty hours a week. Viewers have a total investment of $27,500,-000 in their receiving sets, and the networks and stations have invested $800,000,000 in transmitting equipment. The top-rated one-hour network program, *Bonanza*, costs $187,000 a week to produce, plus $311,000 for air time, for a total just under a half million dollars; the combined production and time cost for the top network news program, *Huntley-Brinkley Report*, is $75,000 for fifteen minutes; on a major current affairs assignment, the costs are indicated by the $1,000,000 spent by the networks for pooled production of the fourteen-hour visit of Pope Paul to the United Nations, plus the cost in revenue from time preempted from commercial programming estimated at $5,800,000 for television and radio. The gross income for TV broadcasters, all from advertising, was just under $2,500,000,000 last year, and NAB projects $3,000,000,000 by 1970.

plores this lack of diversity, as do I. But I have to concede that it represents an advance over the days when Ambrose Bierce could describe Hearst journalism, and most of the rest, as a form of verbal masturbation matching sensation with lack of reality.

The slowly dawning recognition that they have lost the first loyalty of the mass audience to the simple pleasures of television provides a new kind of freedom for publishers and editors who care to make use of it. If they have made their last king, they still have the rapier of informed criticism. It has always been true that more fortunes were lost than made in newspapering, and the gratified ego is still the ultimate reward. "If I wanted to make money I would go into the bond business," says Eugene C. Pulliam, who owns publishing monopolies in Indianapolis and Phoenix. "I've never been interested in the money we make but in the influence we have." Mr. Pulliam, as it happens, is an arch-conservative, but his premise also motivates Arthur Ochs Sulzberger of the moderate *New York Times*, Barry Bingham of the liberal Louisville newspapers, and other owners dotted along the political spectrum.

It is difficult to fault the prescription of perhaps the most successful of contemporary publishers, the only one who has had gumption enough to roll with the technological punch and use the new computerized gadgetry to produce the country's first national newspaper, simultaneously printed in a dozen major cities: "The newspaper of the future must become the instrument of intellectual readership, an institution of intellectual development—a center of learning." Anyone who tends to discount such a statement because it comes from Bernard Kilgore, president of the *Wall Street Journal*, is trafficking in old stereotypes; the present-day *Journal* is one of the most literate and penetrating newspapers published anywhere, and not long ago rattled the teeth of its special constituency by uncovering the commodity market's great salad-oil scandal.

It is perhaps inescapable to my computation that any hopeful signs born of the newspaper's adversity have been matched by the qualitative decline of the medium that now dominates the mass audience. The continuing loss of excellence is agreed to by almost

241

all of those who are concerned with the quality of television programming, and is not seriously disputed even by the industry spokesmen who measure progress in dollars. Each television season in recent years has ended with the critics denouncing the new low in the general level of programming while the trade journals announced that the broadcasters' income and profits have reached a new high. I have no doubt that the proprietors of TV still prefer a good program to a bad one, all things being equal, and I know that some of them, at least, know the difference. But the things that count are anything but equal. The determining fact seems to be that an audience of multiple millions is necessary to market the commercials that pay the freight, and this requires—or at least can only be maintained by—a common denominator of bland mediocrity.

Not long ago a discouraged member of the Federal Communications Commission, Kenneth A. Cox, publicly described the current run of television programs as ranking "somewhere between undistinguished and calamitous." Lawrence Laurent in the *Washington Post* observed that Commissioner Cox probably wouldn't have been so kind had he spoken after the advent of *Batman*, the sensation of the 1965–66 mid-season. This ABC serialization based on an old comic-book character was launched with a publicity campaign which touted it as "camp"—a current vogue word borrowed from the homosexual, meaning in this case that the program is so bad by all normal standards it is somehow "good," or at least smart. Thus, Mr. Laurent wrote, "the poorest kind of published trash becomes the basis for a worse television series. The excuse for propelling it into the public's airwaves is that it is a kind of grisly joke that a tiny in-group is playing on the people."

Batman provides a particularly revealing measure of television's low estate. The series' executive producer, William Dozier, greets criticism by pointing to the ratings and noting: "It's entertaining a lot of people and we're in the entertainment business." This is the same William Dozier who as a program executive at CBS had a guiding hand in such memorable series as *Studio One*, *Playhouse 90*, and *You Are There*. Of that vanished glory he says, "That kind of thing won't get on TV again, because the medium has become a merchandising business, and not enough people watched those dramas to move the volume of goods to be moved." [2]

As in the proverb that has it that every fat man contains a thin man fighting to get out, there is still a great deal of high-grade creative talent floundering around in the denatured corporate reaches of TV, and an occasional brilliant program still reaches the air. But these breakthroughs grow fewer as the broadcasters improve their ability to extract profits from every moment of the broadcast day. Lawrence Laurent has reported on the bonanza discovered in time segments the sales departments once looked upon as unproductive nuisances:

"Daytime television . . . is a collection of games and shrieking contestants and daytime dramatic serials in which shouting substitutes for projected emotion. . . . Some people call the daytime hours 'cheap time,' meaning that a sponsor spends less for a minute than in the golden hours between 7:30 P.M. and 11 P.M. But network executives will say, softly, that 'Daytime is where the real money is.'" [3]

[2] A similar view has been expressed by a producer of equal rank who went from NBC to ABC's "Golden Gulch." Success in the TV-ad agency business, Paul Henninger wrote in the Los Angeles *Times*, requires a "talent for surrender," and he cites the example of David Levy: " 'The era of the one of a kind show has passed,' maintains Levy. He fondly recalls his accomplishments during his three years as head of programming at NBC. He had a hand in bringing to NBC such shows as Walt Disney's series, *Car 54*, the Dick Powell anthology series, *International Showtime*, and *Sing Along with Mitch*, among others. 'Not long ago I talked to two of the toughest agents in town,' continued Levy, 'and these are men who are not unaware of what makes a good show. You know what they told me when I suggested something unique as a series? Dave, they said, get yourself another Phyfe.' Obviously Levy has had to 'surrender.' His *Double Life of Henry Phyfe* series on ABC followed the spy trend. Likewise his *Addams Family* on the same network crawled out of the monster mold."

[3] A sensational affirmation of network daytime policy was offered in February, 1966, when John A. Schneider took over as group vice-president in charge of broadcasting at CBS and promptly cancelled the scheduled live telecast of George F. Kennan's Vietnam testimony before the Senate Foreign Relations Committee. "The housewife isn't interested in the Senate hearings," Mr. Schneider proclaimed. Fred W. Friendly, the veteran CBS public affairs vice-president, resigned in protest. He reached his decision, Mr. Friendly said, when he looked at his office monitors carrying NBC's live coverage of the crucial hearings while CBS displayed "a fifth re-run of *Lucy*, then followed by an eighth re-run of *The Real McCoys*, I wanted to order up an announcement that said: 'Due to circumstances beyond our control the broadcast orig-

The discovery of the financial possibilities of "cheap time" has now about closed out all the odd corners of the schedule where it cost little or nothing to drop in public-service or cultural programs to placate the minority audience. The old "Sunday afternoon ghetto," which once provided an often fascinating laboratory for experimental uses of the new medium, as in *Omnibus*, has become the ideal spot for highly profitable sportcasts, so much so that the baseball, football, and basketball seasons now overlap right around the calendar and the networks have taken to fabricating their own golf tournaments. The fiscal combination required to unlock Hollywood vaults has been found, and vast stocks of fairly recent movies are now available to space out the commercials in the late evening and family-style weekend hours.

All of this, added to the financial return from prime time, where the network rate for a commercial minute is now more than $60,000, has begun to produce surplus income that can no longer be digested within the broadcasting industry. There is, indeed, no interest in internal expansion, but a built-in resistance to it, since existing TV and radio frequencies cover the whole of the mass market, and the bountiful profits depend upon the broadcasters' ability to keep the present limited competition well under control. The result is that the big broadcasting corporations have begun to take over other substantial segments of the entertainment industry. Professional football has become practically a creature of broadcasting, shaped to the special demands of the camera, and the resulting bull market for talent has pushed the going price for a star college linebacker up to $600,000; one network, CBS, has bought the New York Yankees baseball club outright; and NBC's parent, RCA, recently took over a major book publisher, Random House.

The indispensable fountainhead of these riches is the limited number of broadcasting licenses granted by the Federal Communications Commission under an act of Congress requiring the

inally intended for this time will not be seen.'" Mr. Friendly concluded his letter of resignation with a quotation from the late Edward R. Murrow, with whom he pioneered TV journalistic techniques: "There is no suggestion that networks or individual stations should operate as philanthropies. But I can find nothing in the Bill of Rights or the Communications Act which says that they must increase their net profits each year, lest the republic collapse."

244

licensees to operate in the "public interest, convenience, and necessity." This gives a public utilities cast to broadcasting, and regulation is never questioned so long as the FCC employs its powers to set engineering requirements, police technical performance, and make such determinations as that requiring the industry to standardize on one of several competing systems of color television. However, on the very rare occasions when the Commission has moved into the area of programming, it has run into cries of censorship, invocations of the First Amendment, and appeals to the democratic gods—to such an extent that the agency has had inordinate difficulty with relatively simple matters like obscenity and political fair practice. And, by some legerdemain of public relations, these free speech arguments are carried over to thwart every effort to deal with such purely commercial matters as the frequency of advertising.

Over the years, valiant individual commissioners from time to time have cited poor programming and demanded improvement, offered tangible reforms such as formulas for the allocation of prime time to public service, and even suggested that maybe the government ought to share in the vast profits being derived from the "public air." In every significant test, however, the broadcasters' interest has prevailed. On the few occasions when the FCC as a whole has stiffened its neck, the station owners, network proprietors, and their fuglemen in the advertising industry have had no difficulty in persuading Congress to override.

There can be no doubt that great financial resources, plus the celebrity-making power of the medium, contribute to the broadcasters' ability to checkmate every Washington effort to correct their most evident abuses. But, unlike the other special interests that seek support and/or immunity from Washington, broadcasting enjoys another overwhelming advantage that so far has made it impossible to muster any effective force for governmental reform—the stubborn, democratic fact that the great majority of viewers like their television the way it is.

It follows that complaints about television come only from the minority whose tastes are not accommodated by the level maintained for commercial programming. Now that the novelty of the home screen has worn off, most of these appear to have turned back to newspapers, periodicals, films, recordings, and performing arts designed to meet more sophisticated demands. The Harris poll has recorded the result: "TV appears to be losing its audience among adults who have been to college, whose incomes are $10,000 or over, and among suburban residents." This seems to mean in practice that the influential Americans who have been intellectually disfranchised by the new electronic service have accepted their fate, and no longer provide an effective constituency for those who insist that there is a critical issue here that goes beyond satisfying a given level of public taste. Ideally we have thought of the mass media as bridging the gap between educated elite and general public, and have seen this as a unifying process defining and promoting areas of common good. The ideal hardly can be served under a dispensation that presumes a permanent cleavage of the television audience.

This is an issue, unfortunately, which has not been faced by those responsible for an otherwise hopeful entry in the badly neglected area of noncommercial broadcasting—the Carnegie Corporation's look at the cultural, informational, and educational void left by privately owned television. This is the domain presumed to be covered by channels reserved for educational or community broadcasting. Some one hundred of these ETV stations are now on the air, but almost all operate as undernourished charities, dependent on freewill offerings and a trickle of tax money earned as transmitter for prefabricated classroom instruction. Reluctant to go the whole way, as Great Britain and other European countries have done, and provide a tax subsidy for noncommercial TV, we have created a set of fiscal orphans loosely linked by a feeble foundation-financed cooperative program service. These stations are fully protected by law against the corrupting influence of advertising revenue, but they are also effectively denied any other fixed source of income. The result has been programming of such erratic quality that it has nowhere acquired a substantial, sustained following.

Late in 1965 the Carnegie Corporation underwrote an eighteen-months' study by the National Commission on Educational Television. This private agency was formally charged by President Johnson with bringing forth "a recommendation on not

246

only the facilities and finances of educational television, but also the manpower and organization." Chairman E. William Henry of the FCC pledged his full support, and pointedly observed that "federal funds are a possibility." Finally, as a presumed guarantee of continued presidential interest, a conspicuous member of the Commission was J. C. Kellam, president of the Johnson family's Texas Broadcasting Corporation.[4]

Jack Gould of *The New York Times* has pointed to the hazard in thus isolating the noncommercial stations as a special service and treating them as somehow separate from the mainstream of broadcasting: "The worst fate that could befall American television would be to have educational television turn into a lightning rod to draw away minority complaints against the practices and productions of commercial broadcasters." The fear is not an abstract one; there is good reason to believe that this is precisely the role many commercial broadcasters visualize for ETV. Mr. Gould has revealed how at least one network passed the word to Channel 13, New York's struggling ETV station, that it would withdraw its handsome annual contribution unless the station stuck to "educational" as opposed to "popular" subjects—that is, put nothing on the air that would effectively compete with commercial TV for audience attention. And the Georgia Association of Broadcasters publicly brought pressure against the University of Georgia when an affiliated educational station scheduled an old Gina Lollobrigida movie as part of an art film series.

* * *

For diametrically opposed reasons, every effort to bring government authority effectively to bear on broadcasting has failed in the United States—even when the effort has been as wide of

[4] Other members of the Commission: *Chairman:* James R. Killian, Jr., chairman of the corporation, Massachusetts Institute of Technology; James B. Conant, former president of Harvard; Lee A. DuBridge, president, California Institute of Technology; Ralph Ellison, author; John Hayes, president, Washington *Post-Newsweek* broadcasting stations; David Henry, president, University of Illinois; Mrs. Oveta Culp Hobby, president, Houston *Post*; Edwin Land, president, Polaroid Corporation; Joseph H. McConnell, president, Reynolds Metals, and former president of the National Broadcasting Company; Terry Sanford, former governor of North Carolina; Rudolf Serkin, pianist; and Leonard Woodcock, vice-president, United Automobile Workers.

First Amendment proscriptions against censorship as the effort to prevent stations from turning up the volume during commercials. Hal Humphrey of the Los Angeles *Times* has recounted the dismal history of organized public efforts to save quality programs when their audience ratings fell below an arbitrary number on the Nielsen scale. After failing to impress the networks with a barrage of thousands of letters, these mail campaigns have been directed at the FCC with similar lack of result. Humphrey cites a particularly flagrant case:

"Baskets of mail from irate Los Angeles viewers landed before FCC commissioners after a local hothead with a 'hate-talk' show on Channel 11 displayed a gun on camera during the Watts riot. It was an inflammatory act and the most crass kind of irresponsibility. But the august FCC, which said it was 'particularly concerned' with that show, still managed to give Channel 11 an unqualified three-year renewal of its license, and with no recommendation for changing its programming. . . .

"If the FCC commissioners are protecting the public interest here, they prove it in strange ways. The FCC is supposedly not functioning on the basis of a Nielsen rating, as the networks do, but apparently it has little regard for the voice of the people when a large commercial TV channel (part of the Metromedia chain in this case) is involved. . . . What can the parent-teacher groups and other concerned organizations do to impress networks and the FCC, if the latter won't read their mail?"

Yet the coin does have another side, and the thought of what might happen if government did undertake affirmative intervention in television programming still tends to bring down the blood pressure of libertarians outraged by the sins committed under the presumed shelter of the First Amendment. Ever since Franklin Roosevelt discovered that a radio fireside chat enabled him to go directly to the people and short-circuit the dissident voices of the press, broadcasting has become an increasingly important tool in the hands of politicians. Lyndon Johnson's relentless exploitation of the media has led Ben H. Bagdikian to complain in *Columbia Journalism Review* that the President practices "common, ordinary press agentry." When such an effort is combined with the weight of high public office there is a real threat to Thomas Jeffer-

248

son's free marketplace of ideas. Here is the testimony of Fred Friendly, then of CBS, on the aftermath of his network's critical coverage of some aspects of the war in Vietnam:

"I found myself days later under the fingers of two of the highest men in government, being lectured about, 'Did I not think about what was right for the United States?' . . . As the power and strength of broadcast journalism increases, the desire of people to use and manage and ever so delicately control you increases and increases and increases."

Mr. Friendly's complaint can be regarded as another measure of the shifting locus of power in the communications industry. Many an editor has felt the manipulating finger of officialdom, but if he chose to resist he had not only the First Amendment but an honored tradition of independence to sustain him. A broadcaster in similar straits is not likely to forget that he is dependent upon a renewable government license,[5] and the dominant tradition in his depersonalized industry is that the customer is always right. Moreover, the news and public-affairs side of broadcasting is under special internal pressure because, despite the lucrative return from regular newscasts, this is the only form of broadcasting that operates at a net loss. "Networks can't make news pay, even when the regular programs are sold out to sponsors," says Jesse Zousmer, director of ABC's news division. All of this adds up to a high degree of vulnerability when a television newsman goes up against a President who, as Joseph Alsop has said of Mr. Johnson, has undertaken "attempts at news control . . . so much more aggressive, comprehensive, and, one must add, repugnant to American tradition, than any such attempts by other Presidents."

Aside from the unresolved constitutional questions inherent in the relationship between government and the communications media, the problems raised here cut straight through to the fundamental issues of our time. Free speech, with its inescapable corollary of free communications, provides a far more significant distinction between West and East than the economic differences that have survived extensive renovation of capitalist and Com-

[5] In *Trial by Battle*, Edward Lamb recounts in detail his long and expensive personal fight during the McCarthy era to end the political manipulation of FCC powers intended to deny him valuable broadcasting licenses.

munist theory and practice. An independent source of criticism and untrammeled creative endeavor is essential to a pluralist society, as it is anathema to a collective, unitary society. Thus, even in the face of extreme provocation, only the most desperate of those who have been conditioned by the Western tradition are disposed to join in the cry of young Mr. Al-Gailani of Iraq: "One thing surely must be done about the American press and American TV and American movies. They must be censored! They must be controlled by the government!"

* * *

This is the ultimate reason, I suggest, that those who set themselves up as critics of the media tend to go around in worn circles. The dilemma was defined in the most ambitious and competent analysis of these issues I know, an analysis undertaken twenty years ago by the Commission on Freedom of the Press, chaired by Robert M. Hutchins, then Chancellor of the University of Chicago. The Commission concluded that while the government could not, and should not, act in the critical area that borders on censorship, the public could not continue to rely on the media to set their own standards and police their own performance. The proposed answer was the establishment of an independent agency, without powers of legal enforcement but armed with great prestige, to appraise and report annually on the performance of mass communication—in those pre-TV days defined to include newspapers, radio, motion pictures, magazines, and books.[6]

The Commission's report, published under the title *A Free and Responsible Press*, was greeted by a storm of protest from the media, and as a result its supporters failed to arouse enough financial aid to carry through its recommendations. Yet, almost everyone who thinks seriously about the state of our communications system in terms of the public interest sooner or later comes back to some version of the basic idea. Jack Gould, in his report on the Carnegie study of educational TV, concluded that "it is regrettable that the Carnegie Corporation did not go all-out and

[6] The Commission's membership, with the titles then held, and its principal recommendations are set forth in a Note to this article.

set up a National Commission on Television. Such a body could make periodic assessments of all forms of the medium, a variation of a British royal commission. . . ." And Hal Humphrey, putting a pox on both the broadcasters and the FCC, wrote in the Los Angeles *Times:*

> The late President Kennedy was talking about an arts and cultural committee of private citizens who could talk directly to people like TV presidents on their own level. This idea seems to have died with Kennedy, but something like it soon must be revived and fulminated before the public voice in the communications and arts fields is stifled forever. It takes an organized lobby in Washington to get your case heard. . . .

The Commission report did produce one not insignificant by-product. Its publication aroused an immediate response among the group of outstanding young journalists assembled at Harvard under the fellowship program of the Nieman Foundation. Louis Lyons, then curator of the Foundation, has recounted the initial reaction in the introduction to the anthology, *Reporting the News:*

> Responsible was the key word, and freedom and responsibility were linked: only a responsible press could remain free. Responsibility of the press is a concept introduced by the Hutchins Commission, or at least given currency by its report. The publishers who scoffed at it as an academic notion in 1947 have long since adopted it into their vocabulary. I am sure many of them think they invented it. It became at once the basic theme of *Nieman Reports*, and has threaded through the reviews, critiques, and articles occupying seventy-two issues.

For more than fifteen years the Nieman quarterly was the only genuinely critical voice consistently raised in appraisal of the performance of the press. Four years ago the Pulitzer School at Columbia University, acknowledging its debt to *Nieman Reports*, entered the field with its somewhat slicker *Journalism Review*, which pays a good deal more attention to broadcasting than does the heavily newspaper-oriented Harvard publication.

William Benton, who provided funds from his Encyclopaedia

Britannica, Inc. to insure publication of A *Free and Responsible Press*, has maintained an unshakable faith in the utility of a commission to assess the media. His conviction grows out of his experience as a leading advertising executive, and has been reinforced by public service as Assistant Secretary of State for Information, United States Senator, and Ambassador to UNESCO. On behalf of the Benton Foundation I have spent a good deal of time exploring the possibility of establishing the proposed critical agency in association with a university. In a circuit of the Ivy League, and excursions elsewhere, I have found a good deal of sympathy, but no tangible support. There are, of course, good conventional reasons why a university should be reluctant to join in such an unconventional enterprise. But perhaps more compelling is the understandable prudence of administrators who know that the undertaking is inherently controversial, and certain to involve powerful men who have the means to talk back in loud and penetrating voices. One weary university president told me sadly, "Of course it ought to be done, and I'll be glad to sit as an individual on such a commission. But I've just got too damned much trouble on my hands already to think of giving you house-room on this campus."

In *Reporting the News*, Louis Lyons comments on the negotiations with Harvard:

> Although our effort had been stimulated by the Hutchins Commission, we shied away from their proposal for a Commission on the Press. This proposal was kept alive and actively promoted down the years by William Benton and Harry Ashmore, both closely associated with Robert Hutchins. The practicality of this was under recurring discussion. I was never convinced. But beyond that, we resisted involvement in the implication of a board of review that would pass continuing judgment. We wanted a forum of open criticism and appraisal, but drew back from the establishment of a commission to render judgments. We were accused, of course, of doing just that; but so long as we had not presumed to do it, we could stand the accusation.
>
> But we kept the *Reports* open for descriptions of such commissions in Britain and Australia, which to be sure were quite different, and, it seemed to me, of little effect. We pub-

lished with interest a proposal of Arthur Sulzberger's for a "newspaper court" to deal with abuses of pre-trial publicity and the like. Barry Bingham was to suggest a local committee in Louisville for appraisal of the press. . . . But these were very limited applications of the Hutchins idea, as of course was *Nieman Reports* itself.

I have never understood why the idea of collective judgment regularly rendered has aroused so much apprehension among those who agree that stringent criticism of the media is very much in order and, as in the case of Louis Lyons, have long since demonstrated their own courage and integrity. The proposed Commission would have no power to censor, only to expose, complain, praise, and exhort—to perform, that is, on behalf of the mass media the functions the media presume to perform on behalf of all other institutions colored in any way with the public interest. The formal trappings of the Commission, including an annual report, would be intended only to give it sufficient prestige to meet powerful adversaries on fairly equal terms, and guarantee that its findings could not simply be ignored—as, for example, most of the well-intentioned critiques of *Nieman Reports* have been.

It has always seemed to me that the unseemly reaction of the media to the original Hutchins Commission in itself provided a compelling argument on behalf of the proposal. Many publishers and broadcasters uttered outraged protests against "official" intervention in the free press, when, of course, the proposal is the precise reverse of this. There was the equally preposterous argument that the members of the Commission were disqualified because they were not professional journalists—a complaint that not only implied that such distinguished and broadly experienced men were incapable of judging the quality of what they read, see, and hear, but ignored the fact that the Commission was supported by a professional staff and in the course of its deliberations had spent many hours discussing the special problems of the media with leading proprietors and practitioners.

Indeed, the professional associations themselves have long provided the best evidence to support the Commission's premise that effective criticism can only come from those who are outside

253

the media's immediate orbit, and wholly independent of it. I was
a member of the American Society of Newspaper Editors when
A *Free and Responsible Press* was published, and saw the august
membership huddle rumps together, horns out, in the immemorial
manner of, say, the National Association of Manufacturers faced
by a threat of regulated prices. When, in the ASNE *Bulletin*,
I suggested that there might be some merit in the Commission
report I was roundly denounced for fouling my own nest. We had
reached a point where you couldn't tell the ASNE from the
American Newspaper Publishers Association without a program.

This blind reaction to the Hutchins Commission served to
reduce the Commission's proposal to a sort of shibboleth; the
test of loyalty was to denounce it out of hand, and in a curious
way it became the special target of sensitive and frustrated men
who privately recognize the media's grave deficiencies but feel
constrained publicly to deny their existence. The experience of
the past twenty years provides ample evidence to refute the spe-
cious arguments of the early days. Even those who still contend
that the media are doing the best they can rarely argue that the
best is good enough. With the entry of the great, bland behemoth
of television the stultifying tendencies cited by the Commission
have been accentuated; with three giant broadcasting corporations
dominating the bulk of the programming available to Americans, the existence of centralized control, conformity, and vulgarization of public taste has become inescapably self-evident.
We are confronted by a communications system that already
comes very close to providing a circus to accompany the bread
promised to all by the Great Society.

The pursuit of excellence has become a fashionable undertaking, or at least a fashionable phrase. But in a modern society
no man can pursue excellence undeterred and uninfluenced by the
image-building, taste-setting, attention-diverting system of communications that reaches out to him wherever he may be. In
making the case for the Commission to the universities I have
argued that academic self-interest does not deny but rather demands concern and support; teachers have access to their students' minds for only a few hours out of a lifetime, but the
media reach them always and forever; and the values and stand-

254

ards of *academe* cannot long stand inviolate if they are at odds with those that prevail in the marketplace.

No one has ever argued that there is a perfect solution to an issue that is not only critical in its own right but symbolizes, and in a sense summarizes, those that now divide the world. The flyleaf of *A Free and Responsible Press* bears this quotation from John Adams, dated 1815:

> If there is ever to be an amelioration of the condition of mankind, philosophers, theologians, legislators, politicians and moralists will find that the regulation of the press is the most difficult, dangerous and important problem they have to resolve. Mankind cannot now be governed without it, nor at present with it.

The problem has not been resolved, and I do not believe the most sanguine philosophers, theologians, legislators, politicians, and moralists can argue that it has become less urgent. It is in this light that the proposal for a Commission on the mass media deserves the serious consideration it has never had. At the very least it stands as an inescapable challenge to all those who profess concern with the low state of the media along with devotion to the tradition of the free and independent press. I have heard much argument that this is a good idea whose time has not yet come, but I have seen no evidence that this is so, and heard of no alternative.

NOTE

The Commission on Freedom of the Press

In December, 1942, Henry R. Luce of Time, Inc., suggested to Robert M. Hutchins, then Chancellor of the University of Chicago, "an inquiry into the present state and future prospects of the freedom of the press." A year later, the Commission on Freedom of the Press, whose members were named by Mr. Hutchins, began its deliberations, supported by grants of $200,-000 from Time, Inc., and $15,000 from Encyclopaedia Britannica, Inc. The summary report, *A Free and Responsible Press*, was published by the University of Chicago Press in 1947.

255

The members of the Commission were: *Chairman,* Robert
M. Hutchins; *Vice-Chairmen,* Zechariah Chafee, Jr., professor of
law, Harvard University; John M. Clark, professor of economics,
Columbia University; John Dickinson, professor of law, University of Pennsylvania, and general counsel, Pennsylvania Railroad;
William E. Hocking, professor of philosophy, emeritus, Harvard
University; Harold D. Lasswell, professor of law, Yale University; Archibald MacLeish, formerly Assistant Secretary of State;
Charles E. Merriam, professor of political science, emeritus,
University of Chicago; Reinhold Niebuhr, professor of ethics and
philosophy of religion, Union Theological Seminary; Robert
Redfield, professor of anthropology, University of Chicago; Beardsley Ruml, chairman, Federal Reserve Bank of New York; Arthur
M. Schlesinger, professor of history, Harvard University; and
George N. Shuster, president, Hunter College.

Foreign Advisers were: John Grierson, former general manager, Wartime Information Board, Canada; Hu Shih, former Chinese Ambassador to the United States; Jacques Maritain, president,
Free French School for Advanced Studies; and Kurt Riezler, professor of philosophy, New School for Social Research.

The recommendation for a continuing Commission was summarized in ten points set forth in A *Free and Responsible Press:*
*We recommend the establishment of a new and independent
agency to appraise and report annually upon the performance of
the press.*

The public makes itself felt by the press at the present time
chiefly through pressure groups. These groups are quite as likely
to have bad influence as good. In this field we cannot turn to government as the representative of the people as a whole, and we
would not do so if we could. Yet it seems clear to us that some
agency which reflects the ambitions of the American people for its
press should exist for the purpose of comparing the accomplishments of the press with the aspirations which the people have
for it. Such an agency would also educate the people as to the aspirations which they ought to have for the press.

The Commission suggests that such a body be independent of
government and of the press; that it be created by gifts; and that

it be given a ten-year trial, at the end of which an audit of its achievement could determine anew the institutional form best adapted to its purposes.

The activities of such an agency would include:

1. Continuing efforts, through conference with practitioners and analysis by its staff, to help the press define workable standards of performance, a task on which our Commission has attempted a beginning.

2. Pointing out the inadequacy of press service in certain areas and the trend toward concentration in others, to the end that local communities and the press itself may organize to supply service where it is lacking or to provide alternative service where the drift toward monopoly seems dangerous.

3. Inquiries in areas where minority groups are excluded from reasonable access to the channels of communication.

4. Inquiries abroad regarding the picture of American life presented by the American press; and cooperation with agencies in other countries and with international agencies engaged in analysis of communication across national borders.

5. Investigation of instances of press lying, with particular reference to persistent misrepresentation of the data required for judging public issues.

6. Periodic appraisal of the tendencies and characteristics of the various branches of the communications industry.

7. Continuous appraisal of governmental action affecting communications.

8. Encouragement of the establishment of centers of advanced study, research, and criticism in the field of communications at universities.

9. Encouragement of projects which give hope of meeting the needs of special audiences.

10. The widest possible publicity and public discussion on all the foregoing.

XVIII.

What's New, Copycat? *

HUBBELL ROBINSON

A former CBS-TV programming vice-president, Hubbell Robinson was responsible for the development of the *Playhouse 90* series. He is an executive producer at ABC-TV.

∿∿∿∿∿∿∿∿∿∿∿∿∿∿∿∿∿∿∿∿∿∿∿∿∿∿∿

TELEVISION HAS A COMPULSIVE tendency to live off its own fat. The fact that copies of the copies often choke to death on their fraudulence seems to have set few warning lights flashing among the people who concoct them. Television, of course, has no monopoly on this form of self-imitation. In most of the other arts, too, imagination is handmaiden to economics. In the theater, comedy and musicals are the name of the game. During the 1965 season, some fifteen serious plays attempted to make it on Broadway. All failed. Comedies, to pay off, must almost by rote repeat the pattern of a small cast and only one set. Musicals are inevitably adaptations of books or transformed straight plays. In recent years, only *West Side Story* has been able to separate the words "original" and "anathema."

Time, commenting on the theater in 1965, said, "Broadway continued to be beset by urban blight. Part of what was wrong was the audience itself—too old, too prosperous, too complacent to be bothered about the basics of the human condition. These playgoers and, to a degree, the daily New York critics who reflect their likes and dislikes, demand beddy-bye stories for grown-ups—The Theater of Reassurance."

The movies, too, extend the pattern of imitation. They ap-

* Based on an article from *Diplomat,* April 1966, pp. 28, 30 and a speech delivered to the Speech Institute of America in December 1966, by permission of the author.

258

pear dedicated to making what works, work again, retooled as little as possible. The most insistent echo is the relentless attempt to ring variations on James Bond and his spy activities. One of them, *The Tenth Victim*, at least has a scene which seems likely to be a conversation piece of considerable durability. In it, Ursula Andress, a very grown-up sex kitten with claws—and almost everything else in overpowering abundance—shoots a man with two guns concealed in her bra. It's the booby trap of the season.

In still another field of creative effort which speaks to a mass audience—the novel—things are pretty dark out, too. In spite of occasional sparkling performance by John Updike, Mary McCarthy, James Gould Cozzens, Bernard Malamud, Saul Bellow, J. D. Salinger, Katherine Anne Porter, and a few others, the plain fact seems to be that no giant has exploded on the American literary scene with massive and sustained achievement. And the Europeans aren't doing any better. The practitioners of the *"nouvelle nouveau"* are giving it the old Left Bank try. They're original, and that's about where it ends. These concoctions without plot, no discernibly identifiable characters, no beginning, middle, or end, don't appear to be taking the French or anyone else by storm. Two of the cult's leading luminaries recently philosophized about their work. Mme. Nathalie Sarraute described hers as "a new unanism." M. Robbe-Grillet said, "A writer is someone who has nothing to say." This may be pretty saucy stuff in the Beauvoir-Sartre set, but it's not calculated to gladden the hearts of the Messrs. Brentano, Doubleday, and Rizzoli, or send the customers into their stores.

Television's capacity to break through the fog of kitsch which envelops so many of the arts today would seem to be minimal. With its eighteenth season as a major entertainment medium, it is beginning to show unmistakable signs of ennui, fatigue, and creative wear and tear. In the past few years ABC has emerged as a full-fledged contender with CBS and NBC for the home audience's favor. It seems proper to question whether there is enough producing, directing, or writing talent to support that much television. Each network must fill approximately twenty-five hours of evening programming time per week. Actually it's more than that, since many of the hours are split into half-hours. On balance,

259

that means something in excess of 100 shows a week. If the U.S.A.'s total talent pool was available to TV, that would be a staggering assignment. Obviously, it isn't. Only those talents not involved with theater and feature motion pictures are available. It means that at least a third of those laboring in the television vineyards are not talents at all. They are just bodies. It has reduced much of television from an art to a craft, a skill. Any week of steady viewing proves the point with horrendous finality.

Time and money also mitigate against television's chances to emerge from the swamps of mediocrity. Most television hour series operate on weekly budgets in the vicinity of $130,000 exclusive of color. Each picture has a six- or seven-day shooting schedule. Even with continuing characters, a locale, and a running theme or "idea" on which one has only to ring infinite variations, it takes rare gifts to turn out entertainment as satisfying as that possible with a movie budget of $1,000,000 or better, plus a shooting schedule of at least six weeks. More money essentially means more time; more time to improve scripts, more time for principal photography, more time to make each scene better, more time for cutting and editing. It is the reason television "specials," when they have a good idea in the hands of good people, are frequently better than the weekly serials. It is the reason the network "Movie Nights" do well. They seldom draw audiences as big as the top weekly series, but they never do as badly as the series conceived and executed by the short-order cooks of TV's shantytowns. An ancient show-business wheeze reads, "Do you want it quick or do you want it good?" Television rarely has that choice. "Quick" is where the money is, and "quick" is the answer.

Movies and specials obviously can never solve television's programming problems. There aren't enough old movies still unseen. They can't make new ones fast enough to meet the demands. The ideas and people to make "specials" truly special are getting harder and harder to come by. Further answers will have to be forthcoming from the creators and buyers operating in all the other areas of evening television. Before they can move toward solutions, they must indicate some awareness, some acknowledgment that a problem exists; that there is a public which may be reached and moved by programming whose content has more

260

bristle, salt, and contention than that which now consumes all the entertainment time on the networks; that, given sufficient preparation time and the right combination of creative skill, such programming might capture enough audience to pay its own way; that, even if it didn't, the gamble is necessary to the medium's intellectual and creative self-respect; that, if the gamble doesn't work, an occasional proud failure is as worthy as endless mediocre success.

With one or two exceptions this observer is aware of no dialogue, monologue or murmur among the industry's movers and shakers suggesting any such restlessness, any seeking for anything that departs from the formula boilerplate that is our nightly diet. All else continues as usual, and "usual" would appear to be for the most part the product of minds subscribing without question to Pope's dubiously optimistic assurance that "One truth is clear. Whatever is, is right," or to Jeremy Bentham, who synonymized pleasure with profit as an absolute.

Jack Gould of the *New York Times*, Richard K. Doan of *TV Guide*, and John Horn, formerly of the New York *Herald Tribune* are leading practitioners of television criticism. One may quarrel violently with their individual judgments of individual programs, but it seems to me that even if you disagree with what they think, they are thoughtful, articulate, quick to praise the medium's accomplishments and relentless in damning its gaffes. The titles of three of their recent harangues are "Children's Hour, or This Year on Television" by Jack Gould; "Is TV Too Big To Be Hurt by People?" by Richard K. Doan; and "The Wasteland Grows Vaster" by John Horn. In each of these pieces the writers flail away at TV's absorption with triviality; and even within that framework they score its repetitiveness, its limited appetite for adventure, its endless resort to formula rather than to inventiveness. In their view, television is like the Bourbons, who remembered everything and learned nothing.

It is all well and good to have such journalistic surrogates of the public trust hacking away in a good cause. But nothing much is likely to change unless there is what the athletes call "desire" at the top, at those levels where program goals are imagined, crystallized, and implemented. That's where TV's past and present

261

were and are determined—where its future will be modeled. Practically, of course, this means the networks. This is the heartland where the conceiving and shaping must be done. It is the fulcrum where all TV's multiple and manifold interests fuse. Until the top-level decision makers develop a zeal for mixing pride with popularity, the answer to "What's new, copycat?" is likely to continue to be a plaintive "Nothing."

XIX.

What's Bad for TV Is Worse for Advertising*

FAIRFAX M. CONE

Chairman of the executive committee of Foote, Cone & Belding, Fairfax M. Cone has been in advertising since the mid-thirties. He is also chairman of the board of trustees of the University of Chicago.

~~~~~~

TELEVISION HAS GROWN big and rich and flabby.

Some of my best friends are in the broadcasting business, and while I wish them well, I am also distressed at what I perceive to be television's uneven success. Never have profits been better for the operators and never has the product of television, which is programming, shown less imagination or less promise. During television's twenty years, entertainment, which is the principal element in programming, has rarely been explored beneath the surface of old vaudeville routines and motion-picture forms. And only the prospect of repeating all of last year's monotonous attempts at amusement could be more dismal than the prospects for entertainment in the upcoming season.

Gone entirely is the old excitement about great new things to come. (They rarely materialized. But that isn't the point.) The satisfaction of the majority of broadcasters with things as they are is clear. My friends in broadcasting have cast their lot with mediocrity.

It is no wonder, I think, that serious critics call this a dark outlook. And while I would like to be concerned with it as they are,

* Reprinted from *Fortune*, July 1965, pp. 102, 252-4, by permission of the author and the publisher.

263

wistfully, on purely artistic and intellectual terms, there is another side to the matter that I cannot overlook.

This is the conviction on the part of almost all viewers that there is nothing wrong with television that can't be blamed on advertising. As a result, criticism of advertising grows louder and it is more persistent than any other complaint about current business practice. Television is seen as the helpless victim of advertisers' cupidity. It is the advertisers, most people believe, who initiate all program changes; and who but the advertisers, they ask, are the perpetrators of those ghastly commercials?

To suggest that such questions may be a soothing accompaniment to the march of the broadcasters to the vaults is simply to point out the obvious. Advertising is a ready scapegoat. But advertisers must accept half the blame and most of the consequences. Advertising and television are tightly interwoven.

* * *

When Newton Minow, as chairman of the Federal Communications Commission, called television "a vast wasteland" several years ago, this caused some brief consternation in both industries, in advertising and broadcasting. But Minow went back to his private law practice and the hubbub subsided.

Since then questions of any kind about the makeup and the level of entertainment schedules have simply been ignored. Only a few independent station owners and operators appear to be concerned. For the rest, questions about programming are invariably shut off by referring to the audience measurements. The public, it is said, is the sole arbiter of what it shall see and hear: the program schedules are determined by tune-in and tune-out as calculated in the Nielsen Television Index. This, I must admit, is true. The trouble is that audience ratings are based entirely on the programs that are available. They suggest little or nothing about the interests or wishes of nonviewers of the material surveyed.

Acceptance of television advertising by the general public is measured by a similarly defective standard. When people are asked whether the showing of commercials is a fair price to pay for the privilege of watching television, they reply in the affirma-

264

tive in the ratio of four to one. However, this scarcely means approval of television advertising *in toto*.

Roper Research Associates recently completed a study for the Television Information Office in which a large sample of the public was asked: "Which one of these four statements comes closest to describing how you feel about commercials on television?" Each person was then shown a card that listed the four choices corresponding to the attitude range. These are the results from the total sample:

I dislike practically all commercials on television	10%
While some of the commercials on television are all right, most of them are very annoying	26%
There are some very annoying commercials on television, but most of them are perfectly all right	35%
The commercials on television seldom annoy me—in fact, I often enjoy them	23%
Don't know or no answer	6%

While this study can be read to say that favorable attitudes toward TV advertising outstripped unfavorable attitudes by three to two (and this is exactly what the Television Information Office does say), the answers may also be interpreted to mean that seven out of ten people find at least some commercials objectionable. The reasons given for these objections are "too noisy and loud," "many are done in poor taste," and "there are far too many commercials." The study indicates also that while it is agreed that commercials "frequently provide useful information about new products," they "often advertise things that should not be advertised." Altogether, then, it would seem that a considerable part of the U.S. viewing public finds fault with TV advertising on several grounds. This is too bad.

There are unmistakable indications that among college and university students rejection of all advertising is growing; and, of course, there is a great deal of evidence that this is encouraged by teachers. But too few television officials and television advertisers give any evidence of being alert to the hazard involved. If they did, one of the first things they would do would be to outlaw the ubiquitous weasel. The weasel is the flaw in the advertising proposition that makes its promise fuzzy. For instance: *BBB tires are the largest selling tires in the world with their exclusive non-skid tread that gets you there safely in all kinds of weather.* This seems to say that BBB tires have overtaken all other similar tires in popularity and in use. But does it? It does not. It merely says that these tires are the only tires with their own particular tread; so, of course, they are the largest selling in this category. The weasel rests on a slippery claim that is technically correct, and it is a favorite device of foxy TV advertisers.

Another of the indefensible practices of advertising on television is the high level of sound that makes many commercials much louder than the programs in which they are carried. Perhaps even more unpleasant and unnecessary is the quarrelsome nature of so many commercials for headache and stomachache remedies and deodorants and detergents wherein various competitors virtually accuse each other of lying. Denigration is something that surely should be barred from the air.

The greatest offense by television advertising just now, however, is the nonsense with which it is concerned. The only real purpose of advertising is to bring sensible proposals to large numbers of people. And while black eyes suffered in defense of a smoker's choice of cigarettes may call attention to a brand, it is hardly a convincing bit of business. At present, advertising is full of such conceits, and not all are as easily dismissed. While most such indulgences are harmless in themselves, this is not a good excuse. Advertising, by television or otherwise, was invented to present news about products, or to be a pleasant reminder. When it fails in either of these assignments it has little to recommend it to anyone. Furthermore, the end result of massive advertising campaigns based on exaggeration could conceivably be hazardous far beyond the limits of television.

The danger lies in the invitation to the public to be indifferent to advertising. If this were to become widespread, as well it may, the result could be that for a period of time, perhaps years, many products would be bought on experience or word of mouth alone. This would be a huge penalty for business to pay for its apathy in the face of peril, and television would have to look desperately (and probably in the direction of Washington) for support. The economy in which we live, and which most of us would like to maintain, cannot function successfully without advertising. It helps us to choose, and we must be able to do this with confidence. Otherwise advertising will be of no value, and U.S. business will have lost its unique sales tool.

Before the intrusion of radio and television into most of our lives there was more than a little outrage at the ethics of advertising as practiced by makers of patent medicine and vendors of questionable goods and services by mail. *Caveat emptor* as an acceptable policy in business was beginning to be disputed, and several agencies of the government, together with the postal authorities, were actively engaged in running down frauds.

Moreover, the growth of national manufacturers and distributors had from the beginning the requirement that customers be satisfied. The chain store was also an important factor. For all these businesses depended upon the good will of the ultimate consumer. Most products introduced through the supermarket system today are planned for a two- or three-year payout, and this can be accomplished only if a growing number of purchasers become steady customers. This is a fact that is sometimes overlooked by critics of both advertising and marketing. It is advertising that makes the first offer and the initial sale. After that the fate of every product lies in its own performance. No one has yet discovered an advertising mechanism or technique that is more powerful than an unhappy experience. So customer satisfaction is, in effect, part of the guarantee of advertising.

While fraud had been largely eliminated from manufacturers' advertising in all media, television developed brand-new areas of dissatisfaction, as we have noted. Almost all viewers of television who view it with anything less than complete devotion blame advertising for their discontent. They are all aware of the inexorability of the Nielsen averages, and they blame advertising not only for what television does that they object to, but also for what television doesn't do that they want it to. They hold advertisers responsible for the dreadfully low standards of the most popular programs and they hold them accountable for the dearth of art and intellectuality on the new color tubes.

This is on the program side. And it follows that the same crit-

267

ics object vigorously to what they consider to be a carefully calculated commercial exploitation of a struggling captive audience.
It isn't only that the pauses for commercials in most TV programs come at exasperating intervals; or that certain messages
seem interminable. While it is doubtful that the average television viewer is unduly concerned with matters of taste (if he were
he could hardly qualify as an average viewer), he can be insulted,
and his wife, if she is an average viewer, too, can think, and may
very well think, that an awful lot of TV advertising is pretty silly.

Anyway, the chief reason why television advertising arouses
such acid indigestion is its utter inescapability. A dull or unbe-
coming or unpleasant advertisement in a magazine or newspaper
can be dismissed with the quick turning of a page. Unattractive
television advertising is impossible to avoid. The result is that a
large part of television advertising refers cunningly to just those
products that most people find it easy to disregard in print. Understandably, this causes some viewers acute discomfort.

This is not to say that such advertising is likely to be unproductive. On the contrary, it is apt to be extremely successful. It
gets through apathy and ennui. Dull repetition and ugly muta-
tions notwithstanding, it can pay out handsomely. To expect
television to conform to any other purpose would be to ignore a
basic fact. Television is a moneymaking institution; and the institution is doing very well. Nevertheless, the moguls have been
known to make changes, however reluctantly.

What is most disappointing to someone who has no wish at
all to deprive the majority of their choice in entertainment is that
there is so little attempt made to exploit the full potential of the
medium. Only the documentaries cross the soporific line in regularly scheduled mid-evening programs. And these, of course, are
not entertainment; for the most part they are treatises in words
and moving pictures. However well they are done, they do little
to fill the entertainment void.

The principal difficulty both for networks and stations in
satisfying me and other wishful viewers with experimental programming lies in what the broadcast people believe to be their
own rigorous competitive position. If they lose audience, they
face the loss of advertisers, for the advertisers themselves are in

fierce competition; everybody in the business wants to be on top. In the early days of television the advertisers participated in almost all programming, continuing a practice that began with radio broadcasting. The television industry embraced this participation at the outset to help share the financial risks. But as television found its audience, the risks disappeared, and the networks and stations reasserted control over programming. Today the advertisers' participation in programming is almost nil. But their shadow looms menacingly. Probably the strangest suggestion made to date to meet the current criticism of programming is attributed to former FCC Chairman E. William Henry. The Commission had urged that 50 percent of programming be turned over to the advertisers and their agencies. Certainly this would be a backward step. The influence some advertisers and their agencies even now exert is largely responsible for the present sad state of affairs.

* * *

I suggest that we can live with the economic realities and at the same time achieve a reasonable increase in intellectual and experimental programming under a plan that has come to be known as "the magazine approach" to television programming and advertising. When an advertiser contracts for a schedule in a magazine he knows that his copy will appear in certain issues— but where in these issues is not a consideration (except for a few premium positions such as the back and inside covers). Over succeeding issues his advertisements are rotated through the magazine's various features from the first page to the last.

The same procedure could be applied to television's prime time. There are no premium positions in television; within specified hours all time periods are priced alike. So, in a matter of thirteen weeks, which is a typical television-contract multiple, a weekly advertiser might cover as many as thirteen different sets of viewers. If one of these, or perhaps two, were decidedly smaller than average because the network was experimenting or because it had scheduled an unusually selective subject, I think the problem of the low ratings could be offset somewhat by the attraction of new audiences.

Peak-time viewing turns up about 60 percent of U.S. television sets, and over the season in most areas this is divided pretty evenly in the course of a week among the three networks. Without doubt, any substitute for the conventional television diet in any prime-time segment would result in a loss of habitual viewers. However, I believe there is a compensating factor in the 40 percent of families who are *not* tuned in to any station during the average nighttime period. But let us not be concerned now with the number. Rather let us consider that here every night is a group of men and women not usually attracted by formula television, but certainly important to the success of any large sales objective (even for aspirin). If television can attract a fair number of them no more than twice a week, this will help solve its most pressing problem.

The argument that "magazine" scheduling is impossible in television is absurd. Right now, many advertisers place commercials in a collection of programs, instead of sponsoring single shows. There is no reason why the networks cannot direct the same kind of placement on an impartial basis in groups of programs (for example, comedy, variety, drama, children's, etc.). Applying this principle to program categories would preclude the placing of advertisements in entirely inappropriate places. So powerful a medium is television that such a plan could only slightly reduce its effectiveness to the advertisers who pay the bill —and if this were reduced, it would be reduced by the same amount to each one. What seems more likely is that they would find themselves doing business profitably with a number of people who are now tuned out to all their messages.

So there *is* a way to make a place in the network schedules for some of the subjects of restricted interest and for experimentation with new talent and new ideas. This system might not settle every one of television's problems, but it would put some muscle where there is so much flab today.

XX.

National Jukebox or Educational Resource? *

HARRY J. SKORNIA

Harry J. Skornia is Professor of Radio and TV at the University of Illinois. He has served as a member of the Advisory Committee, New Educational Media, U.S. Office of Education. Among his many publications is *Television and Society*.

~~~~~~

ON DECEMBER 17, 1959, I testified before the Federal Communications Commission in hearings on the problems of radio and television network broadcasting. When I implied at that time that the FCC had been something less than generous to education, I was challenged. In the somewhat heated discussion that followed, I indicated that I did not believe that education was only one tenth as important to America as advertising. I thought it was more important. I would not be satisfied, I said, until education had at least as many and as fine facilities for broadcasting as commerce had. I even had the audacity to suggest that half of the Commission—or at least a certain number of the Commissioners —should be educators. This stand has gotten me into difficulty before and since; yet I reiterate my position. I feel that a nation that claims to be civilized and pretends to respect education will not find this position unreasonable.

I find completely contrary to logic and justice the necessity for a public educational group to buy, for over six million dollars, a public frequency for a New York City educational station. The original allocation of a single frequency to New York City—and

* Reprinted from *Audiovisual Instruction* (1964), pp. 223-8, by permission of the author and the publisher.

that in UHF—makes no more sense to me than it would to restrict New York schools to six acres of land for buildings.

With regard to education's rights in the electromagnetic spectrum, I am impressed with the past record of neither the FCC, the Congress, the trade press, nor industry. Many of the failures can, of course, be attributed to past policies and personnel. Present and future signs are more hopeful. Let us therefore examine with optimism a few philosophical and practical considerations of the problems we face. One I shall call the problem of *interaction;* the other I shall refer to as the need for *integration* of all the nation's radio and television services.

To clarify the problem of interaction, let me use as an analogy, alternating and direct current. The earliest type of electricity to find use in the United States was direct current—current which flowed in only one direction. The story of the patent and industrial battles between the DC (Edison) interests and the AC (Westinghouse) interests need not delay us here. Suffice it to say that DC soon proved to be ill-adapted to economical national distribution along long lines and cables in the United States. Even though huge investments had been made in DC, electricity was only half used until national conversion to AC was achieved. A new era in electrical power distribution was opened up with that decision.

I fear that in ETV and ITV [1] we have been concentrating on one-way flow—to the student. We have been concentrating on *teaching* rather than back-and-forth flow, dialogue, or *learning.* It is this interaction that we now need to pay more attention to. As you know, there are rating services that use push buttons to permit the viewer to register instantaneously his approval, disapproval, or other reactions to programs. This may provide a clue to the kind of interplay that might be possible in educational television.

The use of electromagnetic energy could, of course, have been two-way from the first. It would have cost more; it would have reduced the frequencies available for the one-way flow from what

[1] ETV is used here to denote educational television in the broad sense including adult education (and for the most part, broadcast) as opposed to instructional, or inschool, television (ITV).

we now call broadcaster to recipient; it would have been a different system; but it would have been possible. What we now call viewer or listener would then have been "participant." When faced with the alternatives of mass use and small-group or individual use of radio and television, mass use was chosen. These media were then defined as mass media. And generally we don't argue with this decision or even think that the other uses were equally possible. Yet we should, for education can never be a mass operation. Whatever the tools are, in education they need to be used individually.

The 1957 Canadian National Commission Study of Broadcasting (the Fowler Commission) challenges the mass concept. Listeners and viewers must be treated as individuals, not as a mass, we are told. The report goes on: "Packaging individuals for easy handling is a totalitarian device. It is this variety in the individual that gives our society its character and civilized life its richness."

The various British studies (Beveridge, Pilkington, etc.) agree. So do French, Italian, and German studies. Even the Soviet system, in an effort to keep flow going in both directions, emphasizes such programs as "Letters from Listeners" and "Letter and Answer."

Whereas in the United States we usually find broadcast officials and staff *speaking to* recipients who question their product, those of many other democratic systems stress *listening to* these voices of protest and inquiry. European stations have huge listener mail departments, for European viewers and listeners do feed back very much.

Communication in any true sense facilitates interaction, not only between broadcaster and recipient but among recipients. Communication facilitates interaction among individuals, between individuals and their leaders (not merely vice versa, which is totalitarian) and among the different institutions of society itself.

For centuries, education was dialogue. Abelard, Rousseau, and Mark Hopkins represent this tradition. Then came the book, ending the regime of dialogue and scholastic philosophy. But now, after 400 years of book domination which has caused some of us to confuse education and information, the electronic media make dialogue again possible.

Communications scholars, like Colin Cherry and Marshall McLuhan, recognize the need for dialogue. McLuhan states flatly: "AC electric circuits are basic dialogue forms."

"With the coming of electronic tools," he tells us, "the Western World has encountered the form of the dialogue in learning and teaching once more. . . ."

Teaching machines, with or without radio or TV, also illustrate dialogue. Although teaching machines have some mechanical features, as Dr. McLuhan notes, their basic feature is dialogue. Radar is also dialogue.

Jerome S. Bruner of Harvard has warned that the textbook, if read only, can produce "chronic somnambulism." The same is true of listening to and viewing TV. "The educator's job," Dr. Bruner tells us, "is to change the student's role from passive to active. Programmed instruction, for example, ends the passive plight of the reader. It requires a dialogue between the printed word and the beholder. . . ."

Is such interaction impossible in the applications of TV and radio? Everyone seems to know that two-way flow is essential, but no one in TV seems to be doing much about it. We keep asking only for more and bigger pumps to increase the one-way flow we already have.

One way to promote feedback, or at least to reduce the totalitarianism of heedless, monolithic, one-way flow, is to insist on more "smallness" as opposed to "bigness." It is well known that new ideas, or educational content, are better accepted and understood if, as early as possible, the recipient is brought into a discussion of them, given an opportunity to question freely, and permitted to make suggestions. The best education seems to involve a partnership between learner and teacher in easy communication, with neither individual deprived of the means to be heard.

Feedback and interaction are not only democratic. They are essential to democracy. They enable leaders and teachers to tap the strengths and ideas of the whole populace. Feedback makes

274

such leaders and teachers stronger than those in a dictatorship in which the channels run in one direction only.

I have a haunting fear that as we concentrate on carving up the spectrum for flow in one direction only, we are condemning the broadcast media to anachronistic, totalitarian uses which posterity will some day denounce. I think new approaches and techniques need to be devised. The public can't devise them; it is not properly organized for such action. Industry won't devise them; present one-way uses are too profitable.

Can we suggest solutions? I don't think we can until we recognize the problem and seek to identify its many aspects so that communications specialists and technicians who might contribute to its solution may join us in at least thinking about it. I do not believe that the new instruments we are discussing will be used fully until the problems of interaction, feedback, and flow from student or viewer to teacher or broadcaster are finally attacked and solved. Some devices exist in raw, undeveloped form to suggest the direction that certain studies of this problem may take. More attention to it is needed, however, if ITV and ETV both are not to indoctrinate instead of educate.

But the problem is indivisible. It goes beyond education and the educational uses of television and radio. It will not be solved by allowing occasional questions to be telephoned to the teacher. Dialogue and democratic dynamics involve interaction to a far greater degree; they call for an AC-TV system in this sense.

*   *   *

I referred earlier to the need for an *integrated* broadcast system for America. By this I mean a system that includes educational broadcasts of all levels and variants, commercial broadcasts and other possible variants such as toll-television, and a publicly owned and operated political and public-affairs network comparable in the print media to the government printing office. But these variants must all be controlled as a single unified system whose parts support rather than fight each other. The FCC grew out of commerce. We might ask whether an agency so conceived can coordinate, or be expanded or changed to coordinate, an in-

275

tegrated system for granting equality if not priority to education, or whether some drastic new concept involving a new regulatory home may not be necessary.

I do not believe that a sum of disunited parts, growing Topsy-like with no policy coordination, can add up to—in either education or commerce—the balanced communications structure this country needs. To replace this Topsy-like growth, some planning involving far more than education is necessary.

We are at a point where the very term *broadcasting* begins to limit our thinking. We need to think in terms of *narrow*-casting as well as *broad*casting. Are not narrow uses of the electronic media, which education sometimes requires, as valid an employment of the electronic spectrum as shotgun uses? Is there any law that says that all casting must be broad? Different kinds of education, of course, require different kinds of uses and techniques—from the widest to the narrowest. I foresee, then, an integrated system, perhaps no longer called "broadcasting." Such a system will be equally efficient in both directions—from people to leaders and students to teachers, as well as in the DC direction they are now restricted to.

I believe the essentially segregated system we now have, in which the educational system promotes certain values (thrift, peaceful solutions, rationality) while the commercial networks encourage their opposites (spending, violence as an acceptable solution to problems, deceptive advertising), is bad. I think that to separate in-school television from educational broadcasting is bad. I think to say that certain levels of schools shall have closed-circuit while others have open-circuit, is ill-considered. Are elementary schools any less entitled to frequency space than 50-kilowatt radio stations that offer little more than the phonograph records anybody can buy? I believe that any agonizing appraisal or reappraisal that includes education should include commercial broadcasting as well. Radio and television are unique. Their uses for all purposes are of sufficient social significance and power to require the utmost of care and planning, whether the label be education or commercial.

In the tug-of-war for educational frequencies—in which internecine warfare between and among the levels and kinds of education is forced by alleged shortages—facsimile, radio, lasers, and a score of other resources and developments are forgotten.

For the kind of coordination required to integrate these fragmented services, national leadership is necessary. In education generally, federal efforts have been necessary to break down the segregation of the races. It is unlikely that many of the "separate but equal" solutions—which are of course not equal at all—will solve the educational problems for which they are offered. Surely there are common goals towards which all the responsible minds in both education and broadcasting can march—goals consistent with the aims of public education and the public interest, not just the interests of the nation's advertisers and those who serve them.

There will of course be mutterings about socialism if commercial broadcasting is restricted to its proper role and resources. Many people still think, as Calvin Coolidge is quoted as saying, that the principal business of the United States is business. But if we are to find the proper role of educational broadcasting—and the proper balance and function of its parts—we must break new ground and challenge old practices. This will require coolness of nerve, sureness of hand, and the utmost of cooperation among all segments of U.S. education: public, private, lower, and higher. The ideas needed are bigger than any one person can develop. But together we can, I hope, generate them, and put each of the possible services in its proper perspective.

The fabric of both communications and education in America will be more varied, and stronger, if we have public and private ownership at least moving in the same direction—towards goals which all Americans recognize as in the nation's interest. Of the four functions generally recognized for broadcasting—to inform, to enlighten and elevate, to entertain, and to sell goods—education is disbarred from the latter. All of the others must be shared. Much of adult education, for example, is political, economic, and public-affairs in nature. These are not concerns of the schools alone, but of the entire nation. The retraining required following automation illustrates this point. It is actually more a problem of industry than of education. School-based facilities and services are no more obligated to fulfill functions of this nature than are the commercial ones. That is what integration means. To integrate American education, only, would hardly do the job.

If we are to have an integrated broadcasting system in which education finds its proper role, and which is communicative rather than merely propagandistic, in one direction, some changes in policy, law, and in the FCC itself must come. Most of the faults of the FCC are not, of course, of its own invention. Congress keeps the FCC as a watchdog over wire and wireless communications, but persists in doing its own barking—and sometimes its own biting. Rarely, however, does Congress bark unless prodded by large and influential firms. Whether pressure group politics of this nature is democracy or its opposite is another important question we need to ask.

Certainly, something better than a hasty decision is necessary. Electromagnetic frequencies are scarce natural resources. They should not be hoarded; but neither should they be committed with undue haste. These are assets of such scarcity that any rush to occupy them for selfish uses must be resisted firmly and finally. Americans are traditionally impatient and incapable of laying out long-range plans. Here, however, so that the growth of tomorrow is not given short shrift, it is essential for the FCC and other agencies to make plans covering a number of years. Areas in the United States that are not yet even settled must be provided for. Someone must speak for the yet unborn. Services which are as yet new, or not yet established in the curricula, need to be kept in mind for the day when we discover their requirements for spectrum space and facilities. The great planners have always reserved resources for the unborn—whether individuals or institutions. We must therefore ask ourselves: Are the plans we make today adequate for tomorrow? For a hundred years from now? For an age of lasers, space satellites, and a federated world? These considerations are more important than those of adequacy for present needs.

The diversity of services needed is all the more imposing when set against the present twin goals of the commercial services: advertising and money-making. At the elementary level, preschool, in- and out-of-school credit, and noncredit teaching must be pro-

278

vided for. At the secondary level, in- and out-of-school course work, in- and out-of-school enrichment, and extracurricular needs must be met. The fact that schedule and bell problems have delayed high school usage of television should not prevent adequate reservation for the future. The needs in ten years—as university rejections press back upon high school standards and floods of students surge at the doors—will be desperate. High schools then will need these new media most urgently.

At the higher educational level, communication media and classroom space have become interchangeable parts of the same problem, whether for direct instruction, formal, or informal uses.

At the adult education level, the need is perhaps greatest of all—and all levels of schools, not just higher education, share responsibilities here. Many of the adults to be educated are of elementary school, or high school level, and can in no sense be considered graduates. Commercial broadcasting, also, must help. There is no reason why the commercial media should be permitted to do the easy, the profitable, and the popular, while educational media are left with all of the opposites. These are not merely tasks: they are inescapable responsibilities. They must be shared in an integrated approach to communication in which private and public interests reinforce each other.

Education's needs, when contrasted with those cited for commerce, are dramatic. Responsible educators in many areas have said they need six, ten, twelve, or fifteen more frequencies. Is commerce to have all it wishes, in the face of this shortage?

There are 40,000 school districts in this country. How do the needs of these units rate as compared to the interests of the owners and operators of the top 50 big commercial stations and networks?

Westerns, detective programs, family comedy, soap opera, sports, news—how many different kinds of programs does commercial television provide? Don't most stations use old films as "filler" at least half of the time? The average 12-grade school, by contrast, has to teach at least 100 different subjects and grade levels. Should it be expected to accomplish this task with mass uses of media and one or two frequencies? If a store or other business wants a piece of land, and educational interests need the same piece of land, who gets it? What is the answer when the frequency spectrum instead of land is involved?

When Sputnik was launched, educators were not alone in saying that education was the most important thing we could be promoting. Politicians, businessmen, and professional men joined in. So did broadcasters. But so far, the actions of the latter have often belied their words. Their opposition to educational frequencies would sometimes lead one to believe that education represents an enemy power.

*   *   *

There is a multiplicity of tools available now to meet the needs of education. There are "regular" VHF and UHF services, such as those tested and proved in the Salt Lake City area. There is what Adler describes as closed-circuit broadcast—the instructional television fixed frequency service. (And I believe tribute should be paid to the firms who are developing these many new and alternative services—low-power and low-cost.) There is airborne: MPATI, which as a condition of its license, promised to develop and test a three-megacycle, split frequency approach. There is wired closed-circuit. Here again I raise the question of why it should be restricted to education. Many radio and TV stations that serve only to deliver records and films—that, in essence, operate as common carriers—could well be limited to such facilities to the same extent that education is.

There is facsimile, used in Japan and elsewhere to advantage, but here, like radio, largely forgotten in our preoccupation with television. There is slow-scan facsimile, experimented with in England, which uses little spectrum space. There are lasers, although it is to be regretted that most experimentation in the laser-maser field—controlled by telephone interests—seems relatively inaccessible to education. There are community antenna approaches that show great promise, if education is not squeezed out. There are toll-TV approaches and there are satellite and other extra-terrestrial possibilities. But most of these are long-range resources. The needs of education won't wait for them. Our children and our schools need help now.

Although there is a pressing need for deliberate and careful study of low-cost, low-power, non-mass approaches, toll and satellite approaches deserve brief additional comment. I am not, as an educator, interested in commercial toll-TV, although I think that two kinds of commercial services—one direct box-office service and one indirect box-office service via advertising—would be a good thing. It would make more direct feedback possible. I am more interested in the ways in which variants of this approach (special keys for doctors, etc.) could make the use of scrambled materials feasible on a more economical scale than closed-circuit is now. Emergency health instruction to public health officers and posts, directions to civil defense authorities, and many educational uses including even pay-as-you-go correspondence courses—these illustrate my interest in toll or subscription TV.

With reference to satellites, I would remind you of the degree to which we have become one world. To see satellites apparently destined for business instead of education is to me a tragedy. What support did Professor Oliver Reiser of the University of Pittsburgh get when he proposed a UN-UNESCO satellite devoted to international, educational, scientific, cultural, and goodwill purposes? His proposal for a "Project Prometheus," made at the Accra Conference in June 1962, was scarcely mentioned in the U.S. press—and certainly not on the network newscasts. As far as I know, reference to it in the press was limited to one letter to the editor of *Saturday Review*. Neither the executive branch, Congress, nor the FCC supported this plea for specific educational uses of satellites. Yet to my knowledge, no more exciting a challenge to this new tool has been advanced. Perhaps we as educators should press more vigorously for such projects, if we are not to be squeezed out of this area, too, by commerce.

In accordance with the Pilkington Report and the government's new policy, Britain, at great expense, is converting to 625-line picture standards for television—the standards used generally in Europe and in the Soviet Union. Should the United States be considering the technical and other compatibilities of its services with those of the rest of the world? What stake has education in such matters?

Returning to land-based facilities, which it appears will be all

281

that education can count on to meet its more immediate problems, several ownership patterns emerge. These include community stations; state or city-system stations; individual university, college, or school stations; stations operated essentially by instructional centers (illustrated by the Louisville Free Public Library FM services to the schools of Louisville); municipal stations like WNYC and WNYC-TV which might form the nuclei for an eventual public-service, public-affairs, noncommercial network separate from educational stations; joint educational-commercial operations like the VHF-TV station of Michigan State University; partially commercial stations like that of Iowa State University; and various other ownership patterns.

Conspicuously absent from the spectrum are joint commercial stations, arrangements whereby several commercial interests pool and share the same facilities, as schools and colleges must do. Before further commercial allocations are decided, the validity of joint arrangements for commerce as well as for education might well be examined. A national study to decide who gets what—a study cutting across commercial and educational lines—is sorely needed. In view of the shortage of frequencies, should any station, educational or commercial, be licensed to broadcast mostly rock-and-roll and old films? Is a national jukebox or second-run moviehouse a valid communications use of the spectrum?

When the courts ruled that broadcasting was not a common carrier, Mr. Sarnoff had not yet said that "of course, broadcasting is only a pipeline"; stations had not yet become essentially retail outlets for records, films, and other canned goods produced by outsiders, or by record and film companies owned by the same corporations—RCA, CBS, and others—who already control stations and programs, either by ownership, affiliation, or syndication. Now that stations have begun to operate as common carriers, are revisions in the allocations and rules not due for consideration? Or are there some choices here, depending upon the kind of operation we define as broadcasting and as common carriers?

* * *

Under the pressure of quantity-oriented industry standards, we need to reconsider whether "bigger" is always "better"; whether TV is better than radio for certain purposes—or poorer;

282

whether color will be an advantage or a distraction for certain types of TV programs; and many other such questions that pose a choice. It has been found in many instances that the concentration possible via one sense permits more penetration and learning than an appeal to several senses in which the senses become blurred and distractions begin to cancel out the supposed advantage of multisensory appeals. The positive superiority of radio, facsimile, and other neglected media for certain purposes in many subjects is notable. Since what we ask is not for ourselves, nor to deprive commerce or any other entity of its just due, we must be sure that in all of our requests, our motives are honest, based on real facts and real needs, not on a mere sense of competition.

Perhaps a word about the real or imagined dangers of federal influence and centralization is in order. Senator Goldwater was quoted as saying on January 22, 1964, that he was less opposed to federal aid to universities and colleges than to high schools and elementary schools because there is less danger of influencing older students than younger ones. I personally believe emphasis on decentralization for education can be carried too far, at all levels.

Programs involving the arts, or expensive talent or production, should certainly be centrally produced. Programs involving ideas, social and human relations, controversial public affairs, discussions, and regional and local problems should, I think, bear the local stamp. But the problem is not one of "either/or." In most of the studies of viewer attitudes towards ETV and ITV, the objections seem traceable to the local type of production, to inadequate quality, not to the educational nature of the programs as such. To condemn any level of TV, whether open- or closed-circuit, to local production is in many cases to condemn it to amateurism. We do need to tap the grass roots and, as commercial broadcasting has generally failed to do, keep local education and participation alive. But the system we call for, whether for elementary, secondary, or higher education, should also provide for significant enrichment and reinforcement by the best centrally produced programs that the collective efforts of American education and broadcasting can come up with. Some of these, most certainly, should be "live."

Whatever changes we press for will be recognized, I trust, as born out of altruistic, professional motives. None of us has anything to gain personally or financially from one decision or another, made now or later. At the Institute for Education by Radio and Television in Columbus in 1963, Professor Ned Rosenheim of the University of Chicago said: "The service of truth can be a lonely, infinitely demanding, even an ugly task. Yet the service of truth is the only task for us . . . teachers and broadcasters . . . entrusted with this magnificent power of communicating wisdom. It is our job. It is our way of life. It is our way simply because, if humanity is to survive, there is no other way." As another educator, I endorse Dr. Rosenheim's statement.

Many efforts in education are too timidly engaged in. Educators are often visualized as milquetoasts, requesting what they ask for with less than required firmness. When I say I believe education deserves more and better frequencies and facilities than private broadcasting, I am not saying it merely for effect, or as a trial balloon. I mean it. I invite all educators, whatever they do or ask for—not for themselves but for unborn generations and our nation's survival—to ask for it with firmness and confidence, the confidence that comes from knowing that there are no selfish motives involved in their requests. Then let all of us reiterate and stand by our requests, firmly, vigorously, skillfully—and if necessary thunderously. Such a position will help, not hinder, the FCC and other agencies interested in education and America's position in the world generally.

The day when education could *dare* to speak with a small voice is past. Let us be sure greatness, not pettiness, characterizes our planning and our requests for the tools we need to do the task expected of us.

XXI.

*The FCC and Program Regulation**

LEE LOEVINGER

Lee Loevinger has been a member of the Federal Communications Commission since 1963. He has also served as an Associate Justice of the Minnesota Supreme Court and as Assistant U.S. Attorney General in charge of the Antitrust Division of the Department of Justice.

~~~~~~

THE PROGRAMMING OF TELEVISION broadcasts, and to a lesser extent radio broadcasts, is a subject of such popular interest that it is almost constantly under formal and informal discussion. No one, it seems, is wholly satisfied with the programs presented and everyone is in favor of better programs. But while there are many voices decrying the quality of present programming, there is no agreement either as to what improvements should be made or as to how improvements can be achieved. Unfortunately, these problems are essential threshold issues.

A desire to improve programming, like a desire to improve character or society, is meaningful in a practical sense only insofar as it suggests some specific course of action. Accordingly, it should be recognized at the outset that the matter of whether or not broadcast programs are good or bad is at best peripheral to the more basic question of what the relationship of the government in general, and the Federal Communications Commission in particular, should be to programming. And if this latter question is to receive any kind of careful and responsible consideration, the problems must be analyzed and the issues specified.

Much of the discussion of broadcast programming and the

* Reprinted from the *Federal Communications Bar Journal*, Vol. XX (1966), pp. 3-15, by permission of the author and the publisher.

function of the government, however, has the form but not the substance of debate. It has the form of a debate because the discussion is conducted by articulate, sometimes eloquent and sometimes vehement, spokesmen for opposing viewpoints. But it lacks the essential substance of a debate because there is an almost total failure to meet in a discussion of specific issues. To quote only slightly fictitious characters, the advocate of one viewpoint says, in substance: "The FCC should not concern itself at all with the character of programming, and any attempt by it to examine or inquire into program content is an unwarranted intrusion into the area of the broadcaster's free speech and constitutes censorship." An advocate of the opposing viewpoint expresses himself in substantially these words: "Program content is of the essence of the service broadcasting provides, and it is impossible for the FCC to determine whether the grant of an application will serve the public interest, convenience, or necessity without considering the overall character of that programming service. So the FCC should be concerned with programming, and in fact is required to do so by its statute."

These statements fairly epitomize both the position and the arguments of a number of those engaged in this discussion. But neither agreement nor clarification is possible so long as there is merely argument on the highly abstract level of whether or not government should have any concern with program content or quality. The basic issue to be faced is what kind and degree of control is proposed or implied by a particular position.

It will not do to say that government has no concern at all with what is broadcast. The existence of laws against obscenity and of libel laws amounts to some degree of government concern with broadcast content. I do not know of anyone who contends that these laws should be abandoned.

On the other hand, the contention that the government should be concerned with the quality of overall programming is meaningless unless it implies some kind and degree of control beyond that of existing obscenity and libel laws. So it becomes necessary to analyze the subject and to attempt a specification of the problems and issues involved in attempting to exert various

286

kinds and degrees of government influence over programming. As I see it, the following are the most important categories and issues:

Illegal Utterances

Should the government punish or prevent the broadcasting of material of a kind that has been officially established as illegal or legally objectionable?

While the term "illegal utterances" is simply a catch phrase, it seems nonetheless to be a useful tool for identifying certain categories that are recognized by law. There are a few legally established categories of such antisocial or illegal utterance which are generally subject to punishment in one form or another. These are generally recognized as (1) fraud, (2) obscenity, (3) incitement to crime, (4) lotteries, and (5) criminal libel.

It is established by precedent and FCC practice that broadcasters cannot broadcast material falling into any of these categories. Moreover, it is generally conceded that the FCC has the authority to punish the broadcasting of such material and, as a practical matter, although not in legal theory, this means it has the authority to prevent the broadcasting of such material where it is possible to know of it in advance of the proposed broadcast. There is no serious issue or dispute about the power of the FCC to take effective action against the broadcasting of such material, with the exception of that material possibly to be considered libelous, but where the classification is in question.

Right of Reply

Should the government require the opportunity for broadcasting contrasting views on public issues and replies to personal attacks?

Present law provides for what is popularly called "equal time" to reply in certain specific situations involving broadcasting. This arises from two wholly separate and distinct sources that are sometimes confused.

The first legal source, and the one commonly referred to by the phrase "equal time," is Section 315 of the Communications

Act.[1] This statute provides that when any broadcast station permits a legally qualified candidate for any public office to use its facilities it must afford "equal opportunities" for use by all other candidates for the same office. The provision applies only to candidates for public office and does impose an "equal time" requirement. While this section is criticized by some broadcasters and others, it appears to have strong political and popular support. The principle embodied in this section is not currently the subject of great controversy.

The second legal basis for a right of reply is the so-called "fairness doctrine" of the FCC.[2] This doctrine originated in a report adopted by the Commission in 1949,[3] which grew out of a dissatisfaction with the earlier Commission holding that broadcast licensees were not entitled to broadcast any editorial opinions. While in the report the Commission ruled that licensees were entitled to broadcast editorial opinions, it went on to say:

> [In] such presentation of news and comment the public interest requires that the licensee must operate on a basis of overall fairness, making his facilities available for the expression of the contrasting views of all responsible elements in the community on the various issues which arise.[4]

The doctrine received statutory recognition in a 1959 revision of Section 315, which provided that nothing in that section should relieve broadcasters from their obligation to afford reasonable opportunity for the discussion of conflicting views on issues of public importance. The "fairness doctrine" has been maintained by the Commission as a requirement that when one side or viewpoint of a specific "controversial issue of public importance" is presented on a broadcast station, an opportunity for reply or presentation of an opposing viewpoint must also be afforded; in addition, when a personal attack is made on any individual a fair opportunity for reply must be afforded that in-

[1] See Dean, *Political Broadcasting: The Communications Act of 1934 Reviewed, infra, at p. 16—ed.*
[2] *Ibid.—ed.*
[3] In the Matter of Editorializing by Broadcast Licensees, 13 F.C.C. 1246 (1949).
[4] Id. at 1250.

288

dividual or his spokesman. The precise scope of this doctrine has never been clearly defined by the Commission and a good many troublesome questions arise in its application.

Some broadcasters oppose the doctrine, as well as Section 315, on the ground that it inhibits their freedom to present viewpoints on controversial issues. A particular example of such effect is illustrated in the report carried in the *New York Times* for September 8, 1965, at page 38. Station WPIX had scheduled a debate between mayoralty candidates Screvane and Beame. At the same time it offered an opportunity to the other two Democratic candidates, Ryan and O'Dwyer, to appear either in a debate between themselves or individually at another time. All appearances were during evening prime time. Ryan and O'Dwyer objected to appearing at any other time than on the same program with Screvane and Beame and demanded that the program be cancelled unless they were permitted to appear. The staff of the FCC rejected this protest and said that the station might choose the time it offered to the several candidates so long as it was fairly comparable.

Other recent cases involving difficult questions under the "fairness doctrine" arise from protests against documentary films. One complainant claims that a documentary on South Africa is unfair to the ruling group in that country and its policy of extreme and rigorous racial segregation. In another case, it is asserted that an interview with an Israeli official presents Israel in an unduly favorable light. A third complaint is from a national organization which asserts that a network documentary on Vietnam is "highly unbalanced" and "biased." These complaints have been disposed of by the Commission with no public exposition of views or rationale. The Commission is apparently either unable or unwilling to clarify and specify its own understanding of the "fairness doctrine." It nonetheless remains one of the principal means by which the Commission influences the content of broadcast programs.

Despite difficult problems of application and the vagueness with which it is enshrouded, and although one broadcaster has recently instituted an action in the U.S. District Court for the District of Columbia to have it declared unconstitutional and its application enjoined, the "fairness doctrine" seems to have rather widespread acceptance and approval.

Objectionable Programming

Should the government punish or prevent the broadcasting of material that is not in an established category of illegality, but is judged otherwise to be objectionable, bad or unworthy?

It is possible to take the position that, aside from the established categories of illegality, the government has no business seeking to punish or prevent broadcasting of any other material. However, there is much popular demand for government action to prevent or minimize the broadcasting of certain types of programs, such as those devoted to crime, violence, or sex. A recent Gallup Poll reports that some 58 percent of the public surveyed thinks there should be stricter laws to control the kind of books that can be sold, presumably in order to prevent the sale of "dirty books."[5] Undoubtedly an even larger percentage favor some form of censorship of broadcasting. Such considerations suggest that this approach cannot be dismissed with general arguments against censorship, but requires detailed analysis and examination.

In the field of broadcasting, it appears that any government action to minimize certain types of broadcasting is legally equivalent to an action to prohibit specific programs, since the total number of broadcasts has a natural limitation and a given category can be minimized only if specific broadcasts included in that category are omitted. As a consequence, a consideration of this possibility leads to numerous more limited problems:

(1) By whom is the definition of "objectionable programming" to be established? Presumably the ultimate decision will be made by the FCC. This raises the question, however, of how the definition is to be arrived at and how it is to be communicated. If the FCC can go beyond established categories of legality, what standards shall it use for determining objectionable broadcasts? Further, assuming that the members of the FCC can agree on judgments, how are these to be formulated and communicated to

[5] Washington *Post*, October 15, 1965, p. A2.

the FCC staff and to the broadcasters who are expected to comply with them?

(2) Assuming that the FCC has been able to establish a standard of objectionable programming, is this standard to be applied to broadcasters on the basis of single programs, of several programs, or simply "overall performance"? If the FCC relies on its appraisal of "overall performance" what percentage or proportion of "objectionable programs" does this imply will be acceptable? Is the FCC to take action based upon its judgment as to how seriously its standards have been violated, or how "objectionable" in degree the program or programs have been?

(3) Assuming tolerable answers to the preceding issues, what kind of action should the FCC take with respect to the broadcasting of "objectionable programs"? Most American lawyers will say that prior restraint is censorship and, therefore, prohibited by constitutional or statutory principles. However, if a broadcaster with a normal expectation of continuing in business is denied a license renewal because of past programming, is there any significant difference between the threat of non-renewal and prior restraint? In *Near v. Minnesota*,[6] the classic case on censorship, the Supreme Court held that it is unconstitutional to enjoin the future publication of a newspaper on the basis of past practice of publishing libelous and malicious stories. Noteworthy here is the fact that the case did not involve an attempt to prevent publication of a particular article, but rather involved an attempted general restraint based upon an appraisal of "overall performance." It is difficult to see any significant difference between forbidding the future publication of a newspaper because of its publication of objectionable material in the past, and the revocation of, or refusal to renew, the license of a broadcasting station for the same reason.

In any event, it is suggested that regardless of any theoretical difference, in view of the value of broadcast licenses and the sensitivity of licensees to Commission opinion, the refusal to renew a license for past objectionable programming will act as the most effective possible restraint upon any future programming of that kind by all licensees. It is further suggested that the continuous

⁶ 283 U.S. 697 (1931).

discussion and intercourse between broadcasters and their representatives and the Commission and its staff result in a constant flow of official, semiofficial and unofficial advisory opinions with respect to a multitude of matters within the Commission's jurisdiction. If licenses can be denied, revoked, or not renewed because of particular programming, then the opinions of the Commission members and Commission staff as to whether or not programs fall within the category of "objectionable programming" will operate certainly and effectively as a prior restraint.

Desirable Programming

Should the FCC encourage or require the broadcasting of programs that are desirable, good, or useful?

The only means by which the FCC can influence programming other than by forbidding or somehow punishing the broadcast of programs judged to be objectionable is by encouraging or requiring programming judged to be desirable. However, such mandatory or rewarding action also involves a number of difficult issues.

(1) The first and most obvious problem is definitional. Simply to say that "good" programs should be encouraged is hardly enough. There must be a determination, first, of the category of programs with which the FCC is concerned, and then, of the standard by which virtue or excellence is to be judged.

From the legal viewpoint it would appear that there are three broad general categories involved in programming: First is the sensitive legal category involving the expression of viewpoints or opinions, especially on political, legal, and social matters. Second is the category of news reporting. Third is the category of entertainment and general culture.

As to the category involving the expression of viewpoints, it should be noted that the right of reply arising from section 315 and the "fairness doctrine" does, in effect, require the broadcasting of diverse viewpoints when public issues are discussed, candidates appear, or personal attacks are made. A serious issue is presented as to whether the FCC can or should go beyond these established principles in requiring or encouraging the presentation of any particular viewpoints or kinds of viewpoints. One who maintains that the FCC should go further in this direction cannot rest upon the vague assertion that the Commission should require the presentation of "diverse viewpoints" or some similar verbal formula. Rather, such a position requires a specification of the situations which incur an obligation to permit the presentation of particular viewpoints, the kinds of viewpoints which are required to be presented, how the standard of required viewpoints is to be arrived at, and who is to have ultimate authority for interpreting and applying that standard.

A contention that the FCC should require or encourage the broadcast of desirable programming in the category of entertainment or general culture involves the same issues, although the subject is somewhat less sensitive than the expression of political, economic, or social viewpoints. However, the contention that the FCC should be concerned with the quality of entertainment or cultural programming requires an ability to define quality in some kind of objective terms, a statement or specification of this standard of quality, a means of ascertaining and declaring either a threshold standard of acceptable quality (or a method of scaling degrees of quality and specifying the degree of quality required), and the maintenance of a staff or organization capable of applying the official standards of quality.

(2) The second issue with respect to mandatory or rewarding government action is the frequency of presentation to be required or rewarded. Shall the FCC require a certain minimum number of hours of programming to meet its specified quality standard? Shall it require that *all* programming meet some minimum standard of quality? Or shall it require that "overall performance" include a specified percentage of programming which meets a particular standard of quality? These seem to be the only alternatives if a standard of quality is used. In fact, however, the establishment of a qualitative standard has been so difficult that it has not yet been attempted, so the quantitative issue has not arisen in this form.

(3) The traditional FCC approach has been to demand minimum amounts of programming in various specified categories. Licensees have been required to report the percentage of pro-

gramming falling in such categories as entertainment, religion, agricultural, educational, news, discussion, talks, and miscellaneous. The 1960 program policy statement[7] listed 14 categories, including some of the foregoing and additional ones such as programs for children and editorials.

This approach is based upon certain implicit assumptions which, simply stated, are these: The public interest in broadcasting is composed of a number of elements, principally those specified in the FCC program reporting forms. Each licensee should serve the public interest. It is the function of the FCC to require each licensee to serve the public interest or else forfeit his license. In order to serve the public interest each licensee must provide all, or most, of the elements which the FCC specifies as serving the public interest. Therefore, each licensee must provide some programming of each type specified by the FCC (or, in exceptional cases, of most but not all types), or risk losing his license.

An important point to note in analyzing this approach is that it is based altogether on category classification and has nothing whatever to do with excellence or merit. A program is classified as "talk" whether it is Einstein discoursing on relativity, Niebuhr discussing morality, or the local bartender talking about the proper proportions for a martini. A program is classed as "entertainment" regardless of whether it is based upon pornography, contemporary crime and violence, or classical drama. Hence it is apparent that a statistical supervision of program categories has about the same relation to program merit as a requirement for hiring employees on the basis of geographical origin does to a civil service merit system. This approach ultimately rests upon an assumption that category diversity is *per se* a desirable quality in broadcast programming.

The hope that excellence, merit, or even genuine diversity might be provided by the requirement of a statistical "balance" or distribution among prescribed categories of programming has been frustrated by experience. For while the FCC has officially insisted on the necessity for such statistical balance virtually since its inception, its insistence has neither discouraged or pre-

[7] Report and Statement of Policy re: Commission En Banc Programming Inquiry, 20 R.R. 1901 (1960).

vented bad programs nor provided or encouraged good programs.

Indeed, the Commission's traditional approach presents a number of special problems. What and how many categories shall be required? How are these categories to be clearly defined? Shall the FCC and its staff accept the category classifications of licensees, or shall the FCC and its staff review the content of programs and make independent conclusions as to classification?

Further, there is this dilemma: If the FCC requires only a few, broad categories, then it is not providing much diversity or exerting much influence on programming. On the other hand, if the FCC requires a statistical distribution among a large number of narrow categories, then, if successful, it confines programming in a straitjacket and prevents the flexibility that is necessary to respond to changing public tastes and needs. In either case, imposing statistical categorical standards implies that the power of licensing is being used to require some programs that would not otherwise be broadcast, and correspondingly, to prevent the broadcasting of other programs.

Another problem inherent in the attempt to require diverse kinds of programming is that such "balance" or "diversity" tends to frustrate public demand and discourage excellence. All the investigations that have been made of public taste in broadcast, particularly television, programming indicate that those members of the public who are dissatisfied with current programming, want more of the kind of programs that matches their own tastes, rather than a potpourri of something for everyone. There is not the slightest indication that any substantial number is willing to watch a "balanced" or diversified series of programs from one station. On the contrary, there is considerable indication that most of those who watch television or listen to radio habitually want a consistently homogeneous kind of programming. The response to this demand is evident in radio programming in large metropolitan areas where the competition of numerous stations has forced all the stations to meet public demand in order to survive economically. In these situations, all stations develop some one consistent format which attracts a substantial audience. The net effect is that the listening public has a choice among diverse kinds of programs presented by different stations, each station presenting mainly a single kind of programming without any attempt at "diversity."

Another aspect of the same problem is that diversity is likely to be the enemy of excellence. It is difficult enough for either radio or television stations to satisfy the apparently insatiable demand of the American public for continuous broadcast service, and still attain, much less maintain, any degree of excellence. However, by specialization and concentration on special kinds of programming, such as classical music, discussion, or what now passes for "popular music," a station may develop enough "expertise" or skill to achieve excellence, at least occasionally. A station that is forced or induced to present a wide variety of program types has a much greater burden imposed upon its program resources, both human and financial, and is likely to be less concerned about standards of excellence. Almost certainly, it will be relatively uncritical about the merit of the coerced types of programming so long as they are of the "right type." Whatever else may be said for it, a required diversity is virtually certain to be incompatible with excellence.

Of course, within this framework, if a statistical balance among categories is not relied upon, the problems inherent in attempting to establish and apply a subjective standard of quality again arises. Conceivably, there could be subjective standards of quality with statistical requirements for minima in various categories. However, this merely compounds the difficulties and does not provide any practical objective standard.

(4) A final issue with respect to mandatory or rewarding action by the government to require or encourage program quality is that of determining the kind of action to be taken. The only real reward or inducement that the government has to offer, however, is the grant or continuance of a license. As a consequence, the practical distinction between mandatory or rewarding action and prohibitory or punitive action is difficult to see. For if the rewarding action consists of the grant or continuance of a license, and punitive action consists of the denial or refusal to continue a license, we are merely saying the same thing in different words. Further, as noted above, once the FCC takes action either to grant or to deny a license on the basis of specific programming,

all those who are subject to its licensing power are, in effect, compelled to comply with the standard stated or implied by that action. If the standard is based upon the broadcasting of a desirable program other licensees are in effect required to broadcast the same or similar programs.

Practical Problems

As a practical matter is it either possible or useful for the FCC to regulate programming in an attempt to improve it?

The preceding issues and discussion are concerned with the relationship between government regulation of programming and democratic ideals and libertarian principles. But there is another important set of issues arising out of any official effort to control or influence programming—the practical ones: What can be done? What result is likely to occur?

As a purely practical matter it seems highly dubious that the FCC can secure the kind of programming that many high-minded and educated people demand. It is even more dubious that a large number of people would often watch or listen to such programming if it were presented. Steiner reports that

> . . . the fact is that viewers who ask for more enlightenment select it only one-fifth of the time they are watching while it is actually available.

> . . . the number-one suggestion for TV improvement—"more information"—that comes mostly and almost unanimously from the educated critics of the medium, is not backed up *by them* in *their own* program selections.

> . . . Serious drama and music . . . still accounts for a negligible share of their television week; and it still fails to capture as much as half their viewing even while such programs are on the air.[8]

Another aspect of the practical difficulties involved is suggested by a recent publication of Time-Life. This corporation reports that when it presented the program *March of Time* in the late 1930's its audio-visual programming totaled four hours a year for this entire film series. In 1964 the corporation operated five

[8] Steiner, *The People Look at Television*, 188, 202, 203 (1963).

television stations and presented 32,000 hours of audio-visual programming. In the heyday of motion picture production the eight major production companies produced a total of perhaps as many as 150 Class A feature films annually, an equivalent of about 300 hours of audio-visual entertainment. The ordinary commerical television station in the United States today, however, presents between 5,500 and 6,500 hours of programming each year. These contrasts suggest that the problem is not so much that of insuring high quality in programming as one of securing any programming of presentable quality in adequate quantity to fill the time which the public apparently demands. Also suggested is that the supervision of the programming of more than 600 television stations and more than 5,000 aural broadcasting stations in the United States is beyond the capability of any moderate-sized government agency, as a purely practical matter.

A final practical comment on FCC efforts to influence programming is best set forth by an observation from my dissent in the case of *Lee Roy McCourry*:[9]

> The Commission majority surely assumes that official intervention in programming will have an uplifting and beneficent effect. This assumption is shared by many well meaning and sincere people. However the instant case should shed some doubt on that assumption. The program proposal here is excellent, at least by my standards. The thrust of Commission action here is to reduce the high level of proposed programming to the mediocrity of the established mixture (or "balance" as it is called in the official euphemism). This seems to me to be a degradation rather than an improvement. It is conceivable that the establishment of official standards of program quality might have an uplifting effect on programming in the long run—but I doubt it. To me it seems more likely that the setting of program standards by official action will merely insure conformity to a dull and undistinguished mediocrity.[10]

Observation of other cases has strengthened the conclusion that FCC efforts to supervise programming tend more to reduce it to

[9] 2 R.R. 2d 895 (1964).
[10] Id. at 906.

the level of a pedestrian uniformity than to enhance its quality or stimulate excellence.

In reviewing the issues presented by this complex problem, it seems to me that the limited government intervention involved in acting against those things that have been grouped as "illegal utterances" and in maintaining the right of reply is generally sufficiently guarded by precedent and principle to prevent serious danger to free speech. Further government intervention in this area involves much greater threats to freedom. Ultimately the basic issue comes down to the relative value to be placed on liberty as weighed against the achievement of whatever other objectives it is desired to have the broadcasting system serve. In deciding this issue, we must keep in view the specific categories and problems involved and the related values on both sides of the equation.

More than a decade ago, Morris L. Ernst said that we have now come to realize that freedom of speech was not made a constitutional right in order to assure men the unrestricted pleasure of hearing their own voices, but rather because it is a necessity for the establishment of representative government.

> While the courts have frequently spoken in terms of the constitutional right of the speaker or listener, there has been throughout our history a growing awareness that the basic purpose of protecting unpopular or even obnoxious ideas is a social purpose. This social purpose took on new qualities as we shifted from a culture of town meetings and one hundred gazettes in 1787 to magazines with circulations in the millions, millions of movies and theatre seats, and tens of millions of receiving sets to pick up ideas on the airwaves.[11]

That popular as well as unpopular entertainment and ideas may need and deserve some protection against official disapproval is only a quirk of circumstance, less surprising than many other peculiarities of our technological democracy. The basic social purpose in protecting the freedom of communications media from government intervention, as well as the legal principle involved, is the same whether the intrusion is aimed at popular or unpopular expressions.

[11] Ernst and Katz, Speech: Public and Private, 53 Colum. L.R. 620 (1953).

One approach to the challenge of adapting constitutional principles in this field to the complexities of social change was suggested in a recent address by Solicitor General Thurgood Marshall.[12] A recent development is what the Solicitor General calls "the lateral expansion of First Amendment protection," so that its protection extends beyond the specifics enumerated to a broader freedom of expression. The extension of First Amendment protection to broadcasting is, of course, part of this development. However, the Solicitor General says, with this expansion there has come some concession to government regulation. This development is, generally, no cause for concern, he says; but rigor is required in order to assure that regulation of the manner of expression remains neutral as to content.

Although it will not dispose of all cases or answer all questions, this principle will certainly serve as a helpful guide in applying First Amendment freedoms to contemporary conditions. The regulation of broadcasting is founded on certain technical necessities, and, whatever other problems engineering requirements may involve, technical standards are most unlikely to involve First Amendment issues. A fair inference from *NBC v. United States*[13] might be that reasonable regulation of the economic structure of broadcasting does not infringe First Amendment principles. Technical and economic rules for broadcasting are permissible under the First Amendment because they are content-neutral. By the same token, however, an attempt to impose any regulatory standard on programming, either by inhibiting objectionable programming or encouraging desirable programming, is not content-neutral and is inconsistent with the First Amendment. It is submitted that law, logic, and practicality all support the principle that, subject to the strictly limited exceptions of "illegal utterances" and the right to reply, government regulation of broadcasting should be completely content-neutral.

Without government regulation of programming, broadcasting will operate as a medium of mass communication controlled by numerous diverse owners and licensees. Some of them will be ignorant, stupid, venal, or—worst of all—politically opposed to

[12] The Constitution and Social Change, 12 Fed. Bar News 284 (1965).
[13] 319 U.S. 190 (1943).

our own enlightened views. This has been true of newspapers and this is the way that newspapers have operated since the nation was founded. But there are more, and more diverse, broadcasters than there have ever been publishers of daily newspapers. If we do not rely upon the diversity achieved by affording these broadcasters a wide area of freedom and independence, then we must rest our hopes for diversity, quality, and freedom entirely on the good will and judgment of the seven men comprising a government commission. Both our history and our philosophy compel the conclusion that liberty cannot safely be rested on a faith in the benevolence of a government agency. The alternative is to accept the risks and endure the faults of mass communications which are controlled in content by numerous private parties.

XXII.

How Drastically Has
Television Changed Our Politics?*

ARTHUR SCHLESINGER, JR.

An eminent historian, Arthur Schlesinger, Jr., served as Special Assistant to President Kennedy. He is the author of *A Thousand Days*, which won the 1966 Pulitzer Prize for Biography.

~~~~~~

THE TIME has come for a preliminary assessment of the impact of television on our politics. More and more Americans, it appears, are forming their impressions of the world on the basis of the things they see on the tiny screen. Recent surveys report television as the main source of news for more than 50 percent of our voters, and *Broadcasting* magazine could plausibly argue in 1964 that television had become the "Nation's primary news medium." This widening influence of television over American life raises the question how TV is affecting the basic character of our political system and whether it is strengthening or weakening the workings of our democracy.

Some observers, for example, claim that television is producing a more alert and better-informed electorate; others that it is reducing our politics to a mixture of high-pressure salesmanship and beauty contests. The assessment is bound to be preliminary because the evidence is inadequate, contradictory and inconclusive. But I wish to offer an historian's tentative thoughts on a complex problem.

* Reprinted from the October 22-28, 1966, issue of *TV Guide*, pp. 6-10, by permission of the author and publisher. Copyright 1966 by Triangle Publications, Inc.

THE CONTROVERSIAL SCREEN

Television touches politics in a number of ways. For purposes of convenience, one may perhaps distinguish four types of coverage: (1) news programs, (2) pseudo-news programs, (3) interpretation, and (4) party programs. It may be well to discuss each category and then attempt a general appraisal.

News

Probably the greatest influence in shaping political judgment is still the reality of events themselves. A depression, a war, a debate over national policy, constitutional rights protected or denied, economic securities enlarged or imperiled, bills passed or defeated. Such facts remain the great determinants of political opinion. And it is in communicating these facts that television has had its most impressive success.

A notable recent example was the coverage of the hearings on Vietnam before the Senate Foreign Relations Committee. I have no doubt that future historians will conclude that these hearings opened a new phase in the Vietnam debate. Before the hearings, most people had suppressed any disquietude they may have felt over the deepening national involvement in Vietnam on the assumption that the President had more information and no doubt knew best. But the hearings had the clear effect, for better or worse, of legitimatizing dissent. If eminent generals, diplomats, and senators were unhappy about our actions in Vietnam, then the ordinary citizen felt free to indulge in his own doubts. And the hearings not only opened up debate over Vietnam; they also ended the taboo which had so long prevented discussion of American relations with Communist China. Would these hearings have had the same effect had they not been on television? I think plainly not—and all the more credit therefore to the NBC network which carried them in full.

Television, through the vivid reporting of actual events, can thus incite new thoughts and emotions in the electorate. It also has the effect in many cases of heightening the sense of popular participation in public matters. Thus the McCarthy-Army hearings undoubtedly made many viewers feel, as they had not before, that the Wisconsin senator was a threat not just to other people but to themselves. When sustained over a long time, this increased

303

sense of popular participaton can alter somewhat the workings of political institutions. It seems already, for example, to have reshaped so basic a device in our politics as the Presidential nominating convention.

For most of our history, the convention was a relatively closed powwow for professional politicians, who got chummily together, discussed their candidates, made their deals and presented the results to a passive public. People might have exclaimed, "Who is James K. Polk?" when they heard (via telegraph) the outcome of the Democratic Convention of 1884; but they did not feel indignant over the fact that the name of the nominee meant so little to them.

Television has changed all that. The dark-horse candidate, emerging unknown out of smoke-filled rooms for nomination on the 46th ballot, is probably a thing of the past. The tiny screen has made the public an active partner. The feedback is too quick and intense to encourage any convention to risk ditching the favorite of the national audience in favor of a crony of the party professionals. In addition, television has had the happy effect of making conventions shorter. It is safe to assume that the nation will never again have to endure 103 ballots, as it did during the Democratic Convention of 1924.

Conventions, of course, with their inherent drama and suspense, are particularly well adapted to the inquisitive camera. But even television's day-by-day reporting of politics has undoubtedly given the electorate a larger knowledge of public personalities and a greater acquaintance with public issues. News coverage, I think, represents television's best contribution to democratic responsibility.

Pseudo-News

By "pseudo-news"—a subclassification of Daniel Boorstin's general category of "pseudo-event" (in his book *The Image*)—I mean the creation of news on the initiative of the medium. Perhaps the term is unnecessarily invidious; for often the news thus elicited is entirely legitimate. Lawrence Spivak's *Meet the Press* and its various imitators, for example, have greatly advanced public enlightenment through the years by their interrogations of national figures.

On the other hand, some pseudo-news is mischievous and irresponsible. When President Johnson issued his challenge to the intellectual community a year or so ago, a news television crew descended on my office in the evident hope that I could be stimulated to denounce the President. This seems a factitious attempt to manufacture conflict (though, in justice to the program, when I said that I considered the President's remarks appropriate, they filmed the interview anyway and put it on the air).

My feeling is that organized shows in a press-conference format serve a useful purpose but that television interviews designed to lure or trap people into sensational statements they would not otherwise make can be dispensed with. It is necessary to add, though, that television did not invent this technique; it is another bad habit it picked up from the press.

Interpretation

Editorialization on television has taken the form of thoughtful personal comment (Howard K. Smith, Eric Sevareid) or, with the recent encouragement of the FCC, of editorials by local stations. Neither form has thus far had very striking results. I do not know whether television has an inhibiting effect on comment; but certainly no television commentator has spoken with the pungency or authority of Elmer Davis on radio, and men like Smith and Sevareid often look more constrained on the screen than they used to sound over the loudspeaker.

In the past, networks have attempted panel discussions, like the NBC series *The Big Issue* a few years back. This is still done a good deal locally and on educational television. Unquestionably these programs have improved the level of political discussion, in part because they permit the suggestion of subtleties and complexities in public problems. But, possibly for this reason, such programs do not seem to have been pursued very diligently by the networks.

What television has done most successfully in the field of interpretation is the analytical documentary—the kind of thing that Murrow and Friendly used to do for CBS, the NBC *White*

Papers, the Bell & Howell shows. At their best, such programs have dealt with problems at a reasonable level of complexity and have been a highly effective form of public education.

Party Programs

By this I mean time purchased by political parties and leaders, or otherwise made available to them. This, I would say, has been the area of television's most conspicuous failure; and the trouble here begins with the nature of the medium itself. For the effect of television has been to cheapen political discourse, steadily reducing its length, its substance, and its rationality.

Sixty years ago an audience which traveled many miles to hear William Jennings Bryan or Robert M. La Follette hold forth on railroad regulation or the tariff would have felt cheated if the oration lasted less than a couple of hours. The coming of radio set in motion the shrinkage of the political speech, first to forty-five minutes, then to half an hour. Then came television. I can recall the insistence of the TV men in Adlai Stevenson's headquarters in 1956 that half an hour was far too long; unless it were a national crisis, fifteen minutes, they said, represented the outer limit of the attention span of an American audience.

Now the fifteen-minute speech is itself almost a thing of the past. The most sinister statistic in political telecasting is the one which records the ominous rise of the spot announcement. Hyman H. Goldin, a former FCC aide, has estimated that 60 percent of the money spent by candidates on television in recent general elections has gone for spots; the proportion of funds invested in program time has been steadily declining.

This development can only have the worst possible effect in degrading the level and character of our political discourse. If it continues, the result will be the vulgarization of issues, the exaltation of the immediately ingratiating personality and, in general, an orgy of electronic demagoguery. You cannot merchandise political candidates like soap and hope to preserve a rational democracy.

While this drift to spot announcements is in great part the preference of the candidates themselves, the industry cannot be held wholly guiltless, for it would much rather sell spots than

306

program time. Both the candidates and the industry, however, prefer to blame the condition on the audience, which, both claim, will simply not sit still for thoughtful disquisitions on public policy. No doubt a large part of the mass audience could not care less about an intelligent discussion of issues. But there remain a substantial number of viewers, even if less than a majority, who do care. Does not television have an obligation to this important minority, too, as well as to the service of democracy in general?

The ultimate answer to this question lies in the movement which must some day come toward the diversification of the viewing public; UHF and pay-TV will no doubt make it easier for the medium to reach specialized audiences. In the meantime, one wonders whether more free time should not be made available to candidates, especially in Presidential elections. If democracy depends on rational communication, if television is now the dominant communications medium and if television licenses are granted, according to the Communications Act, with a view to the "public interest, convenience and necessity," then it would seem that one of the richest industries in the country might make systematic provision for free time for public debate, at least during Presidential elections.

I recognize that informally the industry has done a considerable amount of this. But I wonder whether it is doing enough to discharge the obligations which come with its highly profitable licenses. Is it not really pretty important to give the electorate a chance to hear a man who wants to be President, even if this outrages people who would prefer to see *The Beverly Hillbillies?* [1] In addition to lowering the level of the party debate, television may give an initial advantage to the poised, photogenic, other-directed, manipulable candidate.

The rush of professional actors into politics is an obvious consequence of the television age. One shudders a little to think what would have happened, for example, to the Adamses or Jackson or

[1] I would not exclude the possibility of achieving this result in part through a graduated system of federal subsidies, as proposed by broadcaster Stimson Bullitt, or through tax deductions for a portion of lost revenues, as proposed by former FCC Chairman E. William Henry; and I would support researcher Herbert Alexander's suggestion that Section 315 of the Communications Act be amended to permit a policy of "differential equality of access."

Lincoln if television had existed in the early years of the republic. On the other hand, television is a relatively unsparing medium; it consumes material voraciously, in politics as well as in comedy and drama; and while it may lend itself to slick first impressions, it probably is not hospitable to sustained phoniness and fakery. In the long run, I think, genuine qualities—intelligence, integrity, humor, firmness of purpose—will win out over calculated effects. The Kennedy-Nixon debates of 1960 was a case in point.

The Balance Sheet

Where do we end up? I do not think that television has wrought a revolution in our political system. American democracy will adapt itself to the tiny box as it has to a series of technological changes from the start of the republic. The effects of television —apart from the nominating convention—have been mostly marginal. It would seem that, through news programs and, to some extent, through pseudo-news programs, television has somewhat widened public acquaintance with issues and personalities; but that, aside from documentaries, its efforts at interpreting the significance of news tend to be superficial; and that its party political programs have encouraged the oversimplification of issues and favored the smooth and bland over the rough-hewn candidate. If voters had to depend on television alone for the information on which they base political judgments, the results would undoubtedly be poor for American democracy.

Yet, so long as television is considered a supplement to newspapers, magazines, political meetings, and solitary midnight brooding by individual citizens, and not a substitute for them, it has in certain respects enriched our politics. And it could do so much more. Its power to convey the quality of political leadership is vast; the agony of grief which ran around the world when John F. Kennedy died after a short thousand days as President was obviously in part a result of the way television had made him a cherished figure in remote lands. If television would recognize an affirmative obligation to elevate the level of our politics, and applied as much thought and talent to this as it does to selling detergents, it might play a great role in helping make our democracy more rational and responsible.

308

XXIII.

Beware of TV's Election Monster!*

MAX LERNER

Max Lerner is Professor of American Civilization at Brandeis University. He has served as editor of *The Nation* and on the editorial board of *The American Scholar*. Among his books are *The Mind and Faith of Justice Holmes, America as a Civilization*, and *The Age of Overkill*.

~~~~~~~~~~~~~~~~~~~~~~~~~~~~~~~~~~~~~~

THE COMMUNICATIONS REVOLUTION has been racing so fast that it has lapped the election process itself: barring some action to prevent it there is a real danger during an election year that one or the other Presidential candidate will be declared virtually (though unofficially) elected on TV by the computing machines, on the basis of a small "raw vote" count, before all the voters have had a chance to cast their ballots and the polls are closed.

It is disturbing and even frightening to reflect on what this might do in influencing the final vote in a potentially decisive state like California, perhaps by a hairbreadth margin. There is a good deal more involved here than the display of technical virtuosity by "voter profile" experts, or the competitive prestige race between the big networks. Nothing less is involved than the integrity of the democratic process itself, which depends on every man having the right to make his final choice in the polling booth without any interference.

In the history of political polling there have been several milestone episodes. Two were flapdoodles: the fatally flawed *Literary Digest* poll of 1936 which led to the death of the *Digest*, and the

* Reprinted from SHOW Magazine, September 1964, pp. 29-31, 90, by permission of the author and the publisher. © 1964 Hartford Publications, Inc.

1948 election forecasts when all the pollsters predicted a Dewey victory over Harry Truman and fell flat on their faces. These created a climate of skepticism about the effectiveness of polling techniques. But that is not the problem now.

The new era in projections is symbolized by the California primary of June 2, 1964. At 8:15 P.M., E.D.T. (5:15 P.M. California time) the CBS Vote Profile Analysis sent a streamer across the Red Skelton show with a preliminary prediction that Goldwater was winning. By 10:22 P.M., E.D.T. (7:22 P.M. California time), only 22 minutes after the polls closed in Southern California and with 38 minutes still to go before they closed in Northern California, CBS analysts awarded the state primary to Goldwater. It was all over but the counting. As it turned out, after a "hard returns" count that kept shifting all night between Goldwater and Rockefeller, the CBS prediction held true, although by a smaller margin than originally forecast. It was a brilliant technical coup, whatever might be said against it on political, psychological, and ethical grounds—which is plenty.

The CBS "model" was based on 42 key precincts out of California's total of 32,861 precincts. The "call" of a Goldwater victory was projected from the vote in only 18 of the key precincts, and only two percent of the total raw vote. Yet Bill Leonard and Lou Harris, who made the CBS decision to call, felt "morally certain" that their projection would hold. But all the discussion on this score misses the real point. If the voting analysts on any network were to be proved wrong, they would pull the whole fabric of their world and the prestige of their network down around their ears. It is exactly when they are proved right, exactly because the model and the techniques with which they work are growing more sophisticated, that their danger to democracy increases. The problem is no longer one of the fallibility of the "monster" machines, but of the suggestibility of men's minds. It is not the failures of the machine that threaten the democratic process, but its frightening successes.

For the danger lies exactly in their credibility. As people learn to trust their accuracy, what can only be called the *impact vote* (the voting done under the impact of the "call") will become sharper and more crucial. As the technicians learn to pick the key precincts in each state, to feed into the computers the right geographic, ethnic, economic, social and political information and the right poll performances from the past, they will call the electoral vote of state after state fairly accurately and very early. As each state goes into one or another column of the shadow Electoral College of the voting analysts, perhaps even before the polls have closed, the outlines of victory or defeat will grow sharper. A President may be "elected" not only before the polls have closed in California but before they have closed in other Western and perhaps Midwestern states.

Who or what is at fault here? Americans are given to the fallacy of the instrument—the belief that it is always the instrument that embodies the evil. First we blamed the opinion polls, and then the computer itself, as if it were an infernal machine embodying the evil eye. The fact is that both the polls and the computer are, like power itself, ethically neutral. Everything depends on how they are used, by whom, for what purpose, in what context. What is at fault is a society that allows them to be used against its interests.

We are dealing here broadly with three forces: the elites, including both the politicians and the technicians; the TV and radio networks, and the press also; and the voter. Each species behaves according to its inner nature. The politicians and technicians move toward power and tend to manipulate. The networks and press, however disinterested, move toward profits and prestige and tend to exploit both. The voter, however intelligent and even perverse some may be, is often unsure, runs with the herd, and tends to be suggestible. When you bring together the manipulative, the exploitative, and the suggestible, you have a formidable mixture and potentially a dangerous one. That is why democracy today is a difficult process.

This is what Eugene Burdick tries to get at in his novel, *The 480*, an imaginative projection of what could happen at a political convention if the new techniques of voter analysis (including the insights of the behavioral scientists and the subtlest tactics of marketing research and candidate buildup) were pushed all the way. The people who do the buildup, the new genus of behind-the-scenes kingmakers and manipulators, are not evil in the novel but only a little heady with their success in their craft—but the point is that they could be evil. The candidate is an appealing Willkie-like figure, with a mind of his own resisting their manipulations and with his heart in the right place, not an evil figure —but again, he might have been. The author allows himself a speculative flight—"Let a madman or just some very ambitious power-seeker start to use stuff like this and the whole game is changed"—but in the end he backs away from his own vision of evil and makes things come out just dandy. I won't say that Burdick turns the computer and the 480 categories of voters and the machine tapes into a hero, but he is clearly fascinated by the sorcery of the whole business.

Behind the fiction there is an interesting bit of opinion-analysis history. Instead of the "Simulation Enterprises" in the book there was actually a Simulmatics Corporation, as Burdick acknowledges, that did some work in the Kennedy campaign of 1960. I asked Lou Harris, who had largely done the technical work for CBS which led to the 1964 California primary projection, whether he had also been involved in the Simulmatics venture. (It would have been one of those esthetically neat tie-ups that delights a researcher's heart.) But although he was close to the Kennedys all through the 1960 campaign he had not been part of Simulmatics. The men behind it were Ithiel de Sola Pool at M.I.T., Robert Abelson at Yale, and William McPhee at Columbia. They had done some work for Adlai Stevenson and were commissioned to do a vote study for Kennedy. But as Lou Harris tells the story, Bobby Kennedy and he decided not to use it, and it is not true (as a later magazine article had it) that the Simulmatics "People's Machine" won the election for Kennedy.

Yet it is distinctly true that Kennedy relied on the vote-analysis techniques considerably. In the crucial Wisconsin and West Virginia primaries, Kennedy relied on some Harris polling tests for his decision (which was his own) to push the religious issue into the open and ride it hard. The tactic worked. Just before the end of the election campaign another test poll led him to bear down hard on the issue again. I agree with Sam Lubell's point that we ought to distinguish between these private polls that a candidate commissions and buys, and the poll and voter-analyses that are furnished to the public, whether in the press or on TV. The candidate's private poll is a form of market research, and the principle there is *caveat emptor*: he buys and uses it at his own risk, and the public to which some of the polls are disclosed while others are concealed ought to remember to be skeptical of both.

There is of course the danger that the candidate will be turned by the computers into a kind of computing mechanism himself, that he will cut his views to what the monster machine tells him, that instead of a mind of his own he will have tapes in his brain, instead of eyes he will have punch cards and instead of blood of his own he will have the computer tallies. All this is possible, but there is no way of giving spine to a candidate who had none to start with, while one who does is unlikely to lose it simply because his technicians make use of the computer. As a warning against snap judgments about candidate behavior, it is worth remembering that in the 1960 campaign it was Kennedy (whom the liberals adore) who used the voter analysis studies extensively, while it was Nixon (whom the liberals deplore) who suspected the private polls and their theoretical "models"—although he always kept his eye on the ups and downs of voter sentiment in the public polls.

* * *

It is the public polls and projections that the public has a stake in, and can do something about. Here the principal medium, before the election itself, is the press and not TV. A continuing series of polls, using a big enough sampling to be safe, involves a difficult and costly enterprise even for such widely syndicated polls as those of Gallup, Roper, Harris, and (on a more modest scale) Lubell. The payoff is the closeness of the prediction to the actual result, and the point is that it all has to be done *before* the voting starts. A good deal depends upon the theoretical model which is chosen—that is to say—the key precincts picked, the sample profile built, the questions asked. The machines can do the calculating, but the result will depend on human qualities like insight, judgment, and even legwork. One safeguard against distortions is that the press, which itself carries the poll samplings and predictions from week to week, can also

313

serve as critic of the results, distinguishing between the polls that came close and those that didn't, serving at once as prod, lash, and conscience.

The enemy of the vote analyst is the "non-stable voter," who is too volatile to remain a docile subject for study. He may not have made up his mind, he may veer with every wind, he may not particularly care. To pin him down, the pollsters have had to continue their samplings right up to the tape on voting day. I happen to believe that while the activity of these pollsters need not be harmful—provided you view them with due skepticism—they serve no real social purpose. The picture of America watching itself in the mirror as it prepares to vote, taking its temperature as if it were a sick man, is not especially inspiring. I confess to some private satisfaction each time the poll predictions go wrong, and while I don't respond much to the man who tells the pollster, "I don't know," I cheer when someone answers, "I'd rather not say." By the 1960 elections, according to the *Wall Street Journal*, the latter character had jumped from a ratio of one in 25 or 30 of those interviewed to one in 8 or 10. He is not the apathetic voter nor even the tormented voter: he is quite simply the man who doesn't want you to intrude on his privacy.

* * *

Perhaps in time he will carry the privacy principle into battle, employing every ruse to mislead the tester. He will cheerfully lie about his economic and social group, invent his income, say he is a Mormon or a Holy Roller, when he is actually a Catholic or a Jew, pretend to a passion for a candidate he loathes, and distort everything about himself except his sex and color which are beyond his control. Sometimes I dream of forming a Society of Saboteurs of the Straw Ballot (SOSSB) whose motto will be Subterfuge, Chicanery, and Cunning.

We may win battles in this war of sabotage, but alas, it is probably a losing war, especially in the Election Night projections, which are growing ever more sophisticated. There is a sharp distinction between the vote predictions before the balloting starts and the lightning vote projections while it is in progress. The difference lies in the raw material: in the first case it is a guess about how the voter *may behave* (he may himself not know until he pulls the lever); in the second, it is how he *has actually voted*—or is voting. Even with a small model the technicians, if they have fed the right comparative information to the computer, can discover quickly what the new voting pattern is in a precinct or county or state, how much it differs from previous ones, and what uniformities there are in those differences. In a brief time they can get a projection; as the voting goes on they can make changes in their model and correct it for unforeseen trends; thus in the interlacing of theory and the hard returns of fact, they can make the leap into their call. They insist that this is not the old "probability sampling," because as the returns come in the model is being constantly corrected by human judgment. Lou Harris calls this, in a portentous phrase, "judgmental sampling on a probability base"—and that ought to do for a while.

The trouble with it, as I have suggested, lies not in the model or the machine itself but in a society which allows them to be used against its interests, for the sake of prestige or profit or even the sense of craftsmanship. Sometimes it seems that the important race is not between the major candidates but between the major networks, especially between those Guelphs and Ghibellines of our time—NBC and CBS. Their rivalry has its healthy aspect and is productive of great technical strides, but it is stupid for the public to allow it unchecked rein if it means running the national elections for the benefit of network rivalry. If, in fact, the early calls on TV before the polls have closed induce panic or stampede voting, then the public has the right, the duty, and the power to set the rules that will prevent it.

* * *

I can understand the defense that the major networks make of their right and duty to report news as fast as it happens. "We have no alternative except to report it," Bob Northshield of NBC told me—a moment after he had termed the early CBS call in the California primary a "trigger-happy" one. As for CBS itself, Bill Leonard says, "I am the most conservative guy in the world. I don't want to shoot craps with the reputation of CBS." I found Jim Hagerty of ABC more anxious than either of his rivals about

315

TV's effect upon the late voting. "Might we not," he asks, "be a facility that could influence the voting pattern of the American public in a Presidential election?" His answer is a decided Yes. He fears that the bandwagon vote or the failure of the discouraged voter to vote at all, once TV has awarded the election to one or another candidate, could affect the state tickets as well as the Presidential slates. As an old hand at politics, Hagerty remembers how politicians (including himself) have tried to use early Connecticut and New York returns to influence Western voting, not only through their impact on the voter but on the party worker. Feeling that the election is as good as over when he hears the TV result, the party watchdog at the voting booth may relax his vigilance and go home or go out and get drunk before the polls have closed.

The public interest doesn't have to carry the burden of proof on this, to show beyond doubt that the TV early projections are necessarily harmful. It need show only what might and could happen. We know enough about voter behavior to know that the voter is highly suggestible, the American is a lonely person; he feels less lonely when he is joining others, especially on the winning side. Even granting that some voters are counter-suggestible, the two don't cancel each other out: in both cases the voter's mind is inflammable timber. The voter is modern man, subject to pressures, riddled by anxieties, sometimes apathetic. He may come to the polling booth after a day's work, anxious to get home. It is crucial that he be allowed to resolve his inner debate by himself in the polling booth before he becomes the target for another attack—this time not on how he ought to vote or on how others will vote, but on how others *have already voted.*

Some of our philosophers and social theorists are deeply worried about what will happen in a computer society. One of them, John Wilkinson, believes that when the machines are linked together, "in such a way that the decisions, or outputs, of the one become the inputs of the other a new identity arises, with a mind of its own, pursuing values that are not human values."

* * *

But there is no need for us to turn into machine wreckers and try to smash the computer. He cannot become a tyrant-king unless we let him; and we can make him useful in the service of the society. Technicians like Northshield, Leonard and Hagerty, Harris and Quayle (the guiding technical spirit on ABC) want to get a job done well. The problem is to shape a framework within which they and their techniques and their machines can do the job responsibly. Since it is the states who regulate voting procedures, Hagerty has suggested an agreement by the states (through the Governors' Conference, or perhaps the Council of State Governments) for a ban on any release or reporting of the votes until the polls close. It strikes me as a sensible suggestion. Northshield thought it might be "close to suppression." Leonard thought he might go along, but wanted the ban to apply to all communications, including telegraph and telephone, which would make it considerably harder to enforce. Hagerty's second suggestion was for a system of staggering the closing of polls in each state so that the time differentials would be evened out. This made good sense to Northshield. Clearly the two methods could be done together and would complement each other.

There has been talk of FCC action banning voting projection while the polls are open through the regulatory power of the Commission in the public interest, and I don't see why we should exclude it as a last resort. Representative Oliver Bolton of Ohio has asked for such action, in the absence of a voluntary network agreement, but a solution by state action or by voluntary action by the big media would be better. Senator Barry Goldwater came up early with a proposal for a legislative ban, but his suggestion never reached a vote. Senator Karl Mundt brought it up again after the California primaries. In both cases there may be the conservative Midwestern or Southwestern fear of the impact of early voting in the more liberal Eastern urban areas upon the others; but the motive is less important than the danger itself, which goes beyond parties.

*   *   *

The networks themselves could cut through all the difficulties of state or FCC action by taking joint voluntary action for a self-limiting agreement to delay putting their projections on the air until the polls are closed. They could do this, provided they wish to, without running afoul of restraint of trade or suppression of news. In order to save costs and avoid confusion they have reached an agreement (along with the big press associations) for a pool of their vote-tallying operations, as distinguished from vote analysis and projection. Thus the vast army of people who put together the tallies and keep track of them on election night will now be under a single direction and will service the networks and press associations at a saving of some millions to all of them.

If they can thus set the frame of competition for the actual raw vote count, in effect eliminating competition, they can equally agree on a pattern of ground rules as to when the projections lend audience excitement to the panels of TV experts—at least until the election is "awarded" by them. The early returns come in during the peak viewing period for TV and the networks are understandably reluctant to sacrifice any part of their audience for any part of that period. This may be why LeRoy Collins, then head of the National Association of Broadcasters, was adamant against a voluntary agreement. By the end of the elections in November of 1964 it was estimated that the networks spent from 25 to 27 million dollars on the primary and election campaigns. They wanted to get something for it, and what they wanted was their advantage over the press in instantaneous reporting in results and projections.

Yet, however strong this network self-interest, it must give way before the national interest. Governor Grant Sawyer of Nevada, the current chairman of the Governors' Conference, has been urging it as a strong possibility. If it included agreement also by the wire services and by the associations of publishers and editors, I don't see why it wouldn't work. Given such a voluntary agreement by TV, radio and press, along with a system of staggered closing hours, a legislative ban would not be necessary: it would be possible to release the voting returns to the technicians as fast as they came in, but keep them from the public. The TV experts could do their computing and could even tape their projections and calls in advance of the closing hour of the polls. At that point the computers could go their merry fallible or infallible way, and both gadgetry and marketry could have a field day, without hurting the public interest. There would be some secu-

318

rity problems to make sure that the rules were not broken, but none that could not be solved. As for the "suppression of the news" which both CBS and NBC seem to fear, the fact is that it is not the voting results themselves but the network projections of them that have to be kept under control. If they are not regulated by voluntary agreement, then either the states or the FCC will have to act. There is no reason to fear the machines themselves. What is dangerous is an attitude toward the machines which makes man not their master but the raw material for them to use. It is part of society's task to impose the human ethos which is indifferent to human values as it is to all values. To regard an election as, in effect, over when the technicians demonstrate that its conclusion is a foregone one—that means to surrender the human voter to the indifference of the machine. Those who have to do their voting in this climate, whatever the precinct or state, become a species of captive voter. I go further: they become a surplus voter, asked to cast their vote in a context in which they are certain it will no longer count. If men are made to feel surplus in a democracy they are demeaned, and the society is thereby diminished.

XXIV.

Violence in the Cinema*

PHILIP FRENCH

Philip French works in radio in London. He is co-editor of *Age of Austerity*.

∿∿∿∿∿∿∿∿∿∿∿∿∿∿∿∿∿∿∿∿∿∿∿∿

THE CINEMA is a peculiarly violent form of entertainment, developed in and catering for what we have come to think of as an age of violence. Undoubtedly one of the reasons that we think of our time *as* an age of violence is because of our vivid vicarious experience of destruction and brutality in newsreels and feature films. One can have lived the quietest of lives and yet feel that through the cinema one has looked upon the face of war and civil disruption, participated in bank robberies and murder, witnessed a hundred gunfights and brutal assaults. Of all aspects of the cinema, the treatment of violence is perhaps the most complex, controversial, and in many ways central. It is only equalled as a controversial issue by the often closely related question of sex. The extreme views of its effects are on the one hand those of certain social observers who see it as one of the principal causes of crime and delinquency, and on the other of those psychologists who believe that it plays an almost essential cathartic role in diminishing aggression.

A not untypical reaction is the comment that "anyone who prolongs scenes of violence is only doing so to titillate a small unhealthy section of the audience." This generalization might find wide acceptance, but it does not stand up for a minute to close scrutiny. To begin with, a mass medium does not persistently set out to please small sections of its audience, so if an interest

* Reprinted from *Twentieth Century*, Winter 1964-65, pp. 115-30, by permission of the author and the publisher.

in violence is unhealthy then it is one that is pretty widely shared. Furthermore the most obviously prolonged scene of violence ever made is the appalling carnage on the Odessa Steps in *Potemkin*, the most celebrated single sequence in the history of the movies. Although it is deliberately prolonged beyond the actual time which the real event would have taken, a rare thing in the cinema, no one could accuse Eisenstein of titillation. The view of the popular audience, which is too rarely heard in these matters (it votes with its feet at the box office), is no doubt expressed for them by Sammy Davis in *Robin and the Seven Hoods*, when he dances around a gambling den which he is wrecking with a submachine gun, celebrating the outrage with the mischievous song:

> *I like the fun,*
> *Of reaching for a gun,*
> *And going, Bang! Bang!*

This is the true spirit of the unselfconscious groundlings breaking through the rational carapace of our nervous times.

Cinematic violence can be approached in terms of two closely linked questions: Why is there so much of it? How much of it is justified, and on what grounds? Naturally, some of the answers take one straight into the field of sociology and psychology, and where it seems better for them to be expanded by sociologists and psychologists I shall break off and leave it to them. There are already far too many film critics treating the screen as if it were society on the couch. But these questions can only be posed against a historical background. There never has been a time when the movies have not been preoccupied with violence. (One of the earliest films of the Edison Company in 1893 was a one-and-a-half-minute film for Kinetoscope viewing called *The Execution of Mary Queen of Scots*—the doomed lady walks to the block, an axe swings, a head rolls in the dust.) Before the end of the century it became apparent that the movies would take over the theater's role of providing violence and spectacle, although the theater's immediate response to the challenge was a vain indulgence in greater realism, more elaborate spectacle. But of one such attempt, the chariot race in an 1898 dramatization of *Ben*

321

Hur, a contemporary critic observed: "The only way to secure the exact sense of action for this incident in a theater is to represent it by Mr. Edison's invention."

If one is looking for the origin of the public opprobrium that is attached to movie violence, this too can be found in the 1890s. Terry Ramsaye, who lived through the period and was the American cinema's first serious historian, places it around 1897, two years after the invention of the movie projector. Faced with the limitless possibilities of the new medium, the American pioneers could think of nothing better to do than record prize fights round by round. Of the consequences of this obsession with the ring, Ramsaye observed in his book *A Million and One Nights* (1926):

> One marked effect of the Corbett-Fitzsimmons picture as the outstanding screen production of its day was to bring the odium of pugilism upon the screen all across Puritan America. Until that picture appeared the social status of the screen had been uncertain. It now became definitely lowbrow, an entertainment of the great unwashed commonalty. This likewise made it a mark for uplifters, moralists, reformers and legislators in a degree which would never have been obtained if the screen had by specialization reached higher social strata.

The history of the cinema has since had running through it a continuous battle between the "uplifters, moralists, reformers and legislators" and the practitioners in the medium, its greatest artists as well as its most blatant commercial exploiters, and the battleground has usually been the treatment of sex and violence.

The cinema was not exactly slow to realize its power, though at first a trifle vague about its dramatic uses. When Edwin S. Porter filmed the first important dramatic close-up, it was of a menacing bandit firing his pistol directly into the camera. But he stuck it on to the end of *The Great Train Robbery* (1903) almost as an afterthought, and the Edison Catalogue of the following year, while recognizing that "the resultant excitement is great," suggested to exhibitors that "this scene can be used to begin or end the picture."

Subsequent film-makers became more knowing in every way as they came to understand the nature of the medium, and as the society in which they lived grew increasingly sophisticated in its appreciation of the nature of violence. Since the turn of the century violence has been a constant factor and I fancy that such evidence as there is for periodic increases has been greatly exaggerated. It is the form and intensity of violence that has changed rather than its quantity. This is a minority view, and a more generally accepted one is that the German cinema was particularly violent in the 1920's, the American cinema in the early 1930's and the French cinema in the 1950's. Socio-political reasons— the atmosphere of the Weimar Republic in Germany, the post-Prohibition early-Depression era in America, the national confusion and colonial unrest in France—are usually given. What these backgrounds may have done is to give a unifying character to the bodies of films (i.e. all German expressionist pictures tend to look alike, all American gangster films share similar characteristics) and the violence may have had a more jarring effect through its repetitive, contemporary character. (Whereas paradoxically the repetitive, formalized violence in an established genre, the horror film, say, or the Western, has the opposite result, making it almost cosy.) Yet if we look closely at the work of someone like Fritz Lang we see in the style and the treatment of violence a continuing personal development that links his German movies of the 1920's with his American ones in the following three decades.

As it happens there has never been a time when some critic hasn't been spotting a new upsurge of violence (and sex). There are at least four major instances in the case of the American cinema. First there was the outcry in the 1920's that brought into existence the infamous Production Code. (This followed an alleged cycle of violent movies that included De Mille's popular success of 1919, *The Cheat*, where Sessue Hayakawa branded his adulterous wife with a red-hot iron, a sequence considered barbarous at the time but recently regarded as sufficiently innocuous to be presented during a sycophantic Tribute to De Mille on prime-time TV.) A second outcry came in the 1930's with the gangster films, which contravened—directly or obliquely—almost every section of the Production Code, and yet a third in the mid-forties immediately after World War II. At this point an anonymous "Film Critic" contributed an article to *Penguin New*

Writing (No. 30; 1947) called "Parade of Violence," which contained the following lament:

Gone completely the sophisticated and adult attitude of American film-melodramas such as *Laura, The Maltese Falcon, Mask of Dimitrios*, etc.; instead we have the purposeless parade of violence for its own sake: physical violence unrelated to any known form of life and apparently catering for a supposed audience of sadistic schoolchildren.

Several of these pictures too are considered fairly innocent fare now that they have eventually reached the television screen, and a handful of them are considered minor classics—including two by Fritz Lang which "Film Critic" compares unfavorably with those German pictures of the 1920's that had been accepted as so dangerously prophetic by the adherents of the heady thesis advanced in Siegfried Kracauer's *From Caligari to Hitler*.

It is easy enough now to see these postwar pictures as expressing the black mood of the time and reflecting Hollywood's belated discovery of abnormal psychology. The psychopathic villain had arrived, to be joined soon by the psychopathic hero, and both remain with us. Still, "Film Critic" was in good company, and was talking about what G. Legman described as "Hollywood's New Violence" (*Love and Death*, 1949), quoting "a working abridgment" of the Production Code coined by an American Jesuit: "No tits—blood." Legman's well-known theory about the suppression of sex leading to an increase of violence in all media, although taken much too far, has a certain validity. Clearly the Catholic orientation of American censorship leads to a toleration of violence and an intolerance of sexual frankness which, coupled with the inescapable violence of American life, makes pictures from the U.S. the most violent in the world. (They are matched only, one is told, by a particular genre of sadistic Japanese film which is anyway brewed for Oriental consumption.)

Still, within less than ten years of Legman's and "Film Critic's" assumption that the situation could hardly get worse, there was an article on censorship in *Sight and Sound* asserting as a fact, scarcely in need of support, that "the ferocity of American films has undeniably increased." And in the same issue (Spring,

324

1956) the magazine's associate editor devoted a long essay to the "instinctive rebellion that finds its expression in meaningless acts of violence" that seemed to her to characterize the most significant of recent U.S. social protest pictures. Again, one must observe that there wasn't a real increase in violence but merely that it was more disturbing on account of its confusion with insoluble social problems—*Rebel without a Cause* (1955) is a case in point. At its best it could even be the result of a desperate honesty.

Now we seem to be involved in a similar debate and it concerns movies from all over the world. From this we can draw some obvious conclusions. The most apparent is that yesterday's excess is today's restraint. A 1955 reviewer of *Diabolique*, the film which started a whole cycle of sick thrillers, recoiled with the observation that "rarely if ever has such a wallow in the sickeningly macabre been passed for distribution"; five years later Hitchcock's *Psycho* made Clouzot's picture look almost like a production of the Children's Film Foundation. Though *Psycho* is still going the rounds and scaring the pants off appreciative audiences, it is now regarded as a black comedy.

Another obvious conclusion is that just as screen violence needs to keep getting more intense to compete with preceding shocks in impact—especially where it is only the impact that matters—so there is a lag between national tastes. Where, say, Sweden is some years ahead of Britain in the tolerance of sexual frankness, so America is ahead in the tolerance of violence. Thus the British censor cuts sex scenes from most Swedish pictures and can spot Eva Dahlbeck's nipples behind a screen better than Ingmar Bergman (who had to run this sequence for *Smiles of a Summer Night* through several times before glimpsing them). While he is rarely troubled in this way by imports from the United States, around two out of three American films leave on his floor a few hundred feet of violence of a kind that would scarcely disturb a sensitive youth in Dubuque, Iowa.

Violence on the screen tends, I have said, to take its character and form (if often obliquely) from the mood of the time and place in which it is made. This operates in two ways. On one level is the creative artist who is responsive to the undercurrent of the society in which he works, and reflects it in his personal vision. On another level is the skillful producer of films that are intended to meet what he divines to be contemporary tastes. Naturally there is a good deal of middle ground here. And one is aware that some directors, Hitchcock for instance, have ideas that usually and happily (in commercial terms) match the public mood, while others, such as Luis Buñuel, rarely do. Thus Joseph Losey, although he has worked in England for over ten years, still has the personal approach to violence that was evidenced in his American pictures, though these at the time (the early 1950's) seemed very much of their period and place. The James Bond films, however, are deliberately thought out in terms of exploiting current tastes, and as they get more certain in touch they become more decadent in treatment. If, then, someone wishes to see how violence is dealt with in a personal way, he might go to a Losey film, but if he wants to see the way in which the industry thinks the public wants it served up, *Goldfinger* is a better guide.

It might be interesting, therefore, to look at the opening sequences of a Losey picture, *These Are the Damned*, and of the third Bond movie, *Goldfinger*. Both pictures contain a great deal of violence, but represent quite different approaches to it, and a comparison between the two will bring us on to the further consideration of the questions posed earlier about the amount of violence in the movies and its justification.

*   *   *

These Are the Damned opens with the credit titles presented against the background of pieces of sculpture outside an artist's studio on a deserted cliff. The scene quickly shifts to the promenade of a quiet south-coast resort where a motorcycle gang are swinging on a statue of George III, and singing a rock song. An American visitor is then lured down a side street by the gang leader's sister to be beaten up and robbed. A few minutes later, battered and bleeding, he is carried into a nearby hotel and meets a civil servant (head of a secret atomic research establishment situated beneath the nearby cliffs). "I never expected something like this to happen to me in England," the American says, and

326

receives the reply: "The age of senseless violence has caught up with us too."

The opening sequence in *Goldfinger* goes something like this. The setting is apparently a Caribbean republic—we see a seagull swimming on the water which turns out to be on the head of James Bond as he surfaces in a frogman outfit. With the aid of a rope fired from a dinky little gun he climbs a wall, kicks a Latin American guard in the teeth, and plants a time bomb in a huge gas tank. He then peels off the rubber suit to reveal a white tuxedo, in the buttonhole of which he places a carnation, and arrives at a night club just in time to be relaxing at the bar when the bomb goes off. (A semi-audible line is muttered which suggests that the factory had been, I think, the HQ of drug traffickers.) Mission accomplished, Bond adjourns to the room of a dancing girl. While kissing her he sees the reflection of an assassin in her eye and uses her to receive the blow intended for him. During the ensuing fight the would-be assassin falls into a bath and while attempting to reach for Bond's gun, which is hanging over the tub, is electrocuted by an electric fire (equipped with a conveniently lengthy flex) that 007 hurls across the room. After the obligatory wry crack from Bond we at last get the credit titles— some fancy designs of a gunman firing through an eye-socket against the background of a golden body.

The chief difference between these two sequences is that in *These Are the Damned* every shot is related to themes and incidents that occur later in the picture, while the introductory episode in *Goldfinger* is wholly gratuitous—it exists as a film in its own right and its only function is to excite and amuse, to establish a mood. Both pictures work in terms of what its audience knows and understands, but the aim of *These Are the Damned* is to explore violence, that of *Goldfinger* to exploit it. (But I don't wish to condemn violent entertainment *ipso facto*, and *Goldfinger* is nothing if not entertaining.)

Take the characters in the two films. In *These Are the Damned* the American visitor is immediately recognizable as the two-fisted adventurer (the part is played, incidentally, by an actor associated with private-eye and Western roles), a suggestion of the perennial movie hero who usually carries a gun or a

327

sword and seems not merely prepared for violent encounters but positively to will them, though he is here deliberately thrown into a situation he cannot comprehend. There is the "teddy boy" gang —traditional figures of group menace, creations of social and psychological unrest, but here set against the atomic scientist and *his* uniformed team, men associated with a new destructive force too hideous to contemplate. In *Goldfinger*, Bond is played as a fantasy figure, totally in control of his world, surrounded by stock figures—the loyal American, the sinister Oriental, the treacherous Latin American, the brilliant but deadly German—and when atomic science comes in, it does so as part of an action plot, a contemporary gimmick.

Then compare the treatment. In *These Are the Damned* a sudden outburst of violence in a peaceful setting; the attack shown in brutal close-up, sado-masochistically presented from the point of view of both attackers and victim, disturbing and difficult to enjoy; and in the pickup which precedes the assault is suggested an underlying erotic implication. From the very first frame of *Goldfinger*, on the other hand, we are disarmed—it is all a huge joke. The violence and sex are rapid and perfunctory (rarely lingered over as in the Fleming books), the association with sex is not implied but hammered home in knowing collusion with a pseudo-sophisticated audience, which is never genuinely involved in it. *These Are the Damned* may be deliberately manipulating conventional material in its schematic way and operating at a symbolical level, but it is set in a real world where people get hurt, contaminated; *Goldfinger* is set in a fantasy world, with elaborately dazzling sets, and even the actual locations are made to seem unreal. The tradition in which it works is that of the violence of slapstick farce and of those sadistic cartoons where animals get squashed flat or have their fur blasted off only to reappear instantly, ready for further humorous punishment.

Finally, note the verbal exchange quoted above between the American and the scientist in *These Are the Damned*: it's a trifle portentous, certainly, yet indicative of a serious awareness of the problem of violence on the part of the film-maker and assumed by him in his audience. *Goldfinger*, of course, is equally self-conscious and assumes in its audience a shallow knowledge of psychology, but this self-consciousness takes the form of deliberately sending itself up, of protecting itself against any serious charge by ensuring that no one likely to make such a charge could take the film seriously.

These films represent the two poles of contemporary screen violence. Superficially they have a great deal in common. They also share another quality that is not so superficial—that no other medium could have presented what is contained in these initial scenes so rapidly or with such impact—before, in fact, we had any knowledge in either case of the characters or the story other than that which we bring from other films.

*   *   *

I have dealt at such length with these two pictures because they highlight many of the ways in which violence is handled in the contemporary cinema, and because they help explain why there is and has been so much violence in the movies. The first reason is squarely faced by *Goldfinger*—there is a vast international public for such exercises in brutality, and the cinema is dependent upon the support of a mass audience. Indeed, the cinema (with the recent low-powered assistance of TV) now bears the main burden of satisfying this legitimate and enduring need. Secondly, as *These Are the Damned* illustrates, serious artists are attracted by violent themes, perhaps today more than ever before, because of the urgent social issues involved, the extreme experiences it entails, and (it must be acknowledged) the "terrible beauty" violence has in itself.

There is a sense in which the cinema by its very nature is drawn towards violence. In writing on "Film Aesthetic" many years ago, Sir Herbert Read spoke of the camera as "a chisel of light, cutting into the reality of objects," and it can be maintained that the flickering passage of twenty-four frames per second through the projector, the vertiginous movement of the camera, the continuous shifting of viewpoint, the rapid change of image in both size and character, the very idea of montage, make films—irrespective of their subjects—a violent experience for the audience. Undoubtedly the technique of film is employed

329

in this way. An obvious and conscious example is Alain Resnais' *Muriel*, where banal, undramatic material was deliberately presented in a violent and shocking manner primarily through its style of editing. In a far more obvious sense, however, the cinema —as the best description of it, "motion pictures," suggests—tends towards violence. It is concerned with movement, with the telling of stories, the conveying of sensations, the sharing of experiences, the expression of ideas, primarily in terms of the changing relationships of people and objects. True, sound effects, words and music have since come to play an important part in a medium that was developed without them, but their role is essentially ancillary; when the word dominates, as it too often does, the result is usually disastrous as either art or entertainment. The movies are predominantly about things happening, and the extreme form of things happening is violence. As everyone knows, the final word before shooting a scene is symbolically the director's call for "Action." Not surprisingly to the moviemaker and the moviegoer the words "action" and "violence" as relating to the content of a film are virtually synonymous.

This natural violent bent of the movies as art and entertainment has been compounded by the scenes of violence in the actual world that it has been the lot of the newsreel to record. And when one comes down to it, the task of distinguishing between the nature of newsreel material and that of the feature film is no easy one. We usually rely upon the context to do it for us, yet such is the basic similarity that the images of the two blend easily in our minds, and are frequently mixed in films. Occasionally there is an outcry when illegitimate use is thought to be made of documentary footage. For one thing it can be used to propagate falsehood—the Italian "documentary" *Mondo Cane* (where the individual scenes of violence and degradation were undeniably "real" and "true" in themselves) is an obvious and rather complicated example. And a few years back there were strong objections to actual combat shots of dying marines being inserted into an "entertainment" film, *Sands of Iwo Jima*, despite (or perhaps because of) the fact that few people could have told which were the real deaths and which the simulated ones.

*   *   *

THE CONTROVERSIAL SCREEN

The Oxford Dictionary defines the primary meaning of violence as "the exercise of physical force so as to inflict injury on or damage to persons or property," and this, the generally understood meaning in everyday life, is the sense in which I have been using it here. It shows how close the cinema is to violence in real life that one can discuss the widest possible range of films in these terms.

In most other media, however, it is necessary to extend this meaning. In the 1964 discussions on Violence in Society and the Arts at the Institute of Contemporary Arts in London, categories were devised to give as much (or more) prominence to violence in analytical cubism and the work of Fontana, Appel, and Mondrian as to a painting like *Guernica*, which is after all about violence, if not an act of violence in itself. (It is significant that the short movie *The Reality of Karel Appel* which shows the artist at work is truly violent in a way that one of his completed canvases isn't. As Mary McCarthy said of Harold Rosenberg's theory of action painting: "You cannot hang an event on the wall, only a picture.") In Martin Esslin's lecture on violence in the theater (reprinted in *Encore*, May-June 1964) only one of the five categories he created—his first, "violence that occurs between characters in the play"—fits the dictionary definition and actually relates to the dramatic action itself. And even here Mr. Esslin was concerned primarily with psychological violence. Physical violence within the play he considers to be "relatively unimportant," and it's almost with a sigh of relief that he records that "this most primitive aspect of the theater has devolved almost entirely on to the other media." But the uses to which violence is put in the cinema are far wider than they ever were in the theater, and of course Mr. Esslin's other categories (violence of the author towards his characters, a rallying call for violence from the stage, violence directed against the audience, violence developed by the audience towards the characters on the stage) are also found in the cinema. They all apply to *Potemkin*, for instance.

One must admit, however, that most violence in the movies, notwithstanding the calculation and the frequent skill in presentation, must be deemed primitive in its ultimate provenance.

For every sequence like that in which the architect in Antonioni's *L'Avventura* expresses all his self-disgust and professional disappointment in the simple act of spilling a bottle of ink over a young student's drawing-board, there are a thousand meaningless gunfights, knifings, and barroom brawls. The distinction here is primarily a moral one, for gunfights, knifings, and barroom brawls are among the things we go to the cinema for, and as both art and entertainment they can be justified in themselves and of themselves, whereas the scene I've mentioned from *L'Avventura* has its moral and artistic significance only in terms of the film as a whole. I stress this because it leads on to the justification of violence in the movies. And part of the case must be concerned with what we seek in them. Certainly no one goes to the theater for physical violence any longer, and the Grand Guignol has at last sadly had to shut its doors in the face of the overwhelming competition from two generations of horror picture producers. Unless handled in a stylized way or with a considerable buildup, and even then its use must be sparing, violence no longer works in the contemporary theater and can never be the *raison d'être* or principal ingredient of a dramatic work.

Violence in the cinema can be justified in terms of its necessity to the overall moral and artistic conception of a work, or merely in terms of the artistry with which it is executed. Many of the principal *genres* in the movies—the thriller, the Western, the war film, science fiction, the gangster picture—endure by virtue of the violence they contain but have their own rules about its use. If one accepts the validity of making these types of film, then one is necessarily condoning that violence. Merely to make the films well is then sufficient justification. But to work against the prescribed rules, to challenge the basic conventions, often results in an intensification of the violence. The most determinedly antiwar pictures, other than those that get bogged down in verbiage like *The Victors,* are more violent than the general rule—as was, for instance, Robert Aldrich's *Attack,* with its close-up of the hero having his leg severed by a German tank track.

Westerns that take a more realistic view of character and of the pioneering experience often tend to dwell on wounding

THE CONTROVERSIAL SCREEN

(Anthony Mann's films), sadistic humiliation (Brando's *One Eyed Jacks*), and unheroic viciousness (Henry King's *The Bravados*). This kind of break with convention has perhaps been too rashly applauded. On behalf of the traditional Western the late Robert Warshow, in perhaps the best article yet written on the subject, argued that "it offers a serious orientation to the problem of violence such as can be found almost nowhere else in our culture." Warshow in the same context touched upon a similar problem in the gangster picture and voiced a feeling that I have long had myself, when he observed:

> Some of the compromises introduced to avoid the supposed bad effects of the old gangster movies may be, if anything, more dangerous, for sadistic violence that once belonged only to the gangster is now commonly enlisted on the side of the law and thus goes undefeated, allowing us (if we wish) to find in the movies a sort of "confirmation" of our fantasies.

It is for this reason that the cycle of gangster pictures in the late 1950's which dealt with the careers of Prohibition and post-Prohibition mobsters, were a good deal healthier than the cycle of vicious private-eye and police movies that preceded them, despite the obvious commitment to characters outside the law. It produced two outstanding films, Budd Boetticher's *Rise and Fall of Legs Diamond* and Don Siegal's *Baby Face Nelson* which, partly through their close attention to period detail, had about them, for all their violence, a kind of balletic purity.

It is easy enough to talk about justifying films on moral and aesthetic grounds and approving of perhaps only a small number of pictures. By these standards one would reject, for instance, the bridge being blown up at the end of *The Bridge on the River Kwai*. Destruction is popular, as Cecil B. De Mille profitably discovered, and it makes for a splendid conclusion in a visual medium to have mighty edifices totter and fall. It was into this twofold cinematic trap that the producers of *Kwai* fell, changing the end of Pierre Boulle's novel and utterly ruining the ironic moral comment that the picture was seeking to make.

The beating that Marlon Brando takes in the final reel of *On the Waterfront* seems to me largely gratuitous and detrimental

333

to the film's ultimate effect. It represents another example of an intelligent director falling into the trap of the slam-bang, upbeat conclusion. (When Budd Schulberg later wrote the film as a novel, his ending was quite different, though less powerfully dramatic.) Its success, in terms of impact on the audience, unfortunately confirmed and encouraged a cinematic tendency to administer symbolic physical punishment of a masochistic nature to the hero that we have seen employed, with varying degrees of justification, in many films, such as *Room at the Top* and *Saturday Night and Sunday Morning.*

For those in search of further descriptive and synoptic material I cannot do better than commend the special issue in February 1963 of the British film magazine *Motion*, a "Companion to Violence and Sadism in the Cinema." Like the program at the Institute of Contemporary Arts, it raises the question of the intellectual's preoccupation with violence which is worth an essay in itself. Under "D" alone the Companion lists "Dark Side of the Light Fantastic, The"; "Dassin"; "Deaf Aid, Torture by"; "Dentures, Death by"; "Disease"; and "Doctor No"; and under "F" the editors choose their "Favorite Movie Scars." Even a cursory perusal of this document should save many a busy person the experience of sitting through a large number of tedious if not actually corrupting pictures. As the old saying goes: "The movies have ruined a lot more evenings than they have morals." I was struck by the way in which the author of an advertisement for a recent horror picture touched in striking fashion on a fundamental aspect of screen violence. The film is called *Straight-Jacket*; it's described as "Entertainment Plus," and the poster depicts a screaming Joan Crawford, together with another photograph of that lady swinging an axe, above which is the slogan: "Keep saying to yourself—it's only a film—It's Only A Film—IT'S ONLY A FILM!"

XXV.

The Film Writer and Freedom*

MICHAEL BLANKFORT

Among the scenarios written by Michael Blankfort are *The Juggler, My Six Convicts,* and *The Vintage.* His several novels include *Behold the Fire.*

∿∿∿∿∿∿∿∿∿∿∿∿∿∿∿∿∿∿∿∿∿∿∿∿∿∿∿

MY FIRST EXPERIENCE with censorship took place when I was about 14 years old. I can recall that about that time I was troubled not only by intimations of sex but also by the first rebellion against religious dogma. I had begun to question the God of my fathers—as well as my father, and that took greater courage. In those years I was a buyer of five-cent blue books published by Haldeman-Julius of Girard, Kansas, a powerful educational instrument in the 1920's now forgotten, unfortunately, by the social historians. Some of my favorites were *What Every Young Man Should Know, Poems of Passion,* by those pornographers, Horace and Ovid, and the *Love Sonnets of Shakespeare,* all sent in plain wrappers. To support my burgeoning atheism, I sent my five cents for a copy of *The Philosophy of Spinoza,* who I heard had also broken with the God of Isaac, Abraham, and Jacob, and had been excommunicated for his daring. I thought he would give me all the arguments I needed.

Now, I make no claims for precocity; I am sure I did not understand the God-intoxication of Spinoza. Yet I must have found something in that heretical tract that was embarrassing my parents, for one day I overheard my mother talking about me to our rabbi. At the end of the conversation on the telephone, she said,

* Reprinted from *Seventh Annual Freedom of Information Conference* (1965), pp. 21-5, by permission of the Freedom of Information Center and the author.

"All right, I'll look and see what books he's been reading." The outcome was inevitable. The little blue book of Spinoza and *French Love Stories* by De Maupassant, both of which I had hidden behind *The Boy Scout Manual*, disappeared. It became clear to me that sex and the questioning of religious dogma were forbidden games. I learned my first lesson in censorship—and its worthlessness, for since that day, I confess, both these subjects have had an overriding interest for me.

As I contemplate the present condition of the writer, chiefly in television and to a far lesser degree in films, I have the uncomfortable feeling that behind the policy committees of the major broadcasting networks, the ad agencies, the censorship efforts of the various state boards, and even the self-censorship of the motion-picture industry, my mother is still at work, and, I add, probably with the same results.

So that there will be no question or misunderstanding about where I stand on the subject of freedom and film, I want to say emphatically that I oppose censorship in all its forms, outside or within the industry, unintelligent censorship or intelligent censorship, if there is such a thing. For, in truth, there is no harmless censorship, anymore than there is a harmless cancer.

*　　*　　*

My motives for this stand derive from the principle that in a democracy, taste, like a citizen's franchise to vote, should be free of constraints. In addition, there is the matter of self-interest. For the sake of the freedom I need as a writer to pursue my visions of human behavior no matter where they lead me, I must protest all limitations to freedom. I cannot accede to the idea that any civic or industrial body has the right to impose its taste and standards of morality on the expressed thoughts of any other writer, lest it take advantage of its power and apply them to my work.

Now, if there are other equally responsible citizens who feel that there is a danger inherent in complete freedom of expression, they will do what they can to restrict it. And it is the writer's task to oppose them. The fact that film writers work under the Production Code as a condition of their employment has never meant that we accept it. On the contrary, writers in Hollywood have been fighting against industrial self-censorship since Theda Bara first bared her shoulders.

Parenthetically, I want to point to a curious misapprehension which fills the mind of many of our censors. It is the idea that the opposite of a state of innocence is a state of sin or depravity. It seems to me that the opposite of innocence is quite different. It is knowledge, not sin. And if one argues that knowledge leads inevitably to immoral acts, then I think we are wasting our time supporting universities. When Adam and Eve ate the seductive apple, they learned that the loss of innocence, and I am being nontheological here, opened their hearts and minds not to the enjoyment of sin but to the hard knowing of life. In this sense, the whole force of censorship works to delay if not distort the facing of truths and the maturing of society.

Before going on to a further discussion of the Motion Picture Association Code, I want to reflect for a moment on the fate of some of my colleagues, the writers for television. The hard knowing of life is experienced these days with great agony by the authors of teleplays. (Perhaps it would be more accurate to call their work, "telepathic plays," since there seems often to be a lack of any sensible communication between what the writer has written and what is seen on the glass box.) As for control of his material and his vulnerability to constraints, not so much from the producers, but from the networks and ad agencies, he is far worse off than the film writer ever was, for he has twice as many bosses and even a greater number of pressure groups and censors who set up taboos with a whim as strong as steel. I recommend a book which covers some aspects of the television writer's travail. *Only You, Dick Daring!* is by Merle Miller and Evan Rhodes. It is a kind of *Uncle Tom's Cabin* of the writer in the clutches of the Simon Legrees who run the air-conditioned plantations of television.

Now, let's turn our attention to feature-length films, products of Hollywood. I am pleased to affirm that the old phrase, "Without the writer we are nothing," so often mouthed in the past and so often discarded in practice, is now coming to have some real meaning. There are reasons for this. Stars, free from the old

337

long-term contracts with studios, have now become more powerful, their own bosses and bosses of production, and are no longer
willing to commit themselves to films that haven't yet been written. Directors demand the opportunity of working with writers,
not like in the bad old days when writers were frequently discouraged from discussing their intentions with the man in charge of
communicating them to the actors. Finally, and this is perhaps
the most important of the new elements in Hollywood, there
is the breakup of the old studio oligarchy. More and more writers
have become producers and directors, with greater control over
their material. This has had an enormous impact on all writers
who take their work seriously, giving them an importance and influence they rarely had before.

* * *

More has to be said, however, about the Production Code. In
the old days, the industry's move to censor itself resulted from
the attacks of pressure groups on the morals of the citizens of
Hollywood and its films. These caused the studio executives some
small amount of spiritual distress and a great amount of economic
uncertainty. The question was how to head these censorship
Apaches off at the pass. And so the Code was created on the theory that if any scalping is to be done, the producers knew better
how to do it.

Writers, as I mentioned earlier, write scripts with the provi-
sions of the Code in mind. Sometimes, we hope that the good
scouts of the Code, honorable and talented men like Geoffrey
Shurlock, when they read our manuscripts will miss those lines
and situations which imply a contravention of the Code. But,
with sadness I say, they invariably see through us. True, they try
to help us keep what we want by suggesting some alternative
approach. But in the end, sin has to be punished. And this stric-
ture creates a spurious morality which has little, if any, connection with the contradictory complex morality of real life.

Today there are signs of great changes. One almost feels that
the long, long war against industrial self-censorship has been won.
We have entered a period of new freedom. The list of films which
couldn't have received the seal of the Production Code several

years ago is a long one. I mention only *Irma La Douce*, *Tom Jones*, *The Carpetbaggers*, and *The Night of the Iguana*. The Los Angeles *Times* recently reported a most unusual event. Dialogue was edited out of a film *after* it had received the Production Code seal. I'm shaken almost to unreason by the thought that in these matters Geoffrey Shurlock, the administrator of the Code, is more radical than Billy Wilder.

It would be pleasant to say that this new dispensation came through the splendid efforts of our freedom fighters—the Guilds, the anti-censorship committees, etc.—but it wouldn't be true. While I don't want to deprecate the victories won at this or that civil liberties barricade by the Motion Picture Producers Association and other groups, whatever triumph evolved has come through the ineradicable need of business to "make a buck."

As is well known, the film industry suffered great losses until recently as a result of television and foreign competition. It had no other choice than to make pictures bigger and freer, for the buck remains the *sine qua non*. Not so long ago, an organization of exhibitors pleaded with a group of producers to cut down on sex in films. It must not be understood by this, by the way, that the theater owners are Galahads of purity. They are, in fact, the most easily frightened men in America. No, these gentlemen were looking for a way to appease their local censorship boards by pointing to someone else's guilt. When the producers asked, in turn, whether the theater owners would stop showing films which had not received the seal of the Production Code, these hinterland defenders of our morals accused the producers of trying to force them into early bankruptcy. In hard cash, morals are always the other fellow's affair. If I may rewrite the gospel: "Profit is not without honor, especially in one's own business."

*   *   *

Though the film writer is freer than ever before, he cannot hang up his sword. Civil liberties and civil rights as subject matter are still beyond the reach of Hollywood films. Not because of prejudices or principles, but simply because of the conviction that such films won't make enough money to return their investment. I was told recently by a distinguished writer-director that he was forced to cut out of his finished film, a Western by the way, one of its most meaningful and moving scenes because it showed the hero, a self-confessed quadroon, compassionately touching the cheek of a white woman he loved. The producers feared that the scene would hurt them at the box office.

Basically, the effect of this new freedom on film writers is very good. It permits us to explore more deeply the characters we write about and our own as well. We have more ammunition with which to attack restrictions on subject matter and even dialogue. And while we are not all rushing back to our Krafft-Ebing, we are hopeful of avoiding those script compromises of the past which sometimes engendered more smirk than truth, more leer than light.

Yet can there ever be too much of freedom? To ask the question is to revoke the whole concept of free expression, for if there are limits, there is no longer freedom. But what will come of it in Hollywood? To answer this is not too difficult. In my opinion, Hollywood will enjoy its new vistas for a little while longer and then will lose what it has gained. Lest I be mistaken for an unrecognized prophet, I hasten to add that I am a disciple of that theory of cultural history which some have called cyclical but which a philosopher friend of mine, Professor Abraham Kaplan, described to me as the "ladies' skirts" theory. As far as styles are concerned, skirts can go up just so far, then they have to start going down again. Then they start going up.

I anticipate the time when our hard-won freedom as filmmakers will create a counter force of demand for censorship. And that this demand can, in time, have an effect. Then new forms of old regulations will settle on us again—on the studios as well as the creators—and we will need all the help we can get. But eventually, just as dresses have to start going up after they have become too long for comfort we will have a newer freedom. And if my cynicism can be forgiven, it will come as before, just when business at the box office is threatened.

There is another kind of freedom I feel deeply about, and one that is very little known. I suggest we leave the outer space of society, so to speak, where censorship boards fly around in ellipses of their own, and probe a little into the precious inner space, the heart and mind of the writer who is, by common agreement, the first cause, the creator without whom there is nothing, not even *Beverly Hillbillies*. In that mind and heart, in that inner space, are waged great battles for freedom. In the lonely, heartbreaking struggles to find creative truths, the writer is both hero and victim, for in films, once he has accepted an assignment, he is no longer master of himself and his work. He can fight for days for his conception of theme, but the ultimate decision lies with someone else—producer, director, star; and to the degree that he fights and wins, to that degree the work of the film writer is his own. One of the mildest men I know, and also one of the most talented of film writers, is called "the killer" by some producers. He fights for his script with a zeal and resourcefulness that mark a great quarterback. The fact that, at the moment, he is Hollywood's most successful writer, with the right to select director and actors, may not be the result solely of his talent. The moral is clear.

Don't forget that most of what is seen on the screen has first been written. Don't fall into the trap of that woman I heard say, "The picture was bad, except for Jack Lemmon's wonderful wit." Mr. Lemmon happens to be a witty man off the screen, but his lines in a film are written by someone else.

*   *   *

It is one of the great secrets of the movie-going world that writers write directions to the director, detailed descriptions for mood and setting, suggestions for music, sound, and silence—all this in addition to dialogue, the structure of plot and theme, the relationship of characters and so on.

Despite all the publicity to the contrary, the script is the prime and ongoing impulse that makes the film. And it is created and shaped in what I have called the inner space.

To understand the terrain of these battles of the creator's inner space, we must remind ourselves that the film, like the theater, is a collective art, and not one in which there is a singular and private connection between the creator and his work, as in the novel and the plastic arts. Standing between the writer and his work there is a living wall of other tastes and personali-

341

ties, so massive and involved that it is often impossible to separate the contributions of the writer from the producer, director and actor. It is because of this that the writer writes with an oppressive and sometimes unconscious tension which has little to do with the normal attrition of his labor.

There are some elements in this phenomenon which recall the old movie scene in which the heroine is tied to the railroad tracks by the villain. From the distance comes the sound of the onrushing train. We see the dark smoke curling above the far horizon, and we ask ourselves, "Will she free herself before the train reaches her? Will she be freed by the hero in time?" And as we watch, two factors operate in our minds. Having been conditioned in our American culture not by the tradition of tragedy but by melodrama, we know with absolute certainty that the heroine will be saved in time, yet we are equally convinced that she won't be saved in time, for otherwise there would be no suspense, and we would laugh instead of holding our breaths or biting our nails. As audience, we are held in constant tension between knowledge and belief, tradition and imagination.

*   *   *

The film writer, too, as any writer in a collective art, works in the same kind of tension. He knows with certainty that his script will not be done as he has written it, yet in order to do his best work, he must believe or imagine that it will. He must give his all, while knowing that no matter how good his all may be, it will not and cannot satisfy the tastes of the others who have equal, if not greater, power over his material. But what may be healthy in an audience is schizoid in the writer. Whether he is or isn't aware of this division in him, his work is affected and his freedom to be himself is curtailed. Who can know how seriously this distorts his work? His capacity to pull out from the recesses of his experience all that he has learned about life is diminished. Although he is able to function under this tension—and it is extraordinary how well he does manage—there are areas of psychic inhibition beyond which he may not be able to move. This is the worst kind of loss of freedom, for it is self-inflicted, a misery beyond calculation.

342

It may be that to avoid this subtle and dangerous self-censorship many talented young men are not coming to Hollywood at all but are writing, producing, and directing their own films in New York, Philadelphia, Chicago, and elsewhere. They are in that still-innocent state where they are free to make films as they see them, and also to make mistakes which are all their own.

I am not offering panaceas for the situation I've described. I'm not sure any exist but I think it is worth mentioning, for the inner constraints of film and television writers, so often forgotten, are as important as the constraints imposed by conventional censorship. When there is a considerable loss of creative energy within that precious inner space, we are all diminished.

XXVI.

Should American Films Be Subsidized?*

WILLIAM FADIMAN

A vice-president of Seven Arts Associated Corporation, William Fadiman has had a varied career as a free-lance journalist, lecturer, literary critic and representative, and motion picture producer and executive.

∽∽∽∽∽∽∽∽∽∽∽∽∽∽∽∽∽∽∽∽∽∽∽∽

THE CURRENT artistic state of the film in America has evoked a condemnatory chorus from many sources. Accusations of intellectual sterility, slavish devotion to formulas, lack of imagination, indifference to esthetic values, degrading capitulation to commercialism, blatant disregard of discriminating tastes, deliberate pandering to vulgarity, and emphasis on arbitrary violence are familiar pejoratives to our Hollywood producers. Moreover, the recent *réclame* and popularity of the imported film as a new standard of comparison and contrast have given all these indictments fresh fuel. In a recent issue of *The New York Times*, Bosley Crowther, the *Times's* film critic, epitomized this viewpoint by stating flatly, "Experience has long since prepared us to accept the uncomfortable fact that the best work in motion pictures —the most intelligent, progressive, astute, and alert to what is happening to people—is being done abroad."

Czechoslovakia, Mexico, India, Japan, France, Italy, England, etc., are lauded as producing motion pictures which achieve the quality and distinction conspicuously missing from our home product. Film festivals from Montevideo to Monte Carlo continually honor their artistic excellence, the philosophic profundity, the comic or tragic inventiveness, the fluid (or static—some-

* Reprinted from *Saturday Review*, August 5, 1967, pp. 14-17, 44, by permission of the author and publisher.

344

times it does not seem to matter which) photography, the simplicity (this appears to be highly coveted) of the narratives, the pre-eminence of the performers, the genius of the editing, the technical virtuosity, and, of course, the masked or naked symbolism of the style.

It is true that the foreign films *we see* are indeed frequently superior in many ways to American films. But it is essential to realize that we are seeing only a small percentage of the hundreds of films produced abroad, all methodically culled and chosen especially for American viewers. And that, furthermore, even these selections are by no means made solely on the basis of their putative artistic value, but also for their appeal to the *voyeurs* in our audiences who derive vicarious satisfaction from the sight of bedroom activities not permitted in American films. It is not to be summarily assumed from this observation that foreign art films (the majority of imported films fall into this category) are deliberately fashioned to attract the prurient American moviegoer. This would be a serious distortion of the truth. It remains important to know, however, that we are seeing only those foreign films which are exhibited for two small segments of our population, the *cognoscenti* and the concupiscent.

*   *   *

It is perhaps fortunate for those critics who bewail our cinematic lot that the majority of European and Asian run-of-the-mill motion pictures are not shown in the United States. For it is a lamentable fact that the average commercial film made in Europe or India or Japan or Mexico is as trite, mindless, vapid, and jejune as any of our own offerings in an identical or parallel genre. Nor is there any validity to the happy assumption that all overseas studios are populated by a talented assembly of Fellinis, Bergmans, Kurosawas, Godards, Resnais, Buñuels, Rays, Polanskis, Demys, Truffauts, Reiszes, and Antonionis. The American cinema has no stranglehold on mediocrity; Europe and Asia have their own creative shortcomings.

But it is not my purpose to advance cinematic chauvinism or to demonstrate that the attacks on the sorry artistic condition of the film in America are mere canards. On the contrary, they are

345

true. Gregory Peck, acting chairman of the recently formed American Film Institute, has publicly deplored "our concern with excessive commercialism," and he is not alone in his censure. Mr. Crowther was right when he stated that the best work in motion pictures is being done abroad.

But why is this so?

Does the fault lie with our moviemakers? Are we really uninventive, unoriginal, untalented, and imitative; are we truly artistically inferior to our European competitors; are our technicians wanting in ingenuity; are we afraid to be enterprising and challenging; do our writers and producers and directors and performers lack the mastery we applaud so unstintingly in their European and Asian colleagues? The answer to all of these charges is, of course, no. There is no cinema magic which is uniquely foreign; our creators and craftsmen are fully as gifted as their foreign rivals. Granting that premise, why is our film fare bereft of so many of the values we extol in foreign motion pictures? It may be worthwhile to examine some of the reasons for this situation, reasons which turn out to be differences—differences which effectually prevent the American film from achieving the deserved supremacy of the foreign films we admire.

In the first place, the cost of producing a film in many foreign countries is considerably lower than it would be in America. It has been proved again and again that the charges for a film production abroad compared to those for the identical film in the United States reveal a 10 to 15 percent difference in favor of the outlander country.

There are various explanations for this lower cost factor, some having to do with the price of the physical materials required, such as the raw stock. Another—and more substantial— is that of labor. Labor is cheaper outside of the United States. Unions exist, but their wage scale is less than ours, and in certain nations the film industry does not have to cope with unions at all, being granted exemptions or lowered rates.

*   *   *

As to stars' salaries, the gap is again in favor of the foreign producer. The extravagant sums paid to our leading players simply do not exist overseas, nor are there many duplications of the American system whereby performers share in the profits and even the grosses of their films. A few examples should suffice: Marlon Brando and Burt Lancaster both receive $750,000 plus a participation in the profits or gross receipts of their films; Elizabeth Taylor demands $1,000,000 in addition to a percentage of the film's revenue. Turning to Europe, one finds that the highest salary paid in Sweden to a performer of the first magnitude, Max von Sydow, is $10,000, whereas Mr. Sydow's remuneration for an American film is approximately $250,000.

Another economic variant is that the foreign film is planned to make its profit uniquely in the country of its origin. It is only the unusual foreign film that ventures beyond national borders. The converse is true of American motion pictures; more than 55 percent of the earnings from American pictures comes from outside the United States. Few American films can anticipate a substantial profit from their domestic showings alone. In fact, almost all our films do well abroad, irrespective of merit or mediocrity. (Is it possible that the alleged twelve-year-old audience level of appreciation could exist in Dijon, Gothenburg, Sapporo, Perugia, and San Miguel Allende exactly as it purportedly does in Kokomo, Indiana?)

The foreign film that is exported to the United States usually finds its acceptance in art houses rather than in ordinary neighborhood theaters. For the foreign film this is a supplementary income from an unanticipated quarter, a sizable bonanza which American films do not enjoy in foreign lands where art houses are not found in any quantity. American films, on the other hand, are almost never produced for the limited exposure offered by art houses. From time to time, avant-garde cinema makers create a modicum of films destined solely for art house consumption; these are known as underground films and in almost all instances are purely experimental. They are invariably undercapitalized, attract a very small coterie patronage composed mainly of loyal cultists, and realize negligible amounts in revenue.

Censorship is another sphere which affects foreign and domestic films in quite different ways. Although we are completely free of government restrictions such as prevail in many foreign

347

countries, these restrictions are rarely applied to sexual behavior, which still remains the one outstanding universal ingredient of screen entertainment. In addition, it must be said that the treatment of sexuality in foreign films is invariably on a more penetrating, forthright, sophisticated, and adult plane than can be found in the most progressive of our films, hobbled as they are by taboos. For the American film faces multiple censorship interdictions ranging from its own self-regulatory Motion Picture Association of America and the National Catholic Office for Motion Pictures to literally hundreds of state, city, village, and hamlet prohibitions and proscriptions. Moreover, the American producer is continually harassed by powerful pressure groups and lobbies hampering and impeding any critical portrayals of various professions, industries, and minority groups. Consequently, we simply cannot present films with the same sexual or social freedom and candor that other nations sanction. The recently applied label for what our censor code calls adult pictures, "Recommended for Mature Audiences" (whatever that may mean), is a feeble attempt to solve this dilemma.

Television also exercises a critical and baleful influence on the American film, an influence which is barely existent in Europe and Asia thus far. For television wields a double-edged sword in the American film industry. Primarily it functions as a competitor for audience attention. Secondarily, however, a strange phenomenon has occurred in which television has suddenly become our ally and our support. For television now pays stupendous fees for the privilege of one or two screenings of a motion picture. Hence, very few pictures are made nowadays without serious consideration of their potential sales value to this medium. I do not wish to belabor the inanities of American television; but when films are conceived within the framework of this unholy alliance they necessarily become debased and degraded. Here again is a factor and a force that foreign films do not have to either consider or counter.

A final problem confronting Hollywood films is that of multiple controls or committee-created productions, a situation which does not apply to such a marked degree in foreign films. It has been said that distinguished foreign films invariably bear the

348

stamp and the imprint of a single man, the director, and that this individual control is a decisive reason for their high esthetic content. This is substantially correct. Why can't this be true in America? For the answer we must turn reluctantly but ineluctably to the financial syndrome which dominates our film industry.

American film companies are publicly owned organizations, while most foreign films are either owned by one man or a private corporation. (There are exceptions, but these are not numerous.) This does not mean that foreign film-makers are not interested in a profit; but it does mean that they do not have the responsibility and obligation to satisfy suspicious and cost-conscious stockholders. One-man supervision permits a wide latitude in the making and implementation of all decisions, whereas our motion picture companies are justifiably chary of allowing a single authority to arbitrarily dispose of millions of dollars. Once in a while a director of proven box-office competence is delegated such power. Historically, Chaplin and De Mille come to mind, and, contemporaneously, Wilder and Wyler and Stevens and Hitchcock and Huston, but even these men are not granted the freedom of operation which obtains in Europe, where the very term "film-maker" often encompasses director and producer and writer in one person.

It seems clear that although there are meaningful contrasts between foreign and domestic films in creative autonomy as well as the pressures exerted by television and censorship, the fundamental difference is that of economics, and that brings us squarely to the subject of subsidization. This is by far the most basic, most influential, and most potent cause of the superiority of the better foreign films. For foreign films are frequently partially subsidized by outright money grants to encourage indigenous production. France, England, Italy, Sweden, Spain, etc.—all maintain institutions whereby the producer receives a sum of money which enables him to finance his product with fewer fiscal problems. His risk is calculably and importantly diminished at the outset, unlike that of the American producer who receives no such donation or lagniappe. These subsidies either come from the government directly or from organizations of a semiofficial nature.

*   *   *

349

In France an annual fund is derived from the imposition of a fixed tax of a little less than a franc on every ticket sold at the box office. By utilizing a complicated disbursement pattern, each picture ultimately receives approximately 14 percent of the producer's share of the income collected from this taxation process. Therefore, that producer with a box-office success will receive more money than the one whose picture has failed to attain audience approval. The sum is given to the producer as a credit to be applied to his next production, thus assuring him of a continuity of plans for his succeeding efforts. Similar financial assistance is also accorded to short subjects (money prizes are awarded to a maximum of fifty each year), thus encouraging an area of film apprenticeship which has become a successful proving ground for such cinematic luminaries as Jean-Luc Godard, François Truffaut, Alain Resnais, and Louis Malle, to name but a few. It is irrefutable that the New Wave of French productions could never have come into being without this financial sponsorship.

England, too, supports its national film-makers under the aegis of a procedure known as the Eady Plan. The Cinematograph Film Act of 1957 expressly provides for the proceeds of a theater ticket tax to be used in subsidizing British films. This levy is administered by the British Film Fund Agency, which divides the money among producers in relation to the box-office potency of their respective productions. This has averaged 40 percent or more on earnings and has gone as high as 55 percent. In 1966, for example, a total of $12,357,117 was disbursed.

Japan likewise has a national subsidization program in which modest amounts of money are donated to those producers who sponsor films specifically designed for the taste and enlightenment of the younger generation, i.e., experimental films devoid of formulas. A study is now being undertaken of additional grants of $5,556,000 for the industry in the form of an annual subsidy for three years.

Spanish films are underwritten with a grant of 15 percent of the gross profits of national films, and the percentage occasionally goes as high as 30 percent for films of outstanding excellence. The Film Aid Fund supervising these gifts also maintains a school for film trainees and dispenses annual awards to individual pictures ranging from 2,000,000 to 4,500,000 pesetas ($33,400 to $75,150) —sums which are often nearly equal to half the total cost of a Spanish film. There are also subsidies for directors who create films of "artistic interest."

Italy, too, offers assistance to its films. This aid amounts to 13 percent of the gross earnings of a film in the first five years it is shown. The Italians also finance a production school, the Centro Sperimentale, and distribute annual awards of 40,000,000 lire ($64,000) each to films demonstrating "special or artistic qualifications." Lesser sums are awarded to meritorious short subjects.

Holland's film fare is financed in part by the Netherlands Production Fund, controlled jointly by the Holland Cinema League and the government. A producer may receive $30,000 to $100,000, depending on the viability of the production he envisages and his own capital. This is a loan to be repaid from his box-office receipts, but with no penalty if such receipts are not forthcoming.

Sweden furthers films via the Swedish Film Institute, which awards a series of cash bonuses to "good" pictures selected by a committee of educators, psychologists, film critics, and industry representatives. Of the money collected from a levy of 10 percent of the box-office receipts from all pictures, one-third goes to the Swedish National Film School for experimental films and training of future film-makers, one-third to box-office winners in proportion to the number of tickets sold, and the last third to films which lost money but won recognition or awards for excellence.

* * *

Other countries which donate money to promote national film production include India and Denmark, the latter having donated 1,275,000 kroner ($184,720) for feature films and 225,000 kroner ($32,580) for short subjects in 1965. West Germany provides 4,000,000 marks ($1,000,000) annually in film subsidies supplemented by various Federal Film Prizes, and supports the Association for Young Film Makers. Iron Curtain countries such as Poland and Czechoslovakia likewise allot financial aid to films, principally to those which meet the demands for national propaganda, but also to pictures which are deemed to be cultural assets.

It is obvious that the intent of most of the subsidizations noted above is to foster film-making in general, whether commercial or artistic. It is patent, particularly in England and France, that such financial benefits accrue to the producer in direct proportion to his competence in pleasing mass audiences; but a welcome result of these dividends is that the truly creative foreign producer is thus enabled to gamble occasionally—and he does— on a film of quality (noncommercial) by virtue of having his investment partially protected. He has the privilege and opportunity of making a film, if not completely *con amore*, at least without total dependence on box-office returns for its and his survival.

From the foregoing, two conclusions may be reached: First, that many foreign films—especially those which cultivate the new and the progressive—are importantly aided by money grants, in addition to freedom from creative restraints; second, that the American motion picture industry cannot hope to exercise its full artistic resources and capabilities until it is independent of the necessity of catering to the lowest common denominator of audience acceptance for profitable returns. Putting it in other terms, foreign producers can strive for an artistically rewarding product without incurring a financial penalty if they fail; American films, quite obviously, cannot do so.

*   *   *

Film-making in America is a business. Even though the end product is sometimes an art product and hence permits the production of films to be labeled an art-industry, the critical noun in that hyphenated description remains the word "industry." Like all industries, it survives on its ability to please the majority of its customers—a majority whose judgment and discrimination are of a substantially low order. If we wish to cater to the minority of filmgoers seeking products of a high artistic order, we cannot do so without suffering gigantic losses.

In any case, it is apparent that the vitriolic attacks on the quality of American films as compared to foreign productions

have been based on little understanding of the differing circumstances under which each product is engendered and no consideration of the substantial fact that financial aid to our foreign
confreres may be a significant cause of the discrepancy. As this
discrepancy becomes more evident the question is being asked
more and more impatiently: What can we do about this?

It seems highly probable that subsidization of some kind may
be one, if not the primary, answer. This possibility has been seriously advanced by many members of the film community. Carl
Foreman, one of America's most renowned producers, recently
stated in an interview in *Variety*, "We are faced today with serious competition. Film-making is improving in all other countries
. . . each country helps by giving a subsidy or a grant because
they are faced with the same problems that face Hollywood: 1)
competition and 2) the high cost of production. . . . Our problem in the United States, creatively, is to play it safe." Arthur
Mayer, an eminent motion picture historian and a veteran exhibitor, wrote in the *Producer's Journal*, "Worthy people constantly complain about the low intellectual and artistic standard
of a large percentage of our motion pictures. Unless we adopt a
system of film subsidies as practiced by European governments,
this condition will continue to exist."

* * *

The National Association of Theatre Owners, a powerful
group of exhibitors, has established a special committee to investigate the feasibility of a film production subsidy. A formal and
urgent recommendation by the Screen Actors Guild to all elements of the motion picture industry "to give immediate and
sincere attention to the possibilities of establishing such a plan
(subsidization) for American production within our geographical borders" has given the subject even greater currency.

The inauguration of the American Film Institute under the
auspices of the National Foundation of the Arts and Humanities
Act of 1965, with George Stevens, Jr., as its director, is the first
institutional acknowledgment of America's delinquency in treating film as an art form. This is encouraging, to be sure, with its
contemplated five-pronged program devoted to training, educa-

353

tion, production, publications, and archival activities. Its operations, however, are limited to only three years, and its budget of $5,200,000, of which only $3,900,000 is currently available, is pathetically small for its grandiose aims. (The Ford Foundation gave United States symphony orchestras alone $85,000,000 in 1967.) Nor is the budget automatically renewable. It is a beginning, but little more than that, and most important, it does not encompass either the permanency or the proven value of the outright subsidization formulas existing outside of the United States.

One may well question the broaching of the question of subsidization for an industry which is far from ailing financially. Why should America be concerned with such an artificial and unnecessary stimulus when it is obviously not needed for commerical viability? The answer has to do with our role as citizens. The motion picture is (or could be) as important a contribution to our cultural climate as other forms of performing arts such as music, ballet, and the theater—all of which are the recipients of various grants and subsidies from public-spirited citizens, foundations, city or state funds, and cultural commissions. As responsible members of a community and of a nation, we are pleased and proud to subsidize such institutions as representative of our interest in the arts. Why should we not manifest equal pride and pleasure in the art of the cinema and consider similar subsidizations?

Perhaps government aid may not be the most desirable approach, since subvention could easily lead to subversion. But another avenue of assistance may be worthy of consideration. This would be from the American film industry itself. We might well reflect on the advisability of channeling a specific portion of our dollar gains from commerical (nonartistic) films into art ventures rather than to discuss or seek outside bounty. We could easily install a system of self-taxation, the proceeds to be utilized for the sponsorship and development of art films. It would be ironic if our very skill in producing and purveying mediocrity would provide us with the needed excess funds to abet film-making on an artistic level: Ironic, indeed, if we could be our own Maecenas.

354

The potential advantages of such an undertaking are self-evident, for it is only by experimentation—by trying the untried —that any art form remains vibrant and alive. To liberate our film-makers from continually reinforcing the low taste level of the mass audience would permit them to slowly but inevitably attract new and larger audiences as greater numbers of people are exposed to films of quality. This would not only be a step forward in our cultural progression, but might even become a profitable investment in the long run.

But whether such aid comes from the film industry or from any other source, it seems apparent that subsidization may be the only means for the American film industry to recapture its onetime undisputed leadership in the single new art form produced in the twentieth century. For as Mr. Stevens announced rather bleakly when accepting the stewardship of the American Film Institute, "Let's face it, the art of motion pictures [in America] has seen better times."

PART FIVE

THE EXPANDING IMAGE

O! for a Muse of fire, that would ascend
the brightest heaven of invention!

—W. SHAKESPEARE

Poets are the hierophants of an unapprehended
inspiration; the mirrors of the gigantic
shadows which futurity casts upon the present.

—SHELLEY

"What is the use of this new invention?"
someone asked Franklin. "What is the
use of a new-born child?" was his reply.

∽∽∽∽∽∽∽∽∽∽∽∽∽∽∽∽∽∽∽∽∽∽

UP TO THIS POINT, the essays in this volume have been both descriptive and argumentative regarding the total situation of motion pictures and television. Their emphasis has been on the *contemporary* interrelationship of the sight-and-sound media, various social institutions, communicators, and audiences. But however critical the here-and-now problems raised by the moving image may be, we cannot be so overpowered by the complexity of these controversies that we are unable or unwilling to consider the future. Granted that what is past is prologue, the successes and failures of our previous investments provide us with a credit standing to borrow from the future. And if our future expectations do not "pay off" we run the risk of bankruptcy.

If the self-fulfillment prophecy is credible, and if we are to avoid a repetition of past frustrations regarding the mass

357

media, it seems imperative that we attach more positive expectations to the inevitable expansion of motion pictures and television. Too often the sight-and-sound media have been damned, feared, scoffed at, ridiculed, and generally written off as necessary opiates to mollify the masses. Psychologists have given us ample evidence that if a child is repeatedly reminded that he is merely tolerated and that he will grow up to be worthless, it is all too likely that this low opinion will be substantiated in his future. By the same token, if we keep repeating the elitists' favorite term about the sight-and-sound media, i.e., *meretricious,* we shouldn't be too surprised if these media take on the aspects of whoredom. After all, the word comes from the Romans' word for a prostitute.

One noteworthy step toward a more positive approach toward motion pictures and television is the "film study" (or "screen education") movement which is described in John M. Culkin's article in this final section. Whether we wish to acknowledge it or not, the moving image comprises a "second curriculum" which competes daily for the attention of young people. As Culkin points out, the average American student finishes high school with a backlog of viewing 15,000 hours of television and more than 500 films.

The time is long past due to implement within our schools a method of integrating study of the sight-and-sound media within the traditional curriculum. Just as children are now led up the ladder of literacy by use of "graded" printed material, so should they develop the skills of sight-and-sound literacy. Beginning with the first grade, and continuing through high school, students should examine the moving image from various degrees of experience, aptitude, and "readiness." For example, we might begin in the elementary grades on the "immediate experience" level by discussing such films as *Dream of the Wild Horses* or *The Red Balloon,* and later, perhaps with the same films, develop the skills of more formal analysis. Although there are many films which are particularly suitable for use in various grades, there are those which yield diverse interpretations and which students might see several times as they mature.

If motion pictures and television are to realize their vast potential we clearly must educate a generation of audiences who will demand something more than *Batman* or *You Only Live Twice*. We enjoy an historical advantage: today's children are, in Culkin's phrase, "native citizens" of the sight-and-sound age. They are tuned in to the emotional wavelength of both the large and small screen. We owe them the resources from which they may develop reasoned intelligence to sort out the images which pervade their lives and to separate the banal from the meaningful.

What we, along with Walter J. Ong and John M. Culkin, are urging is a more vigorous confrontation between the educational institution and the sight-and-sound media. This is not a matter merely of accommodation to inevitable forces in our technological age, i.e. "if you can't lick 'em, join 'em." It is a recognition that the traditional classroom and experiences outside the school must be bridged.

This theme is echoed in Kenneth Winetrout's essay where he calls for even further interaction between Academe and motion pictures and television. In an age in which the dominance of the printed word is being challenged by the moving image, he stresses the need for a new breed of researchers whom he calls "the anthropologists of the visible." It is apparent from the diverse backgrounds of the men whom he considers to be pioneers in this new quest (Ong, McLuhan, Kepes, Ames) that this will have to be an interdisciplinary approach. Indeed, if we could accurately define the emotional semantics of sight-and-sound communication we might be able to construct the intercultural picture-language which Stan VanDerBeek considers vital to world peace.

Even further involvement of the educational institution with television, in particular, is seen in the recommendations

359

of the Carnegie Commission for a system of Public-TV, described by Lester Markel in his contribution to this section. What the Carnegie plan envisions is a more enlightened electorate and an enlarged sense of national consciousness. If the functions of a democracy depend on the "unplugging" of informational blocks, it is not very encouraging to learn that during a national CBS current events test nearly three-quarters of the participants flunked on the tenth-grade level. Such data only reiterate what Gallop polls have ascertained from time to time, although it is shocking to learn from Dr. Gallop that less than one-fourth of the respondents in a national sample could identify General de Gaulle.

But any imaginative schemes for expanding noncommercial educational television must be tempered by a realistic assessment of the financial base. While the Carnegie Commission has recommended a manufacturer's excise tax on television sets to provide programming capital for Public-TV, the Ford Foundation has a more spectacular plan. McGeorge Bundy and Fred Friendly have pointed out that the technology of satellite communication can be converted into a "peoples' dividend." The Ford proposal is to launch a television satellite for use by commercial and noncommercial broadcasters alike. The fees paid by commercial broadcasters (which ordinarily would go for hiring coaxial cables and microwave relays) would be used to pay the way of the entire system of noncommercial broadcasting.

Satellites are only one aspect of the "five areas of technical change" which Leo Bogart describes in his look at the future of mass communications. The changes are not mere planning-board speculations but will become realized probably within the next generation. Already upon us are UHF, CATV and various proposals for pay-TV, all of which are additional distribution systems for expanding the moving image.

While these systems are more specifically related to television, they will also affect the motion picture. The successful implementation of pay-TV through a nationwide linking of CATV facilities will certainly create new "box offices" for film producers. Eighty-three percent of the programs used in 1966 in the Phonevision pay-TV experiment in Hartford, Connecticut were motion pictures.

With the inevitable rapid technological proliferation within these communications systems, it is certain that government will become more involved. As FCC Commissioner Nicholas Johnson has stated, we are utilizing nineteenth-century concepts of regulation which are inadequate to serve the public needs. Indeed, we must ask ourselves again if the Communications Act of 1934 is still functional for tomorrow's problems, or whether it has to be revitalized.

In his overview of the evolving mass media, Leo Bogart in his essay in this section shows that the distinction between the sight-and-sound media and the print media is disappearing faster than we realize. Obviously, the expanding sight-and-sound image will not displace books, newspapers, magazines, and other forms of printed communication; rather print, film, and electronics will supplement each other.

New communications systems portend an increase in the quantity and diversity of sight-and-sound messages. Just as there are now motion picture theaters exhibiting films that appeal to specific tastes, it is certainly likely there will be television stations offering programs for specialized interests. There are already radio stations, such as WINS in New York, for example, which program only news. It is not too difficult to envision a television station that broadcasts only news, documentaries, public affairs, and discussions of current events.

With an increasing number of television channels inevitable (already apparent in the burgeoning UHF stations), greater demands will be made upon those who plan and produce programming material. What will be a special challenge is for quality to keep pace with quantity. Unfortunately, we have no assurance that pay-TV, for example, will necessarily provide better offerings. Today's commercial television stations find it difficult to fill the seventeen or eighteen hours that they are on the air without scheduling "B" films and reruns of second-rate series that never should have been telecast the first time. As we note the increasing growth of co-production deals between the business interests of television and motion pictures and the corporate amalgams of the entertainment giants there is the possibility of a larger-scale mediocrity than ever.

Perhaps the most promising aspect of new technology are greater opportunities for instantaneous global discourse via interconnection of international communications satellites. What is to preclude the formation of an International Broadcasting Company, founded under the auspices of the United Nations? Already we have its beginnings in Intelsat (the International Communications Satellite Consortium) made up of fifty-eight nations around the world. If we could share such pragmatic things as weather reports, crop information, and generally nonpolitical information, we might create, as suggested by the *New York Times*, "an atmosphere of international electronic faith," that might eventually alleviate our deep political rivalries. This is not to say that any technological razzle-dazzle is going to lead us into instant Utopia, for we must remember always that the heart of man governs his actions and that human motives can be equally perverted by smoke signals as by satellites.

This belief that it is still possible to build an international faith that man, the creator, will prevail is echoed in Stan VanDerBeek's manifesto for combining sight-and-sound technology into a "culture-intercom." Like Walter Lassally, VanDerBeek recognizes the emotional basis of film communication and sees the possibilities of world peace by stressing the "emotional denominator" that links all men.

Pierre Teilhard de Chardin has described man's discovery

of the electromagnetic spectrum as a "prodigious biological event." We clearly agree. The sights and sounds that flow through these inexhaustible spaces are becoming more and more essential to human society and the ways man discerns his place in the universe. Yet if this discovery is to lead us to any further evolution of the spirit surely it must be used as something more than an *opi*art to narcotize us against the slings and arrows of everyday existence. As E. B. White so aptly put it, in a letter to the Carnegie Commission, television should "restate and clarify the social dilemma and the political pickle. Once in a while it does, and you get a quick glimpse of its potential."

If we are to have a greater awareness of social reality, it cannot come from looking at repetitious reworking of sight-and-sound symbols on television and theater screens. Man is a restless creature, and any respite he may derive from these undemanding images of his reflected self can at best be merely temporary. Whether motion pictures and television will contribute to the *anomie* and boredom which permeate most men, or whether they will help man to break out of the vicious circle of restlessness to understand his existence better: this is the challenge to and the responsibility of the media managers who will be the architects of the expanding image.

XXVII.

Wired for Sound: Teaching, Communications, and Technological Culture*

WALTER J. ONG

Walter J. Ong, S.J., is Professor of English at St. Louis University. He is the author of *The Barbarian Within*, in which this essay appears, and the recent *In the Human Grain*.

~~~~~~

FROM THE TIME of ancient Greece, communication processes have always been at the center of Western education. Early academic study focused on grammar, which gave birth to rhetoric. Rhetoric formed a matrix for dialectic and logic, and all these conjointly help shape physics and medicine, and ultimately modern science. Through the Middle Ages, the Renaissance, and into the nineteenth century, education began with grammar, rhetoric, and dialectic or logic, the *artes sermocinales* or communication arts.

Teachers are still especially interested in communication, not merely because they are incidentally involved with the process but because their work itself is communication *par excellence*. At the point where teaching is going on, the knowledge which men have accumulated and communicated to one another out of the past thousands or hundreds of thousands of years is being communicated again to inexperienced youth, to give this youth that experience reaching far back beyond one's own years which sociologists call culture. But as teachers channel this knowledge to succeeding ages, they do so by talking it over, rethinking it and recommunicating it among themselves. In the person of the

* Reprinted from *College English* (1960), pp. 245-51, by permission of the National Council of Teachers of English and the author.

365

teacher, who is the depository and communicator of knowledge, mankind constantly reviews what it knows, revaluates its knowledge, revises it, detects its deficiencies, and sets up the framework for new discoveries.

The teacher's work involves him in a constant interior dialogue with the past, the present, and the future. Since the only source of knowledge is the experience we have had up to the present time, or in other words past experience, he has to communicate with the past, to raid it for what it has to tell him. With his students, he puts out feelers into the future to orient his knowledge effectively. And he has to bring his knowledge of past and future into focus within the present system of communication, the one in which he has actually to do his teaching.

Hence it is not strange that teachers are sensitive more than other men to changes in communication processes. And teachers in the field of language and literature are most sensitive of all. In these fields a great deal of restlessness is observable today. The furor about why Johnny can or cannot read, the agitation concerning foreign language programs, the tendency of structural linguistics to replace older grammar, and the general overhauling of language-teaching and literature-teaching processes which has been taking place for the past thirty years or more are symptoms that something is stirring. What is it?

Probably a great many things are stirring; but it is certain that many of them can be summed up by saying that we are leaving the Gutenberg era behind us. As we move further into a technological civilization, we meet with abundant signs that the relationship between the teacher and the printed word and hence those between the teacher and a large area of communication, which includes practically all of what we generally mean by "literature," are no longer what they used to be. These relationships were set up in the Renaissance when a typographical civilization appeared, climaxing the intense development of a manuscript culture which had marked the preceding Middle Ages. The present swing is to oral forms in communication, with radio, television (oral in its commitments as compared to typography), public address and intercom systems, or voice recordings (to replace or supplement shorthand, longhand, typing, or print). As a result of this swing, older relationships are undergoing a profound, if not often perceptible, realignment.

Early teaching was aural and oral in cast. Socrates taught by means of person-to-person dialogue. Although Plato in great part extinguished this dialogue when he and his followers captured, stiffened, and mounted it on the written page, he nevertheless thought of himself as preserving dialogue itself by preserving its form or "idea." And although Aristotle seems to have moved further away from the dialogue form than Plato, a careful and astute reading of his works by Werner Jaeger, Joseph Owens, and others has shown how strongly the dialogic approach persists in them. Cicero's whole framework of culture was oral in a way in which the text-oriented Renaissance Ciceronianism could never be. To bring Greek culture to Rome, Cicero did not simply read books but went to Athens to listen to the oral exposition of philosophy there and thus to learn what to transmit viva voce to his compatriots. It is well known that Cicero first spoke what he had to communicate, delivering his orations first and writing them afterwards. St. Augustine remains similarly oriented. He was disillusioned less by Manichean writings than he was at the oral presentation of Manichean teaching by Faustus, who, after exciting the highest hopes, explained so little and so unconvincingly. When Augustine heard the fateful words, *Tolle et lege*— we know from what he has to say elsewhere about reading habits in his day—he took up the Scriptures and read to himself *aloud*.

By contrast with the ancient world, the Middle Ages produced a more purely manuscript culture. But their teaching methods retained massive oral-aural commitments. Socrates' dialogue, to be sure, was reduced to the university master's monologue, eventually styled a "lecture" or "reading," since it was typically a commentary on a written work and itself regarded as something committed or to be committed to writing. Yet the practice of testing intellectual prowess by oral methods alone, such as disputations, was retained. Written assignments or written examinations after grammar school remained unknown and apparently unthought of. A thesis was not something one wrote but something one asserted and defended orally as one's inaugural act upon induction into the teaching profession. Medieval culture is thus a transitional culture, oral-aural at root but scriptural in bent.

The printed page completed the pedagogical shift away from the oral. It silenced the medieval disputation and, as Marshall McLuhan so well put it in the volume *Mass Culture*, "created the solitary student," and the school textbook as well. From the beginnings of printing the greatest source of revenue for book publishers has been the classroom and its purlieus. Early publishers liked to ally themselves with humanist educators. The massive plaque on Erasmus' tomb in the Münster at Basel is erected by three grateful publishers whom he helped make affluent: Amerbachius, Frobenius, and Episcopius. At a time when not more than a few pages of any book could be kept standing in type at any one time, the Wechel firm of Paris and Frankfort-on-the-Main published at least one hundred and seventy-two editions of one or another work, almost all for classroom or academic use, by Peter Ramus and his literary lieutenant Omer Talon (Talaeus). Erasmus, Ramus, and Talon are only three among thousands of textbook authors whose works are published and read more than those of almost any "literary" writer.

The connection between printing and teaching was from the beginning as subtle and profound as it was financially successful. The notion of "storing" unassembled letters (and consequently dismantled words and books) in "fonts" of prefabricated type, which lies at the heart of the typographical developments of the fifteenth century, exhibits a close psychological connection with the doctrine of the *loci communes* ("commonplaces" or simply "places") taught in rhetoric and dialectic or logic classes in fifteenth-century schoolrooms. One "drew arguments" from the places as one drew type from a font. As the printed book took over, and with it faster and faster silent reading habits, the commitment to eloquence and oral expression lingering as a heritage from the Renaissance devotion to classical antiquity became, more and more, lip service. The "elocution contests" of a generation or two ago were the dying gasps of the old tradition. It seemed that the printed book had won the day.

It still seems so in the sense that it is unlikely that printing

368

(or its recent manifold variants such as mimeographing or plano-graphing) will ever be done away with in teaching or elsewhere generally. It is incontestably convenient to have the spoken word frozen in space, and frozen in exactly the same space for everyone among one's auditors. The teacher is not likely to forego the luxury of being able to say, "Everyone now turn to page 83, line 4 from the top, and look at the third word from the left." This luxury is too hard-won. For such a directive was entirely impossible before the invention of printing, when, if the students had manuscript books, every book would have every word in a different place from every other book. Except in certain academic horror stories, no one really seems convinced that the modern world is going to regress into a pretypographical or a preliterate culture. What is happening is more complicated than this. If students are losing their hold on reading and on grammar, this is in great part because, in their relationship to the other items involved in communication, reading and grammar are not what they used to be. They are still there, and will be, but the constellation in which they exist is shifting its formation.

* * *

One of the principal causes of the shift in status of reading and grammar is the increased importance of oral-aural communication in our technological society. It is paradoxical that a society given so much to the use of diagrams and to the maneuvering of objects in space (from giant aircraft to atoms) should at the same time develop means of communication which specialize not in sight but in sound. Yet the signs of a shift are everywhere. Grammar, which was originally the study of written language (*gramma* in Greek means a letter of the alphabet) and which, as normative grammar, has rules based less upon what speaking people do when they talk than upon what literate people do when they write, is yielding to linguistics, which, while it includes grammar, is rooted in the study of oral performance. The trend toward discussion groups has been under way for a long time. It manifests itself not only in the classroom under such guises as "Deweyism," but also in business, where meetings of all sorts have multiplied beyond calculation in the course of the recent managerial revolution. The same elaborate business organizations which solve many of their problems by computing machines have found that back of the Univac there must be large-scale and deliberate confrontation of person with person. Interest in group dynamics serves as a counterbalance to electronic computers. Often the most efficient way to attack a problem has been found to be the "brainstorming" session, where members of a group stimulated by the rest of the group as an audience, suggest orally whatever solution to a practical problem may stray through their heads, no matter how zany the solution may at first blush appear.

Libraries themselves have undergone significant reorientations. The oldstyle Renaissance, public or semi-public library, with its books chained to keep the users from carrying them away, yielded some years ago to the lending library. Both these institutions were spectacularly quiet. The new library makes allowance for noise, and utilizes noise. It includes seminar rooms and all-purpose rooms for larger meetings. Acoustic insulation, of course, has made these possible. But, by whatever means the effect has been achieved, libraries have recently become places where people can get together to talk. Our attitude toward books, our concept of what they are, is sure to be affected by such a change, especially as more libraries are being run on an open-stack plan. Librarians, including librarians of early lending libraries, until recently appear to have existed chiefly to keep books in the library, from which they would issue them with ill-concealed reluctance, placated only by thought of the savage reprisals which would result if the books were not returned by the detested borrower almost immediately. Today's librarians all want books to go out and feel frustrated if they do not. The result is that more and more books are now read in a world alive with sound, to musical backgrounds provided by radios and hi-fi sets.

The oral-aural emphases of today run counter to certain typical phenomena of the Gutenberg era as diverse as the invention of printing and the exploration and observation of the surface of the globe. These activities reached their peak together, and both focused attention in space and thus vaunted sight. The microscope and telescope, developed as epiphenomena of printing and exploration, did the same. But a new age is upon us, and its shift from sight-emphasis to increased sound-emphasis spans this entire area from the diffusion of the word to the exploration of one's surroundings. In the realm of words dictaphones replace shorthand writing, and audio charge systems replace written library records. Exploration no longer depends on moving the human body through space. It is conducted by radar and radio-telescopes (more informative in many ways than visual-type telescopes), and by sputniks, which are launched into space as little speaking voices. In these devices sight, of course, plays a role, but no longer so exclusive a role as before. Press reports on the first nearly successful moon rocket noted that at its apogee it could not be seen even with the most powerful lens telescope on earth, but that it could be heard.

In their whole trend, modern developments in communications, while they have not slighted the visual, have given more play to the oral-aural, which a purely typographical culture had reduced to a record minimum in human life. The sequence of development running from silent print through audio-visual telegraph to the completely aural radio is an obvious instance of increasing aural dominance. Even television belongs partially in this visual-to-aural series, being only equivocally a regression to visualism. For the visual element in television is severely limited. The amount of detail feasible on a television screen is far less than that visible on a movie screen and not remotely comparable to that tolerable and easily discernible in photographs. Details on television have to be filled in aurally, by explicit vocal explanation or by suggestion through music and sound effects. Silent television is hardly an engaging prospect.

*   *   *

Heightening the oral-aural element in a culture does much more than merely deemphasize vision. It subtly heightens the personalist element in a culture. For the plenary development of sound, the human voice, is a manifestation of the person. Even more than it is a manifestation of an understanding of objects, speech is a calling of one person to another, of an interior to an interior. Sight presents always surfaces, presents even depth as a lamination of surfaces, whereas sound presents always interiors,

371

for sound is impossible without some resonance. The post-Baconian preoccupation with sight and "observation" produced the world of the Enlightenment, a world of objects and things without convincing personal presences, giving us the strangely silent universe which Newtonian physics and Deism both supposed. Printing was the harbinger of this Newtonian world, for printing is spectacularly allied with surface or "object" treatment of reality. Picasso's collages use bits of printed posters or newspapers to establish a sense of flat surface because print is sensed as indissolubly allied with surface. Scraps of printing in the collages serve precisely the function of returning the eye from the perspective depths in other parts of the assemblage to the plane surface of the painting—it is unconvincing to imagine print on anything other than something relatively flat and smooth.

Strangely enough, although it is in part a visualist development, television has moved away from this effect of print. It has been a personalizing, not an objectifying, medium. The discussion panel, with its interchange of personalities, is properly a television phenomenon. Such personal interchange was difficult to manage on radio, for there individual persons could only with difficulty be kept distinct. Hence the use of voice was not brought to its fullest fruition. By the same token television is a more feasible means of education than radio. This is not because it can use visual aid devices (figures written on a blackboard on television cannot be seen by any viewer unless the camera is turned on them—they lack the permanent availability of figures on a classroom blackboard). It is because television better implements personal rapport between instructor and student.

But television is not the only manifestation of the growing interest in the human person which accompanies the resurgence of voice in our culture. Another manifestation is the self-conscious personalism of our times. The twentieth century, from one point of view the most mechanized of all the ages of mankind, is from another point of view the most personalized. No other age has generated a whole philosophy of personalism such as one finds in the works of Martin Buber, Gabriel Marcel, and others. At a much less reflective, more superficial, and nevertheless significant, level, no civilization before our technological civilization has given such attention to problems of personnel and personality in matters even of industrial performance. The "I" and the "thou" have never been the objects of more explicit treatment than now. In the future, alongside the digital and analogue computers and other mathematicizing developments such as Western culture has specialized in more and more over the past few hundred years, the human person will receive more and more attention, not in every quarter but in significant milieus and ways.

One may object that earlier civilizations were, and other contemporary civilizations are, more personal in certain aspects of their structure than ours. Modern Arab culture, styled by Marcel Jousse "verbomotor" (*verbomoteur*), is still almost exclusively personal in orientation (as a preliterate culture must be), acting in terms of personal loyalties and without much "objective" insight into issues. Such cultures can be both anarchical and, as Albert Camus well knows, absorbingly interesting from a human and literary point of view. This is because of their personalist orientation. But from another point of view, and an utterly basic one, such cultures leave much to be desired in this same personality orientation. Their respect for the elementary personal right to life can be quite minimal.

*　　*　　*

The influence which the present cultural shift toward the oral-aural is having on language and literature study and teaching is probably most important where it is least crass and striking. To think of adapting courses to present trends by exploiting as gadgets the spectacularly evident new media—radio, television, tape recordings, intercom—is to a certain extent to miss the point. These new media are not just new gadgets to be employed for what we are already doing with other less efficient gadgets. They are part of a shift which is inexorably affecting our very notion of what communication itself is. The question is not how to adapt television or tape recording to present courses in educational institutions or present courses to television and tape, for the present shift is sapping the very notion of a "course" itself. A "course" (Latin, *cursus*) means a running through. The concept of a "course" in a subject, derivative from the process of

373

teaching by "running through" a text, is a relict of manuscript and typographical culture. Moving in a more oral-aural setting, Socrates never gave a "course" in anything, and indeed had no notion of what such a thing as a "course" might be.

This is not to say that "courses" in language and literature or in anything else are on their way out. Evolution does not proceed by jettisoning earlier developments completely in working toward new ones. It tends rather to preserve earlier developments, even though these may have to be given new guises. Courses in language and literature are evidently going to be with us for a long time, perhaps for good. Nevertheless, their psychological significance is undergoing subtle and complex, but inexorable, change.

One way to express the nature of this change is to say that the old focus of literary studies on rhetoric is being replaced by a focus on dialogue. In ancient times, and through the Middle Ages, the cause of literature was the cause of rhetoric—which is to say the cause of the art of oratory. Poetry and all "ornate" expression was commonly referred to as eloquence which was associated basically with the oration or public speech before a group of persons. In contrast, the dialectic which split off from rhetoric and modulated into logic, first in Aristotle but more definitely through the Middle Ages, has pulled away from literature and helped generate modern science. The Renaissance sought to return from dialectic to literature by reemphasis of eloquence and rhetoric, but the Renaissance effort foundered in the combined currents of an always ebullient scholasticism and of the modern scientism so closely related to scholasticism. Rhetoric and the areas of communication which it represented failed to develop any mature theoretical structure viable in the post-Newtonian world where neat theories seemed to account for everything else.

For some time now the Newtonian universe has been broken down, and the result has been a recrudescence of interest in language and literature. But the interest no longer centers on rhetoric, the art of persuasion, which in our day is much more the province of the advertising man and marketing specialist than of the *littérateur*. The more effective ally of literature has turned out to be the sense of dialogue which marks important philosophical developments of our age (and which is notably missing

374

or *ersatz* in advertising). Literature is no longer standing so much alone as it did when "mere" rhetoric was arrayed against dialectic. It is painstakingly picked over by psychologists, physicians, sociologists, anthropologists, theologians, and others. Certain typically modern philosophies of the "existentialist" sort have been described as literary philosophies, conscious of and using literary form, as exploited by Camus, Marcel, Sartre, and others. We have become explicitly aware in our time of the intimate linkage between the process of communication and human thought itself. Many of the illusions of the Enlightenment concerning private thought and psychological privacy generally have been dissipated since the discovery of evolution, of depth psychology, and of the processes involved in the history of human thinking. We are intimately aware, as Gaston Fessard and others have put it, that science itself is only arrested dialogue. Voice is not an accretion, but a necessary adjunct or even a necessary dimension of human thinking. (It should be added that the "dialogue" meant here is neither medieval dialectic nor Hegelian dialectic, although it is related somewhat to both. Dialogue refers here to actual vocal exchange between person and person.)

It is through awareness of the paramount role of voice in human activity that students of English or of any other language today must seek to understand the reactivation of the oral-aural element in human culture. Voice is coming into its own as never before. But the ways in which it is doing so, and the elements in our culture which favor voice as well as those which militate against it, are complex in the extreme. We can arm ourselves and our students only by vigilant awareness of what is going on about us. In particular, teachers and students of language and literature must cultivate sensitivity to the more profound significance of the media of popular culture—which is not the same thing as either uncritical acceptance of popular culture or entrenched hostility to all its manifestations. Any kind of genuine sensitivity to literature of any age or culture has become thoroughly impossible unless a person has grown seriously—not phrenetically— reflective about contemporary communications media. Men today—and, above all, high school, college, and university students —live englobed in a universe of sound emanating from radio and hi-fi sets which surpasses anything any earlier human culture has known, both in the total decibel output at any given moment and in incessancy. Reflection on the condition of the new media and the changes they are effecting in human life will probably produce no pat formulas either to describe the totality of the present situation or to prescribe highly simplified lines of action. But it should enable us to live.

XXVIII.

The New Age of the Visible:
A Call To Study*

KENNETH WINETROUT

Kenneth Winetrout is Professor of Education at American
International College.

~~~~~~

WE LIVE IN THE AGE of the visible, largely because we are so good
at creating the visible. We carry cameras everywhere. We are so dis-
trustful of the inner eye's memory that Polaroid has made a mint
out of immortalizing that which existed a moment ago. Certainly,
for the United States, there has never been anything quite like
television which went from initial marketing to saturation in a
few short years.

*   *   *

We are not the first age of the visible. Huizinga, in *The Waning of the Middle Ages*, makes much, for example, of medieval
man's attentiveness to the eye. "Every order and estate, every rank
and profession, was distinguished by its costume. The great lords
never moved about without a glorious display of arms and liveries,
exciting fear and envy. Executions and other public acts of justice,
marriages, and funerals, were all announced by cries and proces-
sions, songs and music" (1:9). This was the communications system of the Middle Ages.

This was just one aspect of the medieval visualization. Lords
and serfs alike had little education; they were not very sophisticated, and the world they lived in was one of infinite mystery.

* Reprinted from *AV Communication Review*, Spring 1964, pp. 46-52, by
permission of the author and the publisher.

Yet, "mystery seemed to become graspable by the mind when invested with perceptible form" (1:200). "The spirit of the Middle Ages . . . longs to give concrete shape to every conception" (1:152). Death was one of the great mysteries, and the medieval artist did his macabre best to give it concrete expression. Tombs were adorned "with hideous images of a naked corpse with clenched hands and rigid feet, gaping mouth and bowels crawling with worms" (1:140). Efforts to visualize the Trinity were carried to the grotesque. The artists horrified the simple minds of the day with their realistic creations, but medieval men loved this in spite of the horror.

We are not so mystery-minded nor so mystery-surrounded today. We do not visualize because of the need for concretion, but because those who do the visualization are so competent and possess such remarkable tools. And, because this is so, as Joseph Wood Krutch once expressed the worry, we might become so dependent on the visual that if an idea came along which could not be accommodated visually, we would be lost. Krutch was displaying a verbal bias and an audiovisual prejudice, but his fear must not be discounted.

*　　*　　*

In an article in the *Kenyon Review*, George Steiner discusses what he calls "the retreat from the word." "We continue to assume humanistic authority, the sphere of the word, is predominant. . . . The humanist of today is in the position of those tenacious, aggrieved spirits who continue to envision the earth as a flat table after it has been circumnavigated" (5:193).

From the waning period of the Middle Ages, from the fourteenth and fifteenth centuries, to sometime in the post-World War II period, the word was king. Steiner suggests that the decline of the word began in the seventeenth century, but it remained for the present century to effect the rout of the word. Today it is no longer the poets who declare the glories of the heavens, but the mathematicians. If we turn away from the stars and look very practically at our pocketbooks, we discover that the "alphabet of modern economics is no longer primarily the word, but rather the chart, the graph, and the number" (5:195).

If we turn to our leisure, we find not words but nonobjective art and music— ". . . the musical sound and to a lesser degree the work of art and its reproduction are beginning to hold a place in literate society once firmly held by the word" (5:210).

I, for one, will not play the Jeremiah and sound off that visualization is bad; that our retreat from the word is calamitous. But this much I do say: with the word in retreat and the visual in its heyday, it is time we studied what all this means. I suspect many of our studies have been superficial.

As we have moved into the age of the visible, we have grown more and more skillful at production and have been quite content to allow consumption to take care of itself. We educate producers; we don't educate consumers. Some will deny this and protest: "We have our classes in appreciation; we spend hours in critical review of films and TV shows." Let us be honest. These classes are conducted to help us "appreciate" the producer. Our so-called appreciation classes are production oriented. We are schooled in the subtleties of Bergman's techniques and Benny's timing. We are told to note the way the cameraman did this or that. We busy ourselves in generalized and detailed studies of what the producer can and does do to the viewer. The feedback is to help the producer do bigger and more exquisite things to the viewer: how can we hit 'em over the head the next time—with a sledge hammer or a feather?

It is, with significant differences to be sure, the old story. Advertising has an annual budget of ten billion dollars. Consumer research has to get along with limited funds. We could refer to it as a cultural lag. Production has picked up fabulous momentum as the result of technological improvements and the presence of well-paid talent. The other side is rarely seen.

*   *   *

The following suggestions are made in the hope that we might bring production and consumption into a more balanced and equitable relationship to help us make some sense out of this new age of the visible:

1. We have the genetic expression, "In the Beginning there was the Word." Although the word has been with us virtually from

the start, it seems to me that we really never got around to study-ing language until the 1920's and 30's with the work of Edward Sapir, Benjamin Lee Whorf, Malinowski, et al. "Speech is so fa-miliar a feature of our daily life that we rarely pause to define it. It seems as natural to man as walking, and only less so than breath-ing" (4:3). We have taken our language for granted and it re-mained for anthropologists of language in the twentieth century to create an awareness of language. "Actually, thinking is most mysterious, and by far the greatest light upon it that we have is thrown by the study of language. This study shows that the forms of a person's thoughts are controlled by inexorable laws of pat-tern of which he is unconscious. These patterns are the unper-ceived intricate systematizations of his own language . . ." (6:173).

It seems to me that those who would study the effect of the visible could very profitably begin by looking at the large per-spectives that Sapir, Whorf, et al., brought to the study of lan-guage. We need anthropologists of the new visible. We have made a start here in the work of Kepes, Eames, Ong, McLuhan, and a few others. But as is too often the case, their work is known primarily by the producer.

2. A second aspect of our problem is what we may call the histor-ical. As Huizinga put the visualizations of the fourteenth and fifteenth centuries into a historical dimension—"The Idyllic Vision of Life," "The Vision of Death," "Religious Thought Crystallizing into Images," etc.—so perhaps we could place this present phase of man's life into a wider context. George Steiner has made a beginning in his essay, "The Retreat from the Word."

A more ambitious effort, and a quite successful one I feel, is Daniel J. Boorstin's *The Image*. The author tries to spell out the implications of what he calls the "Graphic Revolution." "Man's ability to make, preserve, transmit, and disseminate precise im-ages—images of print, of men, and landscapes and events, of the voices of men and mobs—now grew at a fantastic pace" (1:10). While words remain important in the graphic revolution, Boorstin's very use of the word *image* as the title of his book sug-gests a visual emphasis.

THE EXPANDING IMAGE

To Boorstin, this image-dominated culture has made for secondhandness. "The Grand Canyon itself becomes a disappointing reproduction of the Kodachrome original" (1:14). Fantasy becomes more real than reality. There is a loss of spontaneity. We are busy contriving events, "pseudo events" he calls them. We are so dedicated to creating images from cigarettes to presidents that ideals are secondary, images primary. "Two centuries ago when a great man appeared, people looked for God's purpose in Him; today we look for His press agent" (1:45).

Boorstin has made a significant contribution in this exploration of implications and trends and has tried to give them a historical setting. This book should make for some introspection among producers from tourist to studio photographer. "Photography becomes a form of narcissism. 'Have you seen *my* snapshot of the Mona Lisa?'" (1:170).

3. A further suggestion would be to study the work of Adelbert Ames, Jr., and his co-workers in the field of perception. Anthropologists have shown how language itself becomes a determinant of reality. Ernst Cassirer writes that once man has language, he cannot "confront reality immediately; he cannot see it, as it were, face to face" (2:43).

The revolutionary work of Ames gives us much the same story: there is no visual world, no reality, that is common to all of us. "Reality" says Cassirer, "is not a unique and homogeneous thing; it is immensely diversified, having as many different schemes and patterns as there are different organisms. Every organism is, so to speak, a monadic being. It has a world of its own because it has an experience of its own" (2:41).

Charles Eames has filmed some of the implications of Ames, but it would be my guess that we have never directly and wholeheartedly explored Ames and his philosophy in terms of an age that grows ever more visual. We have whole methodologies to teach reading skills, number skills, a beginning on listening skill; but what about picture skills in a TV world? How do we see?

Sapir writes, "Language is the most massive and inclusive art we know, a mountainous and anonymous work of unconscious generations . . . a summary of thousands and thousands of individual intuitions" (4:220-31). Over the centuries we have built up a considerable visual language: the cross, the serpent, dragons, the sword, the flag, etc. Here, too, we have a mountainous and anonymous work of unconscious generations.

Today we proliferate visual symbols in television, advertising, movies. We need to ask ourselves, Are these new symbols—the bad guy in TV Western shows, the man in the white jacket— transitory, merely temporary shadows cast on the long-lasting symbols of religion, nationalism, and the Freudian unconscious? Or do they in a subtle, unknowing way get into a basic subjectivity which is henceforth mixed with what we fondly call "the objective world"?

Language grew slowly. But the graphic revolution has hit us hard and universally in a brief time-span, and it is not at all the work of unconscious generations. Rather it is the work of very bright men who are quite deliberately aware of the immediate goals. The question one would raise is this: Is there an awareness of final effects?

Boorstin suggests that we live in an age of contrivance, of the illusioned, of the extravagant expectation. I am not prepared at this stage to accept his rather doom-filled prophecy, but his account is certainly plausible enough that we need to do much more thinking than we do presently. Whatever the leagues of decency or the Vance Packards may do, the creators of the visible are going to be in the saddle and ride mankind. The question is, How are they going to ride. Profit may be a good index, but it can be based on disastrously short-termed policies.

4. To effect the study of the visible, we ought to endow an Institute of the Consumers of the Visible. If war is too serious a matter to leave to the generals, perhaps we can say that the visual is too important to leave to the producer. We want a paid group of professional consumers who will approach our problems with the broad and dedicated attack we see in some of our national foundations—for example, polio, cancer—or in the way Leo Szilard would have us study war.

The institute members would study the large perspectives suggested above; they would attempt the long view. They would report to the public; it would not be their goal to prompt producers into improving their wares so much as to make the consumer aware of what was happening to him. We might find the producer's black-and-white delineations creating a serious blurring of man's power to discriminate. We might discover a sharp decline in our ability to make reality-contact. It is possible in the day of automated factories that visual entertainment has become a necessary activity for maintaining mental health. Leisure has become central; working hours, merely perfunctory and insignificant. Language shifts might be noticed.

Consumer-dominated research has its dangers. We should not want a public of resisters. We would want to avoid the result of the propaganda analysis movement which ended up creating skeptics who believed only that everything was propaganda.

These, then, are some tentative suggestions for exploration. For all man's wondrous and integrating communication devices, it is amazing how easily and unconsciously we enter a new era without knowing how we got there—or even that we are there.

References

1. Boorstin, Daniel J. *The Image.* New York: Atheneum, 1962.
2. Cassirer, Ernst. *An Essay on Man.* New Haven, Conn.: Yale University Press, 1952.
3. Huizinga, Johan. *The Waning of the Middle Ages.* New York: Doubleday Anchor Books, 1954.
4. Sapir, Edward. *Language.* New York: Harvest Books, 1949.
5. Steiner, George. "The Retreat from the Word." *Kenyon Review* 23:187-216; Spring 1961.
6. Whorf, Benjamin Lee. "Language, Mind, and Reality." *Etc.: A Review of General Semantics* 9:173; Spring 1952.

XXIX.

I Was a Teen-age Movie Teacher*

JOHN M. CULKIN

Director of the Center for Communications at Fordham University, John M. Culkin, S.J., sponsors annual film-study conferences and teaches summer courses in the art of the film.

~~~~~~

TEEN-AGE movie teachers teach two things: teen-agers and movies. Both are fun to work with. Both need working with. Some TMTs put the stress on teaching teen-agers and some on teaching movies. The former use films as a way of helping the student to illumine his own experience and to develop a personal point of view. The latter use the student as the audience for a course emphasizing the history and esthetics of film. There is a middle ground to be discovered and defended. And, like all teachers, TMTs teach themselves—their own attitudes, prejudices, likes, and dislikes.

There aren't too many TMTs in captivity, but the number of interested candidates is increasing rapidly. Some teach courses; some teach film units within courses; some organize film clubs. Their work is variously described as "motion picture appreciation," "film study," or, when television is included, "screen education." They are constantly confused with audiovisual specialists whose films deal with the dissection of frogs, or with English teachers who occasionally use a feature film like *Pride and Prejudice* to seduce students into reading the book.

The case for film study in the schools can be put quite simply without invoking the intercession of a long list of respectable

* Reprinted from *Saturday Review*, July 16, 1966, pp. 51-3, 72-3, by permission of the author and the publisher.

experts. We live in a total-information culture, which is being increasingly dominated by the image, both moving and static. By the time the average American student graduates from high school today, he has watched more than 15,000 hours of television and seen more than 500 films. The TV figure is the result of an average of twenty hours of weekly viewing for fifteen years; it adds up to two full years of twenty-four-hour-a-day viewing. During this same period, this average student has attended school five hours a day, 180 days a year, for twelve years, to produce a total of 10,800 hours of school time. Only sleeping time surpasses television as the top time-consumer.

Intelligent living within such an environment calls for the development of habits of perception, analysis, judgment, and selectivity that are capable of processing the relentless input of such visual data. At a time when so many of our economic, political, and personal decisions are being shaped by the new visual media, we have to organize a posse to outnumber and surround the vidiots in our midst and to replace them with seeing-eye children. And great films and television, like great anything-else, communicate insights about man that we should want to share with each new generation. From here on out, to be liberally educated is to be "cinemate as well as literate." Schools are where the tribe passes on its values to the young. Schools are where film study should be housed.

Old Plato in his analogy of the cave pictured a generation of people whose lives were spent watching shadows on a wall. Later on they rejected the outside world because it didn't correspond to their shadows. (Television, anyone?) The ability to distinguish between shadow and substance must be part of any cultural survival kit.

TMTs want their students to see as many fine films as possible, in much the same way that teachers have always wanted their students to read great books and experience great art. They want to free students from the narrow confines of their own "I, my, me" world in showing them films that widen and deepen their understanding of what it means to be human. They want to equip the student with ways of analyzing and reflecting upon the constant flow of moving images that flood his world. They want

385

to produce an enthusiastic, intelligent, selective, and mature film and television viewer.

What kinds of films are involved? All kinds. Everyone has his own list of classical favorites.* Classroom discussions also focus on popular films and TV programs like the Bond cycle, *Batman*, *Bonanza*, and *The Man from U.N.C.L.E.* Better to help them analyze what they are seeing than to develop critical standards for films or books they may never see or read.

The schools had a go at the movies once before back in the 1930's. The crusade started fast and faded fast since it was built on a negative approach to film. The second spring of the movement is based on a respect for film rather than a fear of film. It regards film as one of the humanities, as one of the liberating arts, and it strives to produce the largest possible audiences for the best possible films. Its methodology is built around the screening, discussion, and analysis of well-made, relevant films. It believes that a lively art demands lively teaching and it is, therefore, opposed to a pedanticism that would stifle the spontaneity and enthusiasm most of us bring to films. It maintains that in an image-saturated culture *all* students should become their own TV and movie critics.

At present the movement is but a cloud on the horizon, no larger than a man's hand, but it will inevitably grow because it is both wanted and needed. To speak in cinematic terms, we can consider the film study movement at three focal lengths: a *long shot* on its cultural context, a *medium shot* on the changing student, and a *close-up* on the role of the schools.

* Feature-length films that have proved successful for school screenings include both domestic and foreign productions. Some possibilities: *Hud, The Loneliness of the Long Distance Runner, Singin' in the Rain, Bicycle Thief, Henry V, The Hustler, To Kill a Mockingbird, On the Waterfront, The Golden Age of Comedy, La Strada, David and Lisa, Twelve Angry Men, High Noon, Citizen Kane, Ballad of a Soldier, Requiem for a Heavyweight, Raisin in the Sun, The 400 Blows, Shane, Paths of Glory, Nobody Waved Goodbye, Gate of Hell, Spellbound* and *The Treasure of the Sierra Madre*.

Shorter documentary, animated, and art films also afford some exciting cinema while respecting the rigid school schedule. TMTs have scored consistently with films like *Neighbors, Corral, Dream of the Wild Horses, The Red Balloon, Night and Fog, An Occurrence at Owl Creek Bridge, The Hole, Glass, Clay, The Critic, The Flight of the Friendship Seven,* and *New York, New York*.

THE EXPANDING IMAGE

First, a *long shot* of our changing culture. Marshall McLuhan, who has emerged as the oracle of mass culture and the darling of the magazine writers, has been telling us, for a long while and in his own obscure fashion, that we live in a post-literate world. Not *illiterate*, although that has often been suggested too, but *post-literate*—a world in which print no longer has a monopoly of communication either within the culture or within the schools. The new environment created by the electronic media has formed a free-flow, total-information ecology within which people receive their communication through a great variety of media and at a pace not within the control of the established and traditional mediators of culture—the family, the church, and the school. We can get some idea of both the extent and rapidity of this change by imagining the effects of a month-long national experiment in which we would be deprived of all the communications media developed and mass-produced within our own century. Goodbye TV, movies, telephones, record-players, radios, and a whole way of life stitched together by the new media.

McLuhan holds that the introduction of any new medium into a culture inevitably produces two effects: an apparent threat to established patterns, and a change in the perceptual habits of the people. Thus it was with the phonetic alphabet and the printing press. Thus it is with films and television. He suggests that we bypass the tiresome and predictable clashes of the transition by arriving at an early and reasonable synthesis:

> If these "mass media" should serve only to weaken or corrupt previously achieved levels of verbal and pictorial culture, it won't be because there's anything inherently wrong with them. It will be because we've failed to master them as new languages in time to assimilate them to our total cultural heritage.

The ability to lament vice is no sure proof of virtue. In this period of transition, therefore, we can really do without the tedious replay of the glib generalities about the quality and effect of the mass media, the exhortations to bury our TV sets, the unfair comparisons between the best of one medium and the worst of another, and the either-or fallacies which only dig ditches when we need to build bridges. It's a time for *doing* things.

The brief for some kind of media study within the schools normally follows either of two lines of argument: a) make the media seem so *respectable* that the schools have to recognize them as worthy of inclusion within the curriculum; or b) make their impact seem so *lethal* that the schools feel forced to deal with them as a tactic of survival.

Walt Whitman said: "To have great poets there must be a great audience." Great audiences for any art form are not born; they are made. They are created by an exposure to and an analysis of excellence within the medium. Some people are distracted because the movies are "mere entertainment" (as though that were a bad thing in itself). The same tag once kept Elizabethan drama, the novel, and vernacular literature out of the schools. Others stress the number of worthless or tasteless films. The piffle index, however, is high for any medium, and the percentage of poor films is probably about the same as the percentage of poor work in print, paint, and other media. The best within the film medium deserves the same attention to content and style that we accord to the traditional arts.

Although the fancy talk about film as an art form is true enough and suasive enough, it is not without its dangers. There is a Steinbeck quote which is to the point: "Culture is a lousy word to describe what mankind is all about." Too often we let talk about art substitute for the experience of art. Once a false mystique about art gets into the air, people begin to become insecure about their own instincts and to react to the expectations of the high priests of art rather than to their own honest reactions. This is especially lamentable in a nice friendly field like the movies where everyone has for so long presumed that he is an expert.

If Whitman's thesis about the relation of art and audience is true for poems which can be written on the backs of old envelopes by a production staff of one, it holds with multiplied validity for the motion picture and television, which are wild combinations of art, technology, and commerce. The traditional interplay of artist and patron has to be rethought for each of the new media. Numbers have a great deal to do with what can be communicated through any of the media that involve large financial investments. Both risk and success are measured by increasingly large numbers as one moves from print to stage to film and to television. A hardbound book hits the best-seller lists when it sells 20,000 copies; a Broadway play starts making money after the first 100,000 tickets; a commercial film has to have roughly two and a half patrons for every dollar invested before it breaks even—with the result that a million-dollar movie needs two and a half million patrons; and in television, which is the massest of mass media, a series in prime time needs a continuing audience of approximately 25,000,000 viewers to stay on the air. In 1965, for instance, *East Side/West Side* went off the air with a sustaining audience of 14,000,000 regular viewers—an audience that would be astronomical for any of the other media but which is too esoteric to be served by television.

In the commercial media the name of the game is numbers. The one-to-one relationship between De Medici and Michelangelo has given way to a complicated feedback system between the public and the network or the studio. The public is the patron and, distasteful as this may be to the elitists, this numerical approach to taste is the fact of media life. It has its obvious problems. What most want is not what all should get. And just because people take what they get doesn't necessarily mean that they are getting what they want. The public doesn't know what it wants until it gets it and then they may only be accepting what they appear to want. What we need are more choices and more people qualified to make wise choices. Since the quality of films and television depends on the quality of the audience, we should be at pains to improve the quality of that audience. That is what film study is all about.

Second, a *medium shot* of the changing student. It has been said that if Booth Tarkington were writing *Seventeen* today he would have to call it *Twelve*. The mass media have something to do with those five years which we have lost or gained, depending on your point of view. The schools are no longer dealing with the student of 1900 whose sources of information were limited to the home, church, school, and neighborhood gang. Today's student comes equipped with a vast reservoir of facts and vicarious experiences gleaned from the new media. All the analogies comparing the mind to a blank page or an empty bucket died with Edison. The teacher is now in competition with a host of rival communicators, most of whom are smarter, richer, and considerably more efficient. Relevance and competence are educational tactics against which students have not devised a defense.

It is almost sacrilegious to find fault with Bel Kaufman's *Up the Down Staircase* because it is so human and so in sympathy with our own loves and hates. But the lady made me sad on page 198. "I don't think I got through to them, in spite of all my careful paper-plans . . . The trouble is their utter lack of background. 'I never read a book in my life, and I ain't starting now,' a boy informed me."

Honest, Bel, they've got background; it's the one thing we're sure they do have. It may not look much like your background and my background and it isn't spangled with titles from the great books of the Western world. But it's there. We know for sure that it is well-stocked with plenty of TV material just waiting to be tapped with probing questions about phoniness and realness, winners and losers, style and *schmaltz*—all the new ways of talking about the old ideas of the true, the good, and the beautiful. If the school is in business to communicate with these students, it is up to the school to get plugged in to their background. Whatever the eventual goal may be, there is only one place to start and that is—where they *are*.

Teachers have seldom felt more alienated from the kids; yet it has seldom been easier to make contact with their world. We communicate with people by having something in common with them. One thing we can all have in common is the mass media. TV and film help to shape the dreams of today's students. Students often have a kind of defenseless, direct, but interested approach to the media. They love to talk about TV programs and movies. They don't realize how much they're talking about themselves in the process. If the teacher doesn't watch these programs and if he never discusses them with the kids, he's missing the easiest way to wiretap their private world. This is why all this élite versus popular culture business is so important. The snobs pride themselves on not watching television. Too bad. What happens when this culturally deprived teacher starts waxing lyrical about Elizabethan poetry? Not much. The kids have some polite teacher-talk which they dish out dutifully so that the teacher thinks something is going on in the class. If they like the teacher, they are very generous in keeping the truth from him. If they don't like him they still have enough fear for the sanction of the report card to go along with the game. They seldom say what they really think. Nobody wants to hear it, except, of course, the great teacher, who is by definition the relevant person, the one who understands, communicates, gets through.

Third, a *close-up shot* of our changing education. Stanley Kauffmann said it: "The film in this country is possibly the one art form that is *wanted.*" Television may or may not be an art form, but it is wanted too. Why not start where the action is?

Teen-age movie teachers have all kinds of options in their approach to film. My own prejudice at the high school level is for keeping as close as possible to what Robert Warshow has called "the immediate experience." For me this means the vertical interaction between the student and the screen and the horizontal interaction between students who have seen and discussed the same film. Ancillary knowledge about film is less relevant here and is perhaps more appropriate for the specialist or for more advanced programs. A great deal of snobbery takes over once some people learn how to pronounce the names of all the foreign film directors and can recite in chronological order the titles of all 9½ of Fellini's films.

If I had my choice in the schools, I would like to have each student go through a unit on film and television for about thirty hours in his freshman year and then see and discuss one feature film each month during his four years of high school. A modest amount of time compared to the actual viewing hours that he is clocking. The whole process can be broken down into four approaches to films: show them, discuss them, teach about them, and make them.

Show them. The success of literature teachers can be legitimately measured by the number of books their students read. Same for TMT. A film per month for four years would add up to forty films. The celluloid syllabus should include both American and foreign films, 16mm in-school screenings and 35mm theater screenings, and a generous blend of feature, documentary,

SIGHT, SOUND, AND SOCIETY

and animated films. From time to time it should include a dishonest or pretentious film and occasionally there might be a second screening of a film to check out insights or arguments that arose in the discussion of the film. What is important is that the films be well-made, relevant, and representative. Although most of the films should have the texture of reality about them, a steady diet of grim film gets depressing. Musicals and comedies belong in the series.

Discuss them. When a TMT is asked whether he is just sitting around showing films and talking about them with the kids, the prescribed answer is: "Yup." This is where the fun begins. When students are given a free forum to discuss films, they are also invited to discuss themselves. This type of viewer-centered, free-flow discussion is built into the nature of the film medium. Film is literally an other-directed medium. Both the sequence and the pace of the communication are determined by the director. There is no chance to pause, reflect, and relate as there is with a book. In the darkness of the theater the viewer's attention is riveted on the screen and he is swept along by the succession of sights and sounds that impinge on his eye and ear. This primarily sensory experience leaves the viewer with a stack of unsorted images. A group discussion is a great way to interpret and relate these images, and to discover their structure.

This physical and psychological context explains why the same film can affect different individuals in different ways. Each person sees his own film. This paradox is merely the reaffirmation in a new context of the thesis of individual differences, and selective perception. The same film on the screen washes over each viewer as an individual, with individual past experiences, hopes, loves, fears, needs, and intelligence. The psychological mechanisms of identification and projection come into play. We empathize with some character on the screen. For a while we become who he is, and we will fill out the experience by reading our own emotions into the character. The result is a variety of responses to the same stimulus. It is normally not a solipsistic kind of irresponsible and indeterminate variety, but usually a range of responses hovering around the central theme of the film.

If the teacher can resist the temptation to reward and punish

392

"correct" answers (this usually means his own subjective interpretation) and can create a climate in which all opinions are
respected, these free-winging sessions can dredge up some memorable moments. My winters are warmed by memories of some Job
Corpsmen debating the meaning of what it meant to be a winner
or a loser in *The Hustler*, of the understanding that resulted from
a group of parents and students who had seen and separately
discussed the rebellion of Colin Smith in *The Loneliness of the
Long Distance Runner*, of ten minutes of sheer poetry in a Harlem basement by a teacher commenting on Terry Molloy's care for
his pigeons in *On the Waterfront*, of 200 girls discussing the loneliness and purpose of Zampano and Gelsomina in *La Strada*, of the
ten-year-old girl in New York whose favorite scene in *Raisin in
the Sun* was "when the movin' man came, 'cause that meant they
were gettin' out." Nice things happen in film discussions. Some
teachers find that they are talking less and that the kids are learning more.

As the students build up a background of shared experiences,
they can then use these films and discussions as reference points
for making sense out of their own lives or for communicating with
each other. The phrase, "He's a real loser," says everything to
someone who has seen and discussed *The Hustler*. The better
we know each other, the shorter the sentences we can use.

Teach about them. Not everything that *can* be known about
film and television *should* be known about them. Each TMT has
to make his own way in deciding how much the student should
know about film history, techniques, production, and economics.
It is important, however, that students get a feel for what is proper
to the film medium; that they experience how the tone, rhythm,
pace, style, and point of view of a film are determined by the use
of editing, sound, lighting, color, perspective, and composition.
The making of a film is a highly selective process. The best advice
for the teacher is to play it loose and to start with the film-as-ex-
perienced. By some people's standards this will be a sloppy and
subjective approach, but it is better to recognize and work with
the subjectivity than to impose an arbitrary set of objective standards. The approach should be inductive. The standards should
grow out of the experience and not be imposed on the experi-

ence. We can do without abstract lists of criteria that begin: "A great movie is one which fulfils the following requirements . . ." People know what they like. Those who spend their time telling people that they *shouldn't* like what they *do* like have discovered a first-class way of getting tuned out. Pulling rank won't change taste. Lively analysis in a fair game may do it.

Make them. The study of film inevitably leads students to a desire to try their hand at making a film. The results are wondrous to behold. In England films are now being made by eight- and nine-year-olds. There are tentative beginnings of such a development in this country under pioneering teachers like George Bouwman of Horace Mann in New York, Zane Rodriguez of Fordham Prep, Sister Bede Sullivan of Lillis High in Kansas City, and Rodger Larson who has been working with New York's Neighborhood Youth Corps in Harlem.

There are many and varied film projects just beginning around the country. All kinds of respectable organizations and teachers are getting into the act. Within ten years we will wonder what all the fuss was about and will have transcended the need for developing a rationale.

Meanwhile, it is well to remember that to be a TMT, enthusiasm and a pocketful of theater stubs aren't enough. The idea will be as good as the people who make it happen—the teachers who teach it and the people who develop the printed and filmed teaching materials. There is a degree of competence needed which falls between the highly specialized demands of the film purists and the "anybody-can-do-it" school. A summer program would do it. There are books to be read. There are films to be seen. There are people to be consulted—great TMTs like Tony Hodgkinson of Boston University, David Mallery of the National Association of Independent Schools, and Sister Rosalie of Pittsburgh. Opinions on current films can be found by reading good critics. And anyone can get started by getting a buzz session going on *I Spy*. Great movements deserve modest beginnings.

On the national level the movement can get moving through a consortium of talent drawn from the schools and the studios. The medium itself has been called "a shotgun marriage of culture and commerce," and any movement based on the medium will have to talk to both partners. The dialogue must be enlarged among the many groups that are active in the field. The National Council on the Arts, which is blessed by the presence and hard work of director George Stevens and actor Gregory Peck, could be the prime mover in bringing this idea to the schools both through its own activities and those of the American Film Institute. The use of educational television is a natural for an idea that is visual in nature and short on teachers. To my mind the greatest single resource is the creative talent of the directors, writers, actors, art directors, cameramen, and editors who are the real craftsmen within the media. They and their knowledge should be more directly in touch with the audience. Most of them are eager for such contact. A little money and a little organization can make it happen.

And as more and more teachers get involved at the high school level, it becomes increasingly obvious that the idea should be pushed in the elementary grades, almost as soon as the students become steady consumers of television.

Expensive media like films and television cannot get too far ahead of their audience. They have to rely on public acceptance. Americans have spent a lot of time and energy in the past thirty years complaining about the producers of films and television. Much of the energy would have been better utilized in working with the audience. It's not too late to begin.

XXX.

A *Program* for *Public-TV**

LESTER MARKEL

An associate editor of *The New York Times*, Lester Markel
is moderator of *News in Perspective*, a semimonthly television
program.

〜〜〜〜〜〜〜〜〜〜〜〜〜〜〜〜〜〜〜〜〜〜〜〜〜〜〜〜〜〜

THERE IS a great to-do these days about "educational television" [1]
—visions of satellites, projections of a "cultural revolution" more
revolutionary even than Mr. Mao's, a far-ranging Congressional
inquiry, a Ford Program, a Carnegie Report, a Presidential proposal and, in general, a wide variety of dialogue, including a not-
inconsiderable amount of static.

This large concern with the subject arises out of a belief that
the state of the Union, informationally and culturally, is not what
it should be and a conviction that television is not contributing
what it could toward the advancement of that state.

Recent reports clearly indicate the information gap: three-
quarters of the American voters, it is reported, cannot properly
identify the Vietcong; in a CBS current-events test it was revealed that, applying tenth-grade standards, nearly three-quarters
of those tested flunked the examination.

These are deeply disturbing findings. Democracy cannot truly
function without an informed public opinion. The politician
keeps his ear as close to the ground as the laws of physics allow;

* Reprinted from *The New York Times* Magazine, March 12, 1967, pp. 25,
126-30. © 1967 by the New York Times Company. Reprinted by permission
of the author and the publisher.
[1] "Educational television" is not a good phrase; it connotes something highbrow, forbidding, restricted. The Carnegie Report calls it "Public-TV" as
against "Private-TV": that is the better appellation.

if public opinion is enlightened, national policy is likely to be sound; if it is unenlightened, national policy is likely to be both uncertain and unsound.

The cultural area seethes with activity and eloquence, but the return is still scanty. There is, to be sure, brave talk of our "cultural explosion"; of the large amount of cash and the numerous ergs of energy expended in the effort to elevate taste. But one wonders whether what has been called the Edifice Complex —concentration on construction rather than content—is not still the prevailing motif.

Because television has become a potent factor in American life, it can do vital jobs in the improvement of public opinion and the furtherance of public "culture" (the quotation marks are used not by way of apology but solely because the word has been tainted with pomposity; yet there is no other word). But commercial television has not done these jobs and is not likely to do them. Noncommercial television has done better, but its efforts have been limited by lack of funds and scantiness of audience.

The urgent assignment is to enlarge the size of television's minority audience—that segment of the watchers to which better programming appeals. This is not, in my view, an impossible task. Far from it; my belief is based on some sheer, wholly intuitive guesses: probably 20 percent of the population are moronic; another 20 percent are capable of learning, if they had the desire to learn, which they do not; another 20 percent are really informed and culturally alert.

This leaves 40 percent who are willing to learn if the learning is made simple enough and who are ready to absorb culture if it is provided in easy doses. The challenge lies in this gray area of the 40 percent. The hope rests in the strengthening of Public-TV —of what President Johnson has called a "vital natural resource."

*　　*　　*

What exactly is this TV apparatus we talk about? What has been its performance? Why has it not been better? What can be done? Most important, what can Public-TV contribute? These are the questions around which the debate focuses—a debate that

397

engages the educators, the Congress, the TV industry itself and, slowly, the public.

The reach of television is statistically breathtaking. The TV audience is reckoned at over 80 millions; Mr. Nielsen, one of the scientific samplers, estimates that 94 percent of American households own at least one television set.

There are now in operation some 600 commercial stations, of which more than 500 are affiliated with the three networks. In 1965 the revenue of private television totaled almost two billion dollars and profits before taxes almost half a billion. This is Big and Booming Business.

Noncommercial television comprises approximately 125 educational stations in the country; of these more than 80 are school or university or state stations which are devoted primarily to instruction (in this discussion, the instructional aspect of Public-TV is not considered; that is a separate operation and presents no real problem); some 40 are community stations, placed mostly in the large metropolitan areas, which present general programs. Most of these public stations are loosely affiliated with the National Educational Television network (NET), which supplies to them—with only occasional exceptions—taped programs.

At the moment, the contest between commercial and noncommercial television is a decidedly uneven one. On the one side, there is a Goliath armed with a shield of gold; on the other is a kind of David equipped with a puny stone, with no prospect that the outcome will be at all Biblical.

*   *   *

Before any definite accounting of TV is attempted, these three primary aspects need to be ledgered.

First, for the large majority, TV is a medium of entertainment. Anything these viewers acquire by way of information or culture is incidental and almost accidental. Private-TV is intent on giving the public what it wants—or at least what it thinks the public wants. (At this point the matter of ratings enters the picture. This kind of unscientific sampling is held to be gospel even though it is an unholy business.)

Second, Private-TV, because it receives huge public grants

398

from the nation in the form of licenses, should have a large dedication to the public service. But it has never paid more than lip service to the concept and the Federal Communications Commission has never made any sustained effort to force a shift in programming—for various reasons, the most important being the influence of the TV lobby in Congress. (Because of direct financial interest in TV stations or because of pressure from newspaper publishers who also own television stations or, most of all, because television appearances are vital for politicians, the TV industry gets favored treatment.)

Third, Private-TV has done some excellent shows and is fully capable of doing more, but, because of its commercial structure, it will not present enough of these programs and it will not assign enough prime time to those it does present. Therefore, the task becomes one for Public-TV.

What, then, is the performance of the two groups in the two basic areas of information and culture?

A large responsibility for enlightening public opinion rests with the newspaper and television. They supply—or should supply—the information on which public opinion is based. When they fail, we have, instead of public opinion, apathy or, even worse, public emotion.

The newspaper is still the primary source of news. It has decided advantages over television: it can provide perspective; it has the authority of the printed word; it is constantly at hand, rather than requiring, as television does, presence at stated hours.

But newspapers, in too many instances, are not performing their true function, and an improvement in journalism is a prime need. But, even if that betterment is achieved, television has an important role to play. It cannot supplant the newspaper, but, because of its immediacy and its dramatic impact, it can supplement it to a significant degree. Yet television's news performance is far from satisfactory.

In on-the-spot coverage of events—the Kennedy tragedy, the adventures of the astronauts, outstanding sports contests—Private-TV does an often-superb job. But it does not provide interpretation of the news or perspective on it—and in these days of complex affairs, presentation of facts without an exposi-

399

tion of the meaning of those facts has little significance. Interpretation is essential and it must be done in graspable terms so that even the most hurried or elusive TV viewer will stop, look, and listen.

The lack of background is especially marked in the evening news programs, which are almost wholly bulletin services. In what was heralded as a valiant effort, the Cronkite and Huntley-Brinkley programs were increased from a quarter-hour to a half-hour each evening. But the additional fifteen-minute segments have been given not to interpretation but to features which are often hardly relevant to the day's news.

The commercial stations provide a certain amount of local intelligence, but this is usually the same kind of triviality about persons and happenings that swamp the local newspaper—police-blotter stuff or "society news" (the quotes are an understatement) or the presentation of names in the hope of snaring readers.

As for news documentaries on Private-TV, which in the days of Murrow had wide impact, there are still occasional presentations that are aids to understanding, but they are few and they are decreasing. Moreover, such documentaries are likely to be belated and, being generally unmarketable, are presented at hours when most people are otherwise occupied.

Of the 34 new programs on Private-TV that were introduced for the season beginning in September of 1966, not one was related even remotely to public affairs. The fact is that news operations are not rated as Bonanzas and so are relegated to the offhours.

Public-TV's performance in the public-affairs area is even worse; it has the hours but it lacks the content. There is little news and what there is, with few exceptions, is amateurish in concept and presentation and also failing in interpretation. Moreover, the absence of facilities for "live transmission" is likely to be fatal to almost any news broadcast.

Public-TV's documentaries—such as A Time for Burning and the summaries of the Fulbright hearings—have been at times excellent and have shed needed light on long-term trends. But just as urgent are reports presenting without delay the background of events—and these are not being provided.

THE EXPANDING IMAGE

The gaping lack in television, then, is the effective presentation of news. If we are to be able to cope with the baffling problems of the world—possibly the several worlds—of the future, that lack must be remedied.

*   *   *

In the culture area, television, in view of the number of hours spent before the screen, obviously can have a large influence. The difficulty of the task should not be underestimated; yet it should not be overestimated either. The "cultural explosion" may be only in the lip-service stage, but it is at least a start, and eventually the bricks and mortar may be infused with spirit and out of shadow may come substance. Television, here too, has a large opportunity but, on the whole, it fails to meet the challenge.

As for Private-TV's performance in the cultural area, there have been periodic efforts to provide better fare, such as the presentations of *The Glass Menagerie* or *Death of a Salesman* or the *Hallmark Hall of Fame*. But there has been an actual decline in the number of cultural specials, and of the new season's programs, only one had anything vaguely to do with culture.

The serials have become more and more Peyton Placeish and the audience more and more sob-sistered and cloyed. Batman and Batwoman and the various relatives of U.N.C.L.E. continue on their purple courses. And now there is the increasing dose of movies.

The performance of Public-TV in the cultural field has been more consistent; it has brought to listeners good plays, good music, good critical programs, such as *Uncle Vanya, An Enemy of the People,* and the series entitled *The Creative Person.* But the money has not been available to carry out a really impressive schedule.

Moreover, too much of Public-TV's cultural programs have been designed for the small minority; and, too often, a local station, in the effort to be different, has presented indifferent offerings—so far off-Broadway that they are beyond reach or so close "in" that they stifle and suffocate.

Commercial television, precisely because it is commercial, will not really perform in the cultural area until public taste is considerably elevated, the public desire for better entertainment thereby stimulated, and thus the presentation of "culture" made profitable. But these situations are still far in the future, and so the task becomes one for Public-TV, which should be the Lincoln Center (or what Lincoln Center should be) of the television screen.

*   *   *

Now the faults are being recognized and remedies are being discussed. The debate has been stimulated by three proposals —that of the Ford Foundation, under the direction of Messrs. McGeorge Bundy and Fred Friendly, his T.V.I.P.; that of the Carnegie Commission, under the chairmanship of Dr. James Killian; and that of the President in a special message to Congress.

The original Ford proposal was a spectacular; it suggested that a TV satellite be launched to serve both commercial and educational stations and pay for Public-TV out of the fees charged to Private-TV. But mathematics got in the way; it developed that the most revenue such an enterprise might produce would be some thirty million dollars, whereas the cost of doing anything approximating a real job in Public-TV is estimated at more than two hundred million dollars. Subsequently, certain taxes were proposed to increase the total.

The Ford planners decided further that they should demonstrate what Public-TV could achieve if it had the money. So they engaged, with an appropriation of ten million dollars, on arranging a Sunday-night, three-hour program, which is a kind of Sunday newspaper of the air, covering most areas and touching many bases. This program is largely national in concept; community stations that are the backbone of Public-TV are relegated to a minor role.

The Carnegie Report also sees public television as a "great instrument" for the public good. It concedes—too easily, it is argued—that commercial television has not done and should not be expected to do this kind of job. It proposes two or more national production centers, but they are to be supplemental to the local stations, to which the primary responsibility for programs would be assigned. The whole enterprise would be carried on under the direction of a public corporation which would be entrusted with the task of raising the necessary funds, both from Congress and private sources—a proposal endorsed by the President.

This is the essential difference between the Ford and the Carnegie philosophies: the Ford proposal puts the main emphasis on the national approach. It takes too little account of the function and needs of the community stations; the Carnegie proposal, on the other hand, exaggerates the potentialities of the community stations; a central operation is needed, because only it can supply the staff and the expert touch required for effective programs in the public affairs field.

The true approach is something between the two philosophies. The President's proposal seems to advocate this course—a combination of the best features of each of the two programs.

Thus the debate proceeds. But there is one extraordinary and distressing fact about it: there is voluminous discussion of the philosophy and mechanics of the operation but minimum consideration of the content. The basic question—what can Public-TV contribute?—is almost submerged in the morass of rhetoric and technical lingo. What, then, can be done in the way of content?

Because of the pressing need of a better informed opinion, the first assignment should be in the area of public affairs—in supplying news broadcasts, news documentaries (extended news-background reports), and debates over current issues.

Most urgent is the presentation of the news in an understandable way. This means that there should be much more than a bulletin service or background supplied long after the event; it means daily broadcasts at prime hours, in which the news would be given, and in perspective. Two recent events illustrate what is meant by "interpretation."

The commentator (read "reporter") discloses that the bombing of North Vietnam has been resumed. He does not tell the viewer why it has been renewed or what the response of Hanoi is likely to be or what effect Washington thinks the move will have on the whole war-peace issue.

Or the commentator reports that the C.I.A. has secretly been aiding the National Student Association. He does not tell how the C.I.A. functions or indicate how much scrutiny there is of its performance or discuss the basic issue of how a democracy can engage in secret operations.

Included in such broadcasts should be the presentation of local aspects of national or international news (examples: the way the Vietnam draft affects the community; or what the Common Market means to the factory at Fourth and Main Streets) or a discussion of community issues (examples: the problems of the local schools, of juvenile patterns, of civil rights or analysis of civic virtues and vices generally).

News should be defined in the broadest way, to include the significant trends of the times as well as the spot events, the news of achievement as well as of accident, the news of social developments as well as the news of "society." Always it should be kept in mind that there is no longer any such thing as local news; what happens in Hanoi affects Hoboken; an event in Paris, France, will have an echo in Paris, Ill.; this has become indeed one world and no longer is any news "foreign" to us.

The documentaries should adhere to the same general principles; they should be done close to events so that the impact of the headlines, and the consequent interest, are not lost.

Thus a Presidential message on the state of the Union should be followed almost immediately (as it was on NET) with a program that indicates where the proposals leave the Great Society program. Or an election in Germany with a program indicating what forces seem to be operating in the country and what this means for the future of Europe and for the world.

If the national network is staffed as a good newspaper is staffed—with experts in all the important areas—these tasks of interpretation can be carried out without delay, without waiting on the outside authority, who usually asks for time to arrange his affairs and to permit professorial cogitation. (It is my experience that in many instances delayed opinion holds no advantage in expertise over instant commentary; moreover, it lacks the dramatic appeal and the immediacy of the latter.)

A weekly, three-hour show, covering the high points of the news and dramatizing the significant happenings in every field, is a demonstration of what Public-TV can do in certain areas. But it does not solve the day-by-day problems of the community stations, and it cannot possibly deal properly with the local issues that confront a hundred or more communities.

Finally, there are needed well-ordered and well-moderated debates over the pressing issues of the day. These must not be the usual symposia, with their free-for-all, unfocused discussions and with a half-dozen panelists striving to get a half-dozen words in edgewise. (For example, there has been the welter of words about Vietnam. The debate has been uninformed, distorted by emotion, supplying little information and illumination and providing a heyday for the propagandists, doves, hawks, or even owls.) I would opt for two protagonists able to provide maximum light with minimum heat.

*   *   *

Greater efforts and new approaches are required also in the cultural area. One of the great problems of the future—possibly the greatest problem—is the use of nonworking time, which, as a result of automation, is likely to increase sharply. Work will be less stimulating; there will be a need for distraction or even the mere passing of time and for training and method in the use of leisure. Television will surely continue to play a large part in the program of living; it can provide leisure-time programs, and it can supply guideposts for other leisure-time activity.

What is needed is more theater, more music, more art, more discussion of books, more philosophy, if you will. This must be done both for the sophisticate and the uninitiated, in the hope that an increasing number of the latter can become interested. (For the theater, for example, a repertory company might well be a compelling idea. Repertory has not done well on Broadway for reasons difficult to fathom, but on television it might fare very well. There is a basic appeal about good actors playing a variety of roles; that has been amply proved in the movies and on the TV screen.)

None of this rules out entertainment; it suggests only that entertainment be supplied on a somewhat higher level. I believe profoundly that the public taste is far better than the pap-dispensers reckon it to be. If what is provided is not too far above its head, if the art and the music are not too recondite, if the drama is not too morbid or too remotely off-Broadway, I am sure the minority audience for culture will be largely increased.

A change in the temper and tempo of Public-TV is long overdue; too much of it has been "uplift"; too much has been "elite-conscious"; too much has been a waging of a Cult War. Highbrow does not mean that there shall not be a high humor and high spirits. Public-TV does not have to strike out to Batman, to surrender all goldmines to Bonanza or to despair of finding other Lucys to love. Happenings can be picnics as well as events.

In the cultural area, also, the effort should be local as well as national. It is highly desirable, of course, to present great drama, grand opera, grander art; but it is also highly useful to tap the resources of the community universities, to explain the newest show at the art center, to cooperate with the local libraries in indicating the joys of reading.

There should be full realization that, in the beginning at least, the business of education—of acquiring even a smattering of information and culture—has to be virtually painless. You can lead a citizen to the fountains of wisdom, or wonder, but you cannot make him drink. Avoidance of the serious approach in public television is really serious business.

There is a need, then, in both areas—information as well as culture. But a large question persists; how is Public-TV to be financed? I believe that, once the need for it is firmly recognized, the means will surely be found. The principle of classroom education basically applies: that it be Federally financed but operated free of Federal control. Obviously, Congress needs to be convinced that this is indeed "a great natural resource," so that it will appropriate the necessary funds. As in the case of education in general, there should be private and community contributions.

The parallel with the BBC immediately comes to mind— and it is not too farfetched. The British operation is, on the whole, a highly successful one and government interference is minimal. To be sure, British tradition is different from ours but not as dissimilar as the opponents of Federal action would have us believe.

There is much talk these days that Big Brother dominates most phases of our life. It is said that now it is proposed that brainwashing will be added to his demonic devices, and that Federal subsidies for television will automatically bring about some measure of Federal control.

It was to safeguard against this possibility that the Carnegie Commission proposed the establishment of a nonprofit nongovernmental corporation as the directing head of the enterprise, acting as a buffer between those who supply the funds and those entrusted with the programs. The President also called for this kind of public corporation and emphasized that it must be independent.

But the funds he proposed by way of Federal contribution—some nine million dollars for programs—are wholly inadequate. True, it is a start, but it should be recognized for what it is, only "seed money." The amount needed—the fact must be faced—is at least twenty times as much.

The danger, it seems to me, is not Big Brother but Small Sister, who will never raise her voice or suggest any action to meet the constantly growing number of new challenges.

* * *

In sum, then, this is to be said: There is a large assignment for television. Some of that assignment can and should be carried through by Private-TV but most of the undertaking must be assumed by Public-TV.

Public-TV must break new ground and, in fact, achieve new approaches both in information and in culture. To be sure, it has suffered from lack of funds, but it should be recognized that finances alone will not do the trick; imagination also is required, for ideas are often more important than cash. That is why it is essential that the present debate be concerned much more with content than with mechanisms.

Above all, Public-TV must strive to increase the size of its audience. There is no point in preaching to the converted or ploughing the wastelands rather than the potentially fertile acres. Public-TV must attain, if not a majority, at least a large minority; and, in the course of the long road, set up markers to indicate to Private-TV what can be done that is at once inspiring and profitable.

Public-TV has the potentiality of being a "great instrument"; it should be wielded as such, as an essential part of the national service, in the effort to ensure that the nation will develop the kind of public opinion and cultural viewpoint which are the hallmarks of a true democracy.

XXXI.

Mass Media in the Year 2000*

LEO BOGART

A social psychologist concerned with audiences and institutions, Leo Bogart is Executive Vice-President and General Manager, Bureau of Advertising of the American Newspaper Publishers Association. His numerous publications include *The Age of Television*.

~~~~~~

IT IS HARD to think seriously about the future because we take the present so much for granted. We hardly think twice about the fact that throughout the world music is a commonplace feature of daily life, at leisure and at work. We think of it as part of mankind's heritage, like sun, air, and water. Yet this has only come about in the few years since the invention of the phonograph record and radio. It is as hard for my children to realize that I grew up in a world without television, jet airplanes, washing machines, and astronauts as it is for me to realize that in the time of my father's childhood there were no automobiles, airplanes, and moving pictures.

Since the rate of invention grows as the existing base of technology expands, the changes in the next third-century will be even more dramatic than those of the last third. In that last third-century we have had our communications capacities enlarged by web offset and color gravure printing, photocopying, teletypesetting, talking motion pictures, and television (both first black and white and then in color), miniaturized and printed circuitry, communications satellites, audio and video tape recording, micro-

* Published for the first time in this volume by permission of the author. Copyright © 1967 by Leo Bogart.

photography, and electronic data processing. Although the mass media which existed earlier have bent and changed under the pressure of these inventions, they have not vanished. As we try to read the future, it seems reasonable to expect that today's media will continue to exist, but also that their form, function, and content will undergo radical modifications.

Most of the technical changes to which we can look forward in the remaining third-century will represent refinements and combinations of machines and systems which already exist. It serves no purpose to fantasy about technology which is still beyond the horizon. We must rather ask how the techniques which are already feasible in the laboratory will enter and change the communications systems of the future. How soon new techniques will come into widespread use will depend on how soon, through mass demand and mass production, their cost can be reduced to a scale comparable with today's mass media.

It is not enough to think in terms of a rapidly evolving technology. We must also weigh the economic capacity, the cultural receptivity, and the political willingness of society to make the investment required to translate technological potential into reality.

In our developed world we can foresee a steady rise in education; in the specialization of interests; in work productivity; in income; in leisure time. All these forces point to an accelerating demand for information of all kinds—for culture, for entertainment, and for pastimes to fill leisure.

The great cities of the world will continue to expand in size and to absorb an increasing proportion of the growing number of people. Along with the social and psychological problems of a changing, mobile population come the material problems of urban congestion, the choking of transportation networks, the degeneration of the architectural landscape. The resulting changes in the quality of life will profoundly affect the traditional role of the mass media as expressions of a community's identity and spirit.

International press services and space satellite broadcasting are symptomatic of the growing worldwide interconnections in mass communications. If we want to be optimists we might predict that in the shadow of nuclear destruction, international politics will rely more heavily on communications and less on military power. If the future were to take this happy course, it would surely change the function of the mass media as a force for national cohesion, and expand their potential as the principal means of creating a common vocabulary of ideas among all men.

The development of mass media will be profoundly influenced by the global confrontation of rival political forces and by the widening gap between what the eminent poet and athlete Mao Tse-tung calls the "city" and the "country"—the industrialized nations with a firm hold on the emerging technology and the agrarian nations for which this technology represents largely rumors and receding hopes.

The worldwide explosion of population (which shows no serious signs of abatement and cannot be stopped except by emergency measures) will in twenty years outstrip mankind's existing food supply capacities. How, in the case of famine, can we fail to foresee continuing political tensions and upheavals—quite apart from those directly inspired by ideology? How can there fail to be a continuing material and psychological dependence on the technically advanced countries by the impoverished peoples?

The gap between rich and poor nations will for some time to come cause new and old mass media systems to coexist at sharply different levels of technology—just as today there are nations which have no television and even a few without indigenous mass media of any kind.[1]

Parallel to the divergence in outlook between the advanced and backward countries is the growing difference within the advanced countries between the technical elite and the untrained mass, between those who feel a sense of participation and control over the changing course of society and those who think of themselves merely as consumers. The continuing contradictions,

---

[1] The problem is not solved by transplanting the hardware of an advanced technology to a relatively primitive one. A friend who recently returned from an educational television project in Africa reported to me on the fearful problems that are encountered with a magnificent new transmitter, because no one has the skills required to replace a tube or make a minor adjustment.

variations, and antagonisms within human society will in themselves insure the continued existence of parallel mass media systems—primitive and advanced—on both the local and international levels for many years to come.

The Five Areas of Technical Change

The technology of communication is being transformed in five areas: in assembling information, storing it, retrieving it, compressing it, and reacting to it.

1. In the graphic arts, we are getting higher quality color reproduction by a combination of graphic techniques within the same production sequence. Telecommunication makes possible decentralized production and printing at great speed and with simultaneous operations at separated places. Computerized typesetting and photocomposition, already a reality, will be more broadly used to expedite and reduce the effort required to transmit information from its source to its users.

2. Electronic recording instruments, in combination with the computer, make it possible to store aural or visual communications, transmitted at extremely high speed, for rediffusion or playback at the option, and to the specifications, of the individual recipient. This is true not only of communication through the alphabetic symbols of print, but of the direct reproduction of sound and sight which we now experience through radio, cinema, and television. The familiar tape recorder, already adapted from audio to video, is but the forerunner of far more sophisticated home recording systems that permit information to be stored and played back to suit individual specifications, needs, and tastes.

3. Microphotography has given us the economical visual storage of miniaturized records which can be classified, punch-coded, retrieved through the computer, and rapidly enlarged and reproduced. This is already revolutionizing librarianship, business record-keeping, and a host of other activities which require the rapid assembly of related information drawn from varied sources. New processes now make it possible to achieve microfilm quality without developing film chemically. Electrostatic reproduction, in combination with improved data recording mechanisms, provides the means for widely dispersed facsimile reproduction of

412

the conventional forms of print media, giving substance to the old idea of a newspaper produced in the home.

4. We have vastly increased facilities for transmitting huge flows of information. Thirty million words, the equivalent of 108,000 typed pages, can be transmitted in an hour through a television scanning system. Space satellites using solar energy will make it possible for vast quantities of messages to go directly from transmitters to home receivers in any part of the world. The internationalization of the broadcast media will proceed apace, inhibited largely by language and by localized tastes. Throughout the world, radio and television become more and more universally accessible; more homes are linked through the telephone into communication centrals which ultimately will be put to diversified uses, as has already happened in the United States with community cable antenna TV systems. Lasers permit complex messages to be transmitted along hitherto unexploited reaches of the energy spectrum; through holography they allow us to reconstruct three-dimensional images, reduced or magnified in size. The hologram may replace microfilm for information storage, and could permit the transmission of 2,000 typewritten pages a second.

These complex systems of processing communication raise new problems of information cataloguing and retrieval. Eventually these problems will be solved by indexing information successively in terms of cross-reference points which permit progressively finer expositions of detail. The translation of such machinery from the laboratory to the stage of a mass communications system is obviously limited by the fact that greater complexity requires great expansion in the band of electronic frequencies required. But this obstacle too will be overcome.

5. We will soon have the means to make mass communication a two-way process. Through a home or office console unit, tied to a computer, an individual can feed back questions, demands, and other reactions to his communications source. He can control not only the flow of information but the by-products of information. In most countries the public is already accustomed to this kind of feedback in the form of opinion and marketing research. We see it in American pay-television systems, in which

people pick the programs they want and pay accordingly. We see it in automated vending and mail ordering of merchandise. Already there exists in prototype the push-button store in which the consumer selects the items he wants by remote control and has them assembled and packaged for delivery. It is only another step to link the home and the warehouse directly. In short, computerized selective access to goods as well as to information may represent a public utility as generally available in civilized society as water or electricity, metered and paid for by the same kinds of accounting devices.

The home information system of the future may have its visual center in a large mirror on the wall, a mirror which at our command will present an illuminated reproduction of any kind of information we want. This information may take the form of written language—letters and words as they now appear on the daily newspaper or magazine page. We can summon up these messages to our command by predesignated codes which will yield the particular kind of information we are interested in. Through another system of controls (perhaps using an electronic pencil) we might get pictures to illustrate the words which interest us, just as we might be able to get the full story if the headline is intriguing. A news article about a speech by a public figure could give way to a photograph of the occasion—and in either case we could instantly get a facsimile copy. Another control might bring us the sound of the speaker's voice or the filmed visual record.

Today a few pennies can buy a newspaper or magazine, or hours of radio or television. The systems just described would be prohibitively expensive to install and operate in today's economy, and with today's information needs. And yet can anyone doubt that the time is not distant when they will represent reasonable and economical methods?

The Changing Function of Media

The sharp distinction between broadcast and print media, as we now know it, is likely to be dimmed and perhaps even to disappear in the world of the near future. This sharp distinction rests on two essential differences:

1. The difference between the visible, tactile, permanent record of a print communication and the intangible, evanescent, impermanent nature of broadcast messages. This distinction will disappear as the mechanisms for home recording of broadcasts become more simple, inexpensive, and widespread.

2. The distinction between space and time media in the degree of control which the recipient exercises over the flow of information.

The great advantage of symbolic communication through print is that it may be skimmed or scanned and then dipped into selectively for the information that the reader wants to absorb in greater depth. The reader of a newspaper or magazine, like the reader entering a public library, is simultaneously engaged in two different processes of handling information.

1. He has certain expectations and wishes which he can fulfill by turning immediately to the probable source of what he is interested in. In the library he may go immediately to the shelves which deal with books on a certain subject or by a certain author. In the newspaper he can turn immediately to the pages which carry the stock market quotations, the sports results, or the motion picture reviews.

2. But in either case the great advantage of having an open visual display in a storehouse of information is the opportunity for chance discovery of unanticipated treasures which arouse interest and further investigation. The browser in the library finds books on subjects that he had not thought of reading about. The reader of a newspaper or magazine encounters articles on subjects which he could not possibly have expected in advance. We very quickly filter out, from all the information which confronts us visually, the particular bits which arouse our interest and encourage us to further pursuit. This kind of skimming cannot take place with the same efficiency in a time-bound medium. We can flick the radio dial until we come upon the particular kind of music we want to hear or until we hear a station that speaks our language. But to hear a program which we anticipate with pleasure, we must inform ourselves in advance and adjust our time schedule to that of the broadcaster.

Thus, in contrast to the selective pattern of print media, broadcasting is inevitably a matter of mass and uniform exposure. Because of the economics of broadcasting, fewer channels of information can be diffused simultaneously than in print within the confines of a given language and national culture. The result is that the choices for the broadcast listener or viewer have been fewer than in print. This condition changes as a result of some of the technical developments to which I referred earlier. Soon broadcasts on radio or television will be frozen through recordings; they will be automatically sorted; vast quantities of them will be economically transmitted in a tiny fraction of the time required to play them back at normal speed. In short, it is now possible to think of the skimming or scanning process as one which can be applied to broadcasting as well as to print, much as one speeds up the playback on a tape recorder to get at the parts of a tape one wants to hear.

As we increase our technical capacity to manipulate mass communications selectively for our individual purposes, its borderline with private communication becomes more and more indistinct. The essence of mass communication is that it makes possible the wide diffusion of identical messages, but this characteristic is lost as each recipient determines the particular form and sequence of the messages he receives.

The creation of a twilight zone between private and public communications can hardly mean an end to the mass media as we know them. But today's mass media are unlikely to keep their present form and function in the world of the future. The content of existing media may undergo drastic change, just as (in the United States at least) fiction has been almost eliminated from general magazines and drama has almost disappeared from radio as a result of less than two decades of television. We can best assume that for a long time to come there will continue to be diverse systems of media operating in competition with each other at different stages of technological sophistication, subject to different kinds of regulation and financial support.

It would be silly to suggest that the graphic arts which our Western world has used for some five hundred years are doomed

416

to oblivion within the next fifty. The facsimile system does not provide the answer to the tactility and mobility of newspapers or magazines which are picked up many, many times by each reader and taken from one reading location to another to be perused in a different context. The tactile aesthetic satisfaction of good print reproduction will continue to remain important.

Radio and television, with their obvious capacities for instantaneous, direct communication, will continue to be major means for people to enjoy and inform themselves. One great attraction of existing media is the simultaneous sharing of experience which is incompatible with communication that is both one-way and unique in content. There is a basic satisfaction we get from knowing that other like-minded people are reading the same newspaper editorial or magazine article, listening to the same radio concert, or watching the same play on television.

Radio and television acquire much of their force from the fact that the listener who tunes in feels himself in direct communication with the broadcaster, in real-time. He speaks to us *now*. We feel this strongly as spectators of a televised public event. But this sense of immediacy has already been lost in television's stock entertainment fare because the economics of program production increasingly dictate filming in advance. In the United States this accounts for Hollywood's new vitality and for the fact that fewer and fewer evening programs are broadcast live.

The need for specialized broadcasting channels and publications will inevitably continue in the era of entirely new technology. There will always be interests too narrow or local to justify electronic applications in the short-term future.

There may be a new role for the motion picture precisely because of its involving and overwhelming character as an experience for audiences in the mass. The growing opportunities to be selective in our use of the mass media may make us all the more receptive to the live performing arts. People will always want to go out to experience a spectacle away from their usual home environment, within the order and security of an enclosed space and in human company. Even when lasers are used to produce the illusion of having others with us in three dimensions, this will be a different matter from the direct confrontation of performers with an audience or the members of an audience among themselves.

Entertainment and Information

As we move into an age of greater leisure, is there any sense to the conventional dividing lines between the mass media of entertainment and the mass media of information? Information may be taken as entertainment. Poetry, drama, and fiction all inform as well as entertain, since they instruct us on the aspirations, joys, and perplexities of other men. The nonverbal arts—painting, sculpture, music and dance—may also carry over nuances of this kind of communication, but they are not informative in the sense that we can evoke and integrate their meanings in any other ways than memory or imitation.

What is informative for one person may be merely entertaining for another, and vice versa. Nor is the boundary between information and entertainment a matter of what is timely. The fundamental difference is that information exists largely outside of time. Most people would prefer to acquire a knowledge of calculus or Chinese painlessly overnight with the help of some type of magic electrodes inserted into the pillow. To be sure, there is also an aesthetic element involved in acquiring information—the pleasure of discovering the solution to a problem of mathematics or grammar; finding the relationship between something new and something already known. But information is mainly an end in itself rather than a tool for the pleasure of learning. Entertainment and culture are pastimes which must be savored within the time dimension. It seems reasonable to predict that in the future informational media must strive for ever greater economy and speed of presentation, whereas the audio-visual media will continue to stress entertainment that flows through time.

More and more mass media exposures represent uniform messages from the teletype or film archive rather than the individualized messages of the past. Unlike newspapers, television, which in advanced countries makes the greatest demands on leisure time, is national or international rather than local in its content.

418

While the increased demand for information has produced a tremendous proliferation of publications of all kinds, the production of fresh entertainment matter has not kept pace with the requirements. The film libraries of the world are already on the verge of being exhausted by the insatiable appetites of television. Old programs are rerun repeatedly. In developing countries, modern mass media systems are only now arriving at the point of making real demands in the realm of content. We are on the verge of a tremendous expansion in the worldwide market for information of all kinds, for new ideas, for talent, for the arts.

This in turn raises the question of balance between what people want and what is "good" for them in the eyes of publishers and broadcasters. Elite and popular culture are generally regarded in terms of the requirements of different sectors of society, when they really correspond to different aspects of the same people. All of us tolerate cultural experiences below the level of our highest tastes; we even enjoy them. By the same token, people whose routine cultural exposure is at the most vulgar level are not incapable of being reached and moved by art or high purpose.

Today's mass media, even when regulated by the philosophy of giving the public what it wants, permit and encourage accidental exposures to elite culture in the context of programming or texts with broader appeal. Such chance exposures would not take place if people had complete freedom to select whatever interested them. A small child who knows only a few bedtime stories asks to hear the same ones over and over again.

There is a weakness in those mass communication systems of the future which assume a high degree of purposeful choice on the part of the audience, which assume that they know what they want and what they are seeking. This leaves no room for the element of fortuitous discovery, the accidental encounter with stimuli which arouse our curiosity, remind us of forgotten interests, and lead us into new paths of exploration.

Technology and the Control of Information

In the past, new inventions were produced by chance combinations within the existing base of knowledge. Today, the creation of new inventions and new technology is a matter of purpose, of will, of investment, of decisions made by institutions and states rather than by individual inventors.

Mass media are big business. As technology evolves, it requires greater capital investments and greater aggregations of specialized talents. All of this could lead to greater concentration of control within the communications system.

Although, in some countries, several telephone and electrical systems coexist, it is not normal to find the same residents served by two or more suppliers of electricity or telephone service. By the same token, it would be uneconomical in the future to expect home communications facilities to be serviced by more than a single transmission system. There may be, as in English commercial television today, a number of competing companies supplying messages, but the distribution arrangements are likely to be centralized in the form of a public utility, whether or not this is privately or publicly owned.

As enormous resources have to be coordinated and brought into play, we move farther and farther away from the individualistic expressions which are the roots of modern journalism. We are indeed remote from the tradition of the eighteenth-century feuilleton (or, for that matter, of the Red Guard wall newspapers of 1967 Peking).

While complex technology concentrates power, that power is vulnerable to the rise of even more complex technology. In the United States and United Kingdom, the rise of motion pictures and broadcasting has brought up new forces to mold public opinion and taste, and has shaken the preeminence of the great newspapers and magazine publishing houses.

We are already witnessing a rapid obsolescence of existing communications, and of the machines and technical skills required to operate them. The *status quo* may have powerful support from existing institutions (both on the management and labor side), but who can doubt that change will come anyway?

If information tends more and more to flow through centralized channels which have the character of a public utility, how can new (and unpopular) ideas obtain a hearing? How can we engineer the mass media of tomorrow so that they serve the clash of ideas and foster the diversity of expression and experience which is essential for human progress?

We cannot answer this question except in relation to the economic base, in which advertising, in the Western world, has the predominant part. Where does advertising fit into the scheme of media in the future? Obviously advertising's place today differs throughout the world, depending on the economic system, the level of economic development, and the presence, or regulation, of commercial broadcasting. With the rise of the electronic media, advertising has changed its function. Far less of it is aimed to inform the public; far more of it is intended to persuade.

I don't think there can be much doubt that advertising will have an important place in the mass media of the future, since most advertising represents information which consumers actively seek and which they will continue to demand even when they have complete power to select what they want. The effects of technical change in the media are bound to be greatest in the case of advertising on commercial radio and television, since broadcast advertising messages are more likely to be persuasive rather than informative. They are more apt to be imposed on the viewer or listener, and not sought out to the same degree as advertisements in print.

Advertising will have to change radically in the next third-century, not only in its use of media to reach the consumers who are being sold, but also in its content and style, in the very philosophy of selling consumer goods in a competitive market. As advertising changes, so (necessarily) will the economic base of the existing media. Is it really too soon for the leaders in mass communications, in advertising as well as on the media side, to ponder the long-run implications of impending change, as well as the immediate short-run policy decisions, and to begin the serious research required to ease the transition?

The Problem of "Cultural Lag"

Many years ago the American sociologist William Fielding Ogburn described what he called the "cultural lag" between technological innovation and the capacity of society to change its institutions in a way which permits technical change to be used to best advantage. Today, in the field of mass communications, technical changes are feasible far beyond our capacity to take advantage of them. But cultural lag with regard to communications media is especially important because they are such a great influence on the public attitudes and values which must change if mankind is to intelligently master the new technology.

The developments which are in the offing for mass media exemplify the great changes taking place in *all* spheres of life. There seems to be a tremendous resistance to accept the imminence of these great changes and to face up to their social consequences. When the prospects of space flight were familiar only to a relative handful of specialists, policy makers and social scientists alike showed little response, in fact even resistance, to the idea of confronting its social implications. Who, if not the mass media, has the responsibility of preparing mankind to cope with the challenge of technical progress? Who, if not the media, can goad a reluctant society to come to grips with the emerging problems that arise from space exploration, extension of the life span, eugenics, and the development of new forms of energy?

No one knows better than our generation that the most advanced technology can be used on behalf of the most ignoble ends, or that brilliant means may be used to convey banal content. The educational authorities in one of our states recently engaged a firm of specialists in advanced instructional techniques to develop a system to improve the reading skills of children in the elementary school grades. The materials included some drawings of farm scenes with various domestic animals and their names. Among these drawings was one of a fully mature cow, with all of her basic equipment. The authorities took a look at it and ruled that the udders be removed. Perhaps nothing better symbolizes the problem we face than the spectacle of the latest technology of programmed learning being used to teach children how to spell "cow"—without udders. Let us hope that what men have to say in the future will be worthy of the new means by which they will be able to say it.

XXXII.

Culture-Intercom*

STAN VANDERBEEK

Stan VanDerBeek has won many honors here and abroad for his experimental films. His *See Saw Seems* was shown at the 1967 New York Film Festival.

∽∽∽∽∽∽∽∽∽∽∽∽∽∽∽∽∽∽∽∽∽∽∽∽∽∽

> Vision undergoes re-vision; intention, symbol, reality
> are the factors that undergo constant change
> in the appearance of any art form.
>
> Motion pictures—
> pictures in motion—
> seem most suited to the metaphysics of change,
> to life in motion,
> and as such cinema is becoming the most significant of art
> forms.
>
> > One thing that is new is the prevalence of
> > newness, the changing scale and scope of change
> > itself, so that the world alters as we
> > walk in it. . . .
>
> > (Robert Oppenheimer, *The Open Mind*)

I like to think that life is a dissolve . . .

. . . and that seeing is the real illusion, that a sense of reality is a sense of the senses . . .

* Published in this form for the first time in this volume by permission of the author. Portions of this selection have previously appeared in *American Scholar, motive,* and *Tulane Drama Review*.

that a sense of reality is a sense of non-sense . . .
that movies should delight the eye and rearrange the
    senses . . .
that movies are changing the art of seeing . . .
that movies are an art of seeing . . .
that movies are an illusion . . .
that seeing is believing.

The irony of art and life reminds us that "motion pictures"
are really a series of "still" pictures, which are being replaced
in the projector at less than 1/24th of a second . . . reaching
our eye at 186,000 m.p. second.
That we see the illusion of motion is based on the retention
of image, or the eye's inertia.

Motion pictures are apparent motion . . .
The film worker deals with "visual velocity" and "visual
    inertia,"
laws of sight that seem similar to laws in physics—
or at least to definitions of sight that contemporary
artists are exploring.
If movies and "vision" can assume the same meaning
then visions take the path of least resistance, that is,
intuitive logic, intuitive geometry, image-symbol making, art-
city planning of the mind, a form of research
that is just beginning in motion images.

> If confusion is the sign of the time, I see
> at the root of this confusion a rupture
> between things and words, between things and
> the ideas and signs that are their representation. . . .
>
> (Artaud)

The apparent image and the approximate image interrelate in
our national sense of photo-reality. It is not inappropriate
that we have a magazine called *Life*—that we take for granted
that movies are reality.

Motion pictures are just now beginning to come out of the
    literary

424

perspective of the novel and staged drama they were born
in . . .

It is interesting that after nearly 400 years of art that was
preoccupied with realism—growing mostly out of the theory
of
perspective and its effect on the senses—this preoccupation
has at last reached its ultimate form in photography, particularly
motion-picture photography.

It is part of the interesting nature of art that at this same
juncture in the crossroads of art, with the perfection
of a means to capture exactly perspective and "realism,"
the artist's vision is turning more to his interior, and in a
sense to an
infinite exterior (photos of Mars), abandoning the logic of
aesthetics and springing full-blown into a juxtaposed and
simultaneous world that ignores the one-point-perspective
mind
and the one-point-perspective lens.

Another factor of particular interest is that movies represent
a kind of international decompression chamber, being the
only
international art form that is portable, reproducible and
universal in popularity . . .

I am fascinated by one of the current theories about dreams
which holds that dreams are a way for the body to get rid of
body poisons (which get burned up in the dream-act).

If this holds true, it seems likely that motion pictures
might be a way for us to burn up international and national
"toxic" attitudes. Perhaps this is an aspect of the
moviegoing ritual, and of the value of the Hollywood "dream
factory". . . .

Clearly, movies help us to re-experience our experiences,
which
seems to be a basic human need.

425

Motion, metamotion, kinetic identity, body-motor response,
homeostasis, continuity . . .
the movement of the spheres . . .
are to be pinned like a moth stuck in the axis of the mind,
to relieve the tensions of change (doubt)—of the movement
    of
life itself—by studying it . . .
by changing it into a symbolic form that is as real and
    meaning-
ful as life itself.

I have emphasized that motion pictures are the unique art
    form
of the 20th century,
that they have produced a revolution in worldwide aesthetics,
(namely, that motion pictures have produced the new aes-
    thetics of
anticipation, as compared to the older idea of painting and
    art
history as "meditation") . . .
that cinema is just beginning to come into its own . . .

Some of the ideas that are of particular interest to the
current film-maker are:
simultaneous images and compression,
abstractions, superimpositions,
discontinuous information,
social surrealism,
episodic structure,
loop film (continuous projection),
film as a reflection of private dreams, hallucinations . . .

Some of the vastly expanded techniques available now in-
    clude:
8mm (some 6½ million 8mm cameras in America)
super 8mm
16, 35, 70, 120mm (over one billion dollars for photo-services
annually),
video tape for home use,
computer-generated graphics,
stereo and laser pictures . . .

television (4½ hours viewing-time per average family per
    average
day).

The contemporary artist, facing many opportunities in Amer-
    ica,
must find ways to cut across definitions and precensorship of
techniques and media.

The artist must make use of the force of art, with its influence
on human psychology, to communicate and to announce. He
    must find
ways to come out of his isolation from his community. He
    must
find ways to unite technology and the human condition . . .
He must find ways to investigate, to document, to decorate,
to criticize, to love . . . and so add meaning to the life we
    are all
shaping.

We are on the verge of a new world—a new sense of art,
life and technology—when artists shall deal with the
world as a work of art, and art and life shall again become
the same process. When man's senses shall expand,
reach out, and in so doing shall touch all men in the world.

It is imperative that we quickly find some way for the entire
    level of
world understanding to rise to a new human scale.
This scale is the world . . .
The risks are the life or death of this world.
The technological explosion of this last half-century, and the
    implied future,
are overwhelming; man is running the machines of his own
    invention . . .
while the machine that is man
runs the risk of running wild.

Technological research, development and involvement of the
    world community

has almost completely out-distanced the emotional-sociological (socio-"logical")
comprehension of this technology.
It is imperative that each and every member of the world community,
regardless of age and cultural background, join the 20th century as
quickly as possible.
The "technique-power" and "culture-overreach" that are just beginning to
explode in many parts of the earth has put
the logical fulcrum of man's intelligence so far outside himself that he
cannot judge or estimate the results of his acts before he commits them.
The process of life as an experiment on earth has never been made clearer.
It is this danger . . . that man does not have time
to talk to himself . . .
that man does not have means to talk to other men . . .
the world hangs by a thread of verbs and nouns.
Language and cultural-semantics are as explosive
as nuclear energy.
It is imperative that we (the world's artists) invent a new world language.

I propose the following:

That immediate research begin on the possibility of an international
picture-language fundamentally using motion pictures.

That we immediately research existing audiovisual devices, to combine these
devices into an educational tool that I shall call an "experience machine"
or a "culture-intercom" . . .

The establishment of audiovisual research centers, preferably on an
international scale . . .

these centers to explore the existing audiovisual hardware . . .
The development of new image-making devices . . .
(the storage and transfer of image materials, motion pictures,
    television,
computers, video-tape, etc.).
In short, a complete examination of all audiovisual devices
    and procedures,
with the idea in mind to find the best combination of such
    machines for
nonverbal interchange.

The training of artists on an international basis in the use of
    these image
tools.

The immediate development of prototype theaters, here-
    after called
"Movie-Dromes," that incorporate the use of such projection
    hardware.
The immediate research and development of image-events
    and performances
in the "Movie-Drome" . . .
I call these prototype presentations:
                              "Movie Murals," "Ethos-Cinema,"
                              "Newsreel of Dreams," "Feedback,"
                              "Image Libraries."

The "movie-drome" would operate as follows:
In a spherical dome, simultaneous images of all sorts would
    be projected
on the entire dome-screen . . . the audience lies down at the
    outer edge of
the dome with their feet towards the center, thus almost the
    complete field
of view is the dome-screen. Thousands of images would be
    projected on this
screen; this image-flow could be compared to the "collage"
    form of the
newspaper or the three ring circus (both of which suffice the
    audience

with an abundance of facts and data). The audience takes what it can or

wants from the presentation and makes its own conclusions . . . each member

of the audience will build his own references from the image-flow.

The visual material is to be presented and each

individual makes his own conclusions . . . or realizations.

A particular example:

an hour-long presentation in the "movie-drome" using all sorts

of multiplex images, depicting the course of Western civilization since

the time of the Egyptians to the present . . . a rapid panoply of graphics

and light calling upon thousands of images, both still and in motion

(with appropriate "sound-images"). It would be possible to compress the

last three thousand years of Western life into such an aspect ratio that

we, the audience, can grasp the flow of man, time, and forms of life

that have lead us up to the very moment . . . details are not important; it

is the total scale of life that is . . . in other words . . . using the past and

the immediate present to help us understand the likely future.

Endless filmic variations of this idea are possible in each field of

man's endeavor . . . science, math, geography, art, poetry, dance,

biology . . .

endless variations of this idea by each culture group and nationality

that take it on as a project . . . to be presented in turn to each other

culture group . . .

The purpose and effect of such image-flow and image density (also to be

called "visual-velocity") is to penetrate to unconscious levels
  and to deal
with and logically understand those levels. The use of such
  "emotion-pictures"
would be to reach for
the "emotional denominator" of all men:
the basis of human life thought and understanding that is
  nonverbal.
These "emotion-pictures" would provide images that inspire
  basic intuitive instincts of self-
realization and inspire all men to good will and "inter- and
  intro-
realization."

When I talk of the movie-dromes as image libraries, it is
  understood
that such "life-theaters" would use some of the coming techniques
(video tape and computer interplay) and thus be real communication
and storage centers; that is, by satellite, each dome could
  receive
its images from a worldwide library source, store them and
  program
a feedback presentation to the local community that lived
  near the
center. This newsreel feedback could authentically review the
  total
world image "reality" in an hour-long show that gave each
  member of
the audience a sense of the entire world picture . . . it would
  be the
world's "work of the month" put into an hour.
"Intra-communitronics" or dialogues with other centers would
  be likely,
and instant reference material via transmission television and
  tele-
phone could be called for and received at 186,000 m.p.s., from
  any-
where in the world.

Thus I call this presentation a "newsreel of ideas, of dreams, a
movie-mural" . . .
an image library, a culture decompression chamber, a "cul-
      ture-intercom" . . .

My concept is in effect the maximum use of the maximum
      information
devices that we now have at our disposal.

Certain things might happen . . . if an individual is exposed
      to an over-
whelming information experience . . .
It might be possible to reorder the levels of awareness of any
      person . . .
it certainly will reorder the structure of motion pictures as we
      know
them.

Cinema will become a "performing" art . . . and image
      library.
I foresee that such centers will have their artist-in-residence
      who will
orchestrate the image material he has at his disposal . . .
and will lead to a totally new international art form.
In probing for the "emotional denominator," it will be pos-
      sible
by the visual "power" of such a presentation to reach any
      age or
culture group regardless of culture and background.
The "experience machine" could bring anyone on earth up
      to the 20th
century.

As the current growth rate risk of explosives to human flesh
      continues,
the risk of survival increases accordingly.
It now stands at 200 pounds of T.N.T. per human pound of
      flesh . . . per human
on earth.
There are an estimated 700 million people who are unlettered
      in the world . . .
we have no time to lose

or miscalculate . . .
The world and self-education process must find a quick solution to
reorder itself, a revision of itself, an awareness of itself . . .
that is, each man must somehow realize the enormous scale of human
life and accomplishments on earth right now.
Man must find a way to measure himself, to grow simultaneously and keep
in touch with himself . . .
Man must find a way to leap over his own prejudices and apprehensions.
The means are on hand . . . here and now . . .
in technology and the extension of the senses.

To summarize:
My concern is for a way for the over-developing technology of part of the
world to help the under-developed emotional-sociology of *all* of the world
to catch up to the 20th century . . . to counter-balance technique and logic—
and to do it now, quickly . . .
My concern is for world peace and harmony . . .
the appreciation of individual minds . . .
the interlocking of good wills on an international exchange basis . . .
the interchange of images and ideas . . .
a realization of the process of "realization" of self-education
that now must occur before the "fact" of education.

In short: a way for all men to have fore-knowledge
by advantageous use of past and immediate knowledge . . .
mankind faces the immediate future with doubt on one hand
and molecular energy on the other . . .
he must move quickly and surely to preserve his future . . .
he must realize the present . . .
the here and the now . . . right now.

The development of a nonverbal international picture
language that makes use of cinema and other image-

transmission systems is of utmost importance in the
consistent crises of world peace.

But to realize the possibilities of this new art form
(cinema is only approximately sixty years old) many more
artists and poets must become aware of this medium and
attempt to work with it.
I hope that artists from all over the world will do so
and quickly, so that we can realize and enjoy our differences
in a "culture-intercom."

Sights and sounds, the changing illusion of the world in
      which
we live, and the world that lives
only in the mind, are the basic materials of film creation . . .
The full flow of color, sound, synthesized form, plastic form,
      light, and
picture poetry have in no way begun to be explored in man's
range of experience.

APPENDIX

The Literature of Motion Pictures and Television: A Critique and Recommendations *by Richard Averson and David Manning White*

∿∿∿∿∿∿∿∿∿∿∿∿∿∿∿∿∿∿∿∿∿∿∿∿∿∿∿∿∿∿

The preceding divisions of this book have dealt with the interrelationship of the sight-and-sound media and various social institutions. This section is concerned with bibliographic material and those organizations actively involved with films and TV. It will suggest sources of information for those readers wishing to explore more deeply the juncture of the moving image and American society.

In preparing a motion picture-television bibliography, there is always the tendency to classify publications according to such topics and categories as the history of these media, production techniques, effects on audiences, criticism, etc. While we do not deny the usefulness of this bibliographic approach, we consider it contrary to the purpose of our anthology. We prefer to arrange this Appendix under the headings of (1) The Arts, (2) Education, (3) Government, and (4) Business, thereby maintaining our institutional perspective.

The Arts

An extensive literature exists on motion pictures and television as "communication arts."

In terms of the nature of film and its special requirements for creative expression, the following books are essential: Ernest Lindgreen's *The Art of the Film* (revised edition, 1963);[1] Rudolf

---

[1] Publishers and prices of books mentioned may be found in *Books in Print, U.S.A.* and in *Paperbound Books in Print. N. W. Ayer & Son's Directory of Newspapers and Periodicals* contains addresses and subscription rates of magazines. Another reliable source of information is *Organizations, Publications and Directories in the Mass Media of Communications*, compiled by Wilbur Peterson and published by the School of Journalism, State University of Iowa.

Arnheim's *Film as Art* (1957); Sergei M. Eisenstein's *The Film Form* and *Film Sense*, both available as a single paperback (1957); Raymond Spottiswoode's *A Grammar of the Film* (1950); Siegfried Kracauer's *Theory of Film* (1960); John Howard Lawson's *Film: The Creative Process* (1964); and André Bazin's *What Is Cinema?* (1967). Dealing more specifically with writing and film-making skills are Lewis Herman's *A Practical Manual of Screen Playwriting* (1963); W. Hugh Baddeley's *The Technique of Documentary Film Production* (1963); and Karel Reisz's *The Technique of Film Editing* (1953).

Books on television as a "communications art medium" are primarily manuals for producing and directing programs. (Unfortunately there are no TV equivalents to the above-named books by Arnheim and Kracauer.) We recommend Herbert Zettl's *Television Production Handbook* (1961); Stasheff and Bretz's *The Television Program* (complete edition, 1962), and Gerald Millerson's *The Technique of Television Production* (1961). In the area of scriptwriting for various program-types, especially valuable are Robert L. Hilliard's *Writing for Television and Radio* (1962) and Gilbert Seldes' *Writing for Television* (1952).

There are several anthologies which contain articles and essays written by sight-and-sound communicators giving insight into the creative problems of film and TV. Among them are *Film: An Anthology* (1959; edited by Daniel Talbot); *Film: A Montage of Theories* (1966; edited by Richard Dyer MacCann); *Television: The Creative Experience* (1967; edited by Bluem and Manvell); and *Film Makers on Film Making* (1967; edited by Harry M. Geduld).

The life and work of film producers and directors are examined in such biographies and critical monographs as *The Cinema of Alfred Hitchcock* (1963) by Peter Bogdanovich; *The Films of Akira Kurosawa* (1965) by Donald Richie; *The Innocent Eye: The Life of Robert J. Flaherty* (1963) by Arthur Calder-Marshall; *D. W. Griffith: Film Master* (1965) by Iris Barry; *Luis Buñuel* (1963) by Ado Kyrou; *Lessons with Eisenstein* (1962) by Vladimir Nizhny; *The Personal Vision of Ingmar Bergman* (1964) by Jorn Donner; *Michelangelo Antonioni* (1963) by Pierre Leprohon; *Samuel Goldwyn: The Producer and His Films* (1956) by Richard Griffith; *Hollywood Rajah: The Life and Times of Louis B. Mayer* (1960) by Bosley Crowther; *The Films of Josef von Sternberg* (1966) and *Interviews with Film Directors* (1967)

APPENDIX

by Andrew Sarris; and *Hitchcock* (1967) by François Truffaut. Most of these contain "stills" from the films of these producers and directors as well as useful "filmographies" listing complete credits, release dates, and casts. Further material concerning these and other film-makers may be found in the occasional publications issued in conjunction with retrospective screenings at such centers as the Gallery of Modern Art, the Museum of Modern Art Film Library, the National Film Theatre of the British Film Institute, George Eastman House, and La Cinémathèque Française.

Also valuable are books of memoirs and recollections written by sight-and-sound communicators giving firsthand accounts of their experiences in motion pictures and television. The most perceptive are *My First Hundred Years in Hollywood* (1965) by Jack L. Warner; *A Tree Is a Tree* (1953) by King Vidor; *Fun in a Chinese Laundry* (1965) by Josef von Sternberg; *Good Evening!* (1964) by Raymond Swing; *It Sounds Impossible* (1963) by Slate and Cook; *The Education of a Broadcaster* (1965) by Harry Bannister; *This Is Eric Sevareid* (1964); *Fear on Trial* (1964) by John Henry Faulk; and *Due to Circumstances beyond Our Control* (1967) by Fred W. Friendly.

Screen personalities and "the art of the actor" are the subjects of numerous pictorial volumes such as *The Films of Greta Garbo* (1965; Conway, et al.), *The Films of Charlie Chaplin* (1965; McDonald, et al.); *The Films of Marilyn Monroe* (1964; Conway and Ricci); *Bogey: The Films of Humphrey Bogart* (1965; Clifford McCarty); *The Films of Laurel and Hardy* (1967; William K. Everson); *The Films of Bette Davis* (1966; Gene Ringgold); *Harold Lloyd's World of Comedy* (1964; William Cahn); *The Stars* (1962; Richard Schickel); and *Immortals of the Screen* (1965; Ray Stuart).

Other such volumes worthy of interest because they contain photographs of performers and "stills" from memorable films are *The Movies* (1957; Griffith and Mayer); *Classics of the Foreign Film* (1962; Parker Tyler); *Classics of the Silent Screen* (1959; Joe Franklin); *A Pictorial History of the Silent Screen* (1953), *A Pictorial History of the Talkies* (1958) and *A Pictorial History of Television* (1959) by Daniel Blum; *The Academy Awards* (1964) by Paul Michael; and *The Great Films* (1967) by Bosley Crowther.

For books concerning the "behind-the-scenes" anatomy of film-making and TV program-production, we recommend *Case*

437

History of a Movie (1950) by Dore Schary; *Picture* (1952) by Lillian Ross; *The Journal of The Loved One* (1965) by Terry Southern; *The 200 Days of 8½* (1965) by Deena Boyer; *The Cleopatra Papers* (1963) by Brodsky and Weiss; *Salt of the Earth* (1965) by Herbert Biberman; *The Story of The Misfits* (1963) by James Goode; Jean Cocteau's *Diary of a Film* (1950); *Only You, Dick Daring!* (1964) by Miller and Rhodes; and *To See the Dream* (1957) by Jessamyn West.

Publications containing scripts and scenarios of significant films are *To Kill a Mockingbird* (1964) by Horton Foote; *Four Screenplays of Ingmar Bergman* (1960); *Last Year at Marienbad* (1962) by Alain Robbe-Grillet; Federico Fellini's *La Dolce Vita* (1961) and *Juliet of the Spirits* (1965); *Hiroshima, Mon Amour* (1961) by Marguerite Duras; *Screenplays of Michelangelo Antonioni* (1963); Jean-Luc Godard's *The Married Woman* (1965); Eisenstein's *Ivan the Terrible* (1962); *Five Film Scripts* (1960) by James Agee; and *Tom Jones* (1964) by John Osborne. John Gassner and Dudley Nichols have edited several collections of screenplays: *Best Film Plays, 1943–1944; Best Film Plays, 1945; Twenty Best Film Plays* (1943), and *Great Film Plays* (1959). Those publications containing scripts for television are *Harrison, Texas: Eight Television Plays* (1956), and *Three Plays* (1962) by Horton Foote; *Television Plays* (1955) by Paddy Chayefsky; *Best Television Plays* (1956), edited by Gore Vidal; *Patterns: Four Television Plays* (1957) by Rod Serling; *Other People's Houses* (1956) by Tad Mosel; and *Six Television Plays* (1956) by Reginald Rose.

For "cross-media analysis," *All the Way Home* (1963), which contains both the play and the scenario, is recommended.

Commentaries on films, written by important critics, have been compiled into such books as *I Lost It at the Movies* (1965) by Pauline Kael; *The Dreams and the Dreamers* (1962) by Hollis Alpert of *Saturday Review*; *A World on Film* (1966) by Stanley Kauffmann; and *Private Screenings* (1967) by John Simon of *New Leader*. The most rewarding collection of film criticism remains *Agee on Film: Reviews and Comments* (1958), articles by James Agee written originally for *The Nation* and *Time*. *The Eighth Art* (1962), with an Introduction by Robert Lewis Shayon of *Saturday Review*, contains essays on television.

Several books deal with film and television as media for reporting, news analysis, and social persuasion. The best of these are *Documentary Film* (third revision edition, 1952) by Paul

Rotha, et al.; *Grierson on Documentary* (revised edition, 1966), edited by Forsyth Hardy; *Factual Television* (1966) by Norman Swallow, and *Documentary in American Television* (1965) by A. William Bluem.

The significant periodicals in the United States dealing with the sight-and-sound media, with primary emphasis upon criticism, are *Film Culture, Film Quarterly, Film Comment, Film Heritage, Films in Review*, and *Television Quarterly*. The leading foreign periodicals are *Cahiers du Cinéma* (also published in an English edition), *Movie, Sight and Sound, Films and Filming, Film, Bianco e Nero*, and the *Journal of the Society of Film and Television Arts*. A unique American quarterly, *Cinema-TV Digest*, summarizes film and television reviews appearing in numerous international journals.

Two further indispensable resources must be mentioned: *The Film Index: A Bibliography* (Vol. 1, *The Film as Art*, originally published in 1941 and now being made available by the Museum of Modern Art Film Library); and *International Film Guide*, an annual edited by Peter Cowie, which contains current information on film schools, archives, and festivals. Finally, we suggest the catalogs of the Larry Edmunds Book Shop in Los Angeles which list available literature and memorabilia regarding the art of film and television.

Education

This section is divided into four subcategories: (a) the "film study" movement in both high schools and universities; (b) the incorporation of television programs and films into established curricula, e.g., the language arts, social studies, the sciences; (c) the uses of television and film as a basic medium for teaching within formal classroom situations (ITV) and for general adult education (ETV); and (d) the training of professionals for careers in motion pictures and television.

THE FILM-STUDY MOVEMENT

Much of the impetus for the film-study movement has come from UNESCO, because of its concern with the influence of the screen on children. Two UNESCO publications which should be cited initially are J. L. M. Peters' *Teaching about the Film* (1961), a handbook of techniques and examples of film-teaching in several different countries. A later study by A. W. Hodgkinson, *Screen Education*, is derived from papers written for the International

Meeting on Film and Television Teaching in Oslo, Norway, in October, 1962. This publication discusses methods for developing a critical approach to cinema and television, emphasizing "the language of the screen."

In the United States, much film-study activity has originated at Fordham University's Center for Communications, under the direction of John M. Culkin, S.J. In addition to sponsoring conferences for film teachers, the Center has issued several valuable aids. Among these is a "cinematic care package" consisting of reprints of articles on film as well as related paperbacks.

A great many associations are concerned with film study. They include the National Association of Independent Schools, which has made available David Mallery's *The School and the Art of Motion Pictures* (1964). This booklet contains discussions of outstanding films now available in 16mm for rental to schools.

In addition to substantial film-study activity on the high school level, there is equal concern at the college and university level. The American Council on Education has published a resource book entitled *Film Study in Higher Education,* based on reports at the Film Study Conference held at Dartmouth College in 1965.

Perhaps the major thrust for film study at universities has come from the American Federation of Film Societies, an association of campus film groups. The Federation publishes a monthly journal of news and criticism, *Film Society Review.* Two other periodicals, useful for film study at various educational levels, are *Screen Education,* distributed by the Federation's Screen Education Division, and *Media and Methods.*

Helpful suggestions for organizing film societies and selecting films for screening in high schools and colleges are given in catalogues of major 16mm film distributors such as Brandon Films; Films, Inc.; Twyman Films; the Museum of Modern Art Film Library; Royal 16 International; National Film Board of Canada; Film-Makers' Cooperative; Contemporary Films, and Janus Films. The Educational Film Library Association provides several compendia of films available in 16mm from the majority of American distributors.

CURRICULAR USE

Although the film-study movement *per se* is relatively new, there has been an active involvement of educational institutions

440

with the screen since the 1930's. In several states, attention to the mass media is stressed within syllabi for the language arts. Much work in film appreciation and in incorporating films into the curriculum has been done by the National Council of Teachers of English. In conjunction with the Television Information Office, the NCTE has published *TV as Art* (1966) edited by Patrick D. Hazard, and *Television and the Teaching of English* (1961) by Neil Postman. A companion volume, *The Motion Picture and the Teaching of English* (1965) by Harold Owen, et al., was published by the NCTE under a grant from Teaching Film Custodians, Inc. *Television for Children* (1967), published by the Foundation for Character Education and *For the Young Viewer* (1962; edited by Ralph Garry, et al.) are also useful for teachers.

INSTRUCTIONAL MEDIA

The educational confrontation with motion pictures and television goes beyond emphasis upon content and the teaching of skills for more critical evaluation. Many schools and universities have been using film and television as instructional media, sometimes in "total teaching" situations or for supplementary purposes. Three of the most reliable books related to what we call instructional television (ITV) are Robert M. Diamond's *A Guide to Instructional Television* (1964); *Teach with Television* (second edition, 1965) by Costello and Gordon; and *Using Television in the Classroom* (1961) prepared by Mary Howard Smith for the Midwest Program on Airborne Television Instruction. All of these contain advice on preparing and utilizing tele-lessons.

We also suggest in this regard two helpful pamphlets published by the National Education Association: *And TV, Too!* and *Opportunities for Learning: Guidelines for Television*. A crosscultural survey of uses of TV for formal educational purposes is Henry Cassirer's *Television Teaching Today* (1960, UNESCO). Bridging both closed-circuit ITV and open-circuit ETV is Philip Lewis' *Educational Television Guidebook* (1961), which gives data on legal, technical, and programming aspects.

Television is also being used for what we might call "informal educational purposes" on community-owned and university-based TV stations (ETV). For those interested in the history of educational television (on both noncommercial and commercial stations), John Walker Powell's *Channels of Learning* (1962) and

441

Charles A. Siepmann's *Television and Education in the United States* (1952) are recommended. A worthwhile anthology dealing with the problems of ETV-program improvement, financing, and facilities is *Educational Television: The Next Ten Years* (1962), published by the Institute of Communications Research at Stanford. The possibilities for expansion of noncommercial, educational television—with recommendations for support—are explored in *Public Television: A Program for Action* (1967), the Report of the Carnegie Commission on Educational Television.

The audiences for educational television are examined in depth in *The Impact of Educational Television* (1960) edited by Wilbur Schramm; and *The People Look At Educational Television* (1963) by Schramm, et al.

Agencies that provide publications dealing with various aspects of ITV and ETV are The Ford Foundation; the National Association of Educational Broadcasters; the Department of Audio-visual Instruction, NEA; and the Joint Council on Educational Broadcasting. The U.S. Department of Health, Education and Welfare has supported, under Title VII of the National Defense Education Act, the majority of research studies concerning the effectiveness of television as a teaching tool. These and other studies are summarized in *Research in Instructional Television and Film* (1967) by Reid and MacLennan.

A similar volume for film is *Instructional Film Research, 1918–50* (1953) edited by Hoban and Van Ormer; an additional summary is *Learning from Films* (1958) by Lumsdaine and May.

Various journals provide necessary data on research and utilization of film and television as instructional media. They include *Audiovisual Instruction*; *AV Communication Review*; and *Educational Broadcasting Review* (formerly *NAEB Journal*).

CAREER TRAINING

It is estimated that nearly 140 colleges and universities have radio-television-film departments concerned with preparing undergraduate and graduate students for careers in both commercial and noncommercial broadcasting and motion pictures. Courses offered deal with history of the sight-and-sound media, criticism, writing, announcing, production, performing, advertising, station and theater management, research, and the social aspects of the media. In addition to many books listed under other headings of this Appendix, basic texts for such professional training are *Television and*

APPENDIX

Radio (3rd edition, 1963) by Chester, et al.; *Broadcasting and the Public* (1966) by Robert E. and Harrison B. Summers; *A Tower of Babel* (1966), the first of an important series by Erik Barnouw detailing the history of broadcasting in America; *The Rise of the American Film* (1939) by Lewis Jacobs; *A Million and One Nights* (reissued, 1965) by Terry Ramsaye; *The Film Till Now* (1949) by Rotha and Griffith; *The Liveliest Art* (1957) by Arthur Knight; *Behind the Screen* (1965) by Kenneth MacGowan; *Hollywood in Transition* (1962) by Richard Dyer MacCann; and *The Contemporary Cinema* (1963) by Penelope Houston.

Books we recommend for courses dealing with the social and cultural aspects of the sight-and-sound media are *The Public Arts* (1956) by Gilbert Seldes; *Mass Culture* (1957) edited by Rosenberg and White; *Hollywood Looks At Its Audience* (1950) by Leo A. Handel; *Culture for the Millions?* (1961), edited by Norman Jacobs; *Television and Society* (1965) by Harry J. Skornia; *The People Look At Television* (1963) by Gary A. Steiner; *Television in the Lives of Our Children* (1961) by Schramm, et al.; *Television and the Child* (1958) by Hilde T. Himmelweit; *The Age of Television* (1956) by Leo Bogart; *Understanding Media* (1964) by Marshall McLuhan; *The Immediate Experience* (1962) by Robert Warshow; and *The Image Industries* (1959) by William F. Lynch, S.J. David Thomson's *Movie Man* (1967) is an important contribution to the sociology of film.

In regard to the emerging study of international communications, two germinal books are *Television: A World View* (1966) by Wilson P. Dizard and *Mass Media and National Development* (1964) by Wilbur Schramm.

Of special interest to professors and students in broadcasting and film are such periodicals as *Journal of Broadcasting; Journal of the University Film Producers Association; Public Opinion Quarterly;* and *EBU Review,* published by the European Broadcasting Union in Geneva.

Government

In the complex interrelationship between television and government, the standard historical and interpretive source is Walter B. Emery's *Broadcasting and Government: Responsibilities and Regulations* (1961). A concise history of the development of the Federal Communications Commission's authority is *Freedom and Responsibility in Broadcasting* (1961), edited by John E. Coons. Supplementing these books is an informative collection of speeches by Newton N. Minow made during his tenure as Chairman of the FCC, *Equal Time: The Private Broadcaster and the Public Interest* (1964), edited by Lawrence Laurent.

As the broadcasting media increasingly have become a political modality, social scientists have concerned themselves with their effects on Presidential campaigning and voting behavior. The Kennedy-Nixon debates of 1960 motivated numerous books and monographs analyzing their impact. The most comprehensive is *The Great Debates* (1962), edited by Sidney Kraus. Within a larger context, stressing the role of the broadcast media as political instruments, is Bernard Rubin's *Political Television* (1967). An earlier collection of research essays, edited by Burdick and Brodbeck, is *American Voting Behavior* (1959).

Two books, which contain citations and interpretations of governmental censorship of films and television, are Murray Schumach's *The Face on the Cutting Room Floor* (1964), and Ira H. Carmen's *Movies, Censorship and the Law* (1966).

The majority of information concerning the interplay of government and broadcasting and film will be found in periodicals and pamphlets provided by a number of organizations. Available from the Center for the Study of Democratic Institutions is *The Great Debates* (1962) containing essays by Earl Mazo, Malcolm Moos, Hallock Hoffman, and Harvey Wheeler, and *Broadcasting and Governmental Regulation in a Free Society* (1961). The National Association of Broadcasters makes available both to broadcasters and scholars two publications which give guidelines for meeting political responsibilities, *Editorializing on the Air* and *Political Broadcast Catechism*. The Academy of Television Arts and Sciences has published *Television and Politics: A Forum* (1960). Herbert E. Alexander's *Political Broadcasting: What's Its Impact on Elections?* (1964) is available from the Center for Information on America. Several reprints of speeches and conference proceedings are published by the Motion Picture Association of America, Inc.

In addition to the FCC, numerous other governmental agencies are involved in the sight-and-sound media. Among these are the Federal Trade Commission, the United States Information Agency, and the Department of Justice. Their reports, as well as proceedings of various committees of the Congress, are available from the U.S. Government Printing Office, and are annotated in two excellent bibliographies prepared by the Library of the Television Information Office under the titles of *Television in*

444

Government and Politics (1964) and Television: Freedom, Responsibility, Regulation (1962).

Business

The business aspects of television and motion pictures are explicitly examined in specialized books and trade publications. Among the books we recommend are Warde B. Ogden's The Television Business (1961); Yale Roe's Television Station Management (1964); Harry W. McMahan's The Television Commercial (1957); Jacob A. Evans' Selling and Promoting Radio and Television (1954); Seehafer and Laemmar's Successful Radio and Television Advertising (1959); and Gertrude Jobes's Motion Picture Empire (1965).

Various materials are periodically issued by such service agencies as the Television Bureau of Advertising, the Schwerin Research Corporation, A. C. Nielsen Co., and the American Research Bureau.

The most widely used sources of business news regarding television and motion pictures are such trade publications as Broadcasting, Television, Television Age, Sponsor, Boxoffice, Film Daily, Motion Picture Herald, The Exhibitor, Billboard, and Variety. Sources of statistics are found in such annuals as International Motion Picture Almanac, International Television Almanac, Boxoffice Barometer, Broadcasting Yearbook, Television Factbook, Film Daily Yearbook, and Fame.

Recommendations for Further Scholarship

One of the limitations inherent in any annotated listing of a field's literature is the fact that a bibliographic critique serves merely to trace what has already been written. Certainly "a sense of the past" is indispensable to the interested observer of motion pictures and television; but the scholarly vitality of these media depends not only upon a continuation of established directions of inquiry but also upon untried methods. Therefore, although we are aware that we are "speculating" and that the financial backing for our proposals may be lacking presently, we wish to indicate some areas in which new publications seem needed.

What appears as immediately, almost obviously, necessary is a multivolume series concerning the history of the American film, organized, not chronologically, but perhaps according to the issues raised in this book; e.g., the film as art, as an industry, as an educational force, as a political instrument, etc. Although these separate volumes might be written by specialists in such matters, a general editor for the series would ensure an integration of purpose and approach. We visualize a similar series for American television.

As we review the literature regarding film aesthetics and film-makers we find that European scholars have treated the American motion picture far more seriously than many of our own critics. Such directors as Howard Hawks, Alfred Hitchcock, and John Ford receive greater attention abroad than at home. There are many American directors worthy of critical monographs who generally have been overlooked, such as Clarence Brown, Raoul Walsh, Preston Sturges, Henry King, Frank Capra, George Stevens, and King Vidor. More recent directors such as Richard Brooks, Blake Edwards, and Robert Wise might be the subjects of future monographs. Certainly definitive biographies of producers David O. Selznick and Samuel Goldwyn are long overdue. These studies might be published under the auspices of the American Film Institute.

For additional scholarship concerning sight-and-sound communicators, we suggest a book dealing with those European producers and directors who have made films in Hollywood. Among them are Alexander Korda, Fritz Lang, Jean Renoir, René Clair, and Max Ophuls. Analysis of their American films—e.g., *Lydia, Scarlet Street, The Southerner, It Happened Tomorrow, The Reckless Moment*—within the context of their total work may reveal the influences of different cultural, economic, and political circumstances on artistic style. We might make similar investigations of American producers and directors who now make films abroad; e.g., Jules Dassin, Carl Foreman, and Joseph Losey.

This method of inquiry is not unlike George Huaco's in his *The Sociology of Film Art* (1965). Instead of examining individual directors and their films, Huaco's point of departure is three European "schools" of film-making which he considers "stylistically homogeneous clusters" shaped by their respective sociohistorical situations. This methodology could be applied to what we might call the "American school of social realism," best represented by Warner Bros. films made during the Depression and New Deal period of the 1930's, such as *I Am a Fugitive from a Chain Gang, They Won't Forget, Black Legion,* and *Marked Woman.* Stylistic unity and socioeconomic conditions might also be explored in the proletarian plays written during the "Golden Age of 'live' television drama" in the early 1950's.

In view of the many changes in Hollywood as a result of the advent of television, it is regrettable that there have not recently been books like Hortense Powdermaker's *Hollywood, the Dream Factory* (1950), Leo Rosten's *Hollywood: The Movie Colony, the Movie Makers* (1941), and Lillian Ross's *Picture* (1952), all of which give us insights into the problems of creative and managerial decision-making. Under the heading of "To Be Commissioned" perhaps we might persuade Leo Rosten to write a *Hollywood Revisited: 1968.*

Similarly, Martha Wolfenstein and Nathan Leites should be induced to "update" their extremely perceptive *Movies: A Psychological Study* (1950). (Has the good-bad girl been transformed into Doris Day?)

The British used to say, "Trade follows the film." What *else* follows? To find out, we suggest a cross-cultural study based on the international release of a major American motion picture. Our research team would visit several cities in which the film is exhibited—say, London, Rome, Stockholm, Moscow, Cairo, Nairobi, New Delhi, Tokyo, Brasília—and by means of attitude-scales and structured interviews obtain information on the opinions of the United States derived from the film. Are these opinions, as Edward R. Murrow feared, negative ones? If so, how do they perpetuate the "cold war" of misunderstanding among nations?

In regard to American audiences, and especially children, there is much research to be done. It is our view that most of the studies and surveys sponsored by networks and motion-picture companies —and such trade organizations as the National Association of Broadcasters and the Motion Picture Association of America— have been overly concerned with meeting the requirements of marketing operations and favorable public relations. We are reminded by Harry J. Skornia, in his *Television and Society* (1965), of the extensive Payne Fund Studies on films and their effects on children, published in several volumes between 1933 and 1935.[2] Although the findings of these studies are still valuable

[2] Representative titles are *Motion Pictures and the Social Attitudes of Children* (1933) by Peterson and Thurstone; *The Emotional Responses of Children to the Motion Picture Situation* (1933) by Dysinger and Ruckmick; *Movies and Conduct* (1933) by Herbert Blumer; and *Movies, Delinquency and Crime* (1933) by Blumer and Hauser.

(primarily because, as Skornia notes, the films of that period are regularly shown on television), recent alterations in the Motion Picture Production Code make a new series of investigations mandatory. We direct this suggestion to The Ford Foundation.

The NAB and the MPAA might consider jointly underwriting a twenty-year longitudinal study of the effects of movies and television on the attitudes and behavior of children of different intelligence and socioeconomic levels. The methodology exists for collecting information, over a period extending from preschool age to adulthood, on their viewing habits and viewing preferences. This information would be correlated with scholastic accomplishment, social activities, hobbies, and career choices. Such a study would demand a great deal of money and patience, but would provide a more exact understanding of "what motion pictures and TV are doing to our children."

In 1960 the Television Bureau of Advertising announced a competition for imaginative strategies in television research. To our knowledge none of the award-winning plans, submitted by specialists in many different professions, have been put into operation.[3] One plan in particular—Bernard Berelson's *The Great Experiment in Cultural Democracy*—offers exciting possibilities for determining whether people would watch "higher quality" programs if they were broadcast, or if they prefer television's "standard fare." Berelson proposed that the percentage of "higher quality" programs be varied on two commercial stations serving the same community. By interviews of selected panels of people, Berelson would gather information on who watched the "better" programs, their leisure-time activities, the degree of their community participation, their political interests, their attitudes toward commercials and toward television in general. Such a "natural experiment" would entail the close cooperation of the FCC, networks and stations, and sponsors. Because of the potential importance of such an investigation to the cultural vigor of our democracy, we see no reason why Berelson's proposed study should not be launched immediately.

Another study that should be begun is an investigation of the noncommercial and nonpublic uses of motion pictures in areas such as medicine, psychiatry, group therapy, social work, and in amateur use. We have no way of knowing the volume of motion-

---

[3] Of the 147 plans submitted, 18 were selected for awards, and were reprinted in *Television and Human Behavior* (1963), edited by Arons and May.

picture film sold, and the audiences, for such purposes. How is film being used in the treatment of mental disorders? What production techniques are being employed? What are the career possibilities for people engaged in the making of these nonpublic films? What is the American family's financial- and time-investment in home movies?

We have indicated that our proposals will require new avenues of financial underwriting. Also necessary is more ready access to film and television program archives. While it is encouraging to learn of hopes for expansion of facilities at the Museum of Modern Art Film Library and the establishment of additional archives by the American Film Institute, such resources for film and television study are restricted by geography. We propose that the leading museums offer their films and programs to National Educational Television for nationwide showing on educational stations. Certainly this is a way to increase the audience for ETV, and at the same time enable all scholars and the general public to review the significant sight-and-sound art of the past. Movies and television programs have become part of our cultural equipment—part of what Stan VanDerBeek calls our "image bank"; like great books, they should be reexperienced and reexamined.

These recommendations are mere beginnings, a prologue to what may yet be accomplished. As motion pictures and television continue to dominate our time and attention—and with an expanding technology, there is no doubt that this domination will increase—the force of their influence must be matched by an equally vigorous spirit of inquiry.

The purpose of this book has been to describe the extent of American society's involvement with the sight-and-sound media, and to indicate the special problems engendered by that involvement. It is the Editors' belief that these problems are unique to mass communication in a free and open democracy—a democracy in which all institutions are conjoined in a partnership of hopeful expectations. It is also our belief that the solutions to these problems will be unique.

The artist, the businessman, the educator, the politician, and the lawmaker—all have a stake in the course of film and television. With the encouragement of an involved public, all of them must share the tasks and responsibilities of future scholarship.

INDEX OF NAMES

Abelson, Robert, 312
Adams, Henry, 26
Agee, James, 6, 145, 438
Aldrich, Robert, 332
Alexander, Herbert E., 232, 444
Alpert, Hollis, 438
Alsop, Joseph, 214, 249
Ames, Adelbert, 359, 381
Anger, Kenneth, 167
Antonioni, Michelangelo, 79, 88, 91, 105, 112, 204, 332, 436
Arnheim, Rudolf, 100, 436
Ascoli, Max, 233
Ashmore, Harry, 229, 230, 239–257

Bacon, Francis, 155
Bagdikian, Ben H., 248
Baldwin, James, 72
Barnouw, Erik, 443
Barzini, Luigi, 86
Bazelon, David T., 83, 85, 137–149
Bazin, André, 436
Bell, Daniel, 18
Bentham, Jeremy, 261
Benton, William, 251, 252
Berelson, Bernard, 23, 448
Bergman, Ingmar, 79, 95, 97, 103, 109, 167, 204, 325, 379, 436, 438
Biberman, Herbert, 438
Bierce, Ambrose, 241
Bingham, Barry, 241, 253
Blankfort, Michael, 237, 335–343
Bluem, A. William, 436, 439
Blum, Daniel, 437
Blumer, Herbert, 447
Bogart, Humphrey, 143, 184
Bogart, Leo, 19, 360, 361, 409–422, 437, 443
Bok, Edward, 40
Boorstin, Daniel, 380, 381, 382
Boulding, Kenneth, 83
Boulle, Pierre, 333
Bouwman, George, 394

Boyer, Deena, 438
Brakhage, Stan, 168
Brando, Marlon, 194
Breer, Robert, 101
Bresson, Robert, 88, 95, 97, 98, 204
Brinkley, David, 127, 135, 170, 219, 221, 222, 400
Brodbeck, A.J., 444
Brooks, Richard, 174, 175
Bruner, Jerome S., 274
Buber, Martin, 372
Bundy, McGeorge, 360, 402
Buñuel, Luis, 91, 98, 118, 125, 326, 436
Burdick, Eugene, 311, 312, 444
Burke, Kenneth, 13
Burton, Richard, 178, 179

Cagney, James, 143, 146, 184, 190
Camus, Albert, 373, 375
Capra, Frank, 446
Carmen, I.H., 444
Carmichael, Stokeley, 133
Cassirer, Ernst, 381
Cassirer, Henry, 441
Chafee, Zechariah, Jr., 256
Chandler, Raymond, 185
Chaplin, Charles, 90, 98, 168, 349, 437
Chayefsky, Paddy, 169, 438
Cherry, Colin, 274
Chester, G., 443
Chukhrai, Grigori, 124
Clair, René, 95, 446
Clark, John M., 256
Clarke, Shirley, 168
Clay, George, 216
Clément, René, 98
Clouzot, Henri-Georges, 325
Cocteau, Jean, 95
Collins, LeRoy, 318
Cone, Fairfax M., 230, 263–270
Conner, Bruce, 167

Coons, John E., 443
Corman, Roger, 179
Cowie, Peter, 439
Cox, Kenneth A., 242
Crist, Judith, 204
Cronkite, Walter, 81, 127, 135, 216, 400
Crowther, Bosley, 202, 204, 336, 337, 344, 346
Culkin, John M., 17, 358, 359, 384–395, 440
Cummings, E.E., 152

Dassin, Jules, 8, 98, 446
Daves, Delmer, 176, 177
Davis, Elmer, 170, 171, 214, 218
DeMille, Cecil B., 107, 170, 175, 323, 333, 349
Deren, Maya, 205
De Sica, Vittorio, 98
Deutsch, David, 179
Diamond, Robert M., 441
Dickinson, Emily, 99, 100
Disney, Walt, 118
Dizard, Wilson, 443
Doan, Richard K., 261
Donner, Clive, 179
Downs, Hugh, 81
Dozier, William, 242
Dreyer, Carl, 95, 97, 98, 168

Eames, Charles, 380, 381
Edwards, Douglas, 218
Eisenstein, Sergei, 80, 95, 104, 114, 117, 119, 123, 125, 321, 436, 438
Emery, Walter B., 443
Ernst, Morris L., 299
Esslin, Martin, 331

Fadiman, William, 238, 344–355
Fairlie, Henry, 80, 127–136
Farber, Manny, 145
Faulk, John Henry, 437
Fellini, Federico, 77, 79, 94, 167, 204, 391, 438
Ferguson, Otis, 145
Fessard, Gaston, 375
Fiedler, Leslie, 107, 108
Flaherty, Robert, 204, 436
Foote, Horton, 170, 438
Ford, John, 167, 174, 205, 235, 446
Foreman, Carl, 353, 446

Forster, E.M., 100
Franju, Georges, 125
Frank, Reuven, 220, 221
Frankenheimer, John, 82
Freedman, Lawrence Z., 65
French, Philip, 235, 320–334
Freud, Sigmund, 26, 147
Friendly, Fred W., 10, 14, 214, 249, 360, 402, 437
Fromm, Erich, 85
Fuller, Buckminster, 211

Gallagher, Wes, 214
Galton, Francis, 159
Gans, Herbert, 29
Garbo, Greta, 99, 437
Garry, Ralph, 441
Gassner, John, 438
Gerbner, George, 172
Gitlin, Irving, 222
Godard, Jean-Luc, 204, 205, 438
Goldin, Hyman H., 306
Goldwyn, Samuel, 167, 446
Goodman, Julian, 171, 216, 219, 225
Gould, Jack, 17, 231, 247, 250, 261
Grierson, John, 80, 116, 119, 256, 439
Griffith, D.W., 95, 206
Gutenberg, Johannes, 370

Hagerty, Jim, 315, 316, 317
Handel, Leo A., 443
Harris, Lou, 310, 312, 313, 315, 317
Harvey, Paul, 218
Hawks, Howard, 77, 446
Hayakawa, S.I., 28, 68–74, 323
Hazard, Patrick, 441
Hearst, William Randolph, 241
Heatter, Gabriel, 217
Henry, E. William, 247, 269
Hill, George Roy, 15
Hiller, Arthur, 82
Himmelweit, Hilde, 27, 58, 59, 60, 443
Hitchcock, Alfred, 98, 167, 174, 205, 325, 326, 436, 437, 446
Hocking, William E., 256
Hodgkinson, A.W., 394, 439
Hoffman, Hallock, 444
Hogben, Lancelot, 29
Holland, Norman, 79, 103–114
Hopper, Edward, 210

INDEX OF NAMES

Horn, John, 261
Houston, Penelope, 17, 443
Huaco, George, 446
Huggins, Roy, 236
Huizinga, Johann, 377, 380
Humphrey, Hall, 248, 251
Huntley, Chet, 81, 127, 135, 219, 221, 400
Huston, John, 98, 184
Hutchins, Robert M., 250, 252, 253, 255, 256

Ichikawa, Kon, 97, 125
Isaacs, Norman, 240

Jacobs, Lewis, 443
James, Henry, 16, 17, 206
Jennings, Humphrey, 123, 124
Jobes, Gertrude, 445
Johnson, Earl J., 214
Johnson, Lyndon B., 127, 133, 134, 248, 397
Johnson, Nicholas, 361
Johnson, Wendell, 28
Jousse, Marcel, 373
Jung, C.G., 159

Kael, Pauline, 206, 438
Kaplan, Abraham, 340
Kaufman, Bel, 390
Kauffmann, Stanley, 17, 391, 438
Kaye, Danny, 198
Kazan, Elia, 98, 167, 181
Kellam, J.C., 247
Kepes, Gyorgy, 359, 380
Kilgore, Bernard, 241
Killian, James, 402
Kintner, Robert, 171, 213–227
Klauber, Ed, 213
Knight, Arthur, 443
Korda, Alexander, 446
Kracauer, Siegfried, 207, 324, 436
Kramer, Stanley, 124, 174, 175
Kraus, Sidney, 444
Kris, Ernest, 76
Krutch, Joseph Wood, 378
Kurosawa, Akira, 79, 436

La Follette, Robert M., 306
Land, Herman, 232
Lang, Fritz, 205, 323, 324, 446
Larson, Roger, 394

Lasky, Jesse, 99, 176
Lassally, Walter, 76, 87–91, 362
Lasswell, Harold, 76, 256
Laurent, Lawrence, 17, 242, 243, 444
Lawson, John Howard, 8, 436
Lean, David, 13, 98
Legman, G., 324
Leiser, Erwin, 121
Leites, Nathan, 113, 447
Leonard, Bill, 310, 315, 317
Lerner, Max, 234, 309–319
Lester, Richard, 82
Lewis, Philip, 441
Lindgreen, Ernest, 435
Loevinger, Lee, 7, 231, 285–301
Lorenz, Konrad, 235
Losey, Joseph, 8, 326, 446
Lubell, Sam, 312, 313
Lubitsch, Ernst, 205
Luce, Henry R., 255
Lumet, Sidney, 206
Lumsdaine, A., 442
Lynch, William F., 443
Lyons, Louis, 251, 252, 253

McAndrew, William, 216, 217, 219, 223, 224, 226
MacCann, Richard D., 436, 443
McCarthy, Mary, 331
MacGowan, Kenneth, 443
MacLeish, Archibald, 256
McLuhan, Marshall, 5, 12, 78, 128, 172, 211, 274, 359, 368, 380, 387, 443
McPhee, William, 312
Malinowski, Bronislaw, 380
Mallery, David, 394, 440
Mamoulian, Rouben, 99
Mandel, Loring, 169, 208–212
Mankiewicz, Joseph L., 15, 178
Mann, Anthony, 333
Marcel, Gabriel, 372, 375
Maritain, Jacques, 256
Markel, Lester, 360, 396–408
Marker, Chris, 126
Marlowe, Christopher, 150
Marshall, Thurgood, 300
Matson, Floyd W., 84
May, Mark, 442
Mayer, Arthur, 353
Mayer, L.B., 148, 163, 165, 176, 184, 436

Mayersberg, Paul, 17, 163, 164, 165, 173–185
Mead, George Herbert, 76
Mekas, Jonas, 167
Méliès, Georges, 18
Melnick, Dan, 82
Merriam, Charles E., 256
Miller, Arthur, 170
Miller, Henry, 206
Miller, Merle, 14, 337, 438
Minnelli, Vincente, 98
Minow, Newton, 25, 142, 264, 444
Monroe, Marilyn, 163, 176
Montez, Mario, 167
Moore, Thomas W., 128
Moos, Malcolm, 444
Moreau, Jeanne, 106, 109
Morgan, John, 133
Mosel, Tad, 6, 82, 169, 438
Mulligan, Robert, 82
Mumford, Lewis, 84
Murrow, Edward R., 79, 171, 214, 218, 447

Nabokov, Vladimir, 99
Newman, Paul, 185
Nichols, Dudley, 438
Niebuhr, Reinhold, 256, 294
Nielsen, Arthur C., Jr., 398
Northshield, Bob, 222, 315, 317

Odets, Clifford, 165, 176, 186–200
Ogburn, William F., 421
Ogden, Warde B., 445
Ong, Walter J., 359, 365–376, 380
Ophuls, Max, 446
Oppenheim, A.N., 58
Oppenheimer, J. Robert, 423
Ortega y Gasset, José, 152
Osborne, John, 438
O'Toole, Peter, 180
Owen, Harold, 441

Paley, William S., 34, 213, 218
Pearson, Drew, 217, 218
Peck, Gregory, 346, 395
Péguy, Charles, 139, 141
Peters, J.L.M., 439
Pool, Ithiel de Sola, 312
Porter, Edwin S., 322
Postman, Neil, 441
Pound, Ezra, 17

Powdermaker, Hortense, 447
Powell, John Walker, 441
Preminger, Otto, 8, 97, 98, 236
Pulliam, Eugene C., 241

Ramsaye, Terry, 322, 443
Ray, Nicholas, 175
Ray, Satyajit, 98
Read, Sir Herbert, 329
Reagan, Ronald, 133
Redfield, Robert, 256
Reed, Carol, 98
Reiser, Oliver, 281
Reisz, Karel, 98, 436
Resnais, Alain, 88, 125, 330
Rhodes, Evan, 337, 438
Richards, I.A., 54
Richardson, Tony, 168
Richie, Donald, 436
Riefenstahl, Leni, 80, 119, 121, 122, 123
Riezler, Kurt, 256
Robbe-Grillet, Alain, 259, 438
Robinson, Edward G., 146
Robinson, Hubbell, 169, 230, 258–262
Rodriguez, Zane, 394
Roe, Yale, 445
Rogosin, Lionel, 168
Roper, Elmo, 215, 232
Rose, Reginald, 170
Rosenberg, Harold, 205, 331
Rosenheim, Ned, 284
Ross, Lillian, 14
Rossellini, Roberto, 94
Rosten, Leo, 447
Rotha, Paul, 116, 439
Rouch, Jean, 126
Rousseau, Jean-Jacques, 273
Rubin, Bernard, 444
Ruml, Beardsley, 256
Rusk, Dean, 226

Salant, Richard, 171, 226
Sapir, Edward, 380, 381
Sarnoff, Robert W., 218, 233, 282
Sarraute, Nathalie, 259
Sarris, Andrew, 17, 167, 168, 201–207, 437
Sartre, Jean Paul, 375
Schaefer, George, 169
Schary, Dore, 438

INDEX OF NAMES

Schickel, Richard, 437
Schlesinger, Arthur, Jr., 103, 232, 256, 302–308
Schneider, Romy, 109
Schramm, Wilbur, 26, 54, 57–67, 442, 443
Schulberg, Budd, 334
Schumach, Murray, 444
Seldes, Gilbert, 17, 21, 23, 31–49, 436, 443
Selznick, David O., 163, 167, 446
Serling, Rod, 438
Sevareid, Eric, 437
Shayon, Robert Lewis, 11, 17, 438
Sheehan, William, 171
Shih, Hu, 256
Shirer, William L., 214
Shurlock, Geoffrey, 338, 339
Shuster, George N., 256
Siegel, Donald, 173, 333
Siepmann, Charles, 442
Silvey, Robert J., 24, 50–56
Simon, John, 438
Singer, Aubrey, 83, 84, 150–162
Skornia, Harry J., 230, 271–284, 443, 447, 448
Smith, Howard K., 214, 233
Smith, Jack, 204, 205
Smith, Mary Howard, 441
Sokolsky, George, 218
Southern, Terry, 438
Spillane, Mickey, 146
Spottiswoode, Raymond, 436
Stanton, Frank, 43, 44, 234
Steele, Robert, 17, 77, 93–102
Steinbeck, John, 388
Steiner, Gary A., 24, 297
Steiner, George, 378
Stephenson, William, 25
Stevens, George, 15, 98, 446
Stevens, George, Jr., 353, 355, 395
Sturges, Preston, 446
Sulzberger, Arthur Ochs, 241, 253
Summers, Harrison B., 443
Summers, Robert E., 443
Swallow, Norman, 439
Swayze, John C., 218
Swing, Raymond, 170, 437
Sydow, Max von, 109, 347
Szilard, Leo, 382

Talbot, Daniel, 436
Teilhard de Chardin, Pierre, 362
Thomas, Lowell, 217
Thomas, W.I., 76
Thomson, David, 443
Truffaut, François, 19, 98, 437
Trumbo, Dalton, 181
Tyler, Parker, 437

Vadim, Roger, 206
VanDerBeek, Stan, 168, 359, 362, 423–434, 449
Vas, Robert, 79, 115–126
Vicas, George, 222, 224, 225
Vidal, Gore, 438
Vince, Pamela, 58
Vitti, Monica, 109

Wallace, Mike, 81
Walsh, Raoul, 184, 446
Warhol, Andy, 167, 168, 204
Warner, Jack L., 167, 176, 177, 437
Warshow, Robert, 145, 333, 391, 443
Weaver, Sylvester, 219
Weber, Paul, 236
Weiss, Margaret, 18
Welles, Orson, 76, 79, 98, 168, 205
West, Jassamyn, 438
Westin, Av, 11
White, E.B., 363
White, Paul, 213, 222
White, Theodore H., 232
Whorf, Benjamin L., 380
Wiener, Norbert, 77
Wilder, Billy, 198, 339
Wilkinson, John, 316
Williams, Raymond, 55
Winchell, Walter, 217, 218, 220
Winetrout, Kenneth, 359, 377–383
Winick, Charles, 27
Wolfe, Tom, 236
Wolfenstein, Martha, 113, 447
Wyler, William, 98, 179

Ylvisaker, Paul, 29

Zanuck, Darryl F., 15
Zinnemann, Fred, 15, 98, 235
Zousmer, Jesse, 249
Zukor, Adolph, 15

INDEX OF SUBJECTS

ABC (*See* American Broadcasting Company)

Adler Electronics, 280

Allocation of channels for ETV stations, 9; (*See also* Federal Communications Commission: licensing)

America (magazine), 236

American Bar Association: Canon 35 of the, 234

American Broadcasting Company, 23, 128, 170, 242, 259; ABC News, 171, 215, 217–218, 226, 249, 315–317

American Film Institute, 169, 238, 346, 353, 355

American Home Products, 230

American Newspaper Publishers Association, 254

American Society of Newspaper Editors, 254; *ASNE Bulletin* (magazine), 254

Annenberg School of Communication (*See* University of Pennsylvania)

AP (*See* Associated Press)

Art: and motion pictures, 92–102; as institutional force on media, 11–15; *vs.* propaganda in films, 115–126

ASNE Bulletin (*See* American Society of Newspaper Editors)

Associated Press, 213–214, 220

Association for Young Film Makers, 351

Audiences, 31–49; and "total situation" of motion pictures and TV, 4–5; as composed of individuals, 4–5, 16, 21, 85–86; as "unknown" to communicators, 15–16; children, 57–67 (*See also* Children); creation of, 33–39; for daytime serials, 34; for ETV, 11; for "puzzling movies," 103–114; measurement of, 22–24, 36–37 (*See also* Polls; Ratings); responsibility of, 20; socioeconomic and educational data on, 23–24; viewing decisions, 4, 19–20, 24, 54–55; *vs.* "Public," 32–33, 39–42; "wants" *vs.* "needs," 32–47; (*See also* Television viewing)

BBC (*See* British Broadcasting Corporation)

Ben Hur (play), 321

Benton Foundation, 252

Beveridge Report, 273

Big Knife, The (play), 176

"Blacklisting," 8

"Bond, James" (*See* "James Bond")

Boston University, 168, 394

Boy Scout Manual, The (book), 336

British Broadcasting Corporation, 24, 133, 155; parallel with Public TV, 406; *vs.* American system, 160–161

British Film Fund Agency, 350

Broadcasting: and "the public interest," 39–43; commercial *vs.* educational, 9; need for revised system, 271–284; (*See also* Federal Communications Commission; Television)

Broadcasting (magazine), 302

Broken Image, The (book), 84

Business: as institutional force on media, 6–7, 13–14; (*See also* Media managers)

Cahiers du Cinéma (magazine), 167

Camera obscura, 18

Canadian National Commission Study of Broadcasting, 273

Canon 35 of the American Bar Association, 234

Carnegie Commission (National Commission on Educational Television), 246, 363, 407; Report of,

10–11, 360, 396, 402–403, 407; (*See also* Public television)

Carnegie Corporation, 10, 246, 250 (*See also* Carnegie Commission)

CATV (*See* Community-antenna television)

CBS (*See* Columbia Broadcasting System)

Celluloid, the Film Today (book), 116

Censorship: and the FCC, 231–232; of motion pictures, 8–9, 236–237, 323–325, 335–343, 347–348; of television, 337; Production Code (*See* Motion Pictures: Production Code); *vs.* creativity, 237, 335–343

Center for the Study of Democratic Institutions, 229

Central Intelligence Agency, 403

Centro Sperimentale, 351

"Charisma, Incorporated," 233

Chicago Tribune, 240

Children: and motion pictures, 25–26; and TV "fan mail," 27–28; effects of TV on, 25–28, 57–67; (*See also* Audiences; Television viewing)

CIA (*See* Central Intelligence Agency)

Cinéma vérité, 78, 82, 95–96

Cinemascope, 18, 183

Cinematograph Film Act, 350

Cinerama, 18

Citizens' Research Foundation, 232

Columbia Broadcasting System, 34, 43, 170, 213, 234, 242, 244, 249, 259, 310, 315, 360, 396; CBS News, 14, 171–172, 213–214, 218–219, 222, 226, 249, 305, 312, 319; CBS Radio, 34–35; Columbia News Service, 213; Vote Profile Analysis, 310

Columbia Journalism Review (magazine), 248, 251

Columbia Pictures, 179–180

Columbia University, 251, 312

Commercials (*See* Television commercials)

Commission on Freedom of the Press, 250–257

Common Market, 404

Communication: defined, 76; development of, 3; interdisciplinary study of, 75; models of, 75–76 (*See also* Mass communication(s); Mass media; Motion pictures; Motion pictures and television; Television)

Communications Act, 231, 307, 361; Section 315 of the, 233, 287–290 (*See also* Federal Communications Commission)

Communicators: actors, 14–15, 163, 165–166, 183–185, 186–200; and "total situation" of motion pictures and TV, 14–15; directors, 14–15, 77, 79, 82, 92–102, 167–168, 173–179, 184, 204–205, 350; news reporters, 14–15, 80–81, 127–137, 170–172, 213–227, 305–306, 315–317; of the future, 168–169; problems of, 14–16, 169–170, 209–210, 212, 335–343; producers, 14–15, 82, 163–164, 167, 174–177, 184, 352; writers, 14–15, 82, 169–170, 181–182, 208–212, 335–343

Community-antenna television, 360–361

Computers: and TV election coverage, 309–319

Congress, 234, 244, 272, 278, 281; investigations of Hollywood, 8

Constitution: First Amendment, 168, 245, 248, 300; First and Fourteenth Amendments, 9

Corporation for Public Broadcasting, 10

Criticism (*See* Motion pictures: criticism; Motion pictures and television: criticism)

Critics: *vs.* media managers, 31–49 (*See also* Motion pictures: criticism; Motion pictures and television: criticism)

Daytime serials, 33–35

Death in the Family, A (book), 6

Decca Records, 166

Defense, U.S. Department of, 224

Dehumanization of Art, The (book), 152

Eady Plan, 350

Edison Catalogue (book), 322

INDEX OF SUBJECTS

Edison Company, 321
Editorializing on television, 80, 305–306 (*See also* Communications Act: Section 315)
Education: and "film study" movement, 358–359, 384–395; and future of motion pictures and TV, 358–360; as institutional force on media, 9–11, 13–14; effects of technology on, 365–376; need for more frequencies, 271–284
Educational television, 272, 275; and Carnegie Report (*See* Carnegie Commission: Report of); and controversial subjects, 11; and Ford Foundation (*See* separate listing); and Public Broadcasting Act, 10; audiences for, 11; channel allocations for, 9, 271–284; economic support, 9–10; *vs.* commercial TV, 247 (*See also* Public television)
Election coverage (*See* Television news: election coverage)
Encore (magazine), 331
Encyclopaedia Britannica, Inc., 251
"Equal time" (*See* Communications Act: Section 315)
ETV (*See* Educational television)
Expo 67, 18

"Fairness doctrine" (*See* Federal Communications Commission: "fairness doctrine"; Communications Act: Section 315)
"Robert 'Bob' Farrar," 165, 186–200
FCC (*See* Federal Communications Commission)
Federal Communications Commission, 7, 20, 81, 229–231, 235, 242, 244–245, 251, 264, 269, 271–272, 275, 278, 284, 285–301, 305, 317, 319; and licensing, 91, 230–231, 248, 290–292; and programming, 7, 285–301; and satellites, 281; and voting projections, 317–319; Communications Act (*See* separate listing); "fairness doctrine," 287–290 (*See also* Communications Act: Section 315); limitations of, 230–231, 245, 275–276; regulation *vs.* First Amendment, 245, 248, 300

Federal Film Prizes, 351
Film Aid Fund, 350
Film Estimate Board of National Organizations, 25
"Film study movement," 358–359, 384–395
Film-Makers' Cinémathèque, 167
Film-Makers Cooperative, 168
Films: *Actua Tilt*, 125; *Africa Addio*, 80; *Alexander Nevsky*, 80; *All About Eve*, 178; *All Quiet on the Western Front*, 118; *Attack*, 332; *Baby Face Nelson*, 333; *Balcony, The*, 202; *Barefoot Contessa, The*, 143, 178; *Big Sleep, The*, 184; *Birth of a Nation, The*, 116; *Blackboard Jungle, The*, 174–175; *Blow-Up*, 82; *Boccaccio 70*, 109; *Bonnie and Clyde*, 235; *Bravadoes, The*, 333; *Breathless*, 204; *Bridge on the River Kwai, The*, 202, 333; *Cabinet of Dr. Caligari, The*, 206; *Carpetbaggers, The*, 339; *Chapayev*, 118; *Cheat, The*, 323; *Chelsea Girls, The*, 168, 202, 205; *Citizen Kane*, 201, 204; *Cleopatra*, 15, 177–178; *Collector, The*, 179; *Connection, The*, 202; *Cool World, The*, 202; *Cowboy*, 176; *Cranes Are Flying, The*, 80; *Crazy Quilt*, 202; *Dark Passage*, 176; *David and Lisa*, 202; *Destination Tokyo*, 177; *Destry Rides Again*, 144; *Diabolique*, 325; *Dirty Dozen, The*, 164; *Doctor Zhivago*, 166; *Dr. Strangelove*, 147; *Dream of the Wild Horses*, 358; *Earth*, 118; *8½*, 204; *Elmer Gantry*, 175; *Execution of Mary Queen of Scots, The*, 321; *Face in the Crowd, A*, 181; *Fahrenheit, 451*, 19; *Finnegans Wake*, 202; *Fistful of Dollars, A*, 20; *Flaming Creatures*, 204; *42nd Street*, 118; *From Russia with Love*, 24; *Goldfinger*, 180, 202, 326–329; *Goldstein*, 202; *Gone with the Wind*, 166, 180; *Grand Prix*, 82; *Great Train Robbery, The*, 322; *Green Pastures*, 29; *Guns of Navarone, The*, 90; *Hallelujah the Hills*, 202; *Harper*, 185; *Hawaii*, 15; *Hell Is for Heroes*, 173; *High*

Noon, 235; High Sierra, 184; High Society, 185; Hiroshima, Mon Amour, 103, 106–107, 109–110; Hôtel des Invalides, 125; House on 92nd Street, The, 144, 146; Hustler, The, 393; I Am a Fugitive from a Chain Gang, 182; Immoral Mr. Teas, The, 107–108; Informer, The, 235; Invasion of the Body Snatchers, 173; Irma La Douce, 339; Ivan, 118; Judgment at Nuremberg, 174–175; Kameradschaft, 118; La Dolce Vita, 103–104, 106, 109–110; La Grand Illusion, 122; La Guerre Est Finie, 82; La Notte, 106, 109; La Strada, 167, 393; La Terra Trema, 121; Labyrinth, 18; Ladybug, Ladybug, 202; Las Hurdes, 118, 125; Lassie Come Home, 235; Last Year at Marienbad, 79, 87, 91, 104, 107, 109–110; Laura, 324; L'Avventura, 87, 103, 109, 204, 332; Lawrence of Arabia, 179–180; Les Cousins, 103, 110; L'Espoir, 122; Little Caesar, 144, 146, 182–183, 235; Loneliness of the Long Distance Runner, The, 393; Lord Jim, 175, 179–180; Los Olvidados, 121; Lovers, The, 9, 103, 106, 109; Macbeth, 79; Magician, The, 103, 110; Maltese Falcon, The, 146, 183–184, 324; Man for All Seasons, A, 21; Man with the Golden Arm, The, 8; March, The, 80; March of Time, The, 297; Mask of Dimitrios, The, 324; Miracle, The, 9; Mondo Cane, 330; Moon Is Blue, The, 8; Muriel, 330; Mutter Krausen, 118; Nanook of the North, 99, 205; Night and Fog, 125; Night of the Iguana, The, 339; Night Tide, 202; Nothing But a Man, 202–203; Nothing But the Best, 179; O Dreamland, 121; October, 118; On the Bowery, 202; On the Waterfront, 333, 393; One Eyed Jacks, 333; One Potato, Two Potato, 202; Parrish, 177; Patch of Blue, A, 82; Pather Panchali, 121; Petrified Forest, The, 143, 184; Philadelphia Story, The, 185; Place in the Sun, A, 15; Potemkin, 99, 117–118, 201, 206,

321, 331; Pride and Prejudice, 384; Private Property, 202; Psycho, 234, 325; Public Enemy, 143, 182; Queen Christina, 99; Quiet Man, The, 90; Quo Vadis, 201; Raisin in the Sun, A, 29, 393; Reality of Karel Appel, The, 331; Rebel without a Cause, 175, 325; Red Balloon, The, 358; Riot in Cell Block 11, 173; Rise and Fall of Legs Diamond, The, 333; Roaring Twenties, The, 146, 187; Robe, The, 183; Robin and the Seven Hoods, 321; Rocco and His Brothers, 109–110; Room at the Top, 107, 334; Russians Are Coming, The Russians Are Coming, The, 24; St. Valentine's Day Massacre, The, 25, 235; Salt of the Earth, 202; Sands of Iwo Jima, 330; Saturday Night and Sunday Morning, 334; Savage Eye, The, 202; Scarface, 235; Scorpio Rising, 168, 202; Scoundrel, The, 206; Secret Invasion, The, 179; Seventh Seal, The, 103, 109, 167; Ship of Fools, 174–175; Smiles of a Summer Night, 325; Sound of Music, The, 166, 202; South Pacific, 87, 90; Spy Who Came In from the Cold, The, 179, 181; Straight-Jacket, 334; Strike, 117; Summer Place, A, 177; Susan Slade, 177; Swinging the Lambeth Walk, 121; Tenth Victim, The, 259; These Are the Damned, 326–329; Three Little Pigs, 118; 3:10 to Yuma, 176; Through a Glass Darkly, 107, 109; To Have and Have Not, 184; Tom Jones, 339; Treasure of the Sierra Madre, The, 184; Trip to the Moon, A, 18; Triumph of the Will, 119–120, 122; Turksib, 119; Two Men and a Wardrobe, 125; Up the Down Staircase, 78, 82; Victors, The, 332; Virgin Spring, The, 104, 107, 109–110; Viridiana, 87; Vivre, 125; Wages of Fear, The, 90; War Game, The, 80; Westfront, 118; White Heat, 146; Who's Afraid of Virginia Woolf?, 92; You Only Live Twice, 359

INDEX OF SUBJECTS

First Amendment, 9, 168, 245, 248, 300
For the Young Viewer (book), 27
Ford Foundation, 396; and NET, 10; and Public TV, 402–403; and satellites, 360, 402; and the arts, 238, 354
480, The (book), 311
Fowler Commission (*See* Canadian National Commission Study of Broadcasting)
Fox Movietone Newsreels, 170
Free and Responsible Press, A (book), 250–255
French Love Stories (book), 336
From Caligari to Hitler (book), 324

Gallup polls, 313, 360
General Foods, 230
General Mills, 213
Georgia Association of Broadcasters, 247
Government: and film censorship, 9; and Public TV, 10, 407; as institutional force on media, 7–9, 13–14; House Committee on Un-American Activities, 8
Grauman's Chinese theater, 167
"Great Debates," 232–233, 308
Guernica (painting), 331
Gulf and Western Industries, 15, 164
Gulf Oil Company, 223

Harris poll, 310, 312–313; and ETV audiences, 11
Harvard University, 251, 274
Holland Cinema League, 351
Hollywood: "blacklisting," 8; changes in, 163–167, 173–185; "star system," 186–200; (*See also* Motion pictures; Motion pictures and television; Television)
Homecoming, The (play), 211
Hound and Horn (magazine), 145
House Committee on Un-American Activities, 8
Hutchins Commission (*See* Commission on Freedom of the Press)

Image, The (book), 304, 380
Independent Film Movement, 167–168, 201–207
"Independents," 166–167 (*See also*

Independent Film Movement)
Institute for Education by Radio and Television, 284
Institute of Contemporary Arts, 331
Instructional television, 272, 275; problems of, 272
"International Broadcasting Company," 362
International Communications Satellite Consortium (Intelsat), 362
Iowa State University, 282
Italians, The (book), 86
ITV (*See* Instructional television; Educational television)

"James Bond," 24, 26, 160, 180
Justice, U.S. Department of, 166

Kenyon Review (magazine), 378
Kinetoscope, 321

La Vida (book), 26
Ladies' Home Journal, The (magazine), 40, 143
Life (magazine), 424
Literary Digest (magazine), 309
Lolita (book), 99
Look (magazine), 142
Los Angeles Times, 248, 251
Louisville Courier-Journal, 240
Love and Death (book), 324
Love Sonnets of Shakespeare (book), 335
Lubell poll, 313

Making of a President: 1964, The (book), 232
"Mass audiences" *vs.* individuals, 4, 21
Mass communication(s): as emotional collaboration, 76–78, 87–91; development of, 3; future of, 361–363, 409–422; in democracy, 4; motion pictures and TV as, 4; research, 5, 36–37, 66, 75–76 (*See also* Communication; Mass media; Motion pictures; Motion pictures and television; Television)
Mass Culture (book), 368
Mass media: in democracy, 4, 47–49, 84–86; psychological effects of, 5–6; *vs.* elitists, 19, 358 (*See also* Mass communication(s); Motion

pictures; Motion pictures and television; Television)
Massachusetts Institute of Technology, 312
Max Planck Institute, 235
MCA (See Music Corporation of America)
Media managers: as communication elites, 148; economic problems of, 157–158; social responsibility of, 21–22, 363; vs. critics, 31–49
Metro-Goldwyn-Mayer, 166, 184–185
MGM (See Metro-Goldwyn-Mayer)
Michigan State University, 11, 282
Midwest Program on Airborne Television Instruction, 280
Million and One Nights, A (book), 322
Minority groups: and motion pictures, 29; and television, 28–29, 68–74 (See also Negroes)
Motion (magazine), 334
Motion Picture Association of America, 8, 237, 337, 339, 348
Motion Picture Production Code (See Motion pictures: Production Code)
Motion pictures: American vs. foreign, 344–345; and art, 11–13, 92–102; and business, 6–7, 164–165, 177–181, 346–349, 352–353; and controversial issues, 81–82; and education, 9, 358–360, 365–376, 384–395; and emotions, 87–91; and government, 7–9; and minority groups, 29; and values, 19, 143–144; audience responses, 24; beginnings in camera obscura, 18; censorship, 8–9, 236–237, 323–325, 335–343, 347–348; cinéma vérité, 78, 82, 95–96; criticism, 88, 180–181; Independent Film Movement, 167–168, 201–207; "independents," 166–167; need for subsidization, 238, 344–355; "New wave," 79; Production Code, 8, 323, 336–339; propaganda films, 79–80, 115–126; "star system," 165, 186–200; "underground films," 97, 201–207; violence in, 20, 234–236, 320–334; "wide screen," 18, 183 (See also Mass communication(s); Mass media; Motion pictures and television)

Motion pictures and television: and Academe, 359; and democratic institutions, 4, 13–14; and international understanding, 362, 423–434; and mass culture, 11–13, 137–149; and violence, 234–236; criticism, 16–17; critique of literature, 435–445; debate concerning, 3; development of, 3; influence on children, 25–27; nature of media, 83–84; persuasive power of, 3; recommendations for scholarship in, 445–449; relationships to each other, 82–83, 163–164, 348; relationships to print media, 5–6, 361, 377–383, 409–422; structure of messages, 5–6, 83–84; symbols used in, 5–6, 83–85, 363, 382; "total situation" of, 4–16, 357; vs. elites, 19, 358; vs. "reality," 17–18, 83–86, 137–149 (See also "Plato's cave") (See also Mass communication(s); Mass media; Motion pictures; Television)
Movies: A Psychological Study (book), 113
MPATI (See Midwest Program on Airborne Television Instruction)
Music Corporation of America, 166
Mutual Broadcasting System, 214

NAFBRAT (See National Association for Better Radio and Television)
National Association for Better Radio and Television, 25, 229
National Association of Broadcasters, 318
National Association of Educational Broadcasters, 229
National Association of Independent Schools, 394
National Association of Manufacturers, 254
National Association of Theatre Owners, 353
National Broadcasting Company, 13, 15, 19, 27, 81, 171, 215, 225, 259, 303; NBC News, 213–227, 305, 315, 319
National Catholic Office for Motion Pictures, 229, 348

INDEX OF SUBJECTS

National Citizens Committee for Public Television, 229

National Commission on Educational Television (*See* Carnegie Commission)

National Council on the Arts, 395

National Educational Television, 10–11, 398, 404

National Film Board of Canada, 18

National Foundation of the Arts and Humanities Act, 353

National Geographic (magazine), 26

National Student Association, 404

NBC (*See* National Broadcasting Company)

"NBC-MGM-Time, Incorporated," 149

Negroes: and effects of TV news, 5; and motion pictures, 29; and TV commercials, 28–29, 68–74

NET (*See* National Educational Television)

Netherlands Production Fund, 351

"New wave," 79

New York Daily News, 240

New York Herald Tribune, 214, 220, 261

New York Philharmonic, 34

New York Times, 17, 24, 128, 130, 216, 241, 247, 261, 289, 344, 362

New York University, 168

New York Yankees, 244

New Yorker, The (magazine), 142

Nielsen Television Index, 22, 248, 264

Nieman Foundation, 251

Nieman Reports (magazine), 251–253

"Noise" in "communication process," 76–80

Noncommercial television (*See* Educational television; Public television)

Odyssey (book), 27

Office of War Information, 218

Only You, Dick Daring! (book), 14, 337

Oxford Dictionary, 331

Paramount Pictures, 15, 164

Parents' Magazine, 25

Partisan Review (magazine), 138, 145, 207

Pay-TV, 280–281, 307, 360–362

Penguin New Writing (book), 323

People Look At Television, The (book), 24

Philosophy of Spinoza, The (book), 335

Phonevision, 361 (*See also* Pay-TV)

Photoplay (magazine), 165

Picture (book), 14

Pilkington Report, 273, 281

"Plato's cave," 17–18, 385 (*See also* Motion pictures and television: vs. "reality")

Play Theory of Mass Communication, The (book), 25

Poems of Passion (book), 335

Politics and television, 219, 232–234, 289, 302–308, 309–319

Polls: Gallop, 313, 360; Harris, 11, 310, 312–313; Lubell, 313; Nielsen, 22, 248, 264, 267; Roper, 170, 215, 232, 265, 313

Procter and Gamble, 19, 230

Producer's Journal (magazine), 353

"Project Prometheus," 281

Public Broadcasting Act, 10

Public television, 10, 360, 396–408 (*See also* Educational television; Carnegie Commission: Report of; Ford Foundation: and Public TV)

"Puzzling movies," 103–114

Radio Corporation of America, 244, 282

Radio programs: *Amos 'n' Andy*, 170; *Big Issue, The*, 305; *Invitation to Learning*, 35; *Letter and Answer*, 273; *Letters from Listeners*, 273; *March of Time, The*, 214

Random House, 244

Ratings, 36–41, 264; and "cultural democracy," 22; limitations of, 22–23, 36–39; (*See also* Polls)

RCA (*See* Radio Corporation of America)

Reporting the News (book), 251–252

Revue Corporation, 166

Richard II (play), 22

Roper Research Associates, 170, 215, 232, 265, 313

San Francisco Chronicle, 240
Satellites: and educational broadcasting, 281; and Ford Foundation, 360; and international cooperation, 362
Saturday Review (magazine), 17, 281
Screen Actors Guild, 353
"Screen education" (See "Film study movement")
Section 315 (See Communications Act: Section 315)
Senate Foreign Relations Committee on Vietnam, 14, 303
Seven Arts Corporation, 164
Seventeen (book), 389
Sex: and violence in films, 110–111, 325–330; in films, 106–107, 324–325
Show (magazine), 103, 107
Sight and Sound (magazine), 324
Simulmatics Corporation, 312
Social institutions: and "total situation" of motion pictures and TV, 4; art, 11–13; business, 6–7; contention among, 4, 7, 13–14, 78, 80, 237–238; education, 9–11; government, 7–9
"Star system" (See Motion pictures: "star system")
Supreme Court, 234; and censorship, 9, 236, 291; Consent Decree of, 8, 165
Swedish Film Institute, 351
Swedish National Film School, 351

Television: American vs. British system, 160–161; and art, 11–13; and business, 6–7, 157–158, 243; and controversial issues, 81; and education, 9–11, 271–284, 358–360; and government, 7 (See also Federal Communications Commission); and minority groups, 28–29, 68–74; and politics, 219, 232–234, 289, 302–308, 309–319 (See also Television news: election coverage); and technological culture, 150–162, 373–376; and values, 74, 161–162; as addressed to whole

community, 71; audiences, 4, 20, 23–24, 31–49 (See also Television viewing); censorship vs. writers, 337; criticism, 16–17; documentaries, 171–172, 222–224, 305–306, 400, 403 (See also Television news); drama, 169–170, 208–212, 401; editorializing on, 305 (See also Communications Act: Section 315); future of, 19, 161–162, 360–363, 409–422; journalism (See Television news); private vs. public TV, 396–408; programming problems, 229–230, 241–243, 258–262, 263–264, 298; propaganda on, 81; ratings (See Ratings; Polls); vs. newspapers, 239–241; (See also Mass communication(s); Mass media; Motion pictures and television)
Television and the Child (book), 58
Television commercials, 230, 263–270; and racial demonstrations, 28–29, 68–74; "magazine concept," 269–270
Television Information Office, 229, 265
Television news: and Canon 35, 234; and Congressional hearings, 303–304; and editorializing, 217–218, 221–223; and "public figures," 133–134; and racial demonstrations, 5, 129–133, 236; credibility of, 170, 215, 302; election coverage, 232–234, 304–308, 309–319 (See also Television: and politics); responsibility of newsmen, 135, 171–172, 213–227; violence in, 129–132, 236; vs. print journalism, 127–136, 213–216, 399–400; vs. "reality," 80, 127–136, 304–305 (See also Television: documentaries; American Broadcasting Company: ABC News; Columbia Broadcasting System: CBS News; National Broadcasting Company: NBC News)
Television programs: Batman, 27, 164, 242, 359, 386; Ben Casey, 23; Beverly Hillbillies, The, 164, 307, 341; Biography of a Bookie Joint, 222; Bonanza, 164, 386; Boy, 11;

INDEX OF SUBJECTS

Bozo the Clown, 25; *Bus Stop*, 234; *Captain Kangaroo*, 25; *CBS Playhouse*, 170, 210; *CBS Reports*, 81; *Creative Person, The*, 401; *Death of a Salesman*, 170, 401; *Death of Stalin, The*, 226; *East Side/West Side*, 389; *Enemy of the People, An*, 401; *Fugitive, The*, 22; *Glass Menagerie, The*, 401; *Great Highway Robbery, The*, 222; *Hallmark Hall of Fame*, 169, 401; *Hogan's Heroes*, 164; *Homosexuals, The*, 81; *Huntley-Brinkley Report, The*, 216, 219; *I Love Lucy*, 14; *I Spy*, 19; *Kraft Theatre*, 169; *Kremlin, The*, 224, 226; *Legend of Jesse James, The*, 174; *Lion Walks among Us, A*, 234; *Man from U.N.C.L.E., The*, 147, 160, 386; *Mark Twain To-night*, 23; *Meet the Press*, 304; *Mission: Impossible*, 21; *Mills of the Gods, The*, 11, 80; *Mother, The*, 169; *My Lost Saints*, 169; *NBC White Papers*, 305; *N.Y.P.D.*, 82; *Omnibus*, 244; *Peyton Place*, 5; *Philco Playhouse*, 169; *Playhouse 90*, 169, 242; *Public Broadcast Laboratory*, 11; *Rise of Khrushchev, The*, 226; *Run for Your Life*, 22; *Stage '67*, 169; *Studio One*, 169, 242; *Tenement, The*, 171–172; *Thunder on Sycamore Street*, 169; *Time for Burning, A*, 400; *Today*, 219; *Uncle Vanya*, 401; *Untouchables, The*, 26, 147; *You Are There*, 242
Television viewing: and needs of individuals, 4–5; and racial demonstrations, 68–74; as "play," 24–25; circumstances of, 50–56; effects on children, 25–28, 57–67 (*See also* Audiences)
Texas Broadcasting Corporation, 247
Time (magazine), 248
Time-Life, Incorporated, 297
Titus Andronicus (play), 234
Toll-TV (*See* Pay-TV)
Transamerica Corporation, 15
Transradio News Service, 217
TV Guide (magazine), 261
TVQ scores, 23–24

Twentieth Century-Fox, 15, 166, 183

UCLA (*See* University of California at Los Angeles)
UHF (ultrahigh-frequency) channels, 307, 360–361
Uncle Tom's Cabin (book), 337
"Underground films": as non-art, 97; relationship to Independent Film Movement, 167–168, 201–207
UNESCO, 252; and satellites, 281 (*See also* United Nations)
United Artists, 8, 15
United Nations, 362 (*See also* UNESCO)
United Press International, 214, 220
United States Information Agency, 79
Universal Pictures, 166
University of California at Los Angeles, 168
University of Chicago, 250, 284
University of Georgia, 247
University of Michigan, 39
University of Pennsylvania, 168
University of Pittsburgh, 281
Up the Down Staircase (book), 390
UPI (*See* United Press International)

Valley of the Dolls (book), 26
Variety (magazine), 6, 174, 353
VHF (very-high-frequency) channels, 280, 282
Violence: and sex in films, 110–111, 325–330; censorship of, 323–325; effects on children, 25–26, 63–64; in films, 320–334; in motion pictures and TV, 234–236; in painting, 331; in the theater, 331; in TV news, 129–132, 236
Vote Profile Analysis (*See* Columbia Broadcasting System: Vote Profile Analysis)

Wall Street Journal, 241, 314
Waning of the Middle Ages, The (book), 377
Warner Brothers Pictures, 164, 176, 182–185
Washington Post, 17, 220, 242
Weimar Republic, 323

West Side Story (play), 258
WGBH-TV, 9
What Every Young Man Should Know (book), 335
"Wide-screen processes": and "eclipse of distance," 18–19; Cinemascope, 18, 183; Cinerama, 18
William Morris Agency, 166
WINS Radio, 361
WNYC Radio, 282

WNYC-TV, 282
WPIX-TV, 289

Xerox Corporation, 170

Yale Drama School (*See* Yale University)
Yale University, 170, 312
Yale-ABC project, 170